THE **WALLFLOWER**

YAMATONADESHIKO SHICHIHENGE

♥ **6** ♥

Tomoko Hayakawa

TRANSLATED AND ADAPTED BY
David Ury

LETTERED BY
Dana Hayward

DEL REY

BALLANTINE BOOKS • NEW YORK

2005 Del Rey® Trade Paperback Edition

Copyright © 2006 Tomoko Hayakawa.

Published in the United States by Del Rey Books, an imprint of The Random House Publishing Group, a division of Random House Inc., New York.

DEL REY is a registered trademark and the Del Rey colophon is a trademark of Random House, Inc.

Originally published in Japan in 2002 by Kodansha Ltd., Tokyo as *Yamatonadeshiko Shichihenge.*

This publication: rights arranged through Kodansha Ltd.

Library of Congress Control Number: 2004095918

ISBN 0-345-48370-7

Printed in the United States of America

www.delreymanga.com

9 8 7 6 5 4 3 2

Translator and adapter—David Ury

Lettering—Dana Hayward

Cover design—David Stevenson

Contents

A Note from the Author

MY ...

...BABIES
(A FEW
OF THEM)

♥ I heard from a friend that the late night TV show "Ranku Oukoku" ("The Kingdom of Ranking") listed *Wallflower* Volume 5 in their ranking. (I was so sad that I didn't get to see it myself . . . crying) It's all thanks to you guys. Thank you so much. ♥ ♥ ♥ I'll continue to do my best! —**Tomoko Hayakawa**

Honorifics

Throughout the Del Rey Manga books, you will find Japanese honorifics left intact in the translations. For those not familiar with how the Japanese use honorifics, and more important, how they differ from American honorifics, we present this brief overview.

Politeness has always been a critical facet of Japanese culture. Ever since the feudal era, when Japan was a highly stratified society, use of honorifics—which can be defined as polite speech that indicates relationship or status—has played an essential role in the Japanese language. When addressing someone in Japanese, an honorific usually takes the form of a suffix attached to one's name (example: "Asuna-san"), or as a title at the end of one's name or in place of the name itself (example: "Negi-sensei," or simply "Sensei!").

Honorifics can be expressions of respect or endearment. In the context of manga and anime, honorifics give insight into the nature of the relationship between characters. Many translations into English leave out these important honorifics, and therefore distort the "feel" of the original Japanese. Because Japanese honorifics contain nuances that English honorifics lack, it is our policy at Del Rey not to translate them. Here, instead, is a guide to some of the honorifics you may encounter in Del Rey Manga.

-san: This is the most common honorific, and is equivalent to Mr., Miss, Ms., Mrs., etc. It is the all-purpose honorific and can be used in any situation where politeness is required.

-sama: This is one level higher than "-san" and it is used to confer great respect.

-dono: This comes from the word "tono," which means "lord." It is an even higher level than "-sama," and confers utmost respect.

-kun: This suffix is used at the end of boys' names to express familiarity or endearment. It is also sometimes used by men among friends, or when addressing someone younger or of a lower station.

-chan: This is used to express endearment, mostly toward girls. It is also used for little boys, pets, and even among lovers. It gives a sense of childish cuteness.

Bozu: This is an informal way to refer to a boy, similar to the English term "kid" or "squirt."

Sempai/senpai: This title suggests that the addressee is one's "senior" in a group or organization. It is most often used in a school setting, where underclassmen refer to their upperclassmen as "sempai." It can also be used in the workplace, such as when a newer employee addresses an employee who has seniority in the company.

Kohai: This is the opposite of "sempai," and is used toward underclassmen in school or newcomers in the workplace. It connotes that the addressee is of lower station.

Sensei: Literally meaning "one who has come before," this title is used for teachers, doctors, or masters of any profession or art.

[blank]:   Usually forgotten in these lists, but perhaps the most significant difference between Japanese and English. The lack of honorific means that the speaker has permission to address the person in a very intimate way. Usually, only family, spouses, or very close friends have this kind of permission. Known as *yobisute,* it can be gratifying when someone who has earned the intimacy starts to call one by one's name without an honorific. But when that intimacy hasn't been earned, it can be very insulting.

THE wallflower
YAMATONADESHIKO SHICHIHENGE
ヤマトナデシコ七変化♡

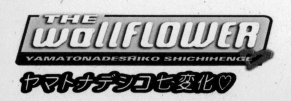

CONTENTS

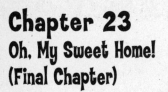

THE wallflower

YAMATONADESHIKO SHICHIHENGE

Chapter 23
Oh, My Sweet Home!
(Final Chapter)

♥ BOOK 6 ♥

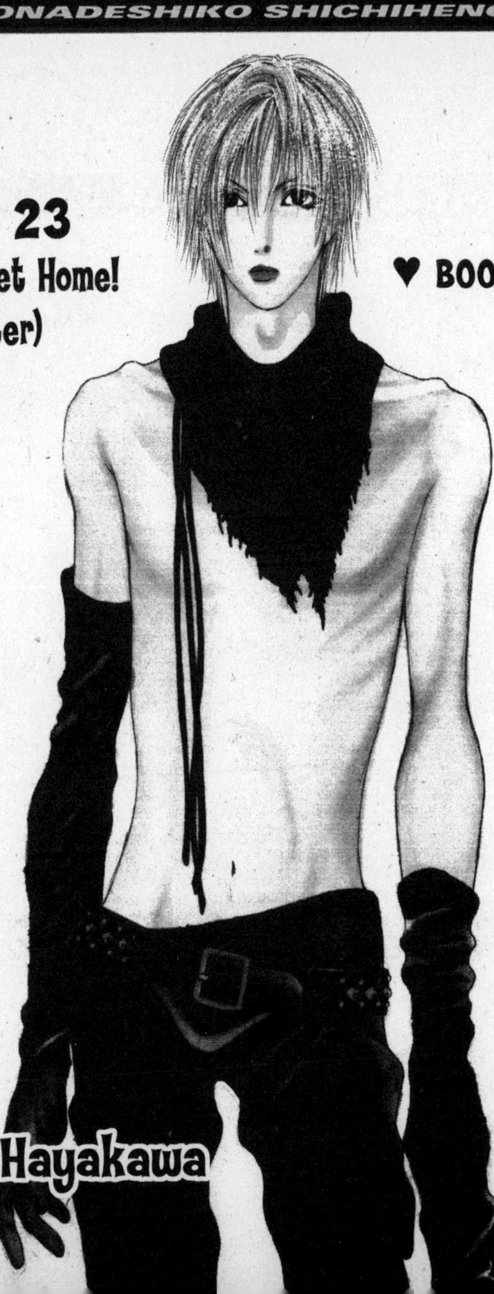

Tomoko Hayakawa

Wallflower's Beautiful Cast of Characters (?)

SUNAKO IS A DARK LONER WHO LOVES HORROR MOVIES. WHEN HER AUNT, THE LANDLADY OF A BOARDING HOUSE, LEAVES TOWN WITH HER BOYFRIEND, SUNAKO IS FORCED TO LIVE WITH FOUR HANDSOME GUYS. SUNAKO'S AUNT MAKES A DEAL WITH THE BOYS, WHICH CAUSES NOTHING BUT HEADACHES FOR SUNAKO. "MAKE SUNAKO INTO A LADY, AND YOU CAN LIVE RENT-FREE."

BUT...HOW IS IT THAT THESE FOUR "CREATURES OF THE LIGHT" CAME TO LIVE TOGETHER IN THE SAME HOUSE? YOU'RE ABOUT TO FIND OUT IN THIS TALE OF DRAMA AND SUSPENSE.

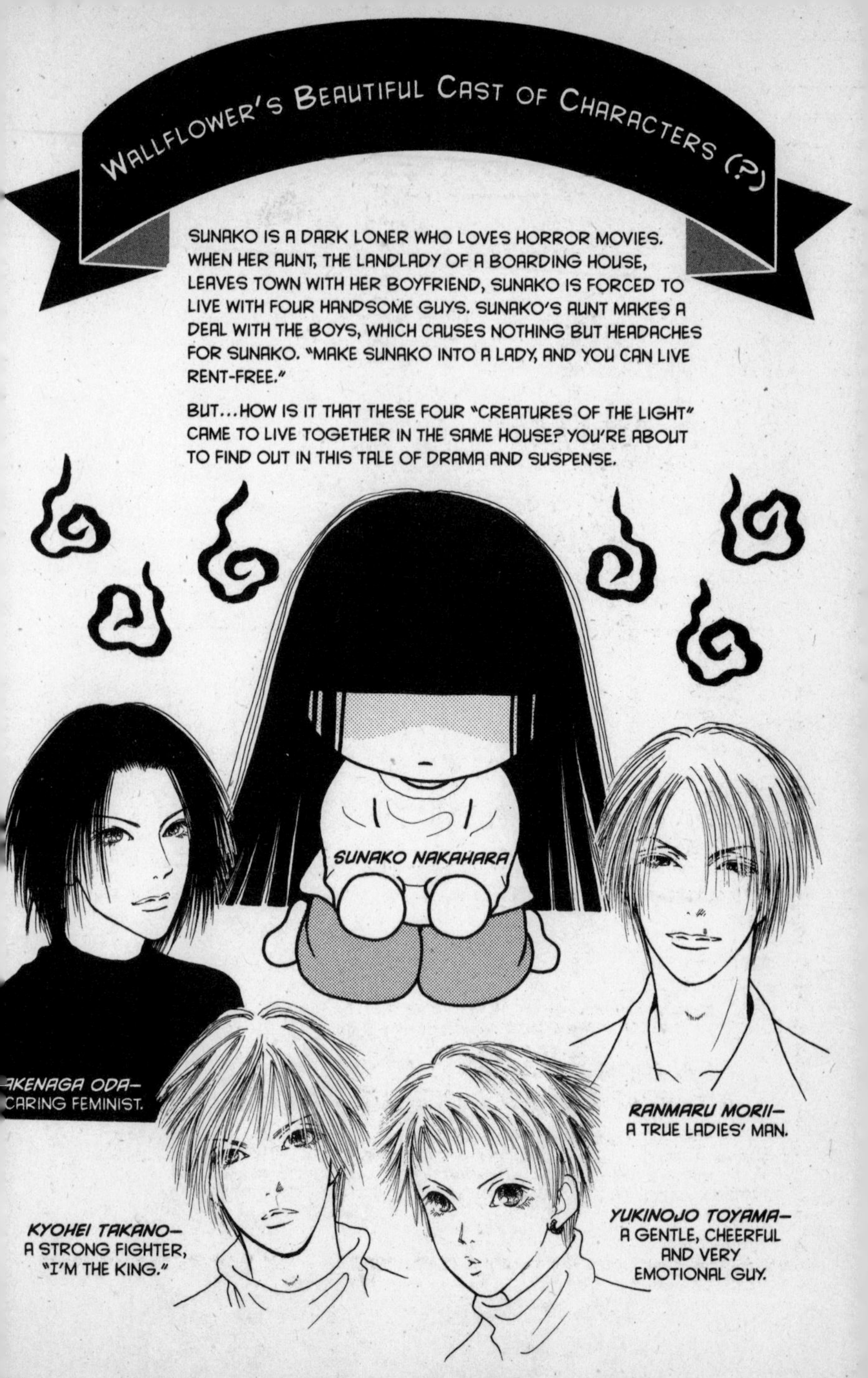
SUNAKO NAKAHARA
RANMARU MORII—
A TRUE LADIES' MAN.
AKENAGA ODA—
CARING FEMINIST.
YUKINOJO TOYAMA—
A GENTLE, CHEERFUL AND VERY EMOTIONAL GUY.
KYOHEI TAKANO—
A STRONG FIGHTER, "I'M THE KING."

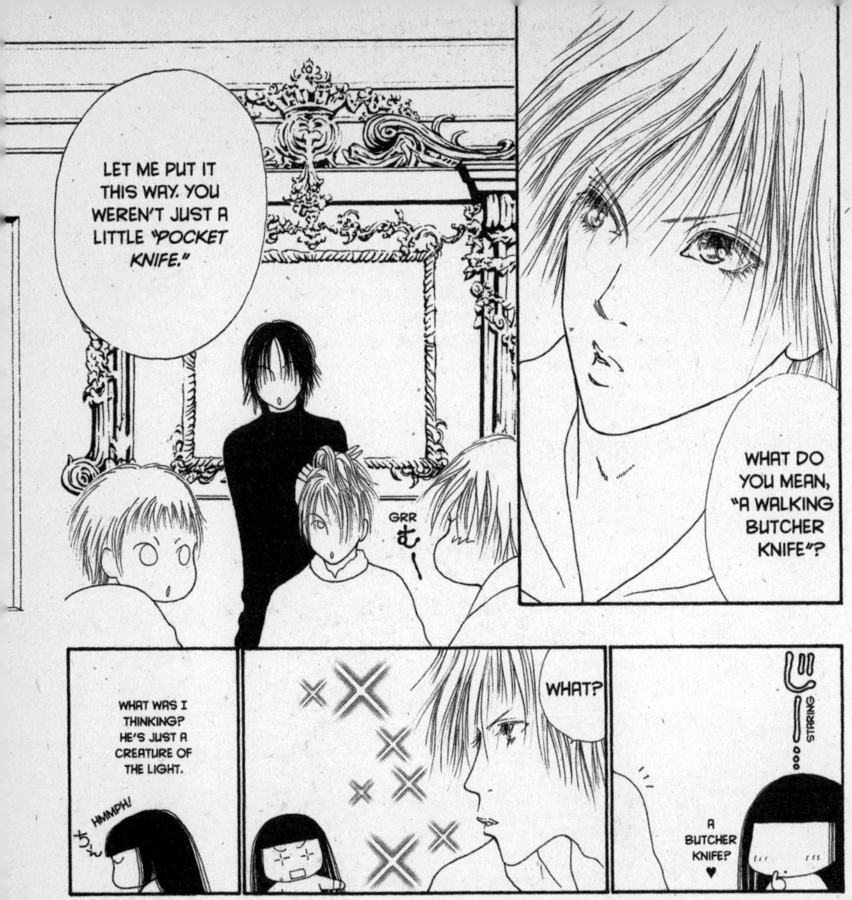
WHAT DO YOU MEAN, "A WALKING BUTCHER KNIFE"?
LET ME PUT IT THIS WAY. YOU WEREN'T JUST A LITTLE "POCKET KNIFE."
GRR
STARING
A BUTCHER KNIFE? ♥
WHAT?
WHAT WAS I THINKING? HE'S JUST A CREATURE OF THE LIGHT.
HMMPH!

BEHIND THE SCENES

WELL ... I WAS PLANNING ON WRITING A "BEHIND THE SCENES," BUT I DON'T EVEN WANT TO THINK ABOUT IT ... I'M SORRY. I WAS EMOTIONALLY UNSTABLE. AND ...

THE SADS CONCERT WAS TWO DAYS BEFORE MY DEADLINE, SO I COULDN'T GO ... *AHH ...*

MY MIND AND BODY WERE BOTH A MESS. IF ONLY I'D BEEN ABLE TO CATCH JUST A GLIMPSE OF KIYOHARU ... SIGH ... I CAUSED MY MOTHER AND LITTLE BROTHER A LOT OF TROUBLE. (ESPECIALLY MY BROTHER) MY LITTLE BROTHER IS SO SWEET. HE'S A REALLY GREAT GUY. (OR IS IT JUST SISTERLY LOVE?) I HOPE HE FINDS A CUTE WIFE SOON ... I WANT A LITTLE SISTER. ♥

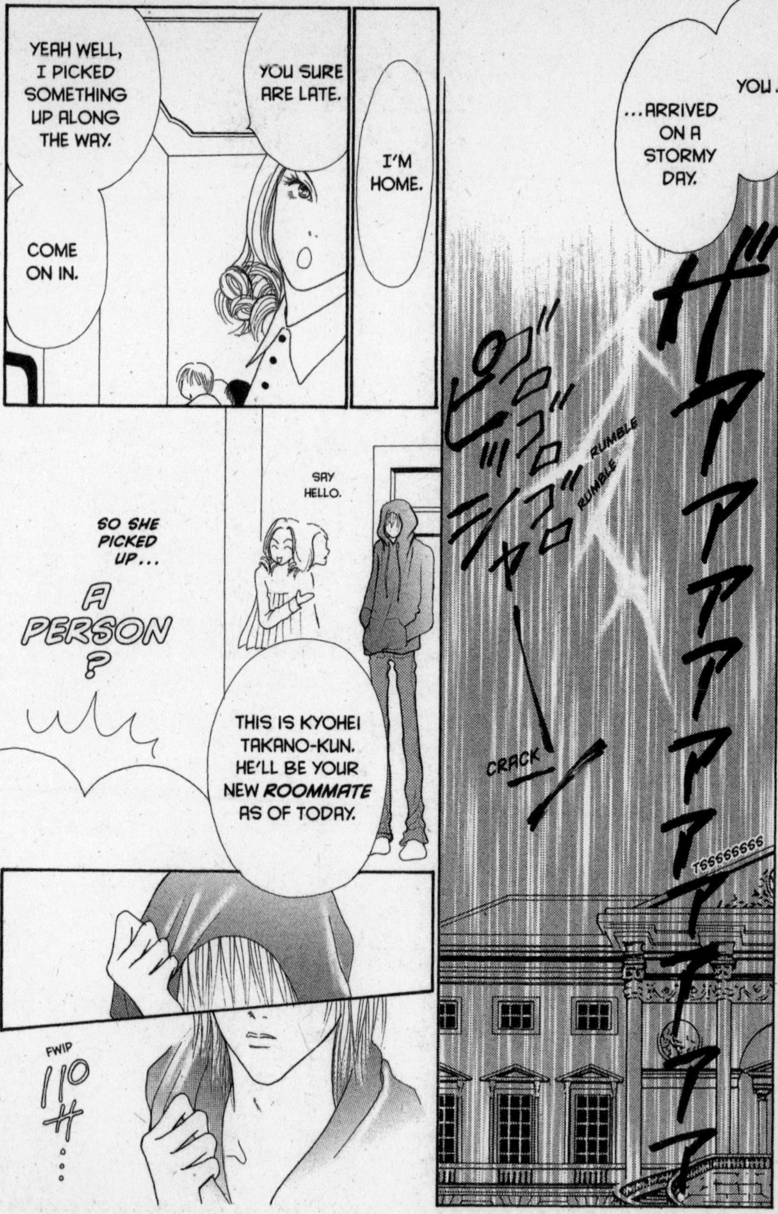
YOU...
...ARRIVED ON A STORMY DAY.
ザァァァァァァァァァ
ピシャーン
ゴロゴロゴロ
RUMBLE RUMBLE
CRACK
TSSSSSSSS
I'M HOME.
YOU SURE ARE LATE.
YEAH WELL, I PICKED SOMETHING UP ALONG THE WAY.
COME ON IN.
SAY HELLO.
THIS IS KYOHEI TAKANO-KUN. HE'LL BE YOUR NEW *ROOMMATE* AS OF TODAY.
SO SHE PICKED UP...
A PERSON ?
FWIP

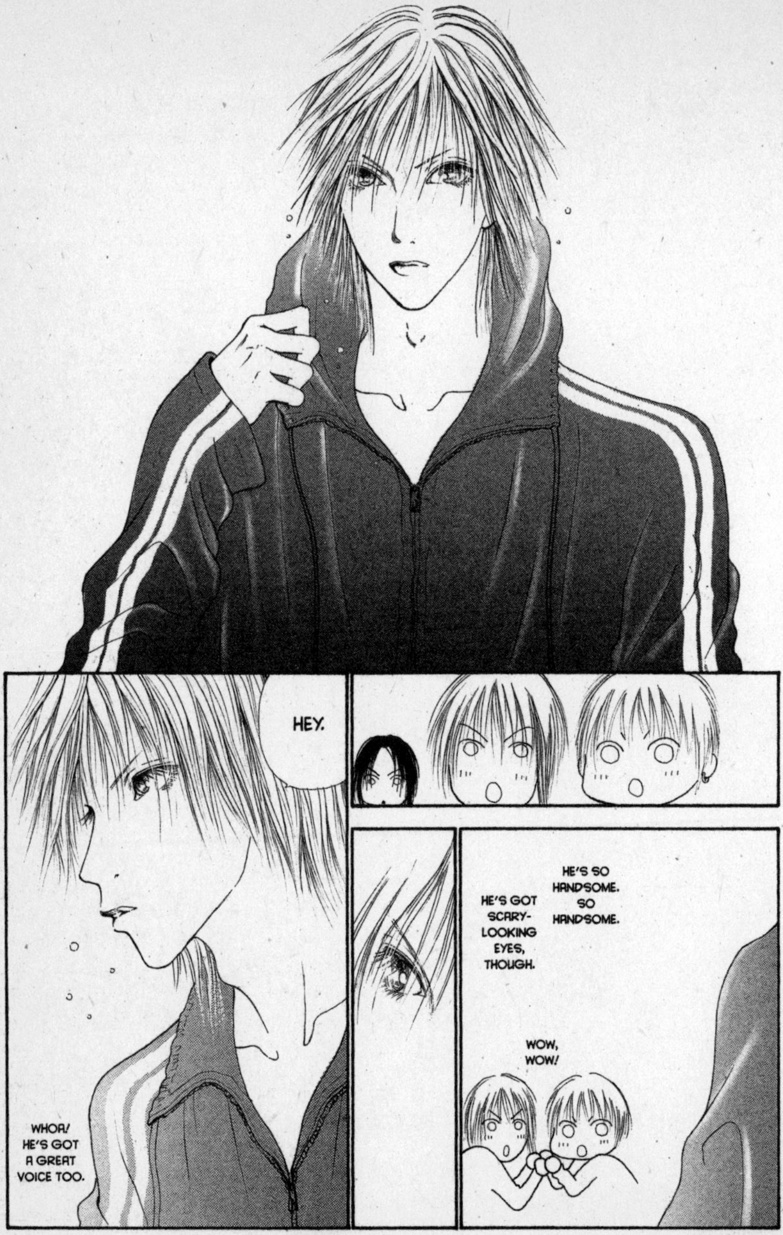
HE'S SO HANDSOME. SO HANDSOME.
HE'S GOT SCARY-LOOKING EYES, THOUGH.
WOW, WOW!
HEY.
WHOA! HE'S GOT A GREAT VOICE TOO.

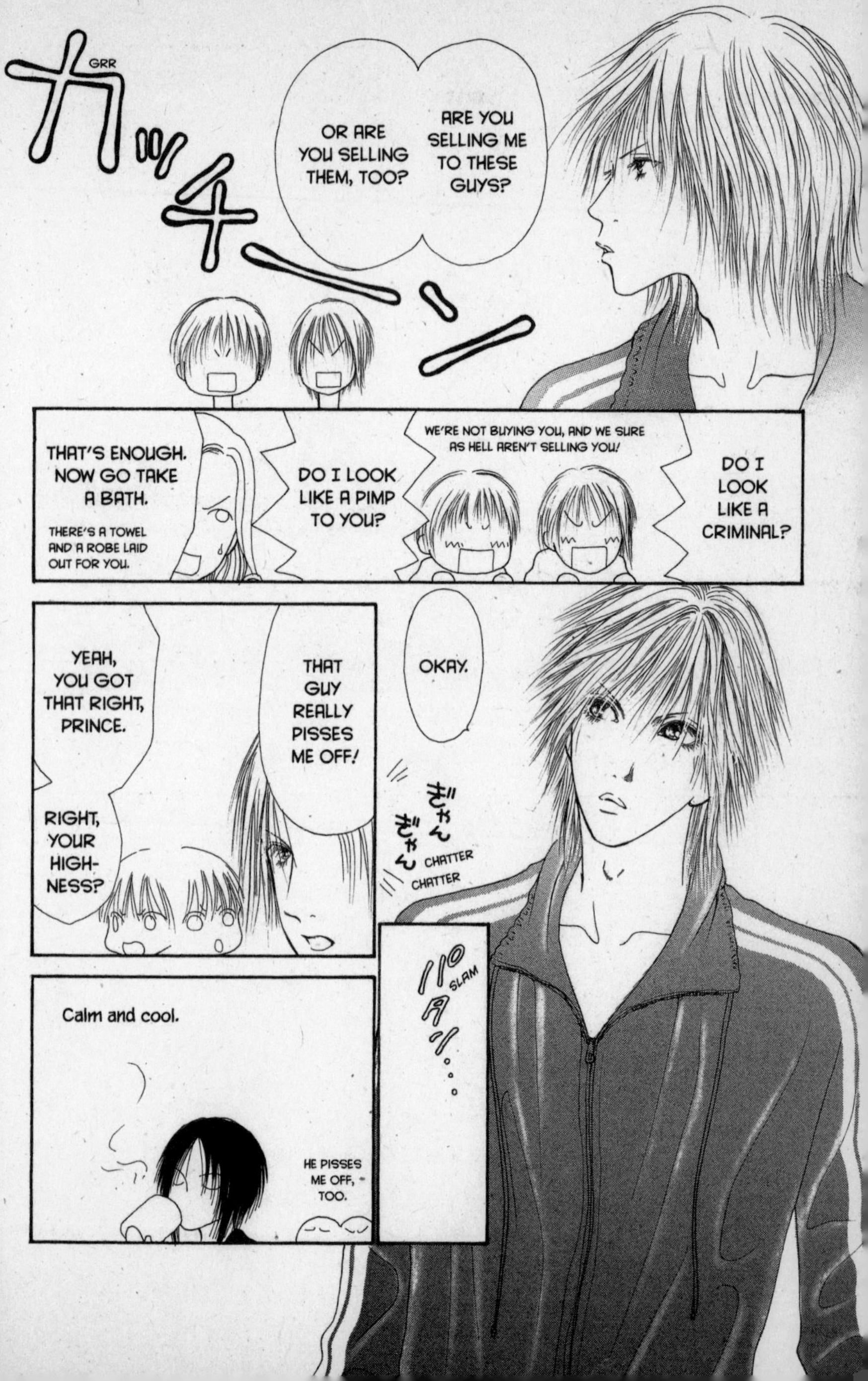
ARE YOU SELLING ME TO THESE GUYS?
OR ARE YOU SELLING THEM, TOO?
カッチーン
GRR
DO I LOOK LIKE A CRIMINAL?
WE'RE NOT BUYING YOU, AND WE SURE AS HELL AREN'T SELLING YOU!
DO I LOOK LIKE A PIMP TO YOU?
THAT'S ENOUGH. NOW GO TAKE A BATH.
THERE'S A TOWEL AND A ROBE LAID OUT FOR YOU.
OKAY.
ざんざん
CHATTER CHATTER
THAT GUY REALLY PISSES ME OFF!
YEAH, YOU GOT THAT RIGHT, PRINCE.
RIGHT, YOUR HIGH-NESS?
パタン。。。
SLAM
Calm and cool.
HE PISSES ME OFF, TOO.

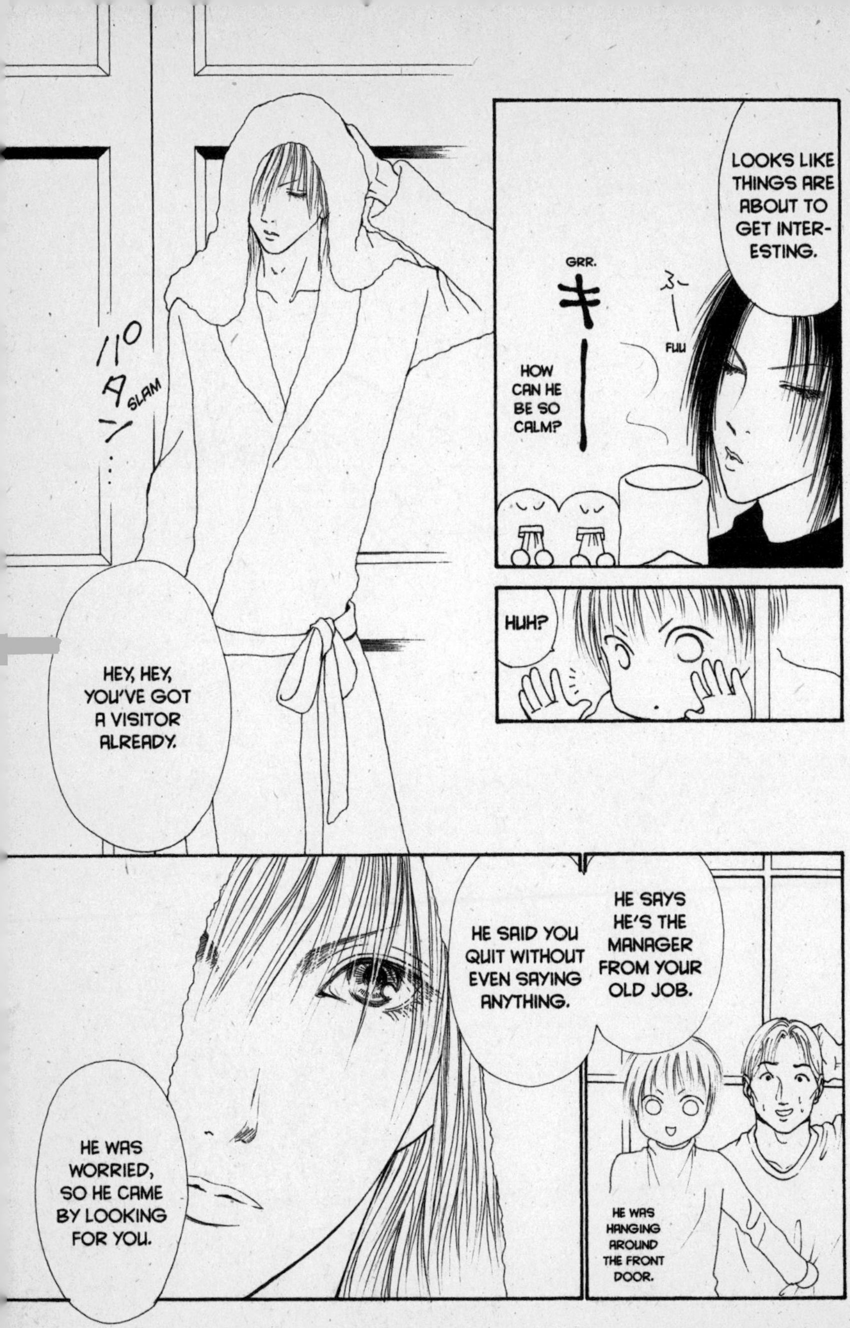
LOOKS LIKE THINGS ARE ABOUT TO GET INTERESTING.
ふー
FUU
GRR.
キー
HOW CAN HE BE SO CALM?
HUH?
SLAM
...
HEY, HEY, YOU'VE GOT A VISITOR ALREADY.
HE SAYS HE'S THE MANAGER FROM YOUR OLD JOB.
HE WAS HANGING AROUND THE FRONT DOOR.
HE SAID YOU QUIT WITHOUT EVEN SAYING ANYTHING.
HE WAS WORRIED, SO HE CAME BY LOOKING FOR YOU.

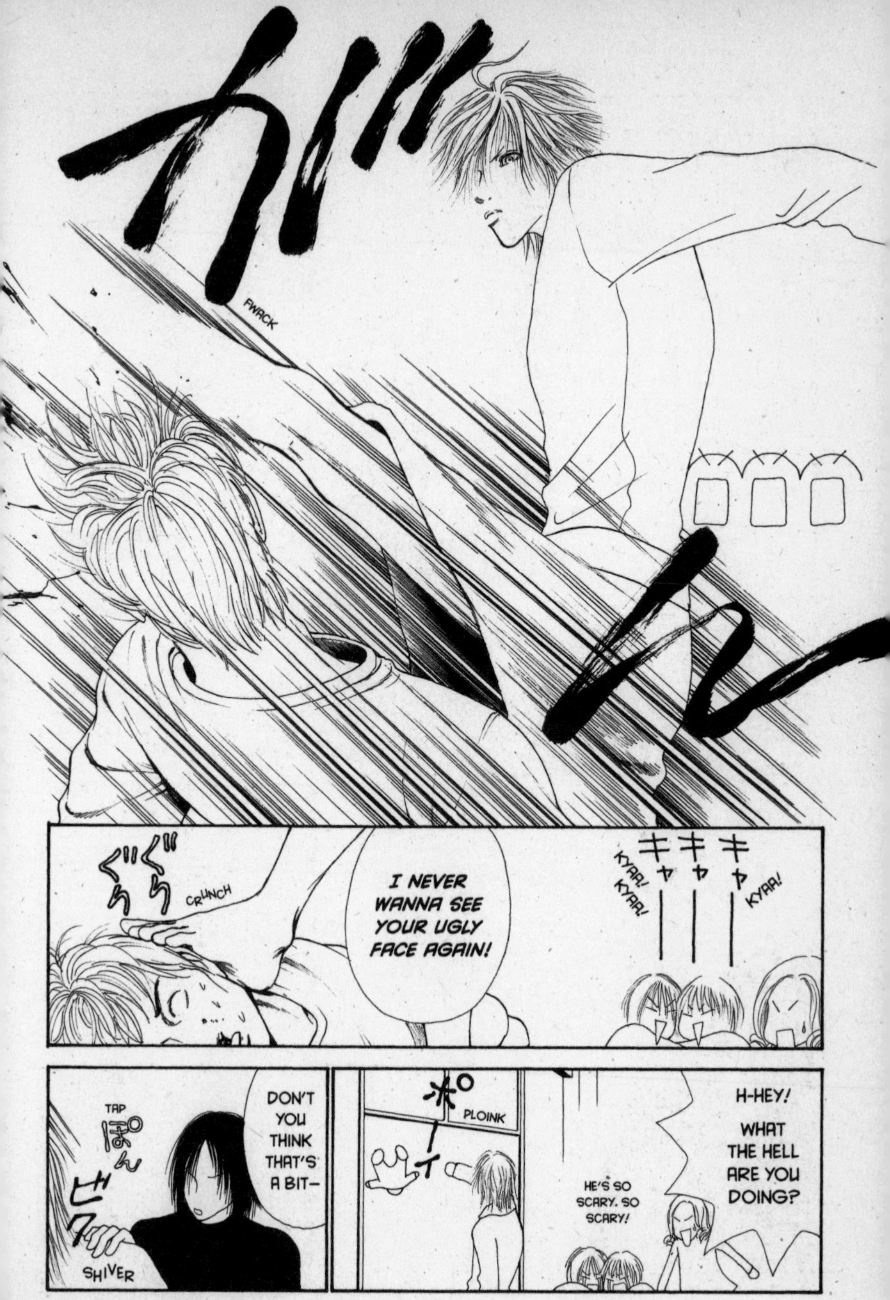
FWACK
KYAA! KYAA! KYAA!
I NEVER WANNA SEE YOUR UGLY FACE AGAIN!
CRUNCH
H-HEY! WHAT THE HELL ARE YOU DOING?
HE'S SO SCARY. SO SCARY!
PLOINK
DON'T YOU THINK THAT'S A BIT—
TAP
SHIVER

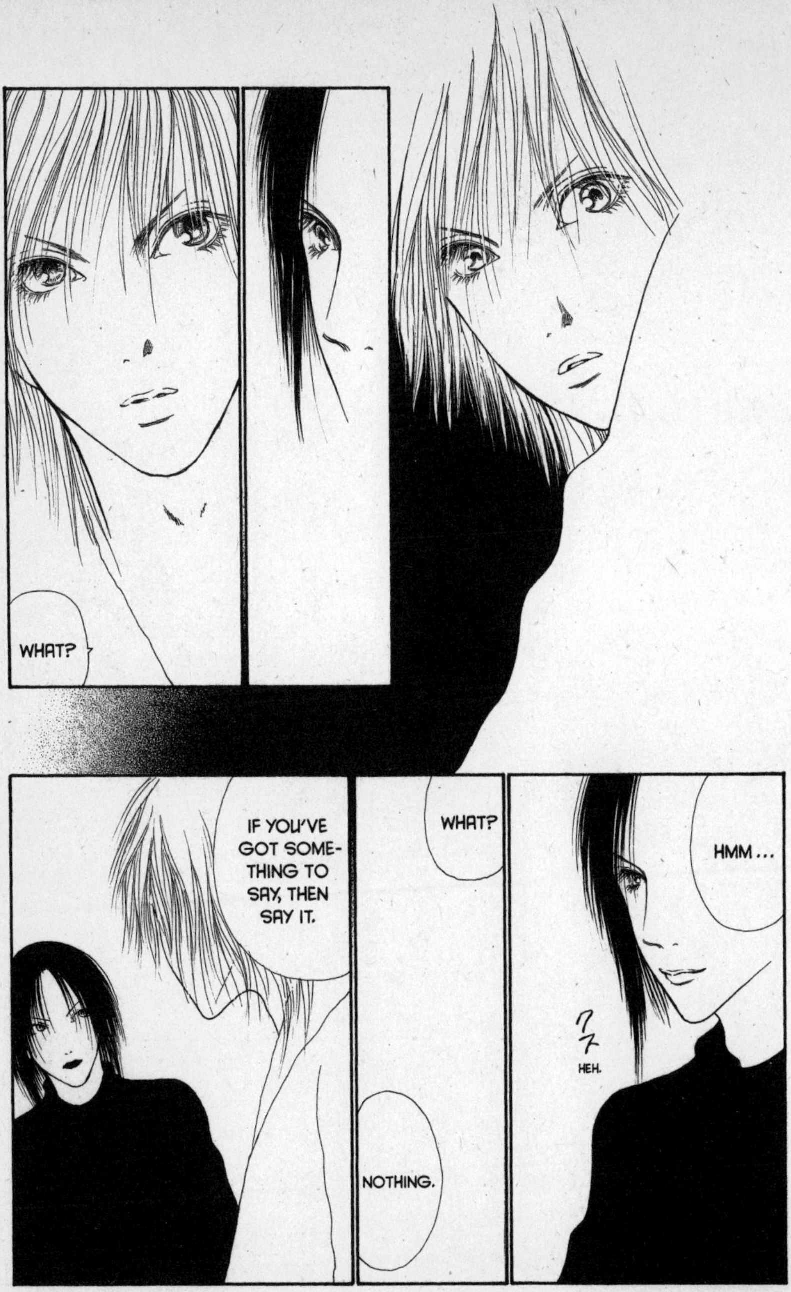
WHAT?
HMM ...
HEH.
WHAT?
NOTHING.
IF YOU'VE GOT SOME-THING TO SAY, THEN SAY IT.

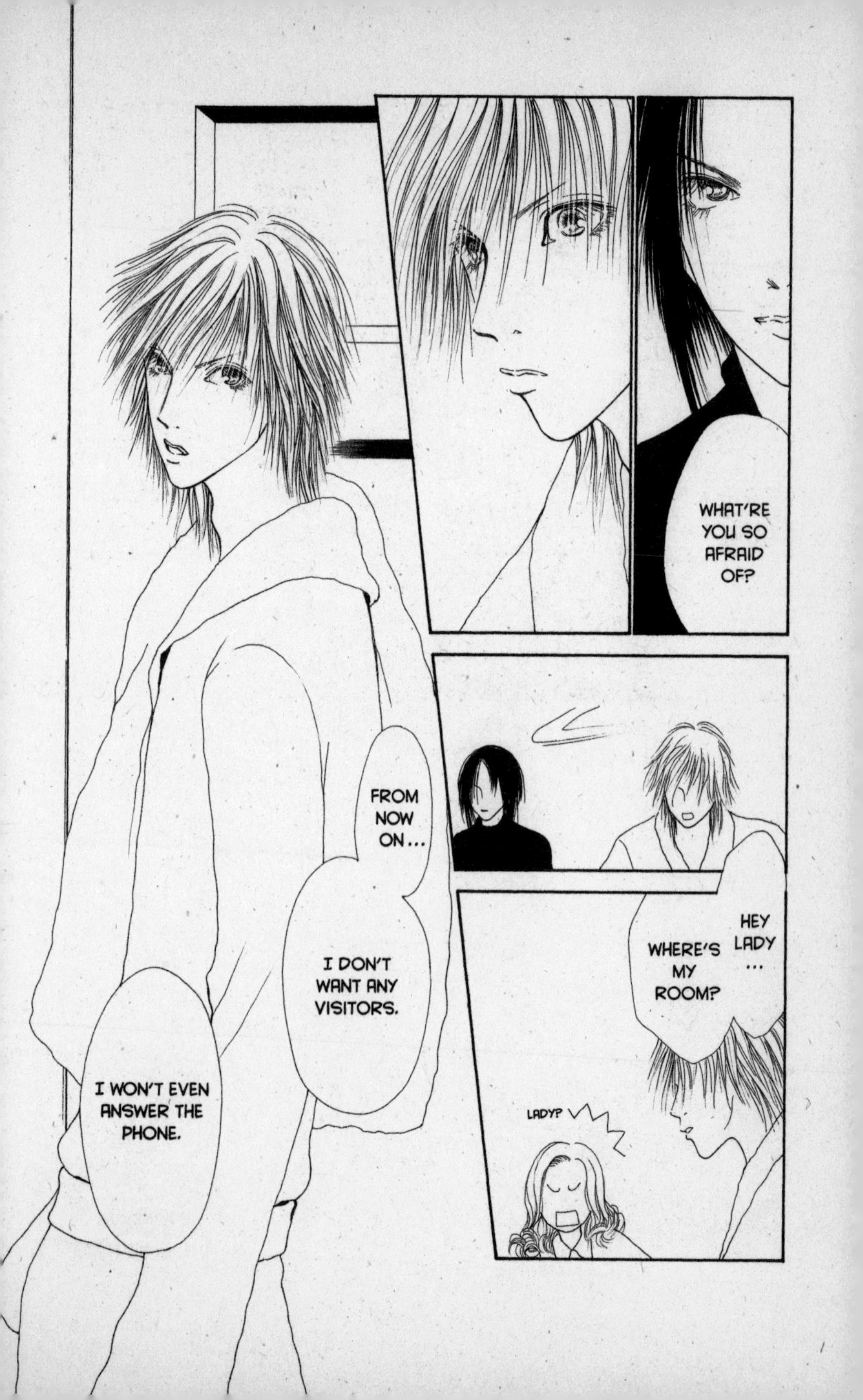
WHAT'RE YOU SO AFRAID OF?
HEY LADY ...
WHERE'S MY ROOM?
LADY?
FROM NOW ON...
I DON'T WANT ANY VISITORS.
I WON'T EVEN ANSWER THE PHONE.

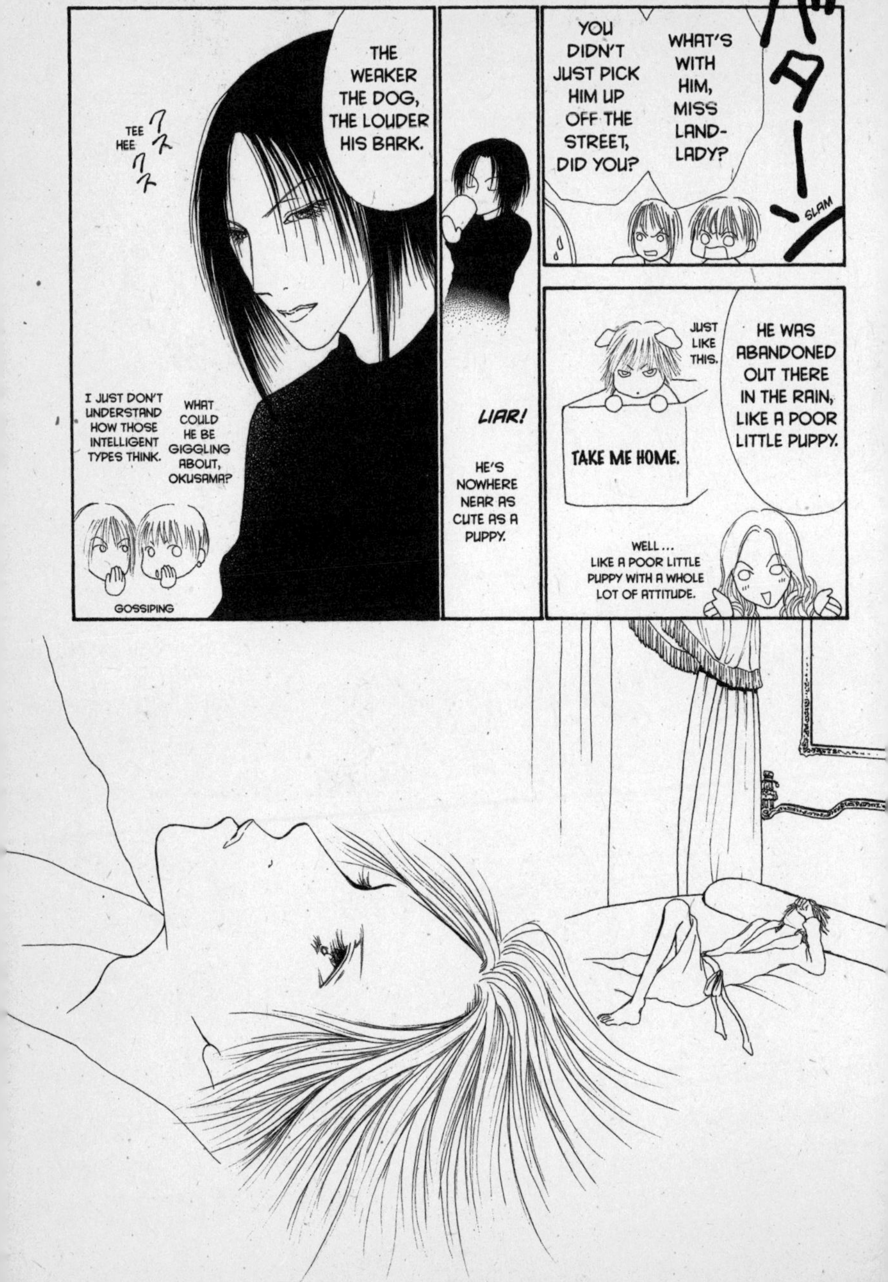
バターン
SLAM
WHAT'S WITH HIM, MISS LANDLADY?
YOU DIDN'T JUST PICK HIM UP OFF THE STREET, DID YOU?
HE WAS ABANDONED OUT THERE IN THE RAIN, LIKE A POOR LITTLE PUPPY.
JUST LIKE THIS.
TAKE ME HOME.
WELL ... LIKE A POOR LITTLE PUPPY WITH A WHOLE LOT OF ATTITUDE.
LIAR!
HE'S NOWHERE NEAR AS CUTE AS A PUPPY.
THE WEAKER THE DOG, THE LOUDER HIS BARK.
クスクス
TEE HEE
WHAT COULD HE BE GIGGLING ABOUT, OKUSAMA?
I JUST DON'T UNDERSTAND HOW THOSE INTELLIGENT TYPES THINK.
GOSSIPING

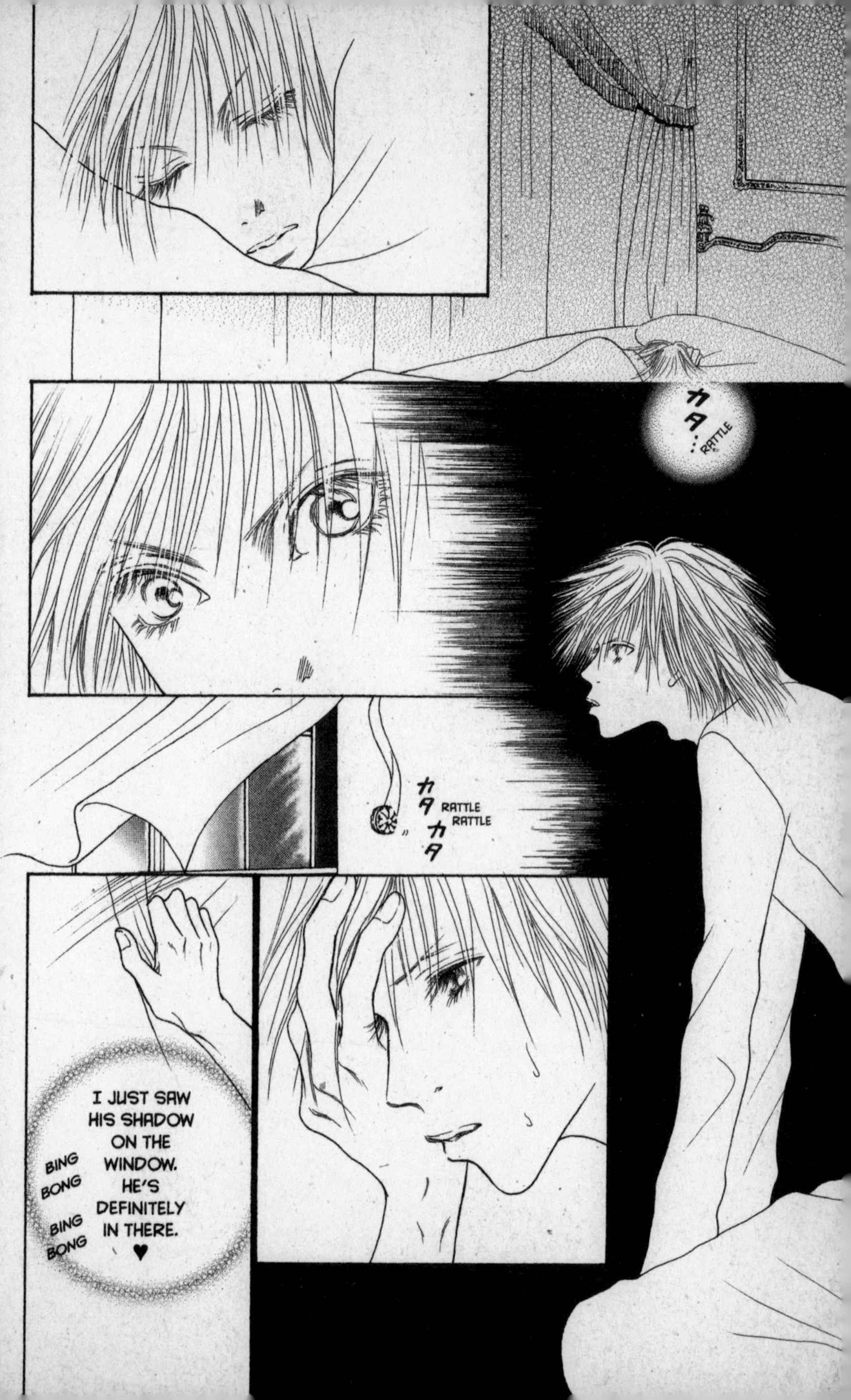
カタ… RATTLE
カタ カタ RATTLE RATTLE
I JUST SAW HIS SHADOW ON THE WINDOW. HE'S DEFINITELY IN THERE. ♥
BING BONG BING BONG

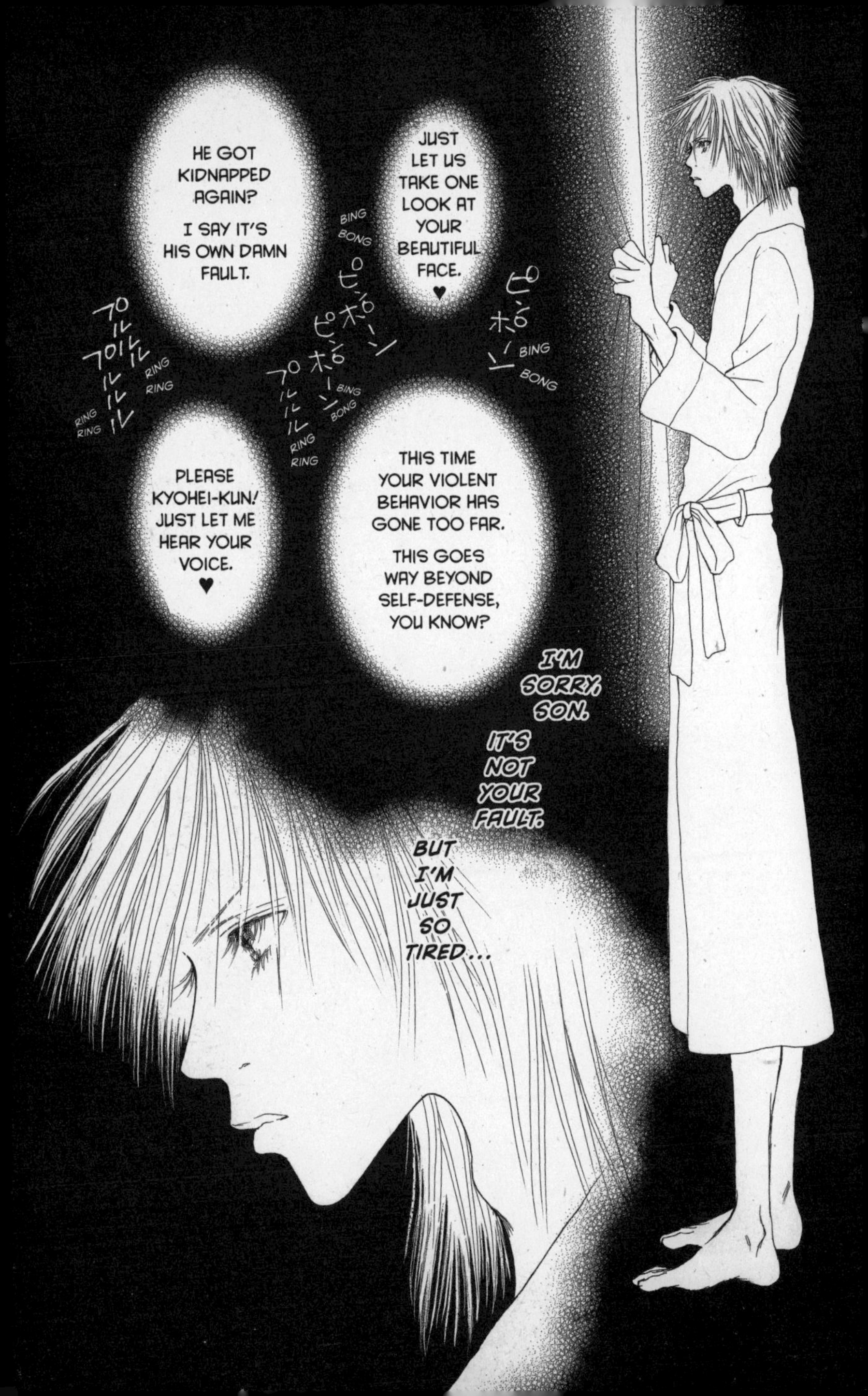
JUST LET US TAKE ONE LOOK AT YOUR BEAUTIFUL FACE. ♥
BING BONG
HE GOT KIDNAPPED AGAIN? I SAY IT'S HIS OWN DAMN FAULT.
BING BONG
BING BONG
RING RING
RING RING
RING RING
THIS TIME YOUR VIOLENT BEHAVIOR HAS GONE TOO FAR. THIS GOES WAY BEYOND SELF-DEFENSE, YOU KNOW?
PLEASE KYOHEI-KUN! JUST LET ME HEAR YOUR VOICE. ♥
I'M SORRY, SON.
IT'S NOT YOUR FAULT.
BUT I'M JUST SO TIRED...

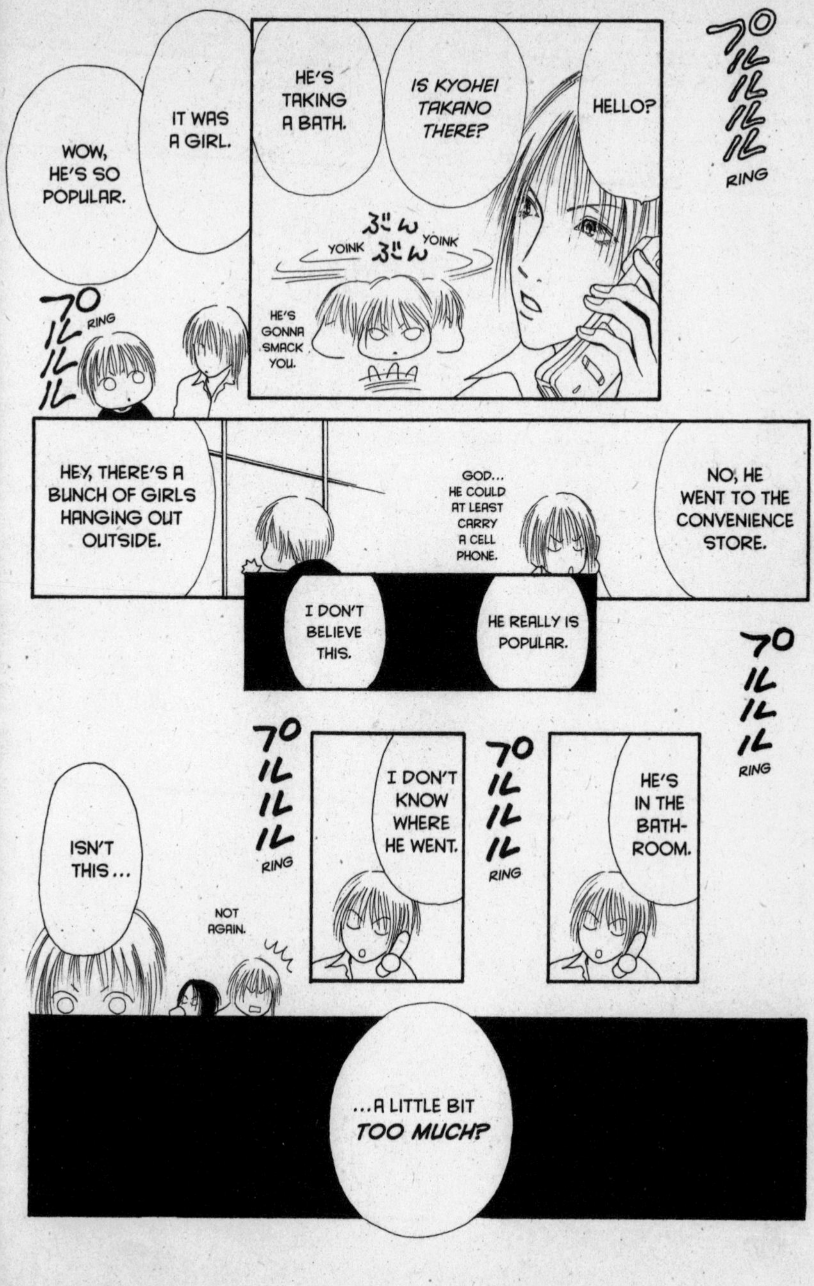

プルルル
RING
HELLO?
IS KYOHEI TAKANO THERE?
HE'S TAKING A BATH.
ぶん ぶん
YOINK YOINK
HE'S GONNA SMACK YOU.
IT WAS A GIRL.
WOW, HE'S SO POPULAR.
プルルル
RING
NO, HE WENT TO THE CONVENIENCE STORE.
GOD... HE COULD AT LEAST CARRY A CELL PHONE.
HEY, THERE'S A BUNCH OF GIRLS HANGING OUT OUTSIDE.
HE REALLY IS POPULAR.
I DON'T BELIEVE THIS.
プルルル
RING
HE'S IN THE BATH-ROOM.
プルルル
RING
I DON'T KNOW WHERE HE WENT.
プルルル
RING
ISN'T THIS...
NOT AGAIN.
...A LITTLE BIT *TOO MUCH?*

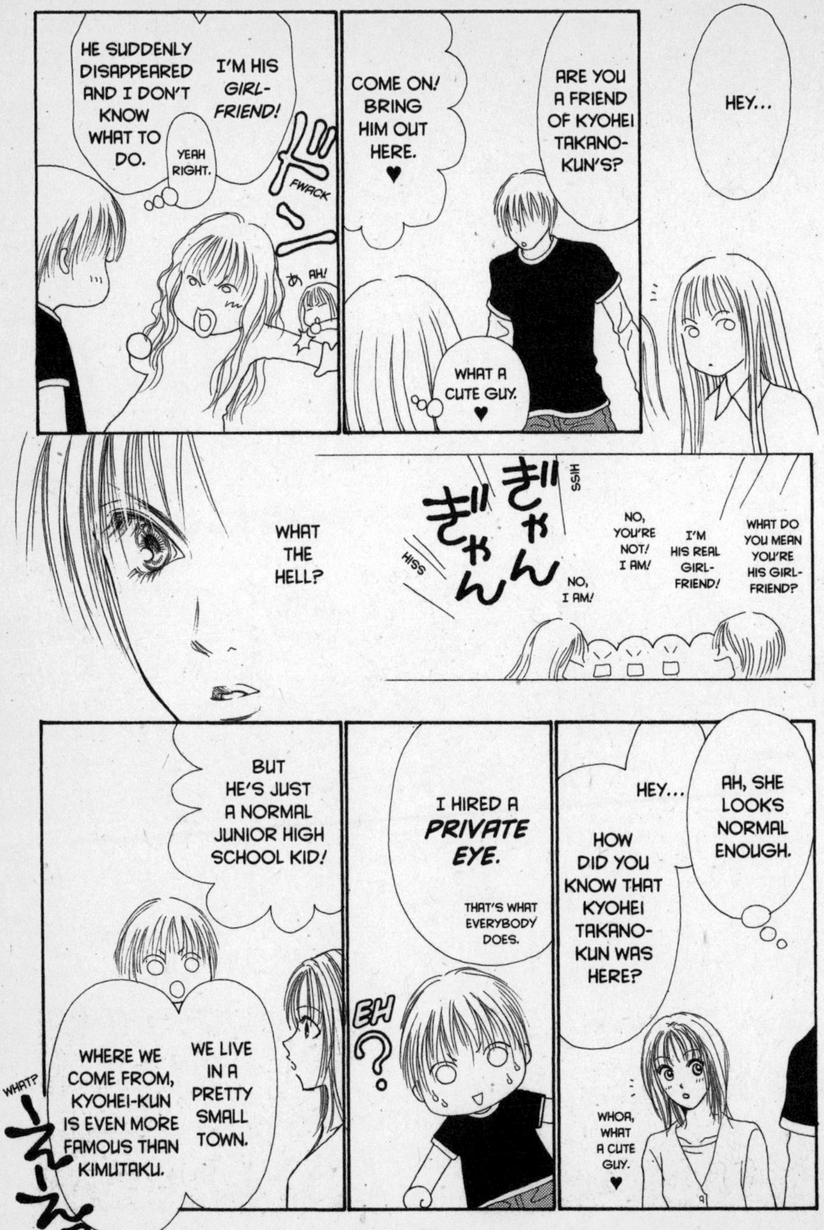
HEY...
ARE YOU A FRIEND OF KYOHEI TAKANO-KUN'S?
COME ON! BRING HIM OUT HERE. ♥
WHAT A CUTE GUY. ♥
I'M HIS GIRL-FRIEND!
HE SUDDENLY DISAPPEARED AND I DON'T KNOW WHAT TO DO.
YEAH RIGHT.
FWACK
あ AH!
WHAT DO YOU MEAN YOU'RE HIS GIRL-FRIEND?
I'M HIS REAL GIRL-FRIEND!
NO, YOU'RE NOT! I AM!
NO, I AM!
HISS
HISS
WHAT THE HELL?
AH, SHE LOOKS NORMAL ENOUGH.
HEY... HOW DID YOU KNOW THAT KYOHEI TAKANO-KUN WAS HERE?
WHOA, WHAT A CUTE GUY. ♥
I HIRED A *PRIVATE EYE.*
THAT'S WHAT EVERYBODY DOES.
EH?
BUT HE'S JUST A NORMAL JUNIOR HIGH SCHOOL KID!
WE LIVE IN A PRETTY SMALL TOWN.
WHERE WE COME FROM, KYOHEI-KUN IS EVEN MORE FAMOUS THAN KIMUTAKU.
WHAT?

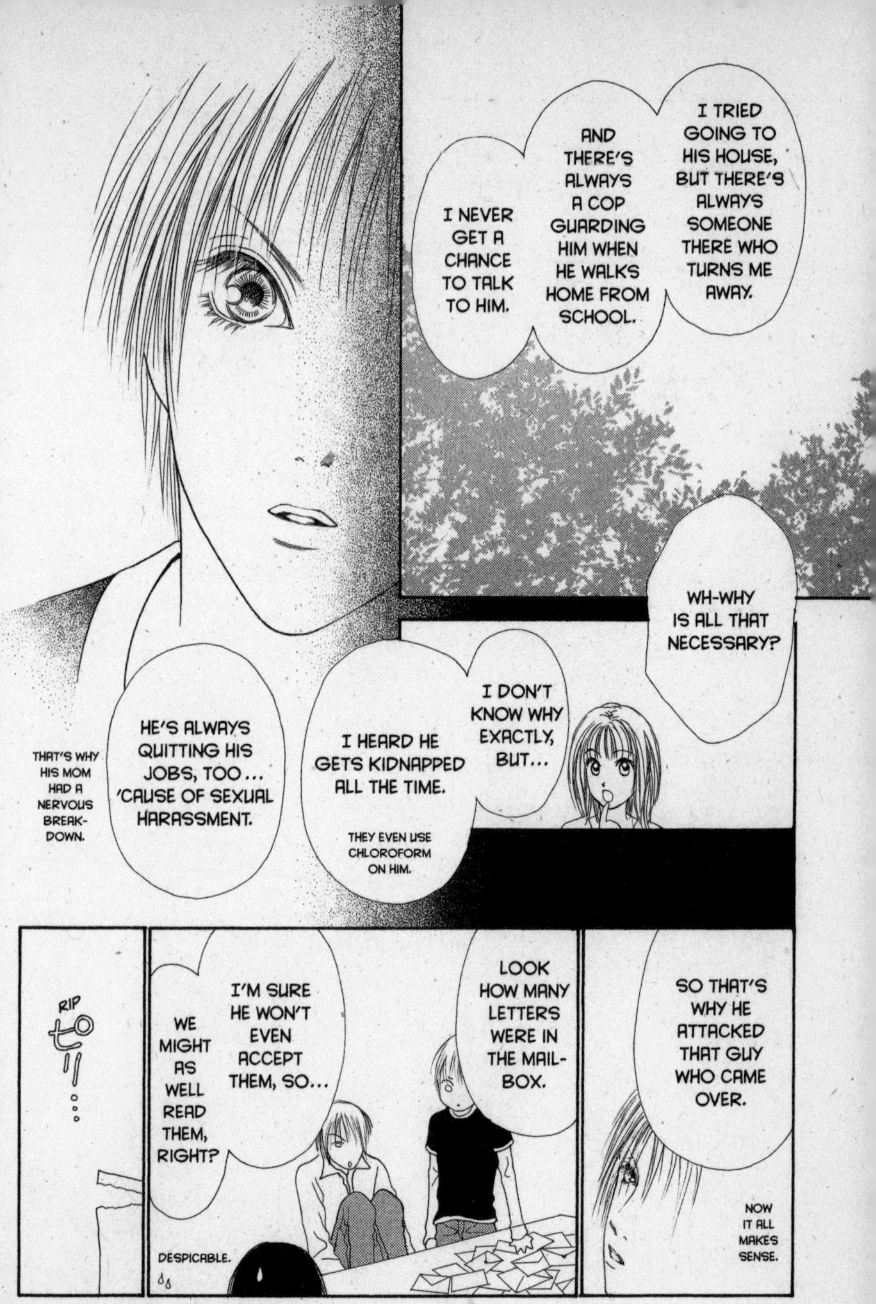
I TRIED GOING TO HIS HOUSE, BUT THERE'S ALWAYS SOMEONE THERE WHO TURNS ME AWAY.
AND THERE'S ALWAYS A COP GUARDING HIM WHEN HE WALKS HOME FROM SCHOOL.
I NEVER GET A CHANCE TO TALK TO HIM.
WH-WHY IS ALL THAT NECESSARY?
I DON'T KNOW WHY EXACTLY, BUT...
I HEARD HE GETS KIDNAPPED ALL THE TIME.
THEY EVEN USE CHLOROFORM ON HIM.
HE'S ALWAYS QUITTING HIS JOBS, TOO... 'CAUSE OF SEXUAL HARASSMENT.
THAT'S WHY HIS MOM HAD A NERVOUS BREAK-DOWN.
SO THAT'S WHY HE ATTACKED THAT GUY WHO CAME OVER.
NOW IT ALL MAKES SENSE.
LOOK HOW MANY LETTERS WERE IN THE MAIL-BOX.
I'M SURE HE WON'T EVEN ACCEPT THEM, SO...
WE MIGHT AS WELL READ THEM, RIGHT?
DESPICABLE.
RIP

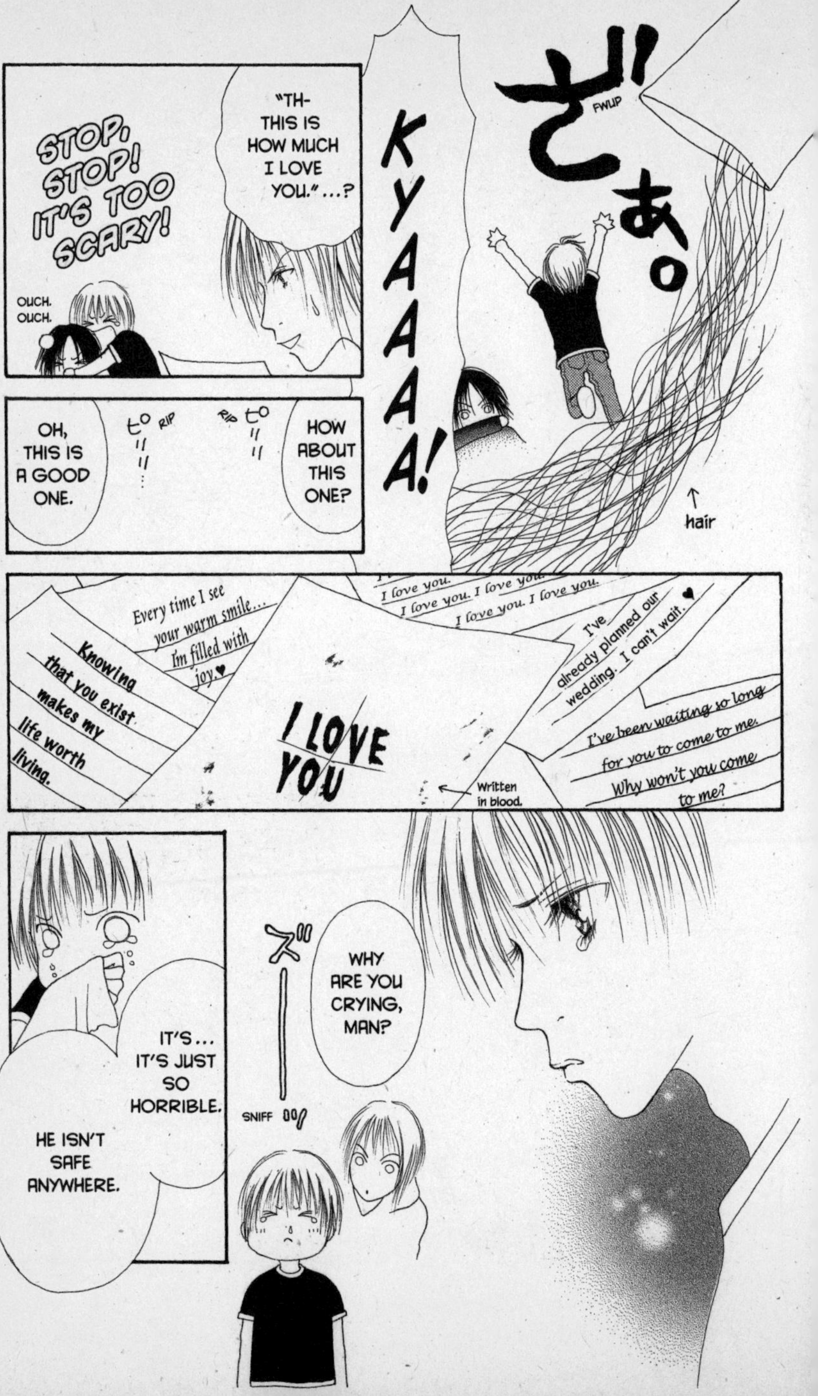
ざあ。
FWUP
KYAAAAA!
↑ hair
"TH-THIS IS HOW MUCH I LOVE YOU." ...?
STOP, STOP! IT'S TOO SCARY!
OUCH. OUCH.
HOW ABOUT THIS ONE?
ピッ RIP
ピッ RIP
OH, THIS IS A GOOD ONE.
I've been waiting so long for you to come to me. Why won't you come to me?
I've already planned our wedding. I can't wait. ♥
I love you. I love you. I love you. I love you. I love you.
Written in blood.
I LOVE YOU
Every time I see your warm smile... I'm filled with joy.♥
Knowing that you exist makes my life worth living.
WHY ARE YOU CRYING, MAN?
ズー
SNIFF
IT'S... IT'S JUST SO HORRIBLE.
HE ISN'T SAFE ANYWHERE.

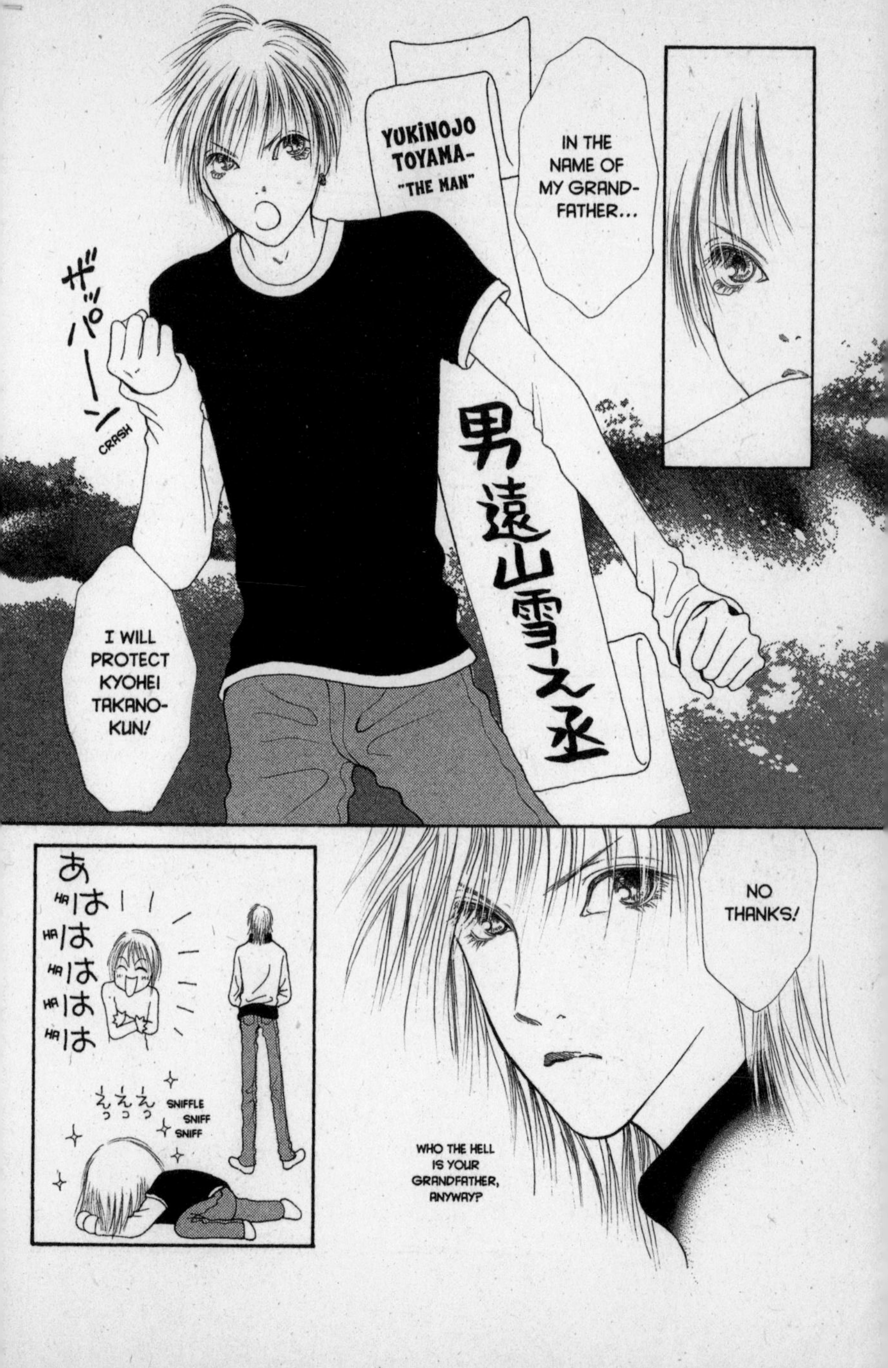

IN THE NAME OF MY GRAND-FATHER...
YUKINOJO TOYAMA- "THE MAN"
男遠山雪之丞
ザッパーン
CRASH
I WILL PROTECT KYOHEI TAKANO-KUN!
NO THANKS!
WHO THE HELL IS YOUR GRANDFATHER, ANYWAY?
あははははは
HA HA HA HA HA
えっえっえっ
SNIFFLE SNIFF SNIFF

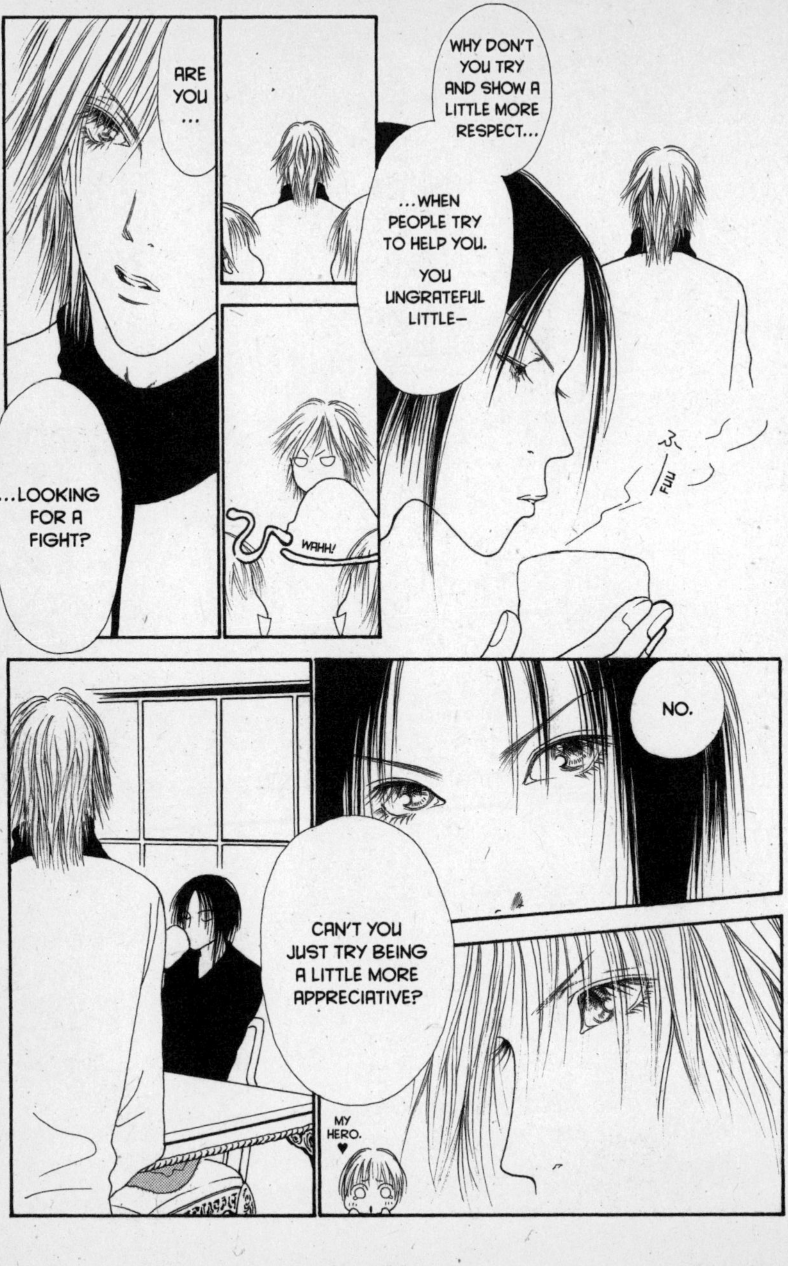
WHY DON'T YOU TRY AND SHOW A LITTLE MORE RESPECT...
...WHEN PEOPLE TRY TO HELP YOU.
YOU UNGRATEFUL LITTLE—
ふ— FUU
WAHH!
ARE YOU ...
...LOOKING FOR A FIGHT?
NO.
CAN'T YOU JUST TRY BEING A LITTLE MORE APPRECIATIVE?
MY HERO. ♥

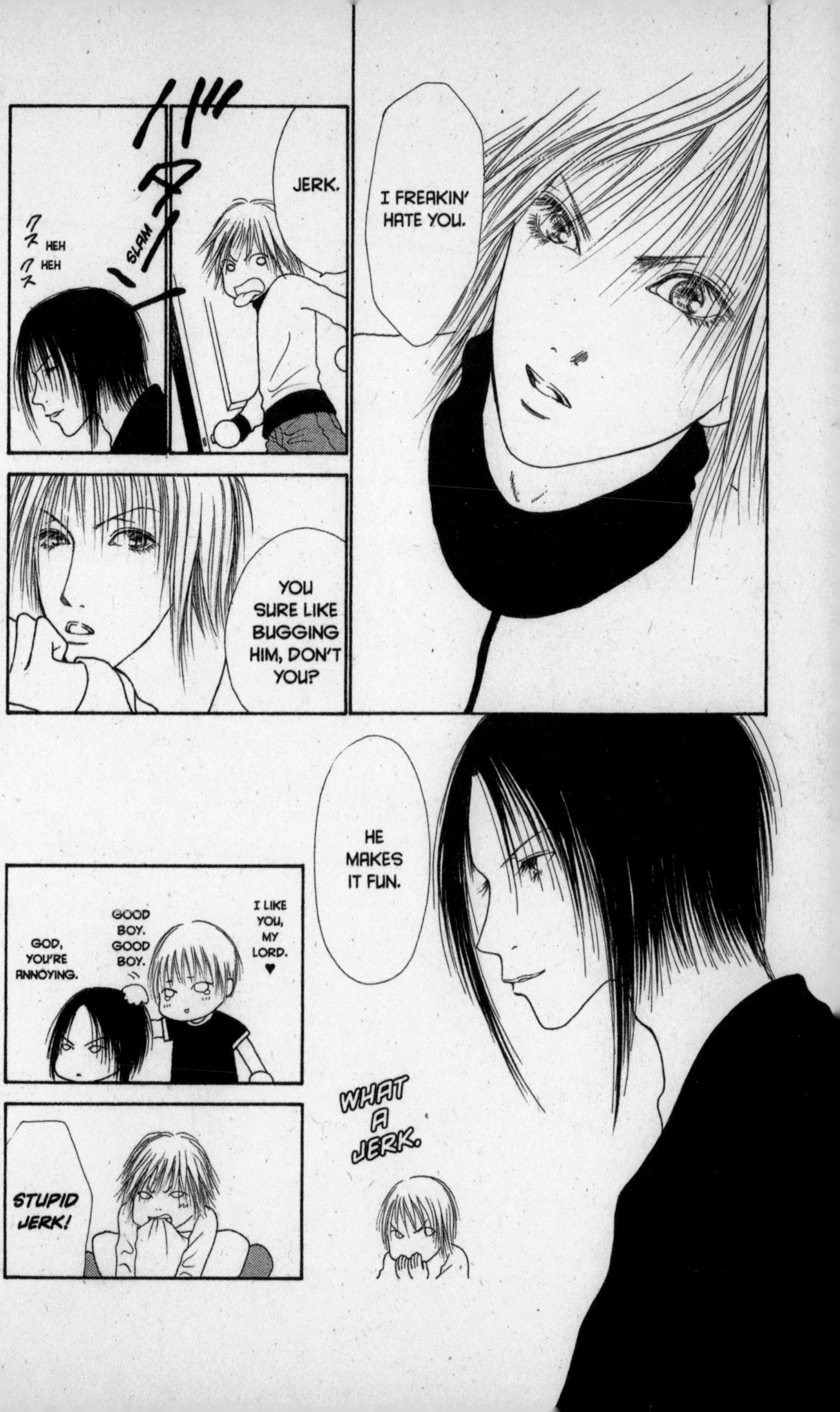
I FREAKIN' HATE YOU.
JERK.
バタン
SLAM
HEH HEH
YOU SURE LIKE BUGGING HIM, DON'T YOU?
HE MAKES IT FUN.
WHAT A JERK.
I LIKE YOU, MY LORD. ♥
GOOD BOY. GOOD BOY.
GOD, YOU'RE ANNOYING.
STUPID JERK!

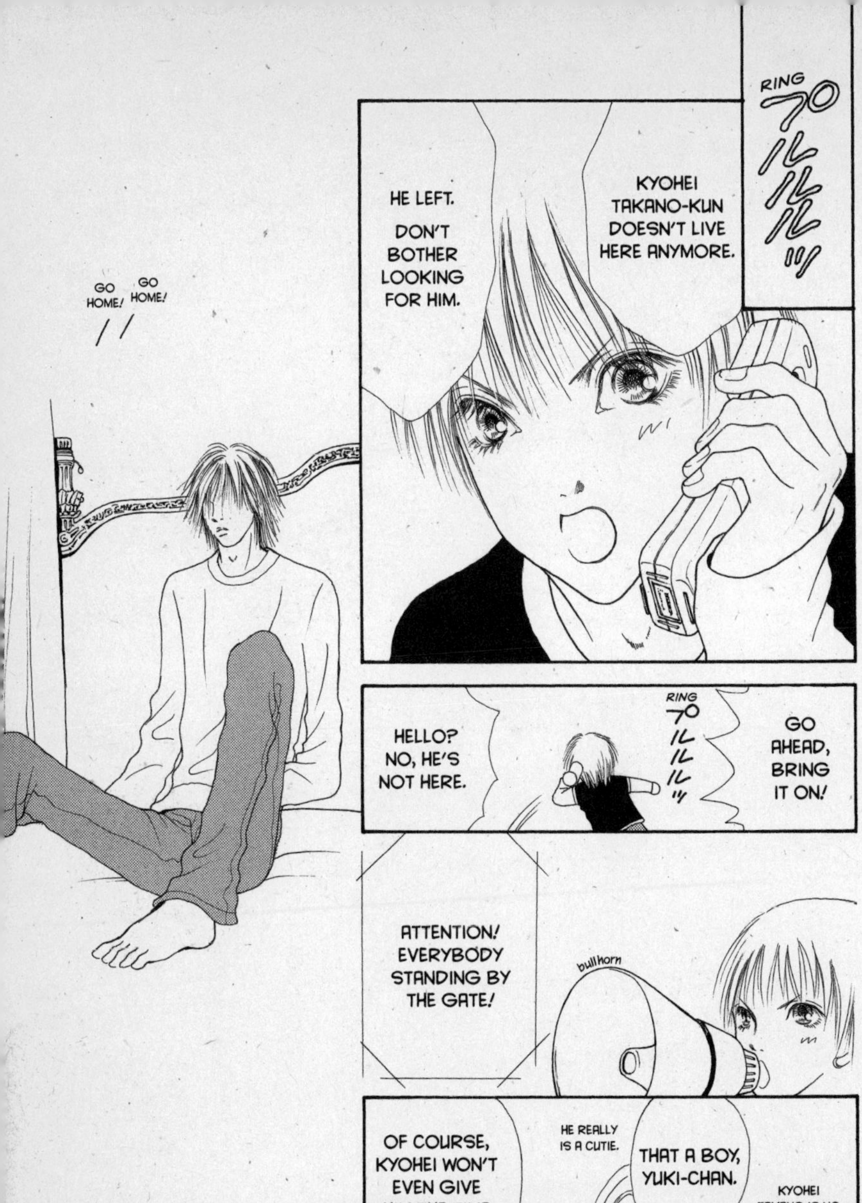
RING
KYOHEI TAKANO-KUN DOESN'T LIVE HERE ANYMORE.
HE LEFT.
DON'T BOTHER LOOKING FOR HIM.
GO AHEAD, BRING IT ON!
RING
HELLO? NO, HE'S NOT HERE.
ATTENTION! EVERYBODY STANDING BY THE GATE!
bullhorn
KYOHEI TAKANO IS NO LONGER HERE! PLEASE, RETURN TO YOUR HOMES IMMEDIATELY!
THAT A BOY, YUKI-CHAN.
HE REALLY IS A CUTIE.
OF COURSE, KYOHEI WON'T EVEN GIVE HIM THE TIME OF DAY.
GO HOME!
GO HOME!

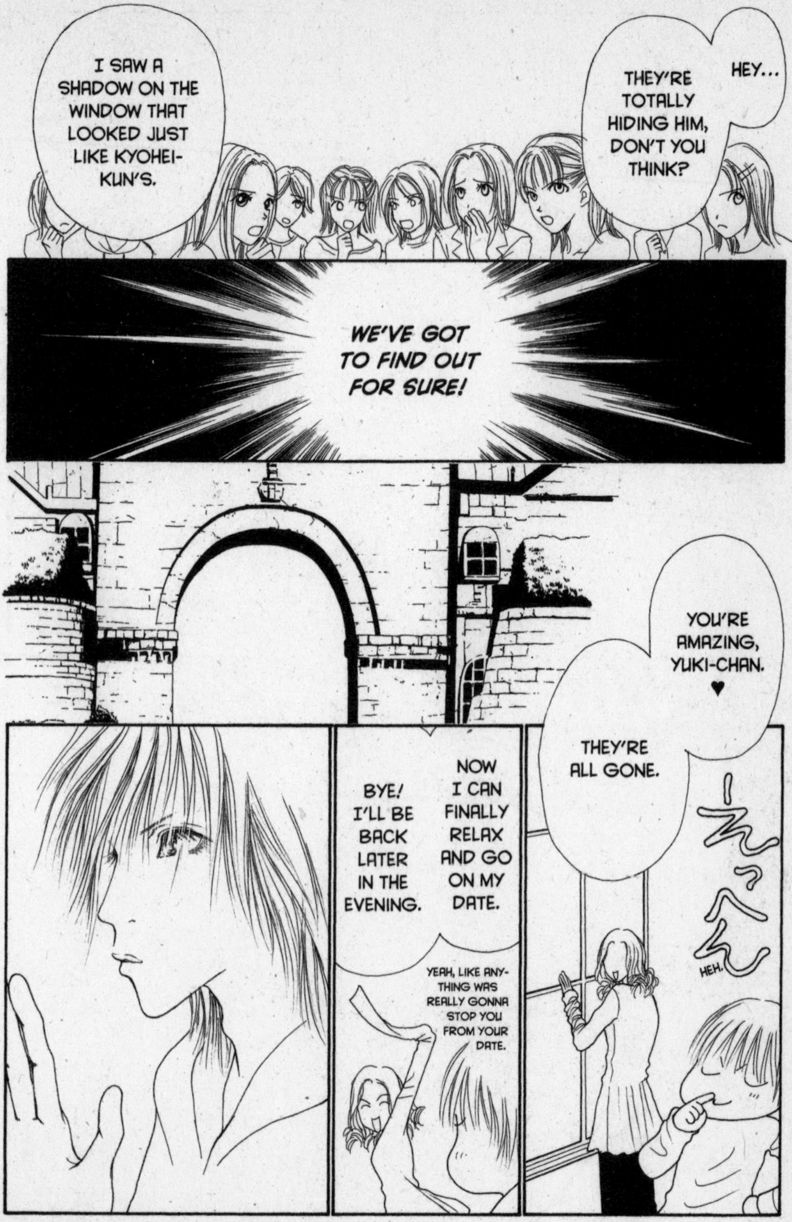
HEY...
THEY'RE TOTALLY HIDING HIM, DON'T YOU THINK?
I SAW A SHADOW ON THE WINDOW THAT LOOKED JUST LIKE KYOHEI-KUN'S.
WE'VE GOT TO FIND OUT FOR SURE!
YOU'RE AMAZING, YUKI-CHAN. ♥
THEY'RE ALL GONE.
えっへん
HEH.
NOW I CAN FINALLY RELAX AND GO ON MY DATE.
BYE! I'LL BE BACK LATER IN THE EVENING.
YEAH, LIKE ANYTHING WAS REALLY GONNA STOP YOU FROM YOUR DATE.

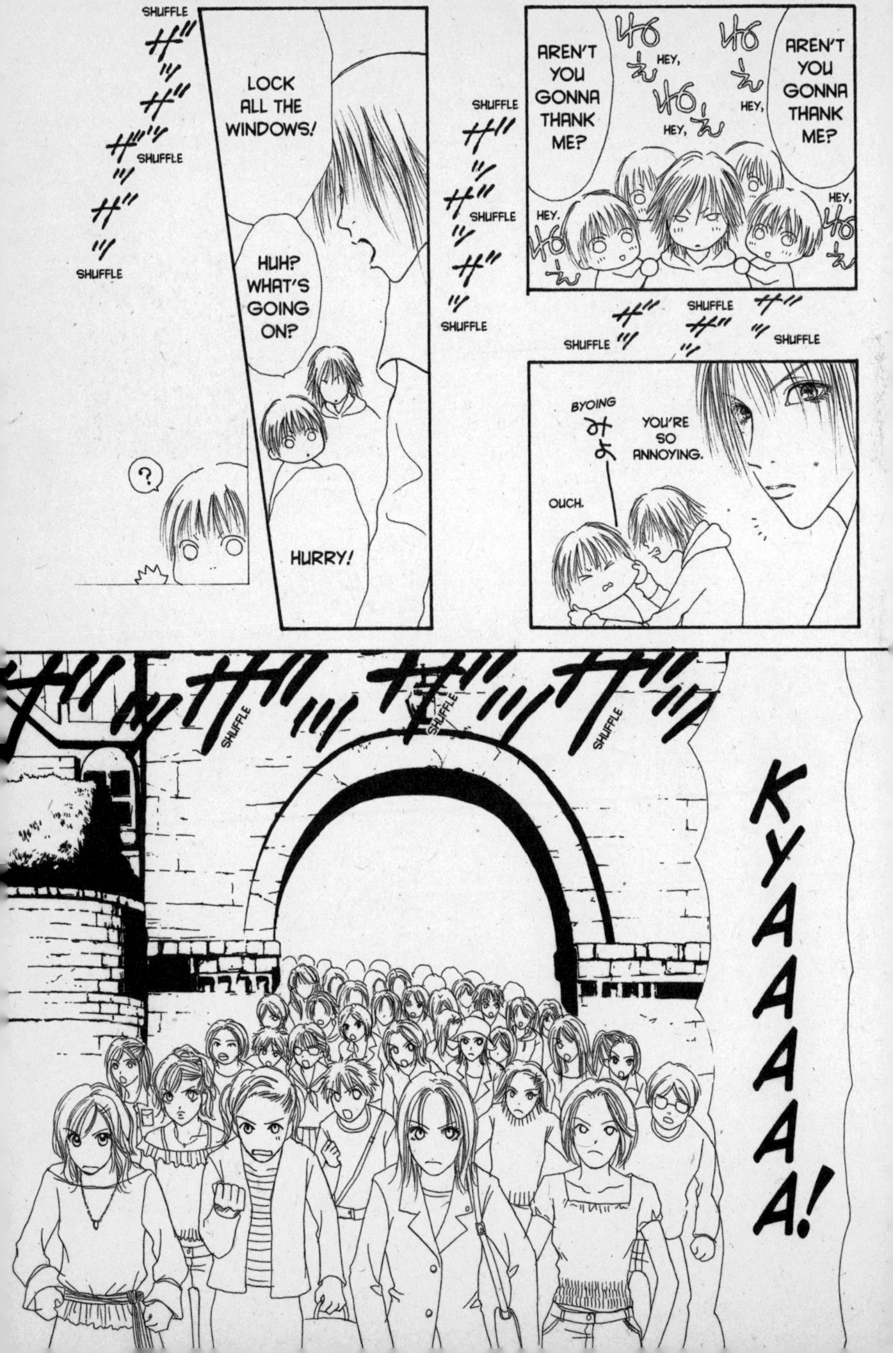
AREN'T YOU GONNA THANK ME?
HEY,
HEY,
HEY,
HEY.
AREN'T YOU GONNA THANK ME?
SHUFFLE
SHUFFLE
SHUFFLE
SHUFFLE
YOU'RE SO ANNOYING.
BYOING
みよ
OUCH.
SHUFFLE
SHUFFLE
LOCK ALL THE WINDOWS!
HUH? WHAT'S GOING ON?
HURRY!
SHUFFLE
SHUFFLE
SHUFFLE
?
SHUFFLE
SHUFFLE
SHUFFLE
KYAAAAA!

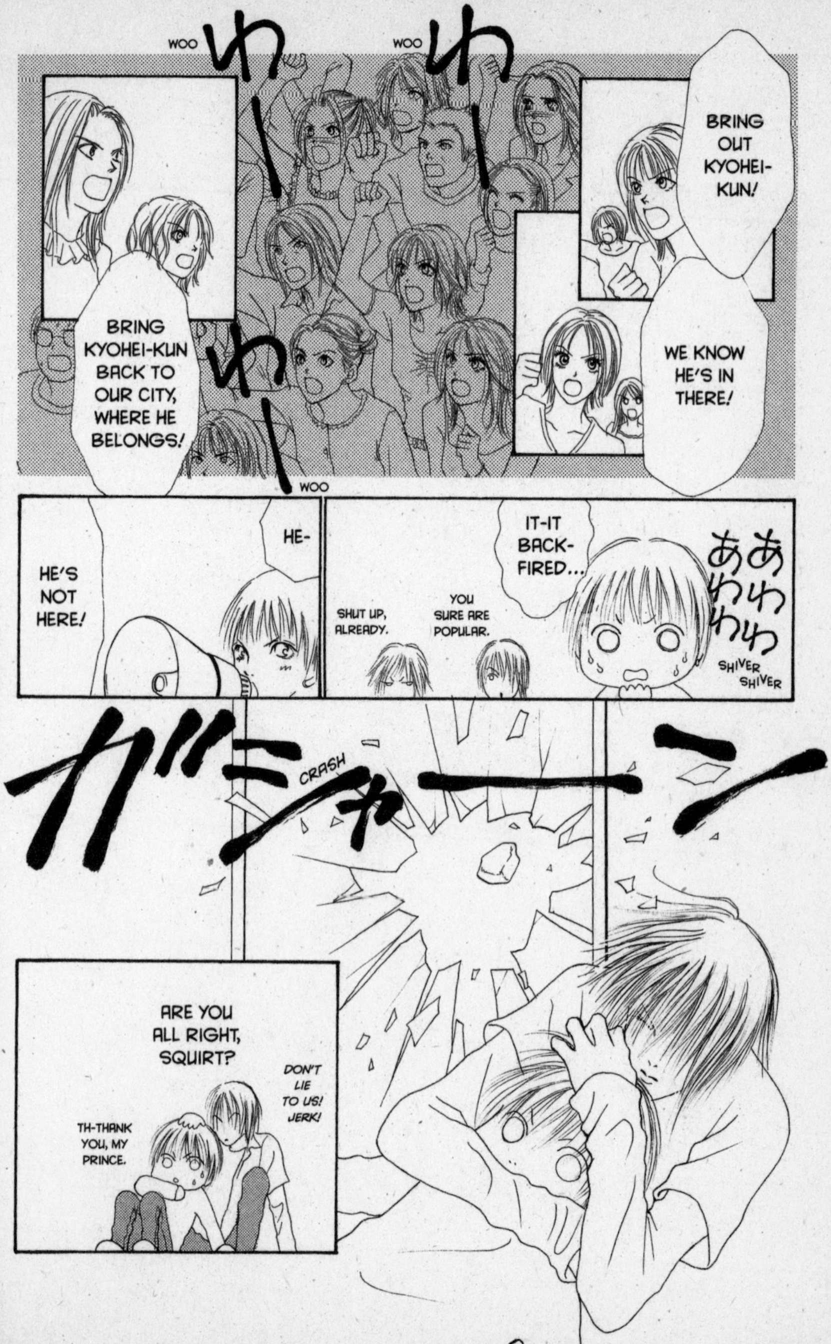

BRING OUT KYOHEI-KUN!
WE KNOW HE'S IN THERE!
わー
WOO
わー
WOO
わー
WOO
BRING KYOHEI-KUN BACK TO OUR CITY, WHERE HE BELONGS!
あわわわわ
SHIVER SHIVER
IT-IT BACKFIRED...
YOU SURE ARE POPULAR.
SHUT UP, ALREADY.
HE-
HE'S NOT HERE!
ガシャーン
CRASH
DON'T LIE TO US! JERK!
ARE YOU ALL RIGHT, SQUIRT?
TH-THANK YOU, MY PRINCE.

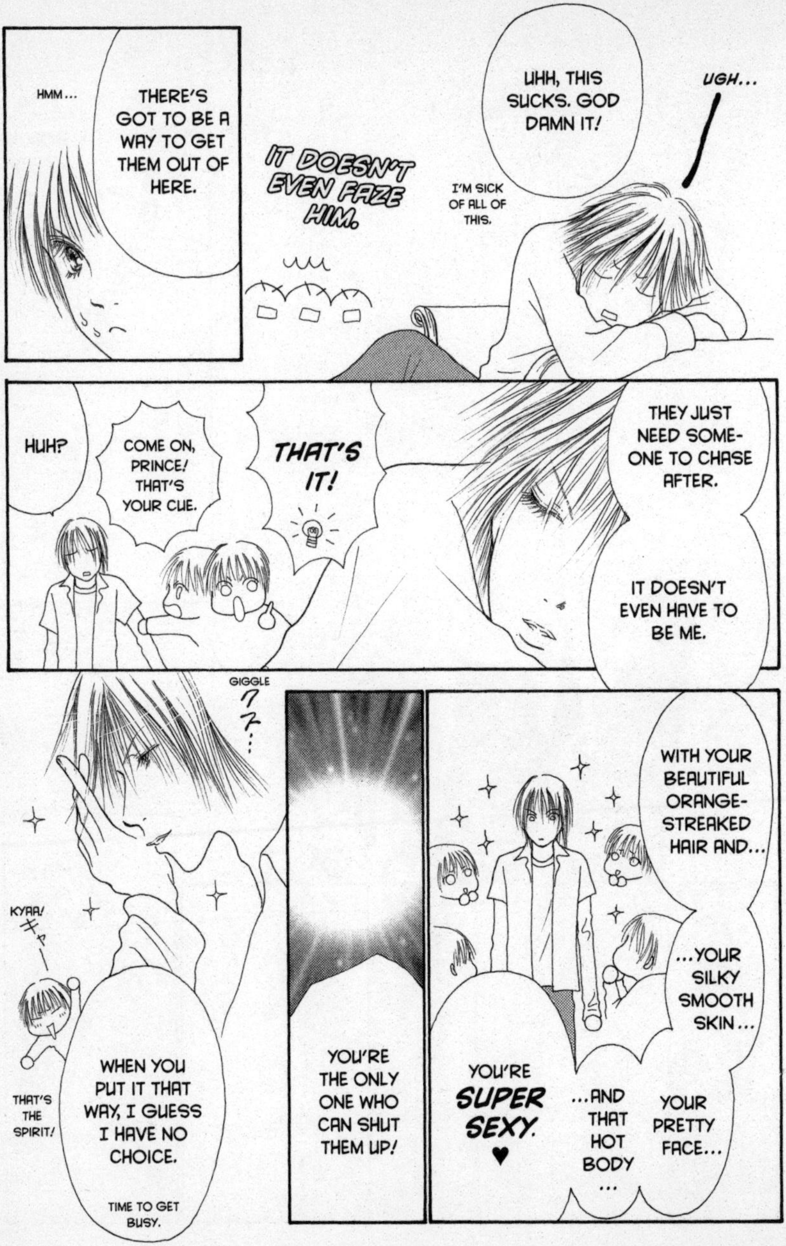
UGH...
UHH, THIS SUCKS. GOD DAMN IT!
I'M SICK OF ALL OF THIS.
IT DOESN'T EVEN FAZE HIM.
THERE'S GOT TO BE A WAY TO GET THEM OUT OF HERE.
HMM...
THEY JUST NEED SOME-ONE TO CHASE AFTER.
IT DOESN'T EVEN HAVE TO BE ME.
THAT'S IT!
COME ON, PRINCE! THAT'S YOUR CUE.
HUH?
WITH YOUR BEAUTIFUL ORANGE-STREAKED HAIR AND...
...YOUR SILKY SMOOTH SKIN...
YOUR PRETTY FACE...
...AND THAT HOT BODY...
YOU'RE SUPER SEXY. ♥
YOU'RE THE ONLY ONE WHO CAN SHUT THEM UP!
GIGGLE
クス…
WHEN YOU PUT IT THAT WAY, I GUESS I HAVE NO CHOICE.
TIME TO GET BUSY.
KYAA!
キャー
THAT'S THE SPIRIT!

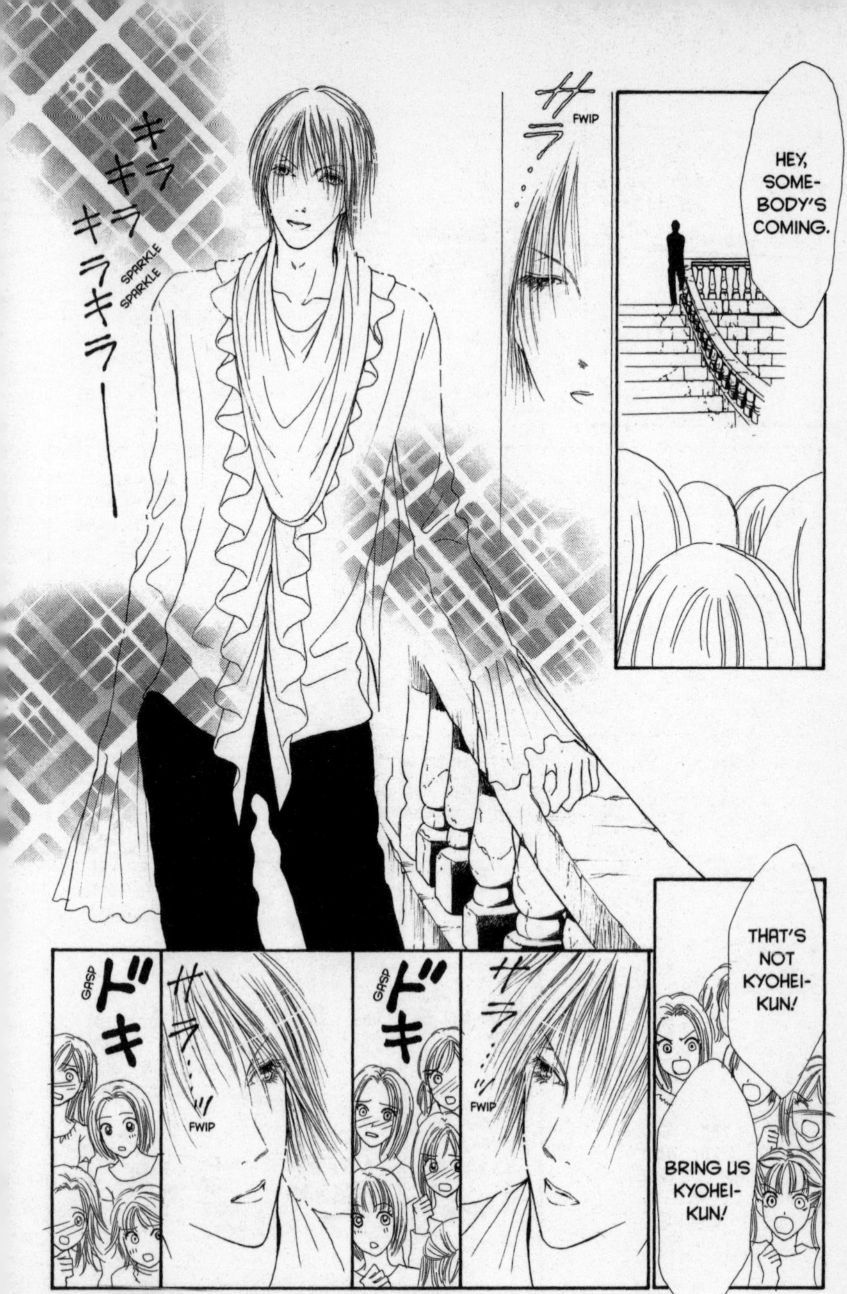
HEY, SOME-BODY'S COMING.
サラ
FWIP
キラキラキラキラー
SPARKLE SPARKLE
THAT'S NOT KYOHEI-KUN!
BRING US KYOHEI-KUN!
サラ…ッ
FWIP
ドキ
GASP
サラ…ッ
FWIP
ドキ
GASP

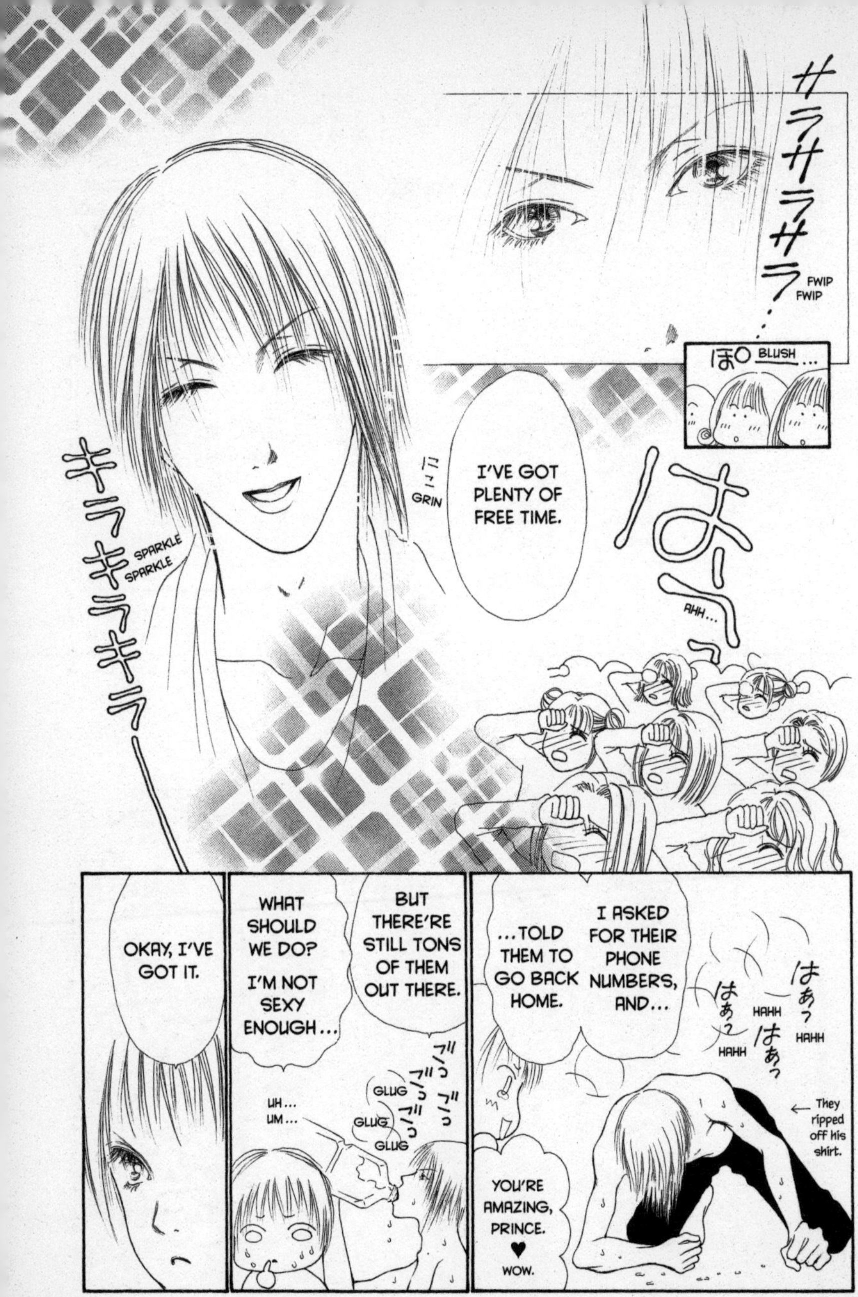
サラサラサラ…
FWIP FWIP
ぽ BLUSH…
I'VE GOT PLENTY OF FREE TIME.
にっ GRIN
キラキラキラ
SPARKLE SPARKLE
はぁ〜っ
AHH…
I ASKED FOR THEIR PHONE NUMBERS, AND…
…TOLD THEM TO GO BACK HOME.
はあっ はあっ はあっ
HAHH HAHH HAHH
← They ripped off his shirt.
YOU'RE AMAZING, PRINCE. ♥ WOW.
BUT THERE'RE STILL TONS OF THEM OUT THERE.
WHAT SHOULD WE DO? I'M NOT SEXY ENOUGH…
ゴッゴッゴッゴッ
GLUG GLUG GLUG
UH… UM…
OKAY, I'VE GOT IT.

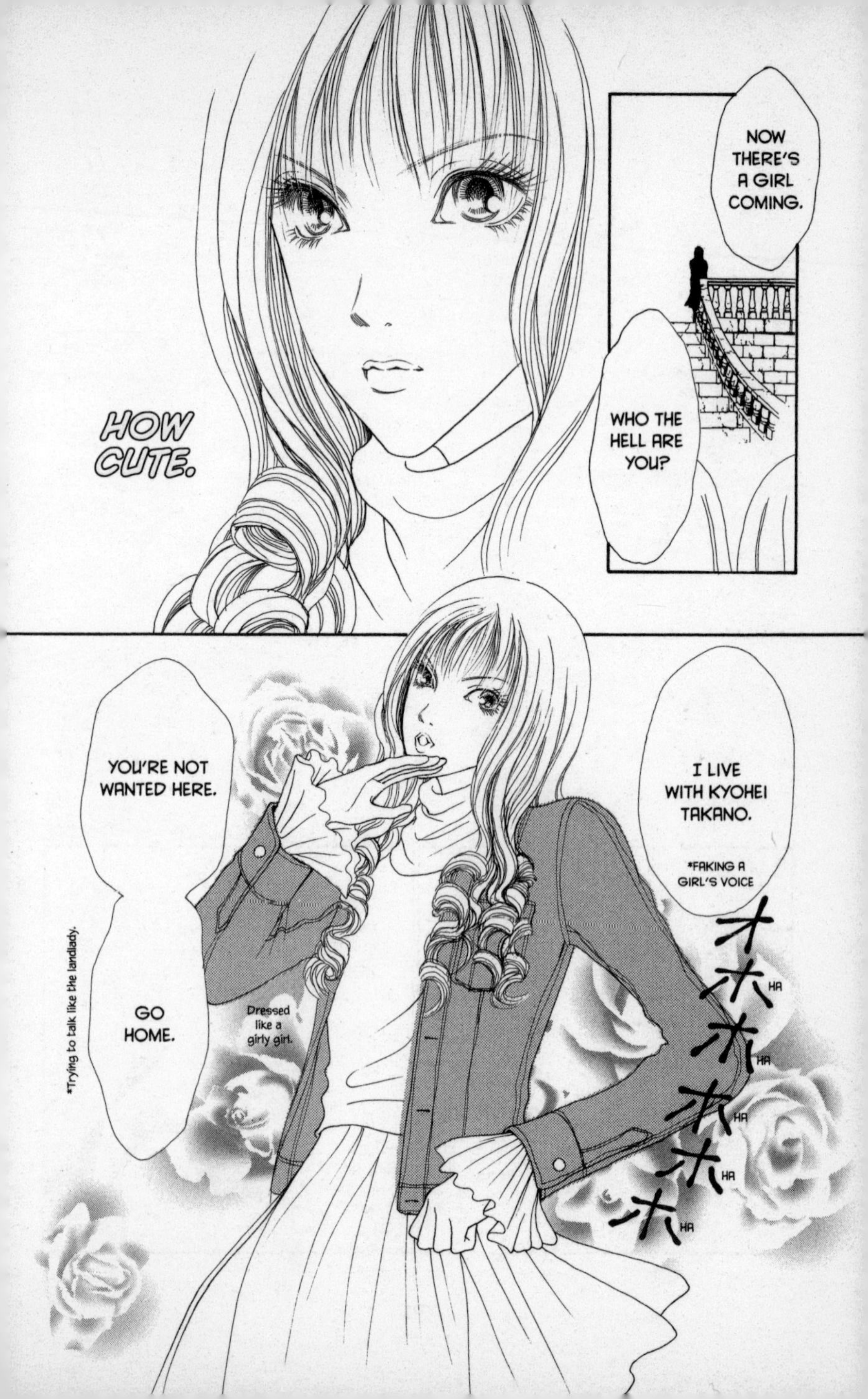
NOW THERE'S A GIRL COMING.
WHO THE HELL ARE YOU?
HOW CUTE.
I LIVE WITH KYOHEI TAKANO.
*FAKING A GIRL'S VOICE
オホホホホ
HA HA HA HA HA
YOU'RE NOT WANTED HERE.
GO HOME.
Dressed like a girly girl.
*Trying to talk like the landlady.

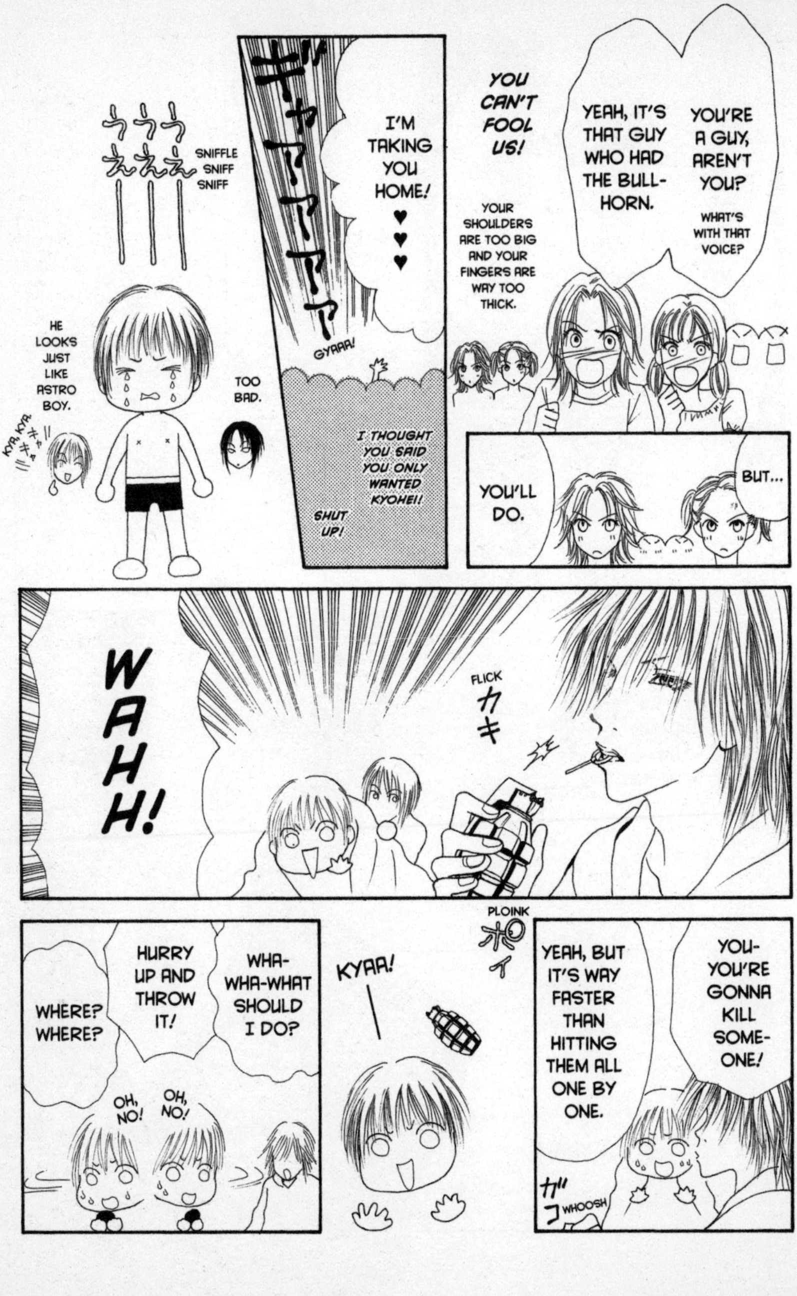
YOU'RE A GUY, AREN'T YOU?
YEAH, IT'S THAT GUY WHO HAD THE BULL-HORN.
WHAT'S WITH THAT VOICE?
YOU CAN'T FOOL US!
YOUR SHOULDERS ARE TOO BIG AND YOUR FINGERS ARE WAY TOO THICK.
BUT...
YOU'LL DO.
I'M TAKING YOU HOME! ♥ ♥ ♥
ギャアアアア
GYAAA!
I THOUGHT YOU SAID YOU ONLY WANTED KYOHEI!
SHUT UP!
うえうえうえ
SNIFFLE SNIFF SNIFF
TOO BAD.
HE LOOKS JUST LIKE ASTRO BOY.
KYA, KYA
キャッキャッ
FLICK
カキ
WAHH!
PLOINK
ポイ
YOU-YOU'RE GONNA KILL SOME-ONE!
YEAH, BUT IT'S WAY FASTER THAN HITTING THEM ALL ONE BY ONE.
ガコ
WHOOSH
KYAA!
WHA-WHA-WHAT SHOULD I DO?
HURRY UP AND THROW IT!
WHERE? WHERE?
OH, NO!
OH, NO!

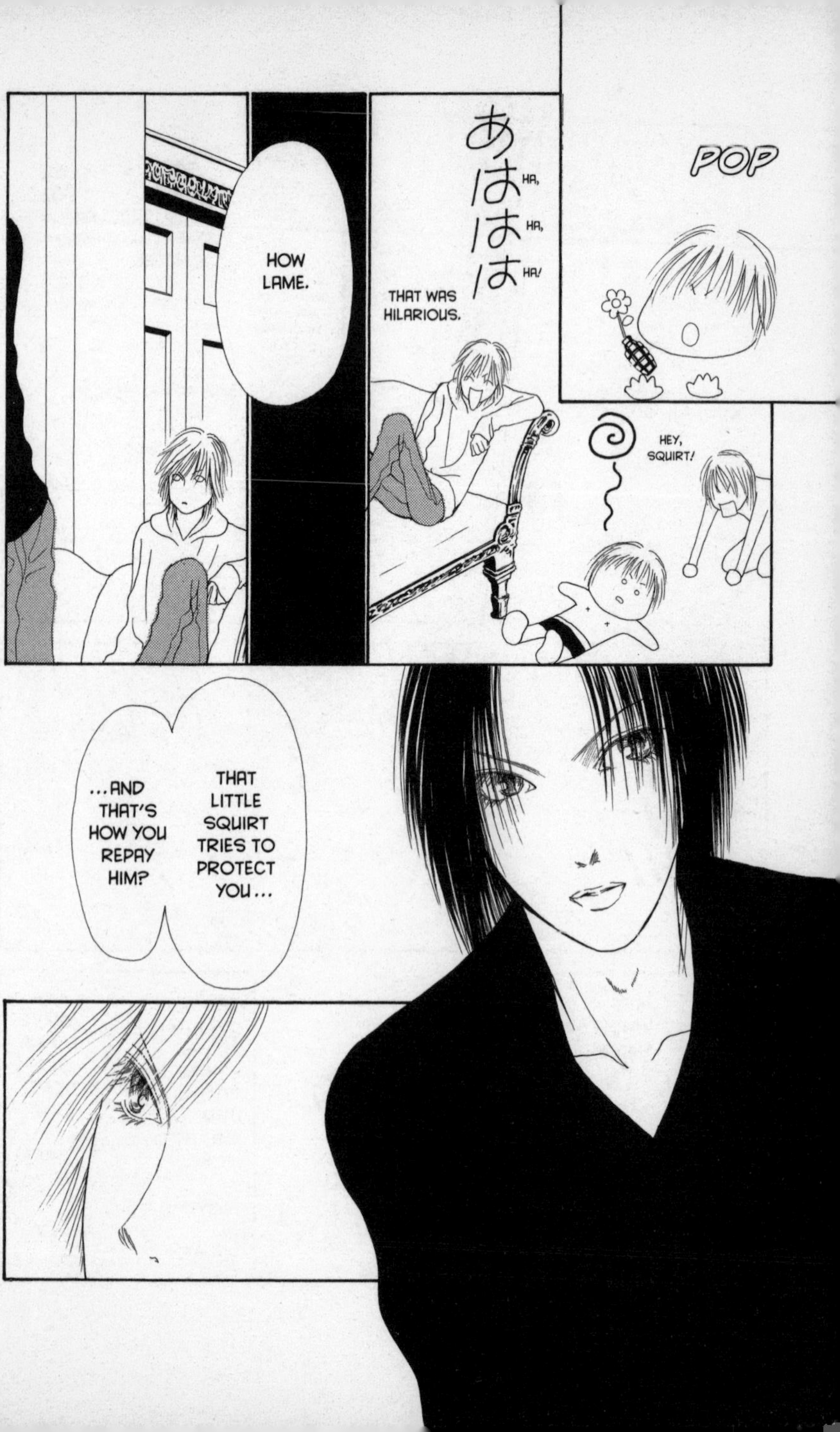
POP
HEY, SQUIRT!
あはは HA, HA, HA!
THAT WAS HILARIOUS.
HOW LAME.
THAT LITTLE SQUIRT TRIES TO PROTECT YOU...
...AND THAT'S HOW YOU REPAY HIM?

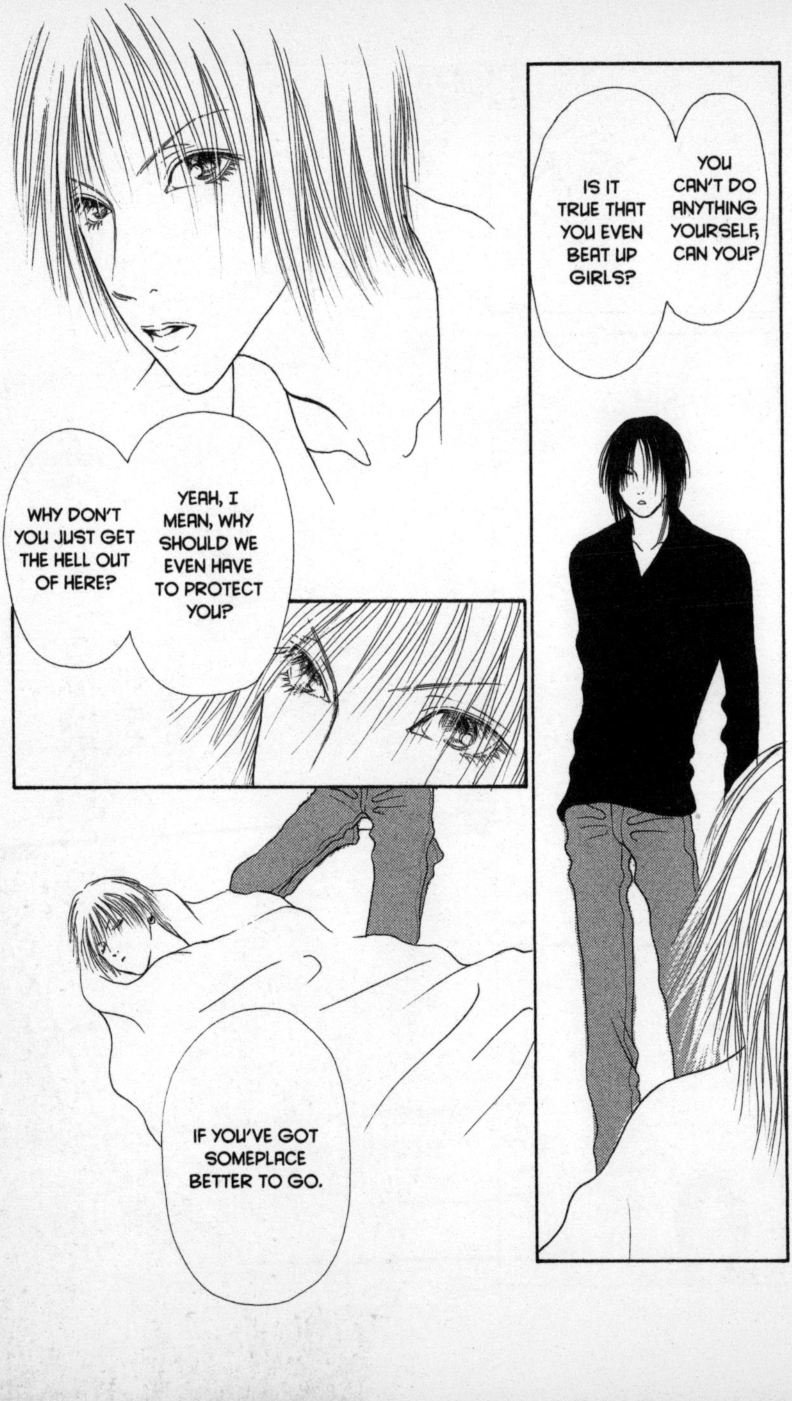
YOU CAN'T DO ANYTHING YOURSELF, CAN YOU?
IS IT TRUE THAT YOU EVEN BEAT UP GIRLS?
YEAH, I MEAN, WHY SHOULD WE EVEN HAVE TO PROTECT YOU?
WHY DON'T YOU JUST GET THE HELL OUT OF HERE?
IF YOU'VE GOT SOMEPLACE BETTER TO GO.

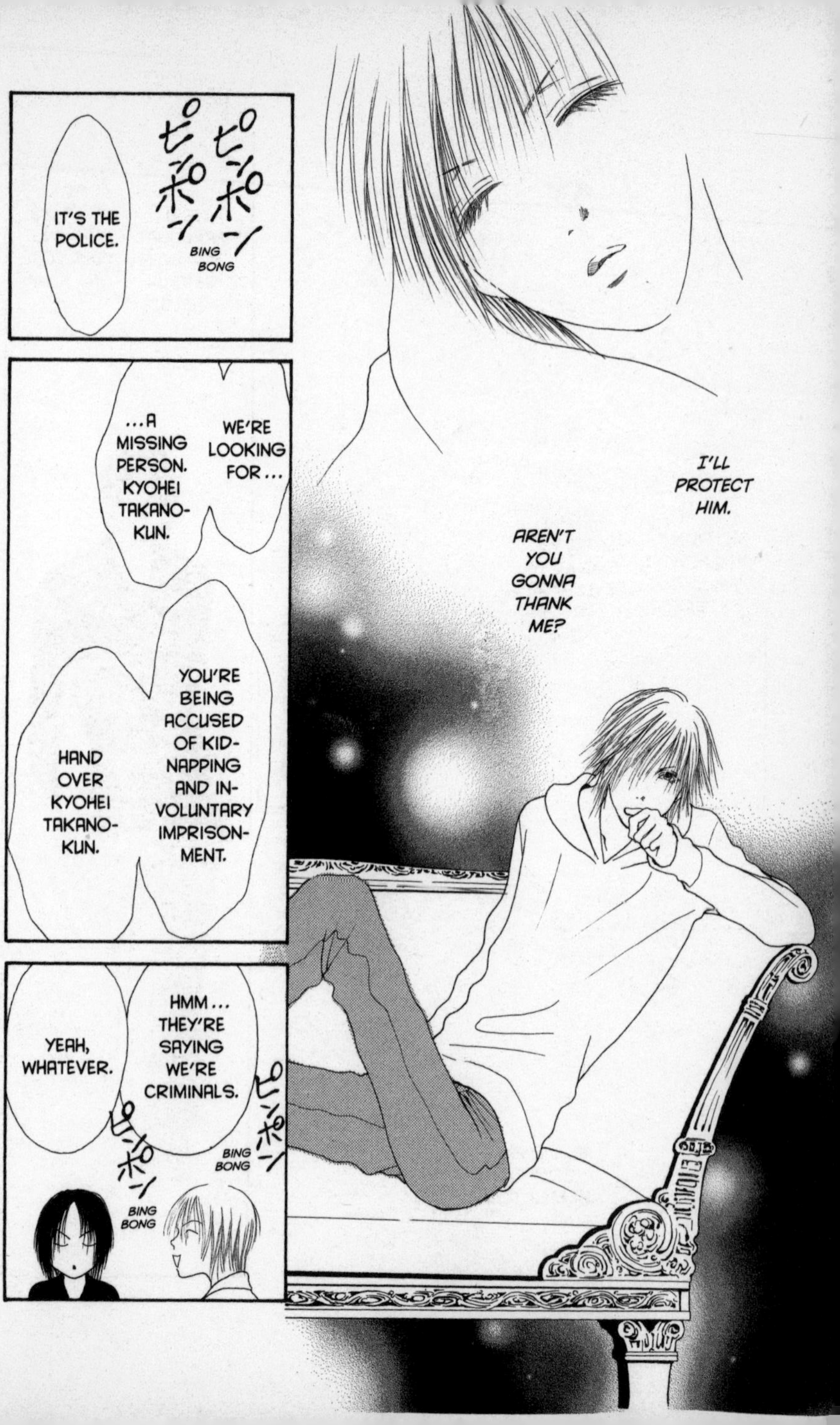
I'LL PROTECT HIM.
AREN'T YOU GONNA THANK ME?
ピンポーン ピンポーン
BING BONG
IT'S THE POLICE.
WE'RE LOOKING FOR...
...A MISSING PERSON. KYOHEI TAKANO-KUN.
YOU'RE BEING ACCUSED OF KID-NAPPING AND IN-VOLUNTARY IMPRISON-MENT.
HAND OVER KYOHEI TAKANO-KUN.
ピンポーン
BING BONG
HMM... THEY'RE SAYING WE'RE CRIMINALS.
YEAH, WHATEVER.
ピンポーン
BING BONG

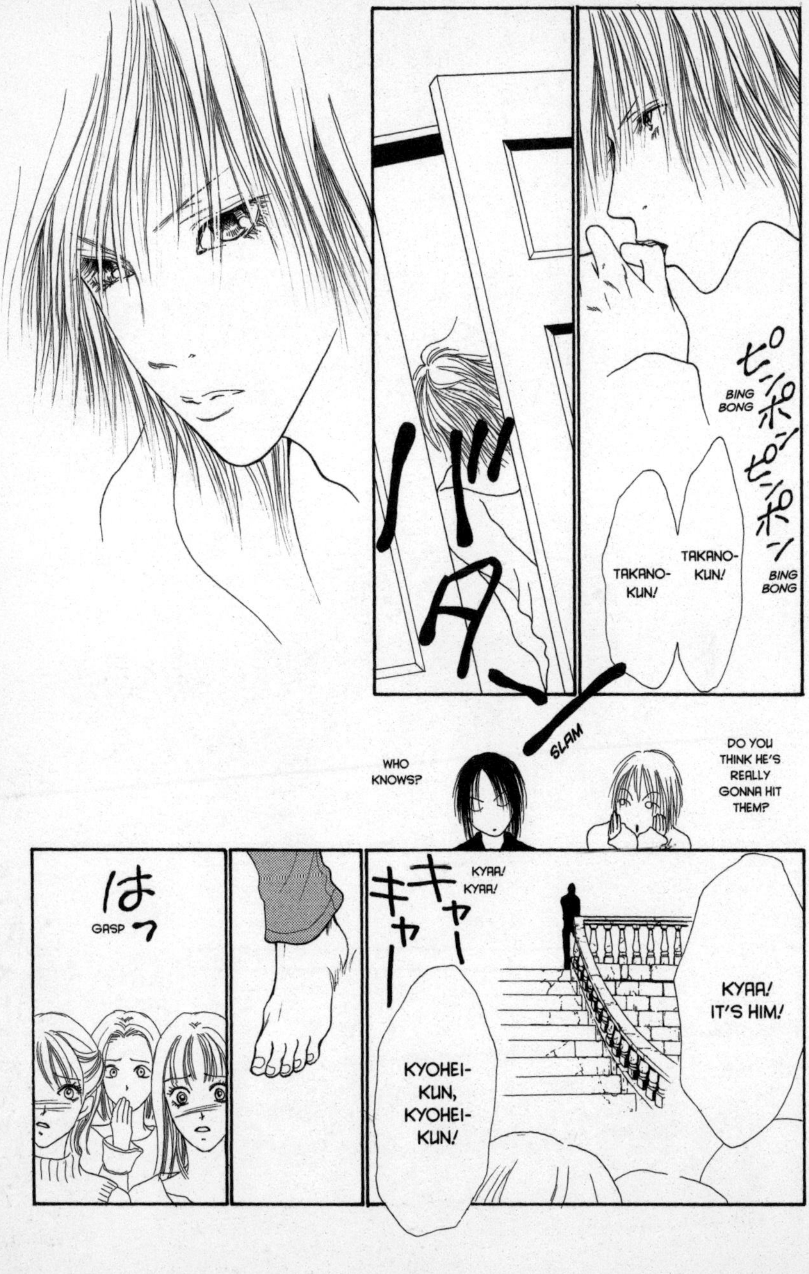
ピンポンピンポン
BING BONG
TAKANO-KUN!
TAKANO-KUN!
BING BONG
バタン
SLAM
DO YOU THINK HE'S REALLY GONNA HIT THEM?
WHO KNOWS?
KYAA! IT'S HIM!
キャーキャー
KYAA! KYAA!
KYOHEI-KUN, KYOHEI-KUN!
はっ
GASP

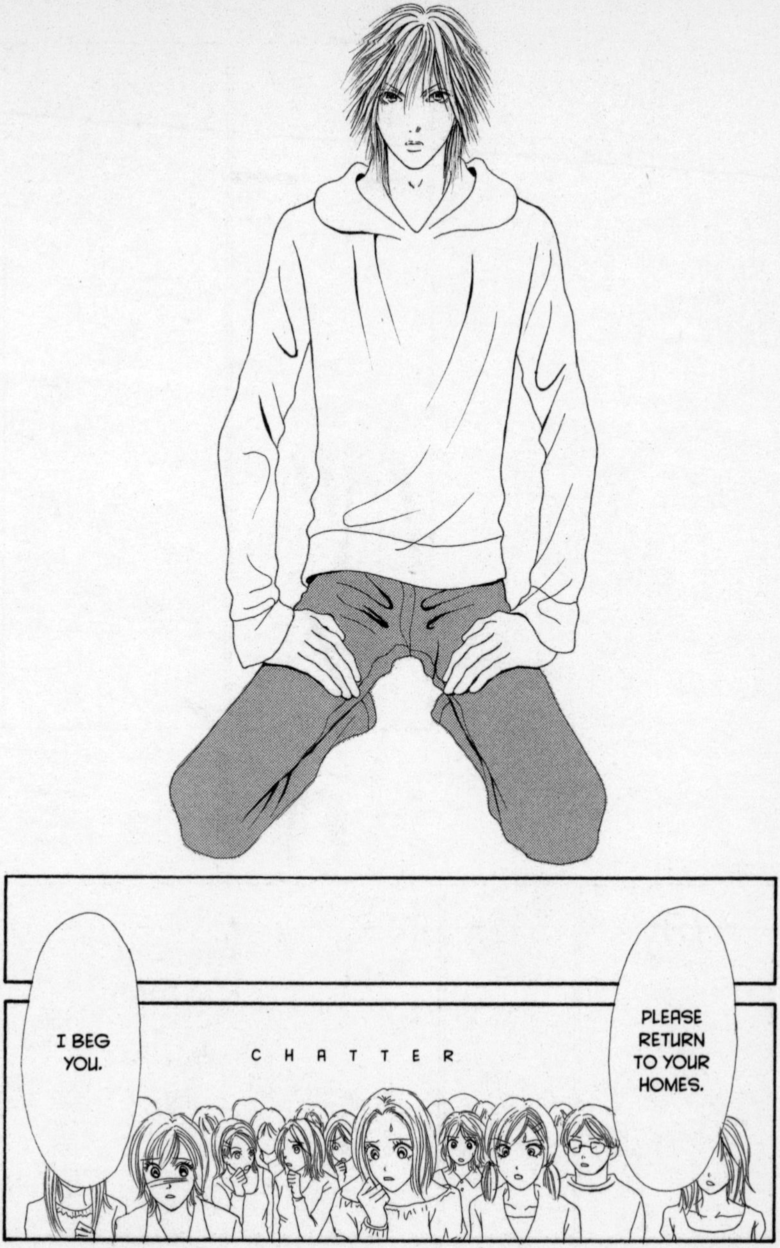
PLEASE RETURN TO YOUR HOMES.
CHATTER
I BEG YOU.

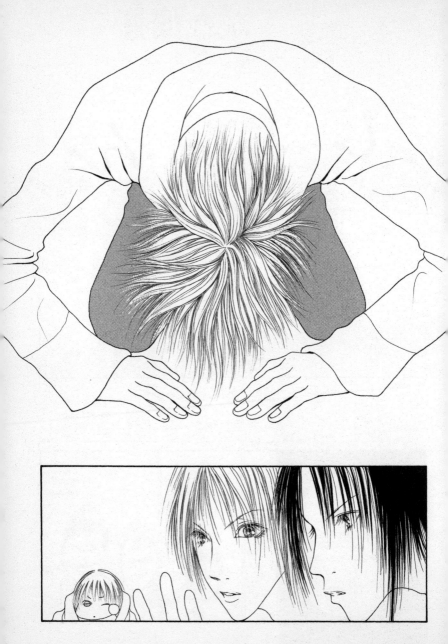

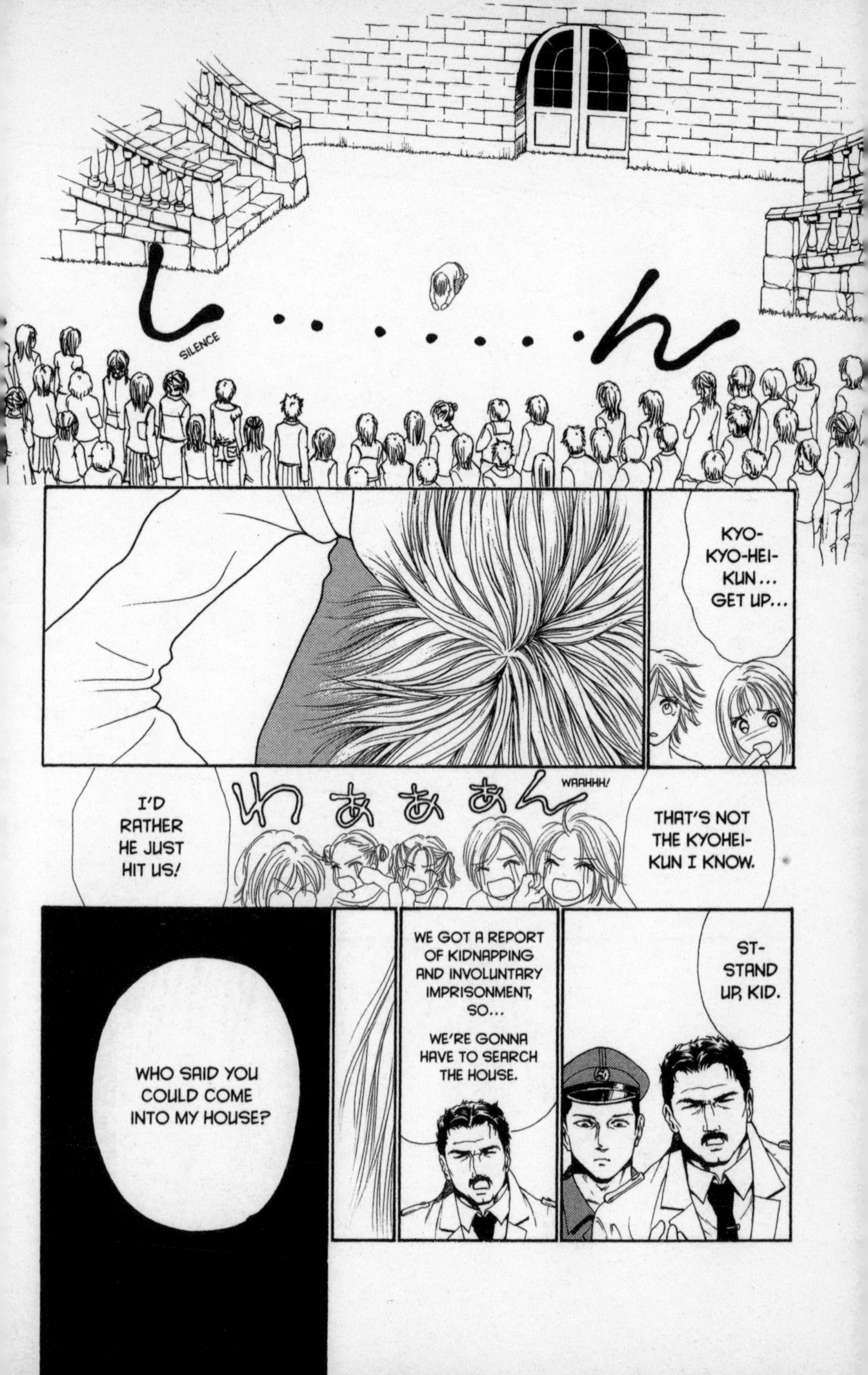

し・・・・・ん
SILENCE
KYO-KYO-HEI-KUN... GET UP...
THAT'S NOT THE KYOHEI-KUN I KNOW.
わあああん
WAAHHH!
I'D RATHER HE JUST HIT US!
ST- STAND UP, KID.
WE GOT A REPORT OF KIDNAPPING AND INVOLUNTARY IMPRISONMENT, SO...
WE'RE GONNA HAVE TO SEARCH THE HOUSE.
WHO SAID YOU COULD COME INTO MY HOUSE?

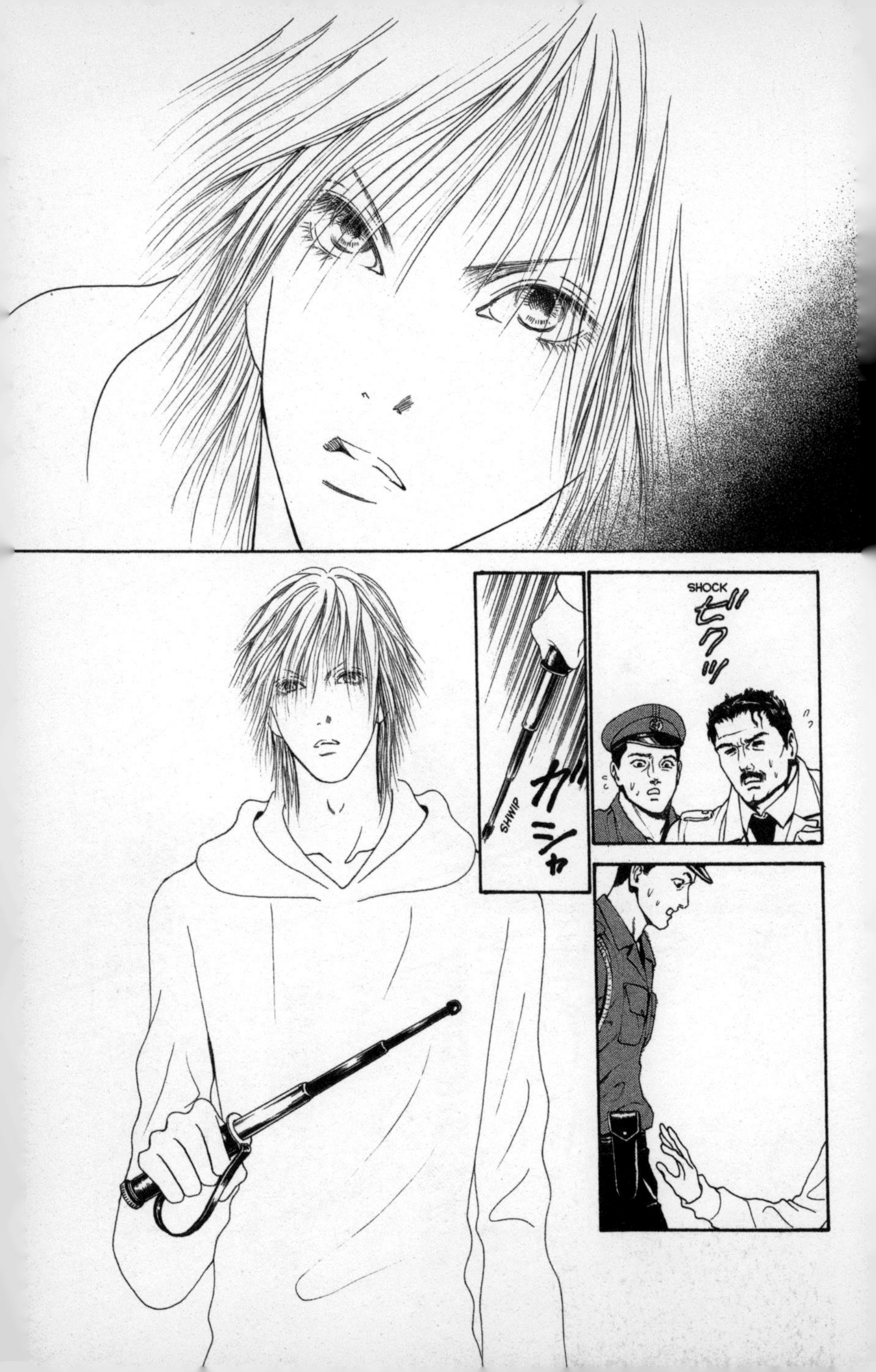
SHOCK
ビクッ
SHWIP
ガシャ

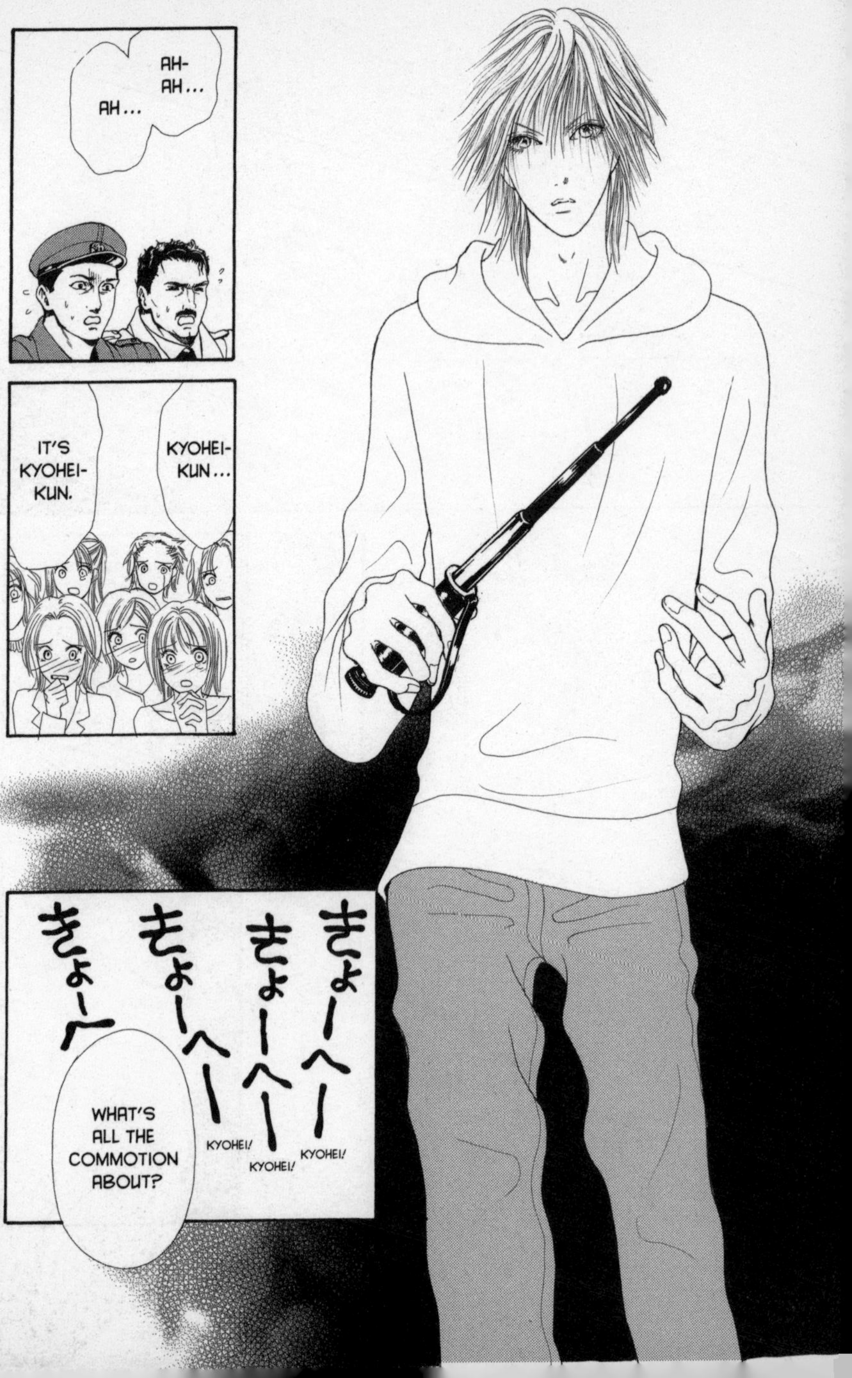
AH-AH...
AH...
KYOHEI-KUN...
IT'S KYOHEI-KUN.
きょーへー
KYOHEI!
きょーへー
KYOHEI!
きょーへー
KYOHEI!
WHAT'S ALL THE COMMOTION ABOUT?

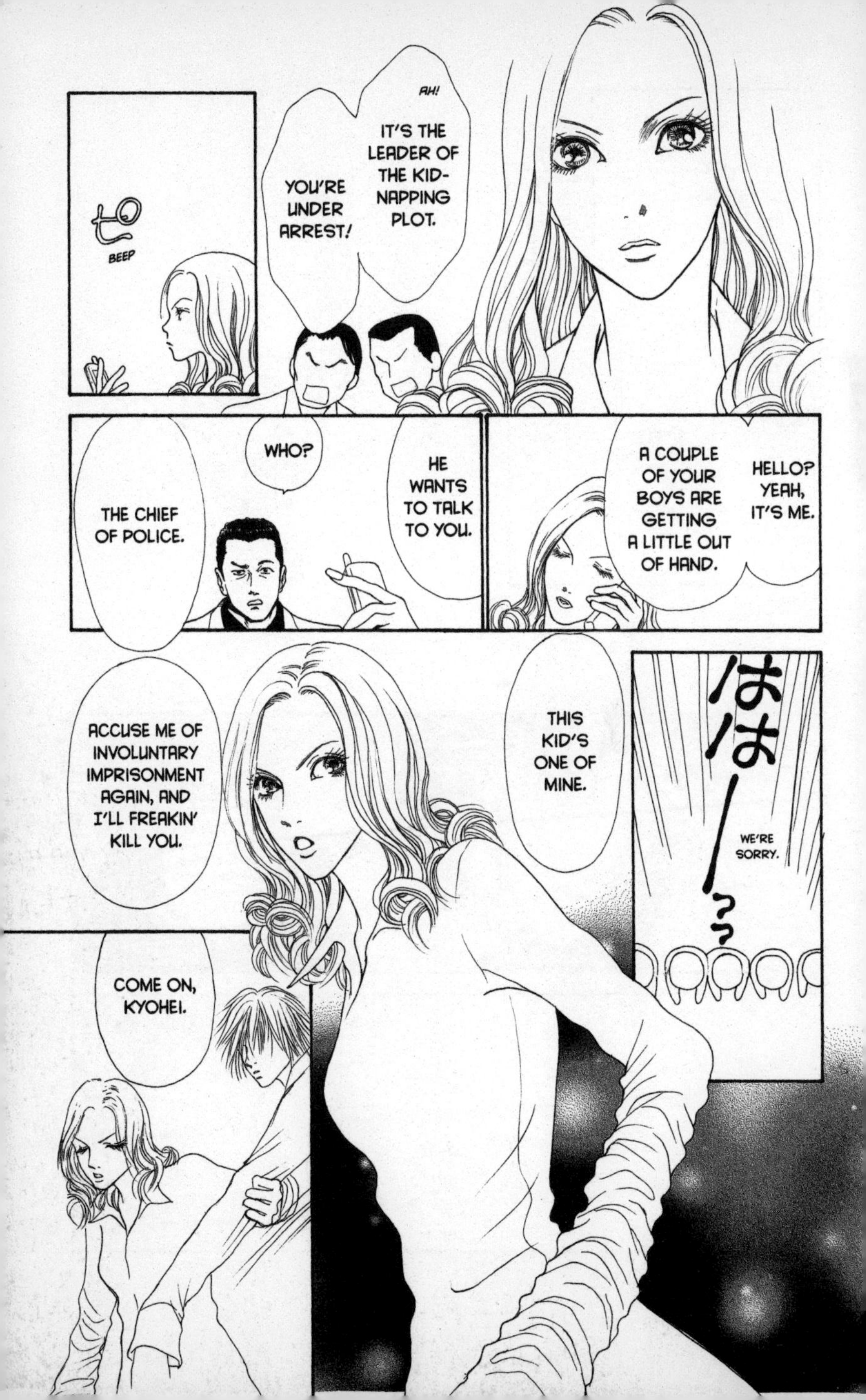
AH!
IT'S THE LEADER OF THE KID-NAPPING PLOT.
YOU'RE UNDER ARREST!
ピ
BEEP
HELLO? YEAH, IT'S ME.
A COUPLE OF YOUR BOYS ARE GETTING A LITTLE OUT OF HAND.
HE WANTS TO TALK TO YOU.
WHO?
THE CHIEF OF POLICE.
ははーっ
WE'RE SORRY.
THIS KID'S ONE OF MINE.
ACCUSE ME OF INVOLUNTARY IMPRISONMENT AGAIN, AND I'LL FREAKIN' KILL YOU.
COME ON, KYOHEI.

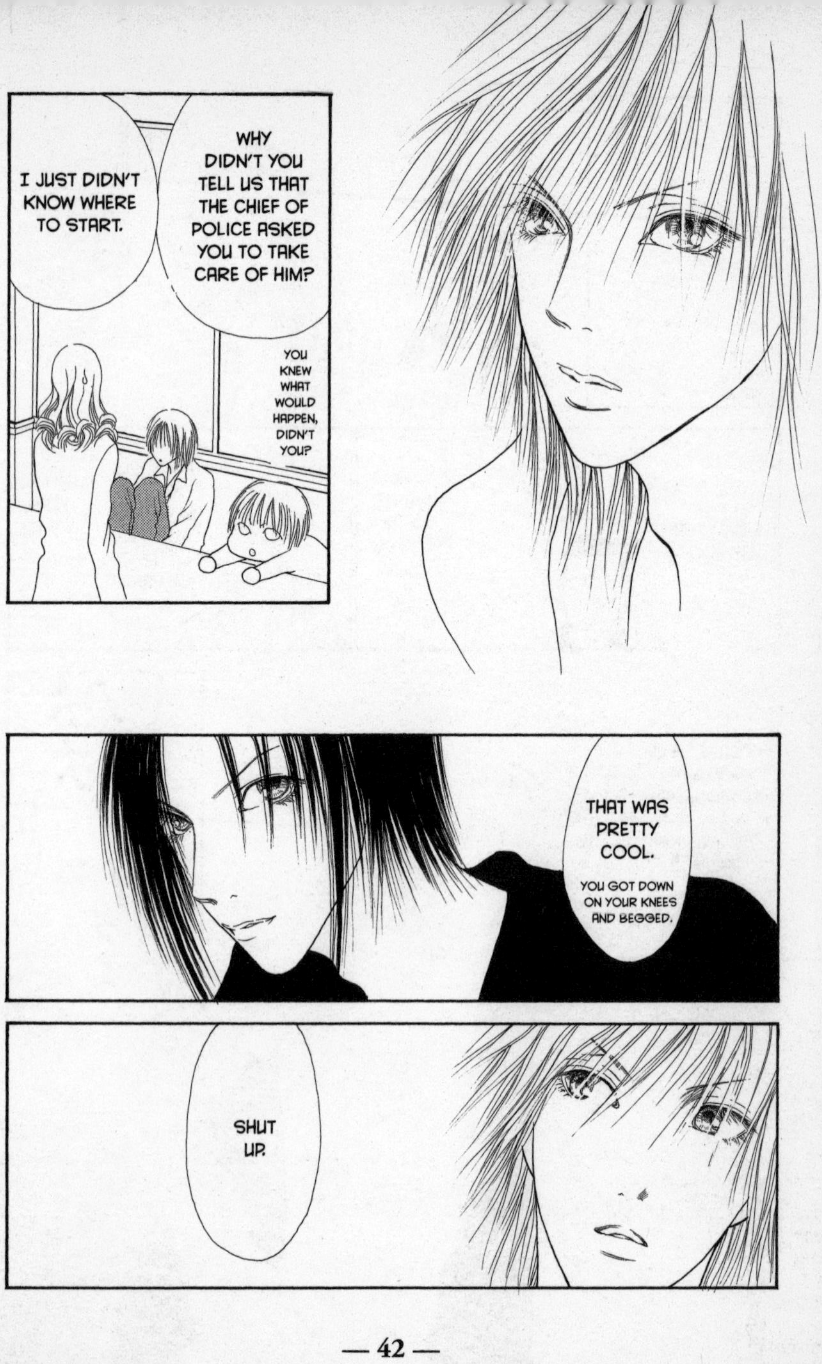
WHY DIDN'T YOU TELL US THAT THE CHIEF OF POLICE ASKED YOU TO TAKE CARE OF HIM?
I JUST DIDN'T KNOW WHERE TO START.
YOU KNEW WHAT WOULD HAPPEN, DIDN'T YOU?
THAT WAS PRETTY COOL.
YOU GOT DOWN ON YOUR KNEES AND BEGGED.
SHUT UP.

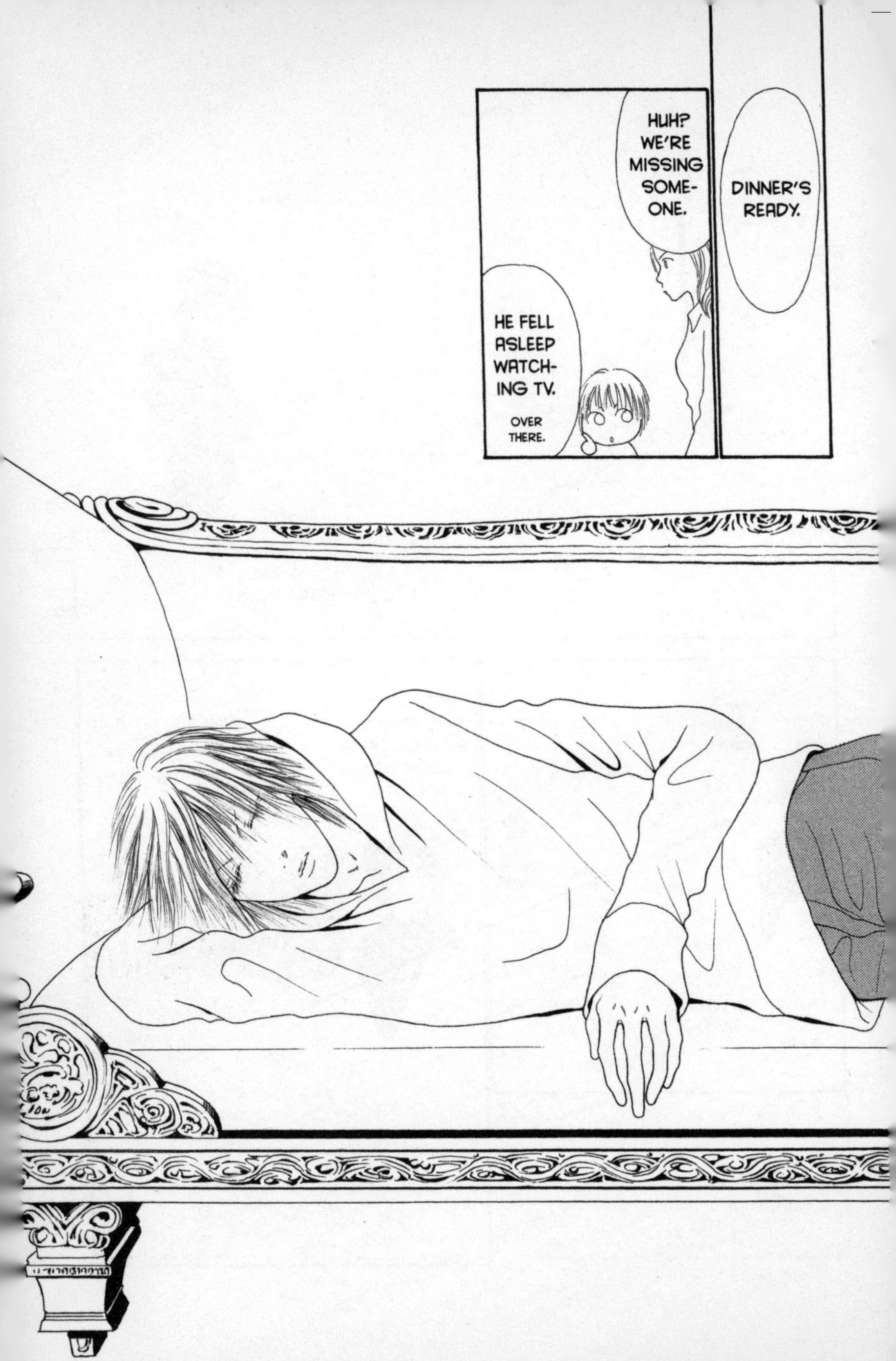
DINNER'S READY.
HUH? WE'RE MISSING SOME-ONE.
HE FELL ASLEEP WATCH-ING TV.
OVER THERE.

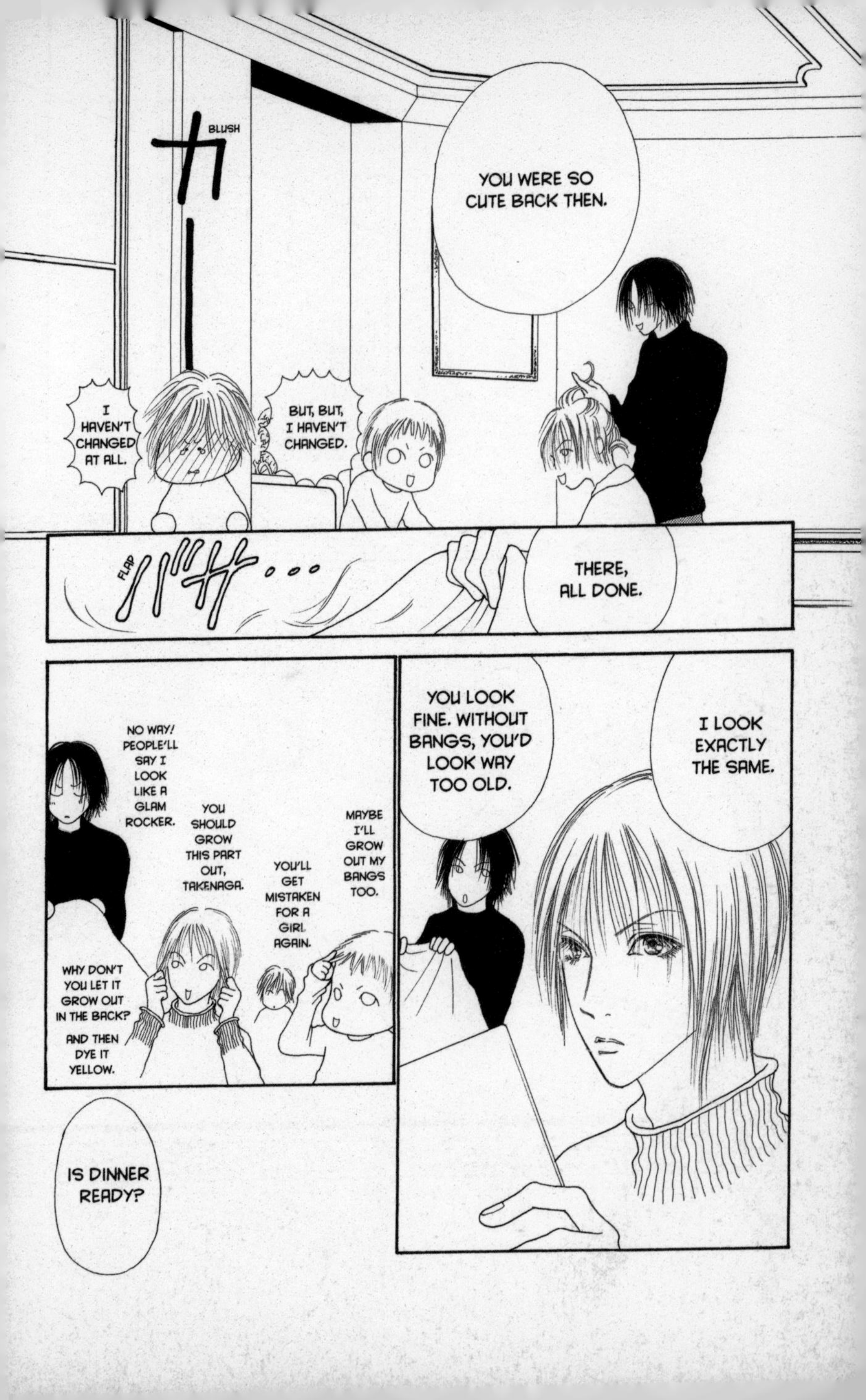
YOU WERE SO CUTE BACK THEN.
BLUSH
BUT, BUT, I HAVEN'T CHANGED.
I HAVEN'T CHANGED AT ALL.
THERE, ALL DONE.
FLAP
I LOOK EXACTLY THE SAME.
YOU LOOK FINE. WITHOUT BANGS, YOU'D LOOK WAY TOO OLD.
MAYBE I'LL GROW OUT MY BANGS TOO.
YOU'LL GET MISTAKEN FOR A GIRL AGAIN.
YOU SHOULD GROW THIS PART OUT, TAKENAGA.
NO WAY! PEOPLE'LL SAY I LOOK LIKE A GLAM ROCKER.
WHY DON'T YOU LET IT GROW OUT IN THE BACK?
AND THEN DYE IT YELLOW.
IS DINNER READY?

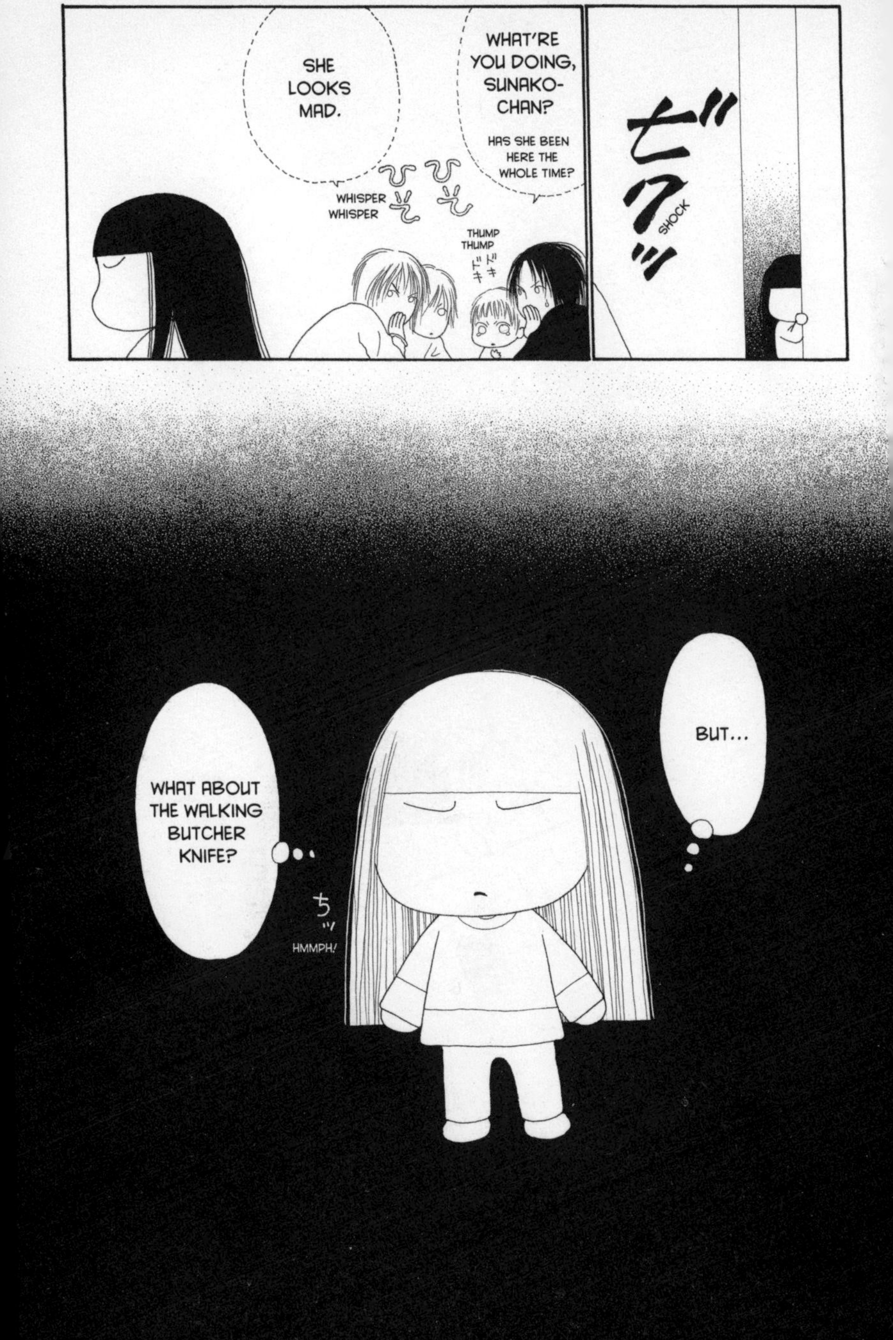
ゾクッ
SHOCK
WHAT'RE YOU DOING, SUNAKO-CHAN?
HAS SHE BEEN HERE THE WHOLE TIME?
SHE LOOKS MAD.
ひそひそ
WHISPER WHISPER
ドキドキ
THUMP THUMP
BUT...
WHAT ABOUT THE WALKING BUTCHER KNIFE?
ちッ
HMMPH!

WALKING
BUTCHER
KNIFE

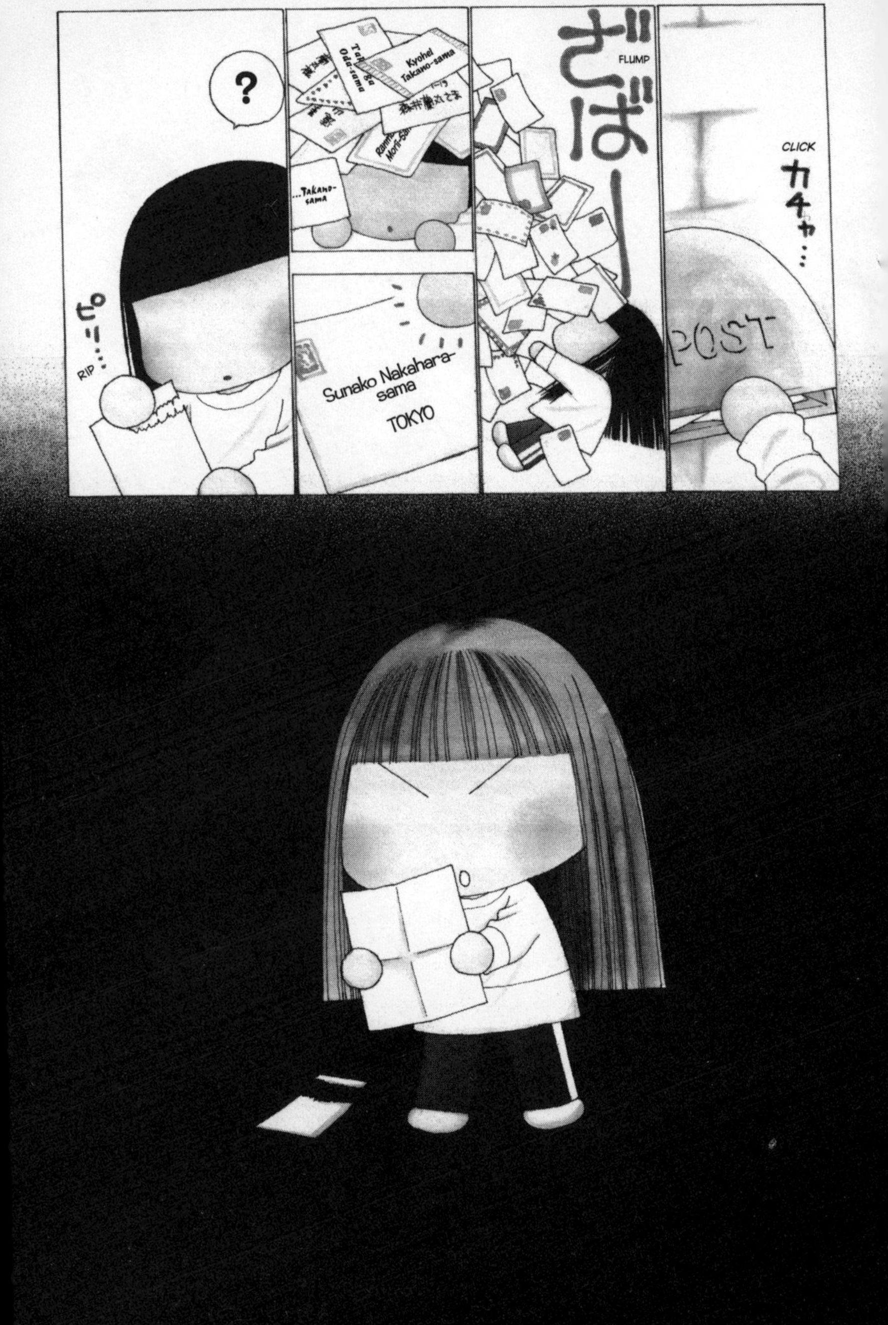
CLICK
カチャ…
POST
ざばー
FLUMP
Kyohei Takano-sama
...Takano-sama
Sunako Nakahara-sama
TOKYO
?
ピリ…
RIP

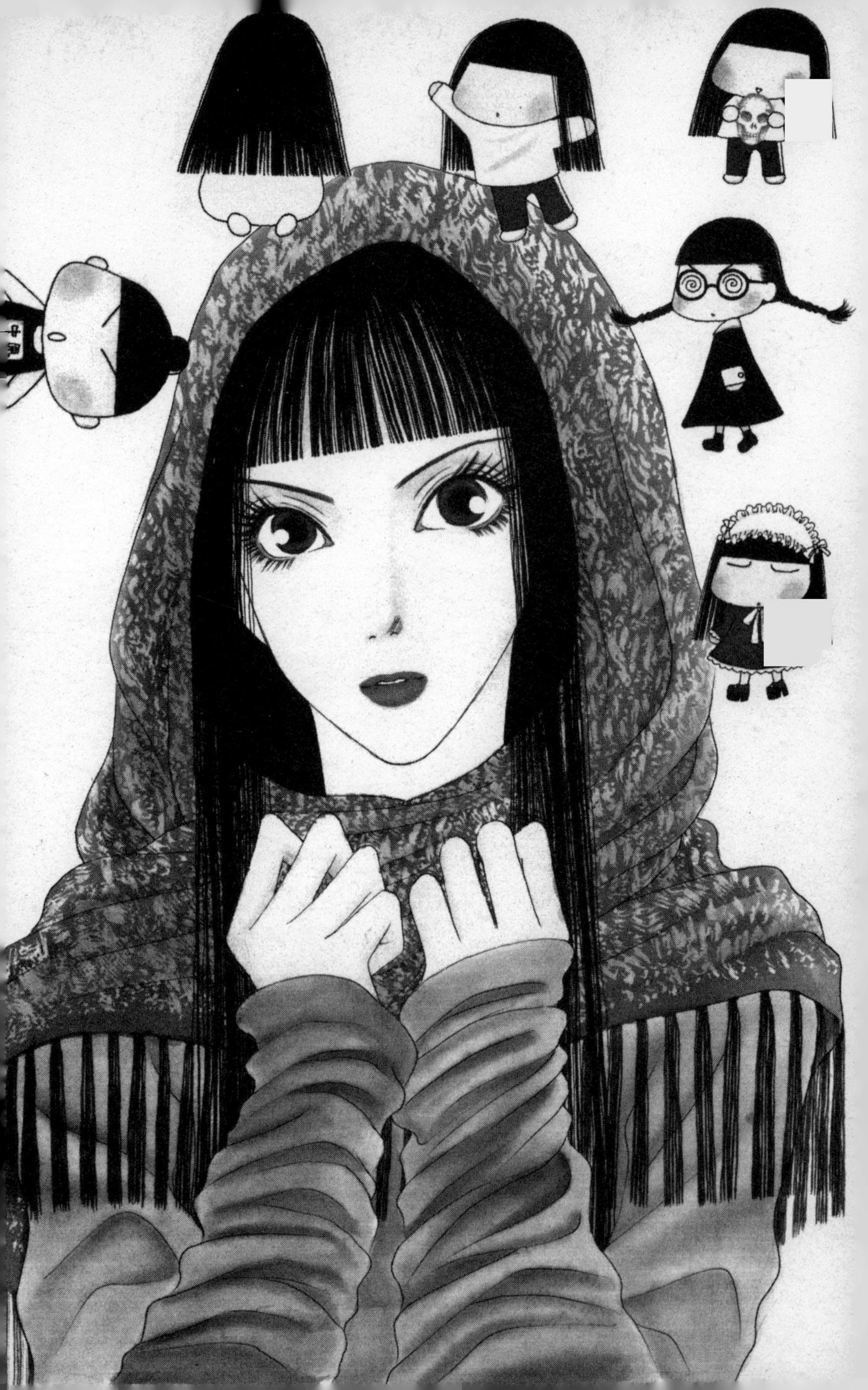

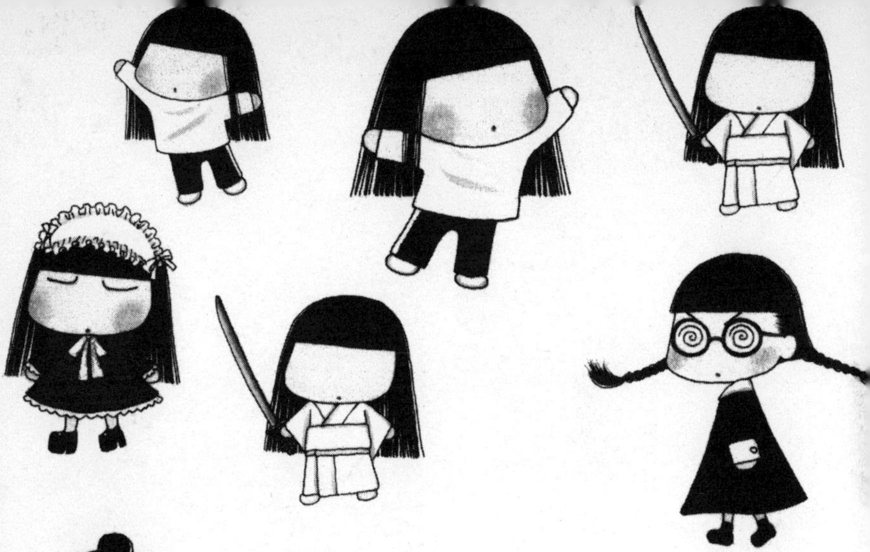

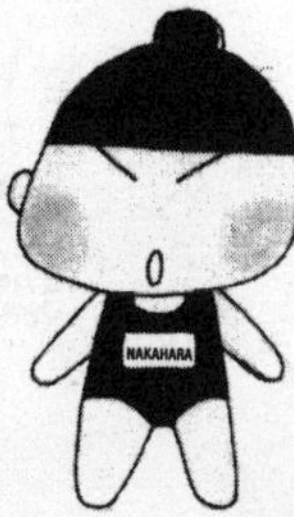
NAKAHARA

Chapter 24
Forever Old Friends

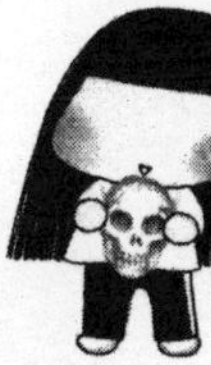

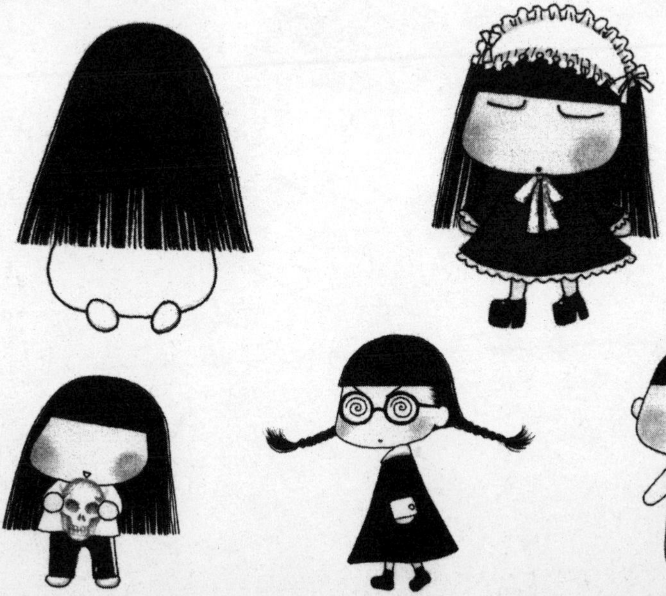
中原

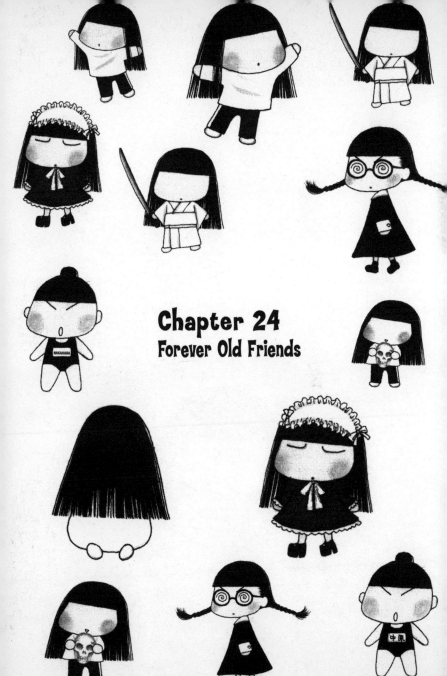

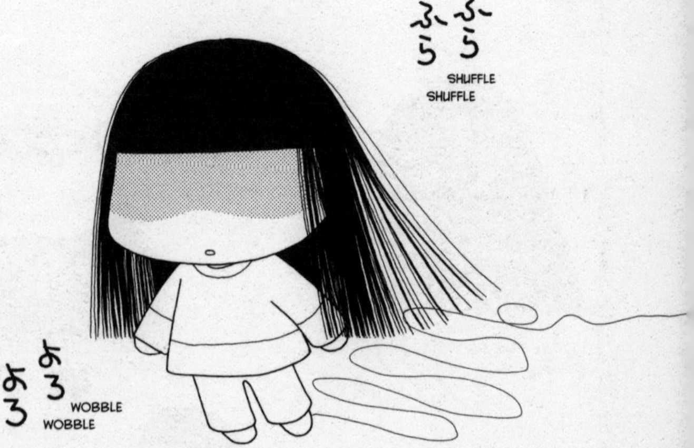
ふらふら
SHUFFLE SHUFFLE
よろよろ
WOBBLE WOBBLE

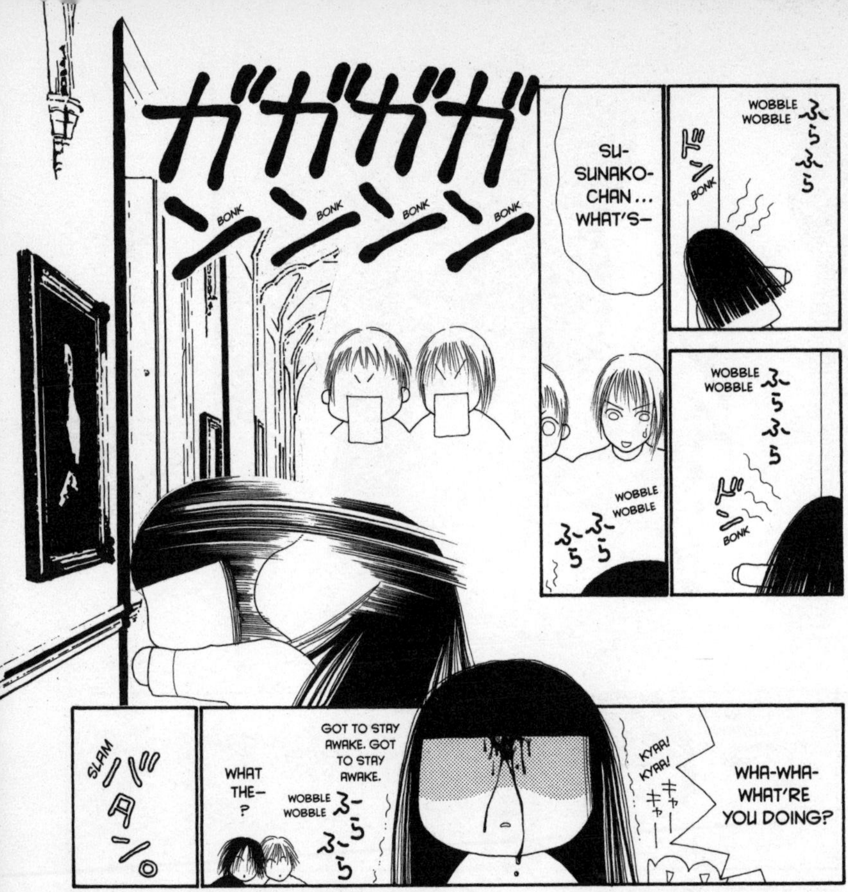
WOBBLE WOBBLE
ふらふら
ドン
BONK
SU-SUNAKO-CHAN... WHAT'S—
WOBBLE WOBBLE
ふらふら
WOBBLE WOBBLE
ふらふら
ドン
BONK
ガガガガンンンン
BONK
BONK
BONK
BONK
WHA-WHA-WHAT'RE YOU DOING?
KYAA! KYAA!
キャーキャー
GOT TO STAY AWAKE. GOT TO STAY AWAKE.
WOBBLE WOBBLE
ふらふら
WHAT THE—?
SLAM
バターン。

BEHIND THE SCENES

UNLIKE LAST TIME, I WAS TOTALLY HAPPY ♥ WHEN I WROTE THIS. I WAS IN THE MIDDLE OF CHANGING MY PERSONALITY AND MY LIFESTYLE. (I ENDED UP NOT CHANGING ANYTHING.) MY LITTLE DWARFS DID ALL THE INKING FOR ME WHILE I WAS ASLEEP. THESE TWO DWARFS ARE NAMED AYU WATANABE AND MACHIKO SAKURAI. ♥

HAVING TWO CUTE YOUNG GIRLS AROUND MAKES THE OFFICE FEEL MUCH MORE LIVELY. ♥ (THEY'RE BOTH BISHOUJO GIRLS.) THEIR FACES ARE REALLY SMALL. I HOPE NO ONE IS COMPARING THEIR LOOKS WITH MINE.

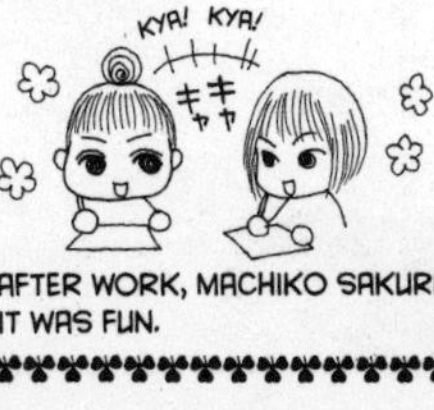
KYA! KYA!
キャキャ

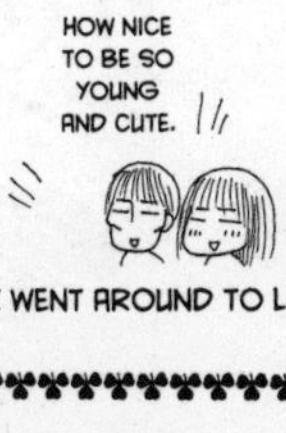
HOW NICE TO BE SO YOUNG AND CUTE.

AN OLD LADY AND AN OLD MAN ENCHANTED BY YOUTH. (ME AND THE GENIUS HANA-CHAN.)

AFTER WORK, MACHIKO SAKURAI AND I WENT AROUND TO LOTS OF DIFFERENT TOY STORES. IT WAS FUN.

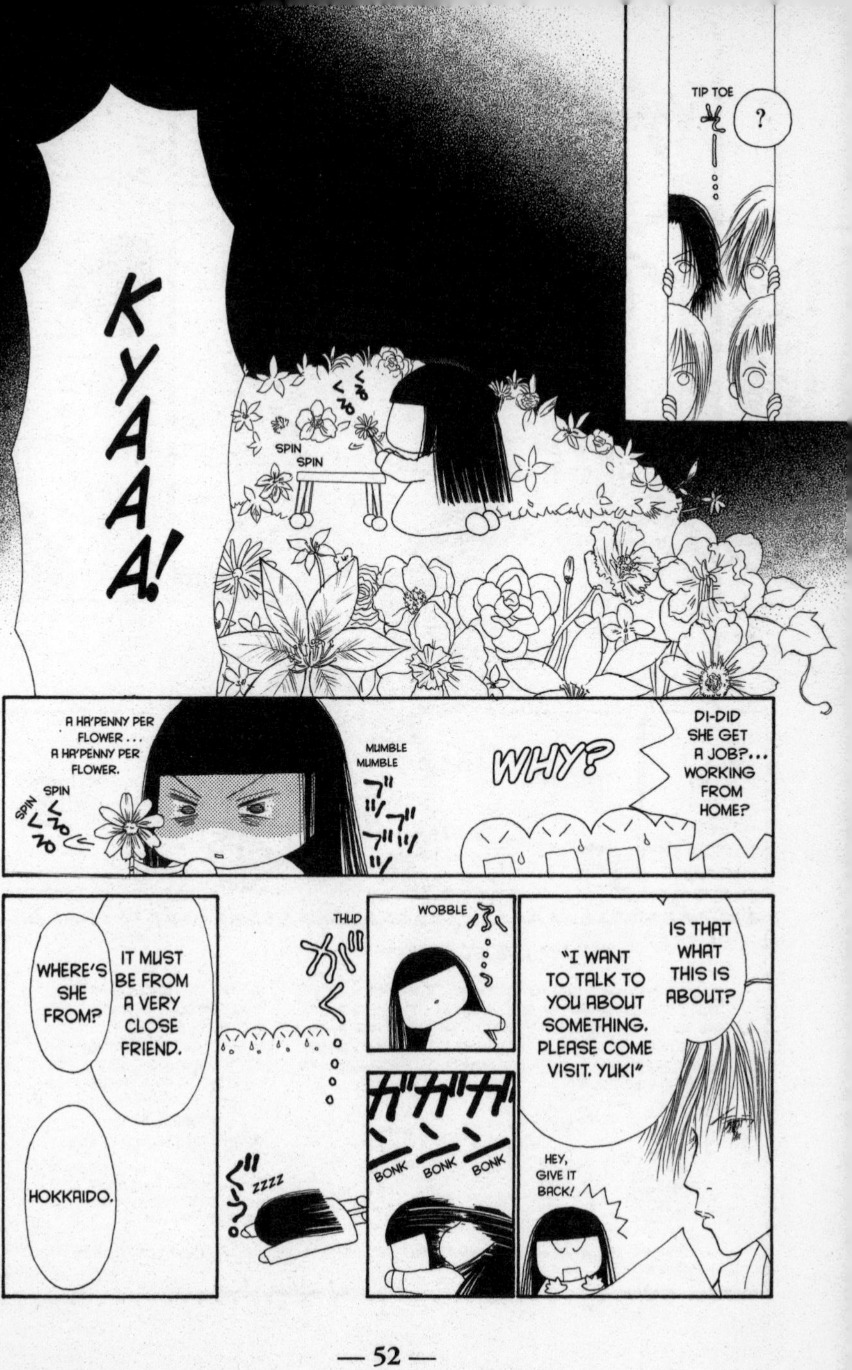
TIP TOE
?
KYAAAA!
SPIN SPIN
DI-DID SHE GET A JOB?... WORKING FROM HOME?
WHY?
MUMBLE MUMBLE
A HA'PENNY PER FLOWER... A HA'PENNY PER FLOWER.
SPIN SPIN
IS THAT WHAT THIS IS ABOUT?
"I WANT TO TALK TO YOU ABOUT SOMETHING. PLEASE COME VISIT. YUKI"
HEY, GIVE IT BACK!
WOBBLE
BONK BONK BONK
THUD
ZZZZ
IT MUST BE FROM A VERY CLOSE FRIEND.
WHERE'S SHE FROM?
HOKKAIDO.

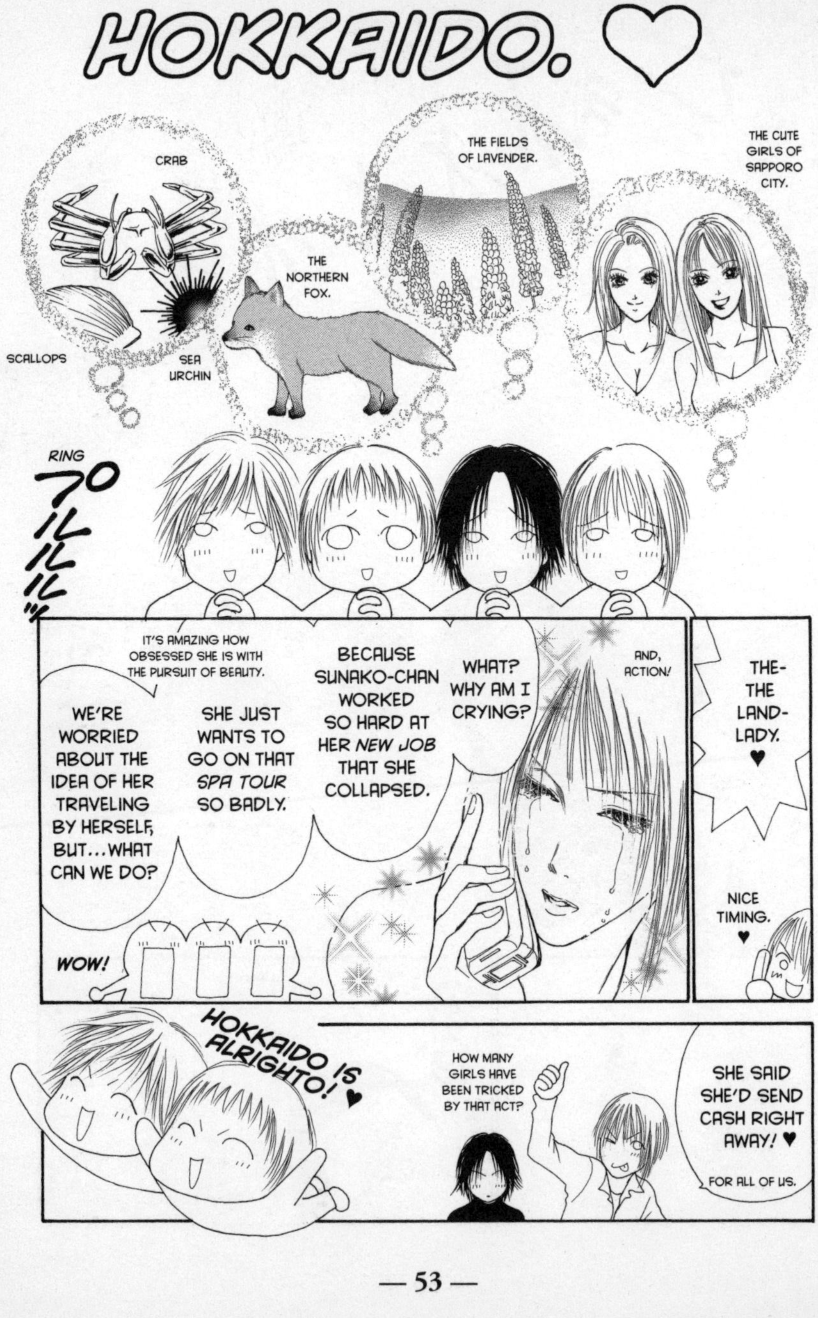
HOKKAIDO. ♥
THE CUTE GIRLS OF SAPPORO CITY.
THE FIELDS OF LAVENDER.
THE NORTHERN FOX.
CRAB
SEA URCHIN
SCALLOPS
RING
プルルルッ
THE- THE LANDLADY. ♥
NICE TIMING. ♥
AND, ACTION!
WHAT? WHY AM I CRYING?
BECAUSE SUNAKO-CHAN WORKED SO HARD AT HER *NEW JOB* THAT SHE COLLAPSED.
IT'S AMAZING HOW OBSESSED SHE IS WITH THE PURSUIT OF BEAUTY.
SHE JUST WANTS TO GO ON THAT *SPA TOUR* SO BADLY.
WE'RE WORRIED ABOUT THE IDEA OF HER TRAVELING BY HERSELF, BUT...WHAT CAN WE DO?
WOW!
SHE SAID SHE'D SEND CASH RIGHT AWAY! ♥
FOR ALL OF US.
HOW MANY GIRLS HAVE BEEN TRICKED BY THAT ACT?
HOKKAIDO IS ALRIGHTO! ♥

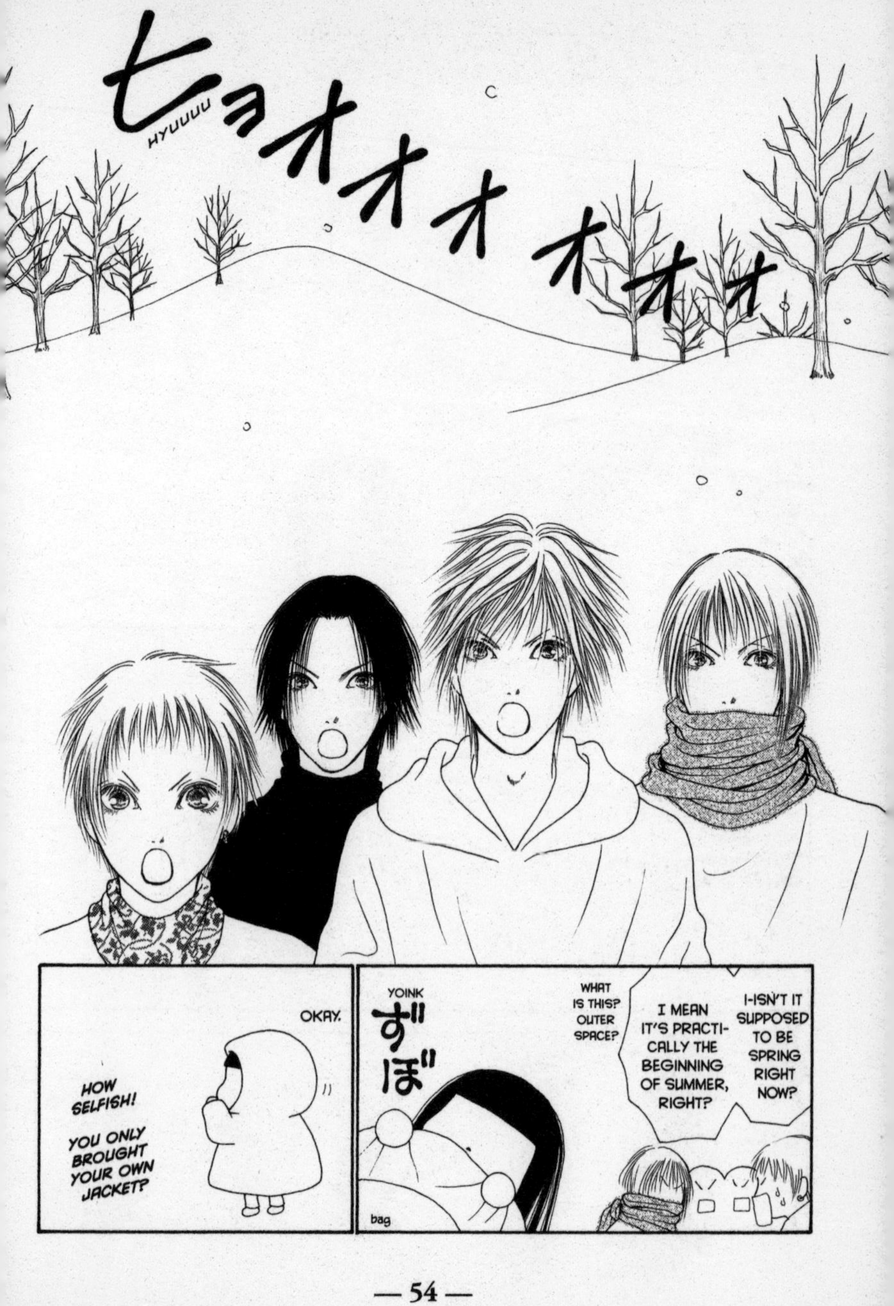
ヒョオオオオオオ
HYUUUU
I-ISN'T IT SUPPOSED TO BE SPRING RIGHT NOW?
I MEAN IT'S PRACTI-CALLY THE BEGINNING OF SUMMER, RIGHT?
WHAT IS THIS? OUTER SPACE?
ずぼ
YOINK
bag
OKAY.
HOW SELFISH! YOU ONLY BROUGHT YOUR OWN JACKET?

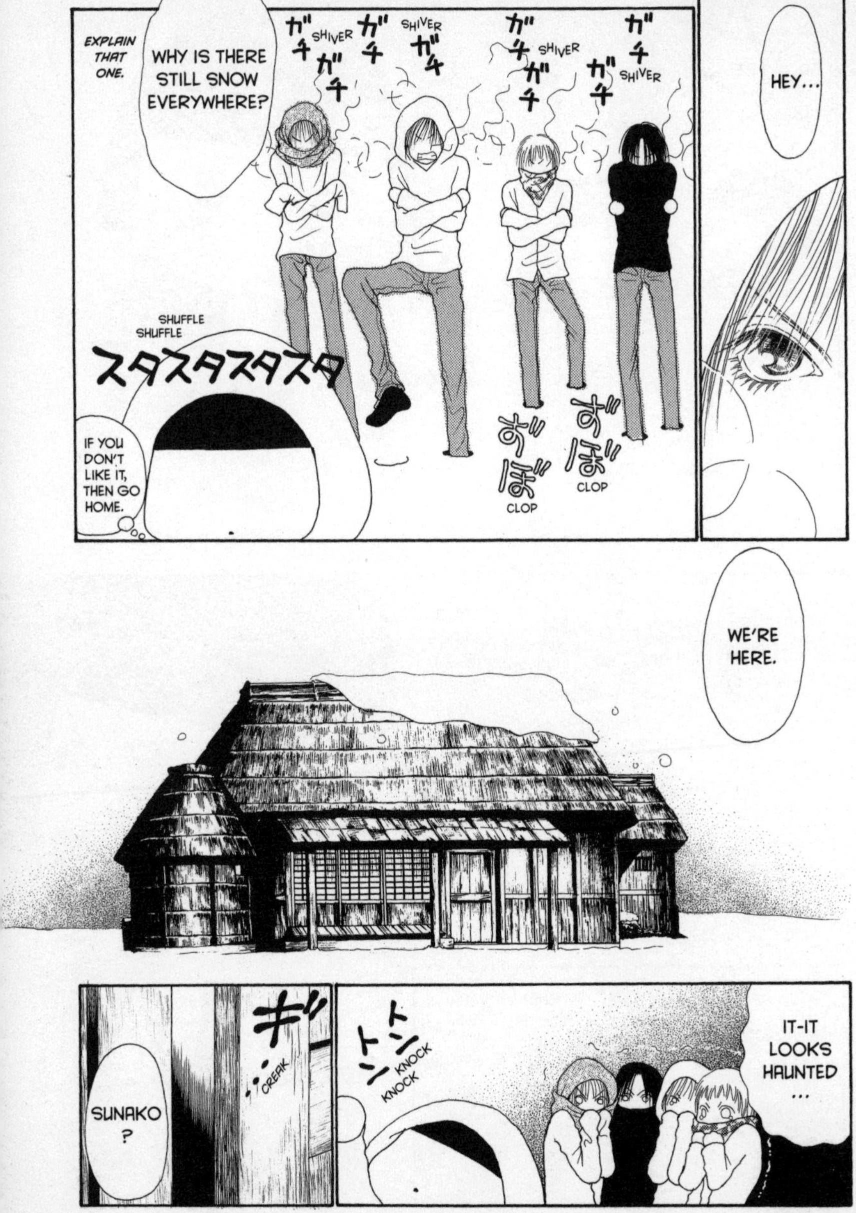
HEY...
ガチ SHIVER
ガチ SHIVER
ガチ SHIVER
ガチ SHIVER
ガチ ガチ ガチ ガチ
WHY IS THERE STILL SNOW EVERYWHERE?
EXPLAIN THAT ONE.
スタスタスタスタ SHUFFLE SHUFFLE
ずぼ ずぼ CLOP CLOP
IF YOU DON'T LIKE IT, THEN GO HOME.
WE'RE HERE.
IT-IT LOOKS HAUNTED ...
トントン KNOCK KNOCK
ギ CREAK
SUNAKO ?

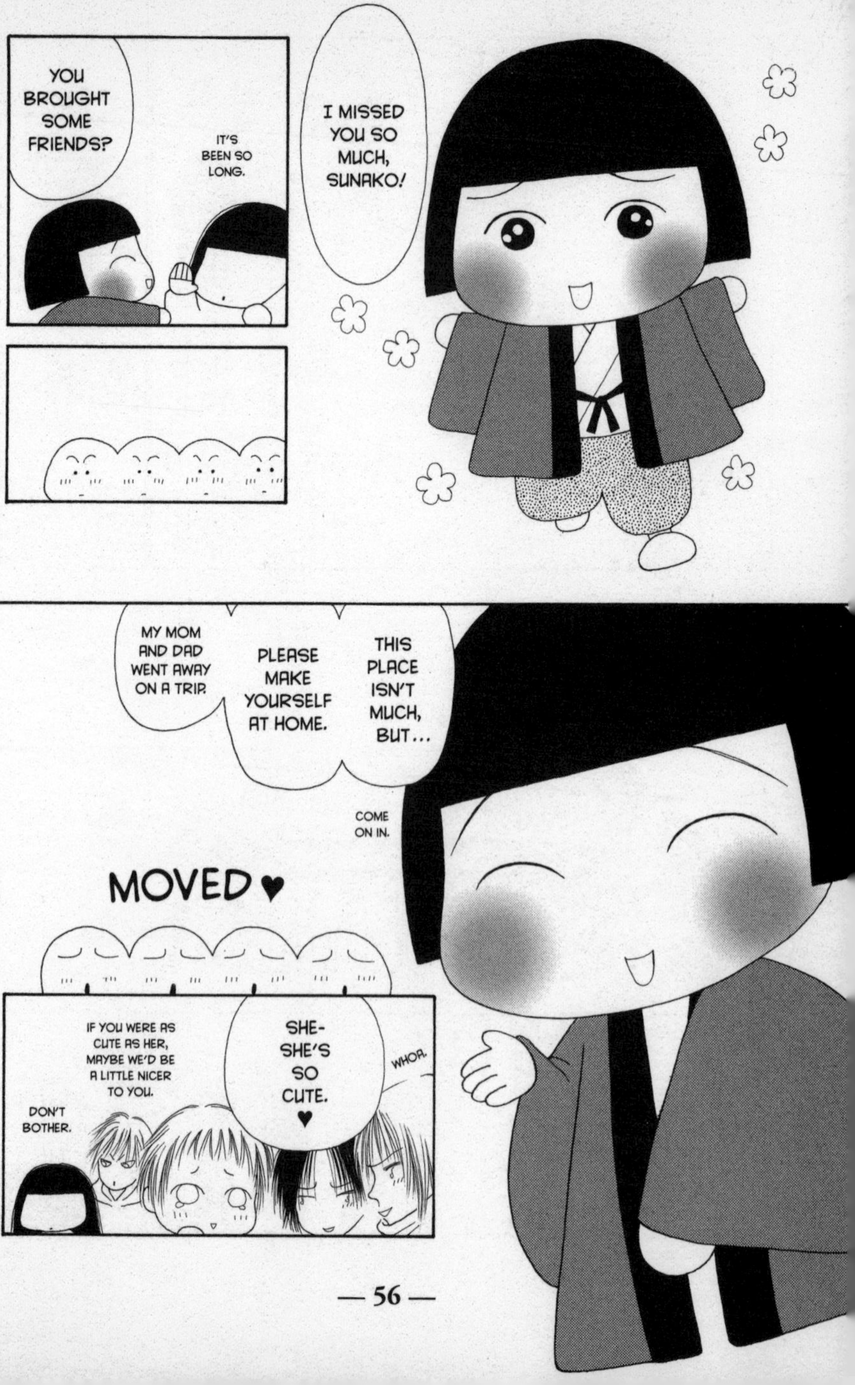
I MISSED YOU SO MUCH, SUNAKO!
IT'S BEEN SO LONG.
YOU BROUGHT SOME FRIENDS?
THIS PLACE ISN'T MUCH, BUT...
PLEASE MAKE YOURSELF AT HOME.
MY MOM AND DAD WENT AWAY ON A TRIP.
COME ON IN.
MOVED ♥
WHOA.
SHE-SHE'S SO CUTE. ♥
IF YOU WERE AS CUTE AS HER, MAYBE WE'D BE A LITTLE NICER TO YOU.
DON'T BOTHER.

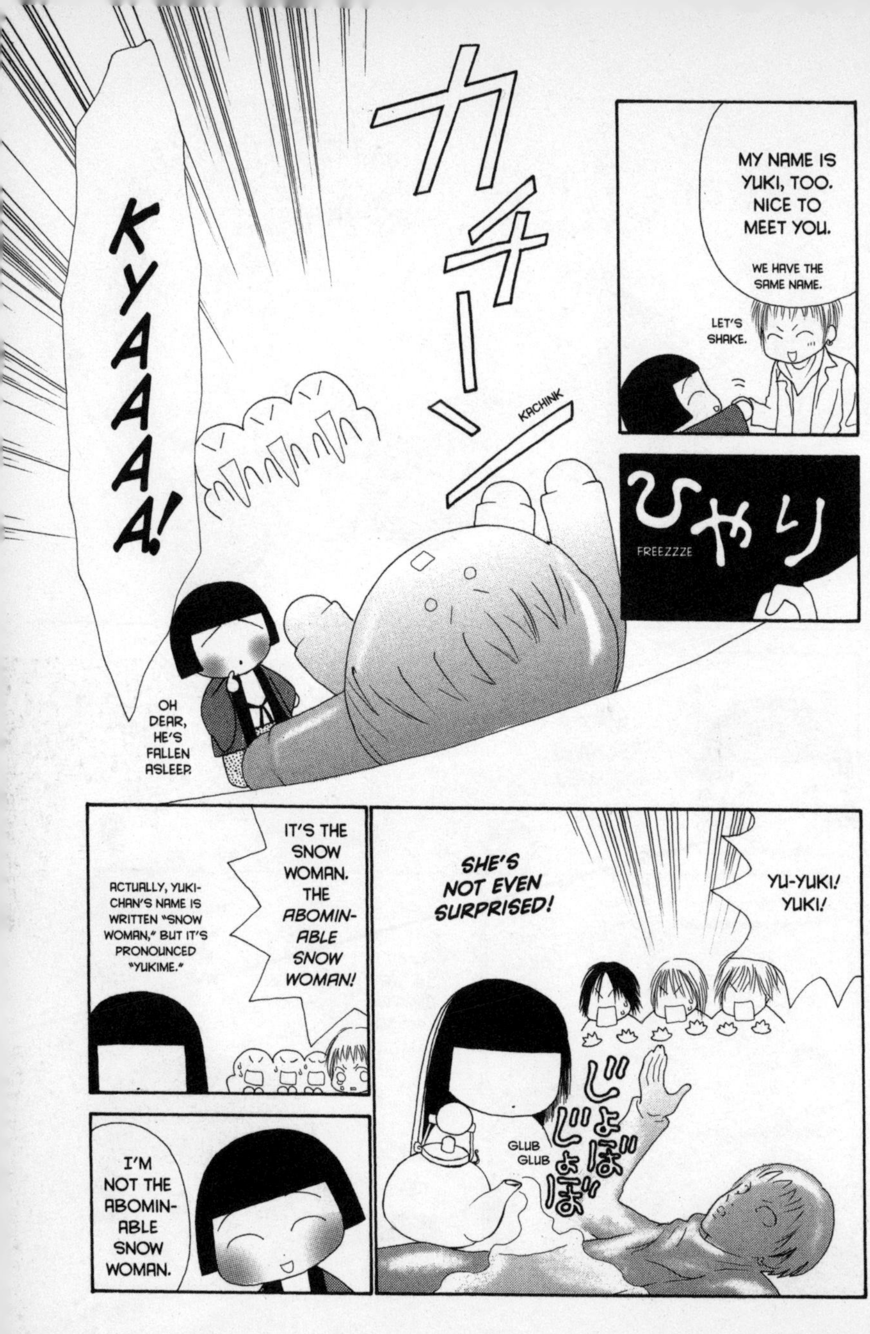
MY NAME IS YUKI, TOO. NICE TO MEET YOU.
WE HAVE THE SAME NAME.
LET'S SHAKE.
ひやり
FREEZZZE
カチーン
KACHINK
KYAAAAA!
OH DEAR, HE'S FALLEN ASLEEP.
YU-YUKI! YUKI!
SHE'S NOT EVEN SURPRISED!
じょぼじょぼ
GLUB GLUB
IT'S THE SNOW WOMAN. THE ABOMINABLE SNOW WOMAN!
ACTUALLY, YUKI-CHAN'S NAME IS WRITTEN "SNOW WOMAN," BUT IT'S PRONOUNCED "YUKIME."
I'M NOT THE ABOMINABLE SNOW WOMAN.

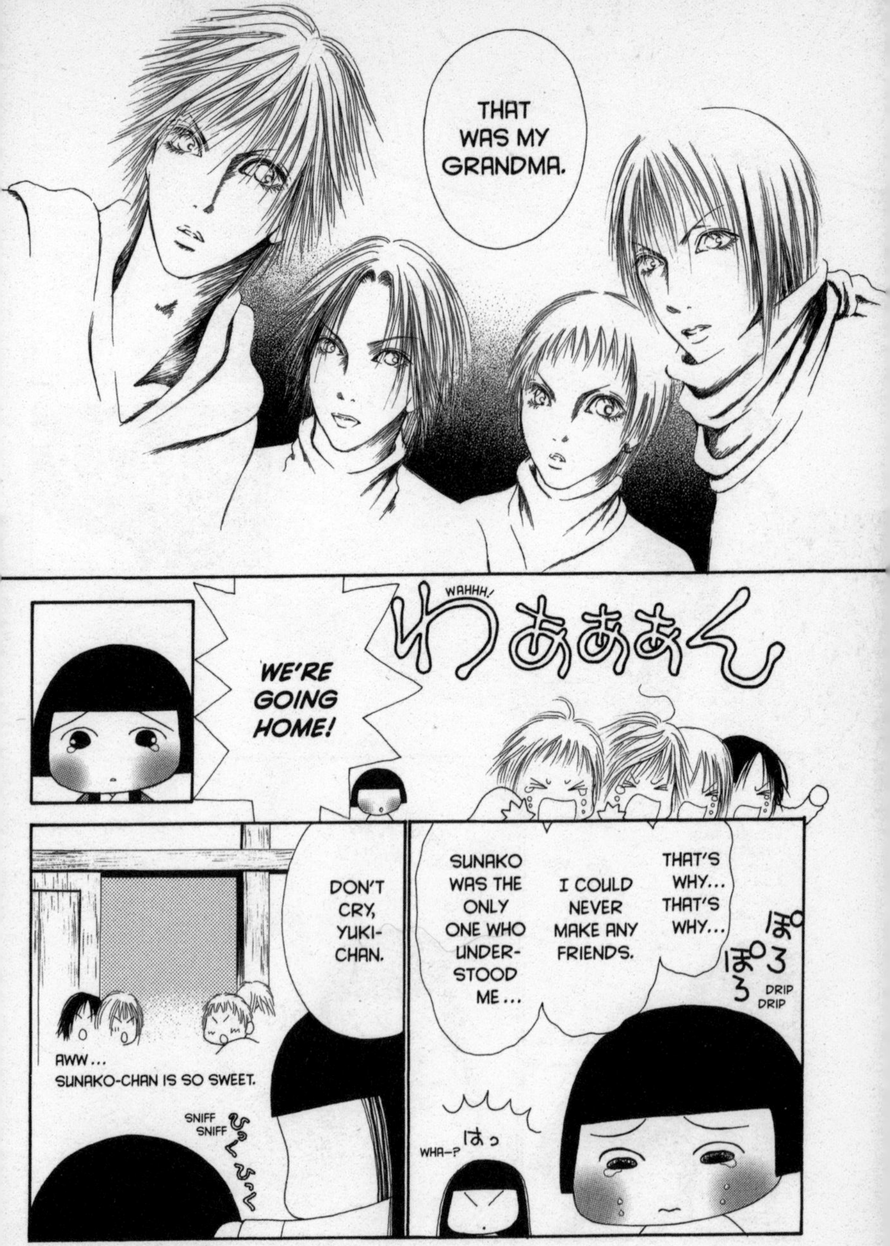
THAT WAS MY GRANDMA.
わあああん
WAHHH!
WE'RE GOING HOME!
THAT'S WHY... THAT'S WHY...
I COULD NEVER MAKE ANY FRIENDS.
SUNAKO WAS THE ONLY ONE WHO UNDERSTOOD ME...
ぽろぽろ
DRIP DRIP
はっ
WHA-?
DON'T CRY, YUKI-CHAN.
AWW... SUNAKO-CHAN IS SO SWEET.
ひっくひっく
SNIFF SNIFF

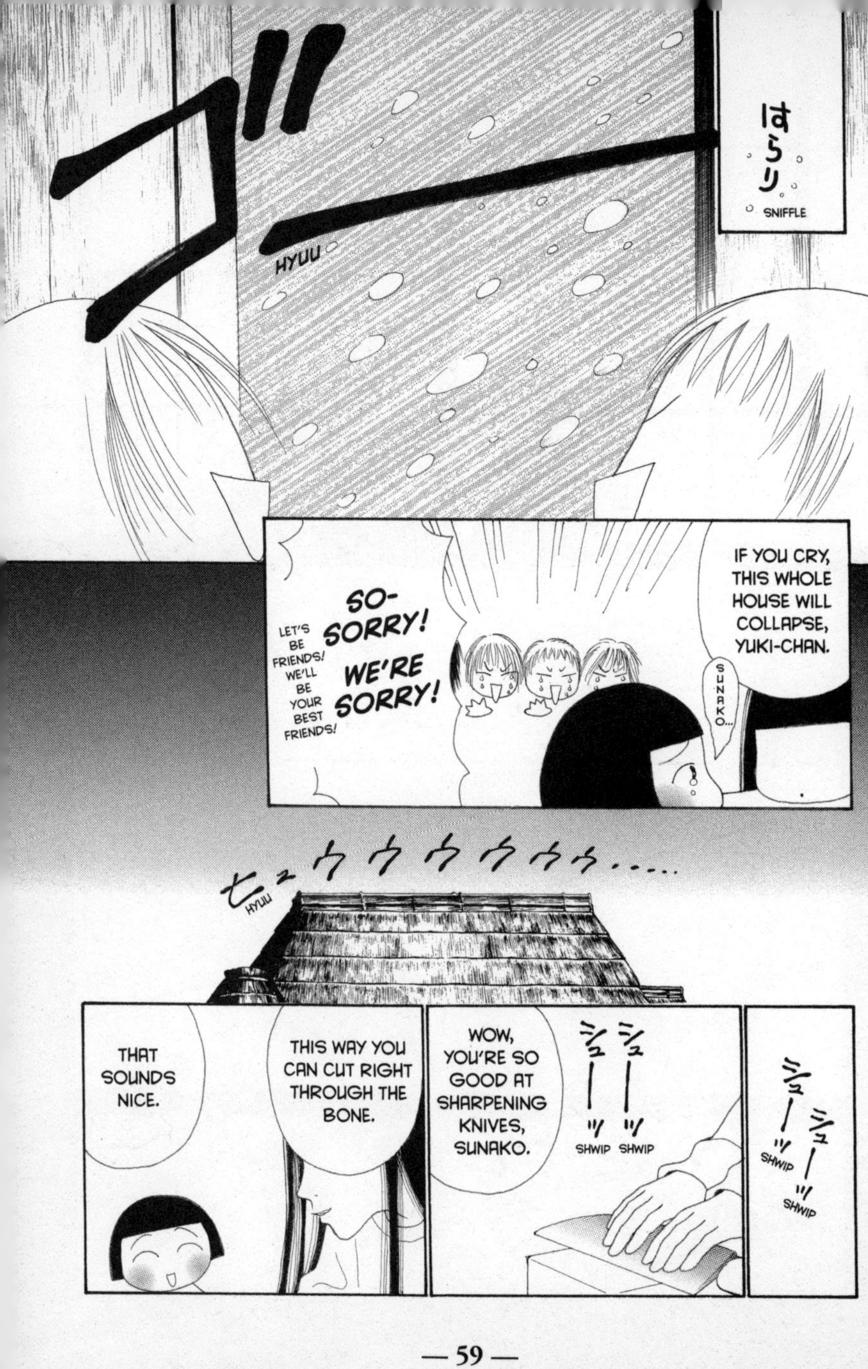

はらり
SNIFFLE
ゴー
HYUU
IF YOU CRY, THIS WHOLE HOUSE WILL COLLAPSE, YUKI-CHAN.
SUNAKO...
SO-SORRY! WE'RE SORRY!
LET'S BE FRIENDS! WE'LL BE YOUR BEST FRIENDS!
ヒュウウウウウウ....
HYUU
シューッ
SHWIP
シューッ
SHWIP
シューッ
SHWIP
シューッ
SHWIP
WOW, YOU'RE SO GOOD AT SHARPENING KNIVES, SUNAKO.
THIS WAY YOU CAN CUT RIGHT THROUGH THE BONE.
THAT SOUNDS NICE.

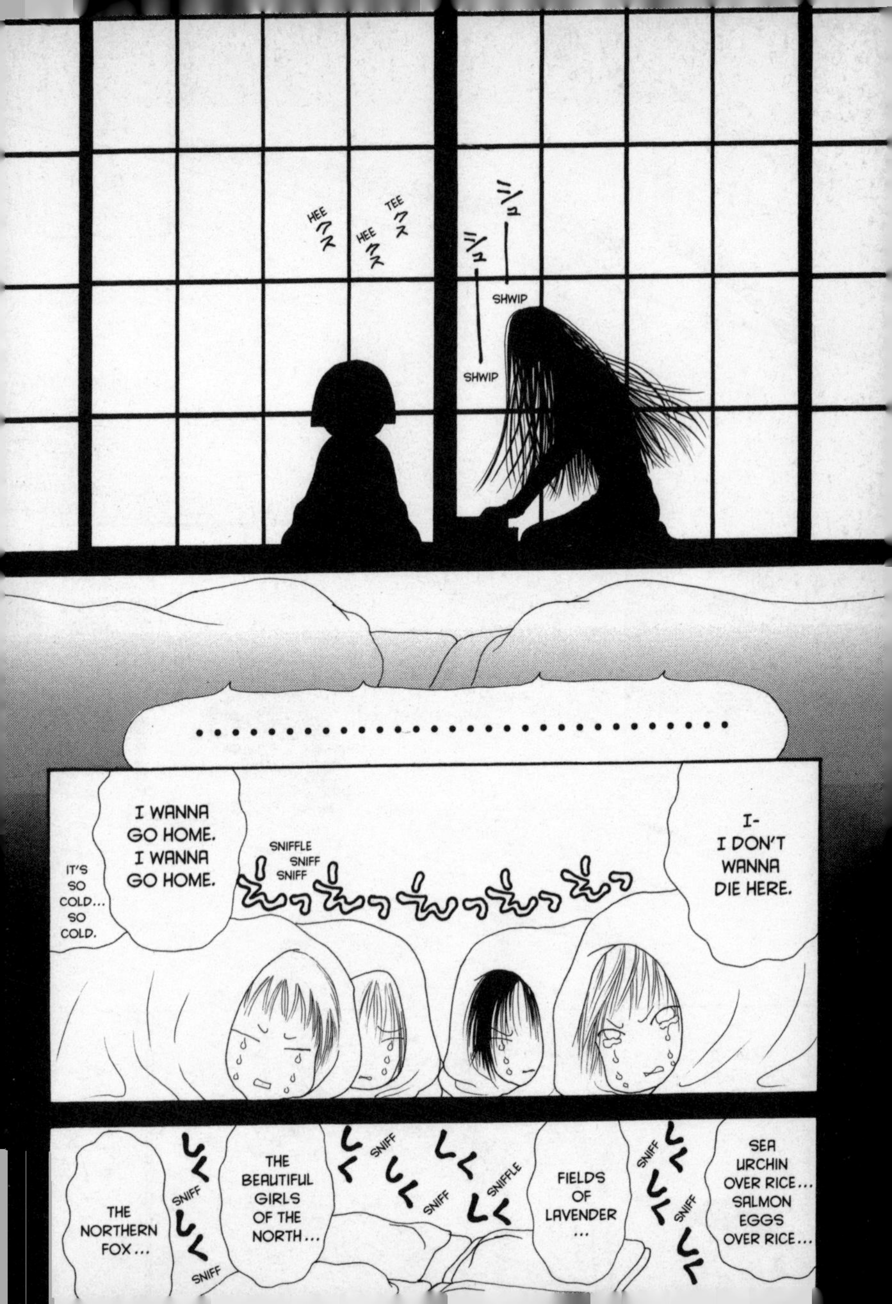
シュー
SHWIP
シュー
SHWIP
TEE クス
HEE クス
HEE クス
....
I- I DON'T WANNA DIE HERE.
SNIFFLE
SNIFF
SNIFF
I WANNA GO HOME. I WANNA GO HOME.
IT'S SO COLD... SO COLD.
SEA URCHIN OVER RICE... SALMON EGGS OVER RICE...
SNIFF
SNIFF
FIELDS OF LAVENDER ...
SNIFFLE
SNIFF
SNIFF
THE BEAUTIFUL GIRLS OF THE NORTH...
SNIFF
SNIFF
THE NORTHERN FOX...

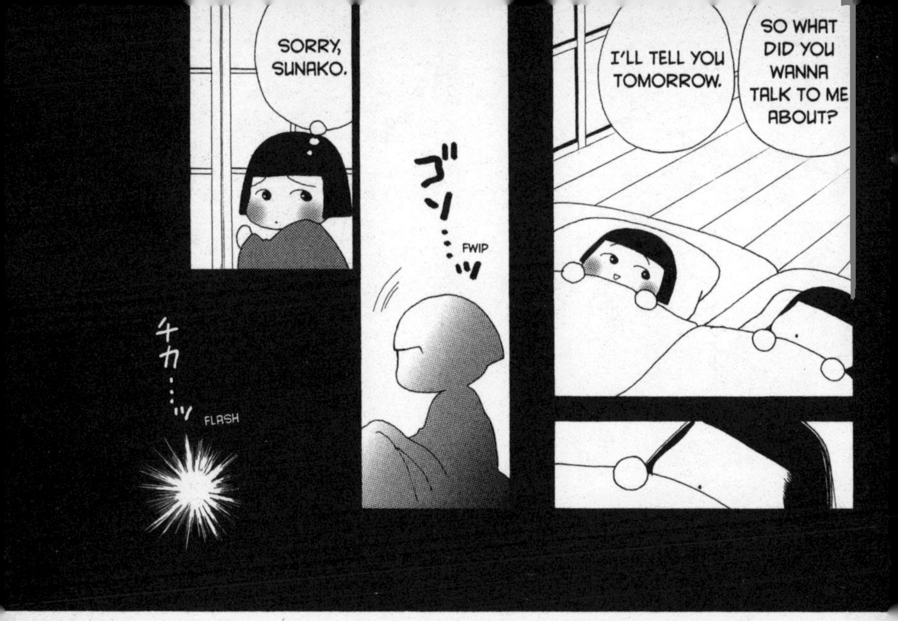
SO WHAT DID YOU WANNA TALK TO ME ABOUT?
I'LL TELL YOU TOMORROW.
ゴソ…ッ
FWIP
SORRY, SUNAKO.
チカ…ッ
FLASH

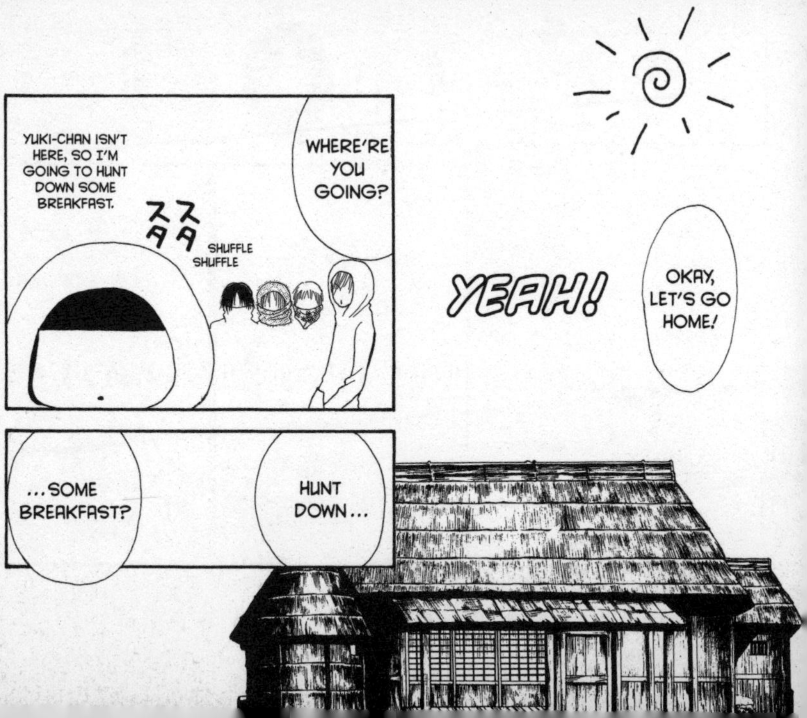
OKAY, LET'S GO HOME!
YEAH!
WHERE'RE YOU GOING?
YUKI-CHAN ISN'T HERE, SO I'M GOING TO HUNT DOWN SOME BREAKFAST.
スタスタ
SHUFFLE SHUFFLE
HUNT DOWN...
...SOME BREAKFAST?

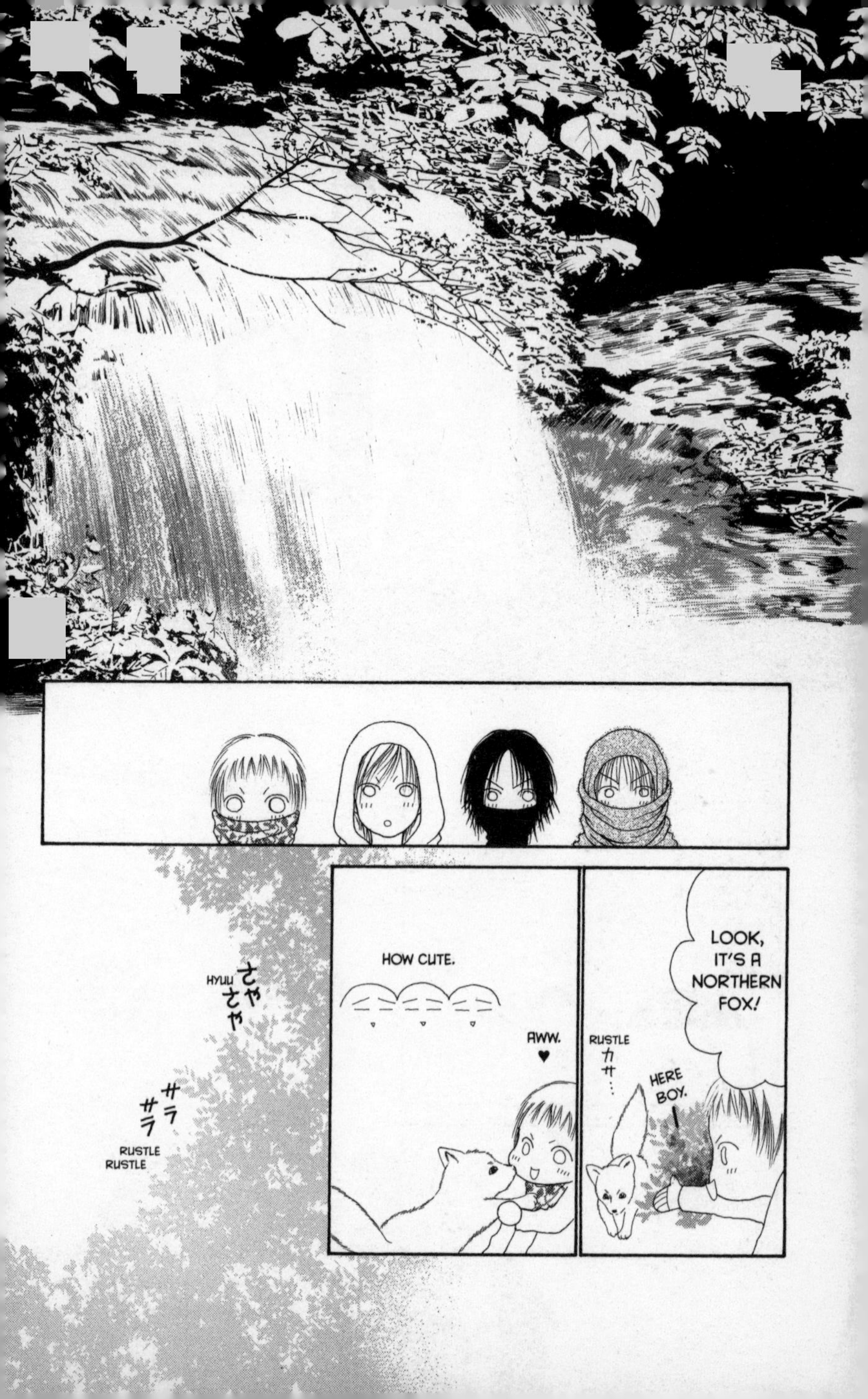
LOOK, IT'S A NORTHERN FOX!
RUSTLE
カサ…
HERE BOY.
HOW CUTE.
AWW. ♥
さやさや
HYUU
サラサラ
RUSTLE RUSTLE

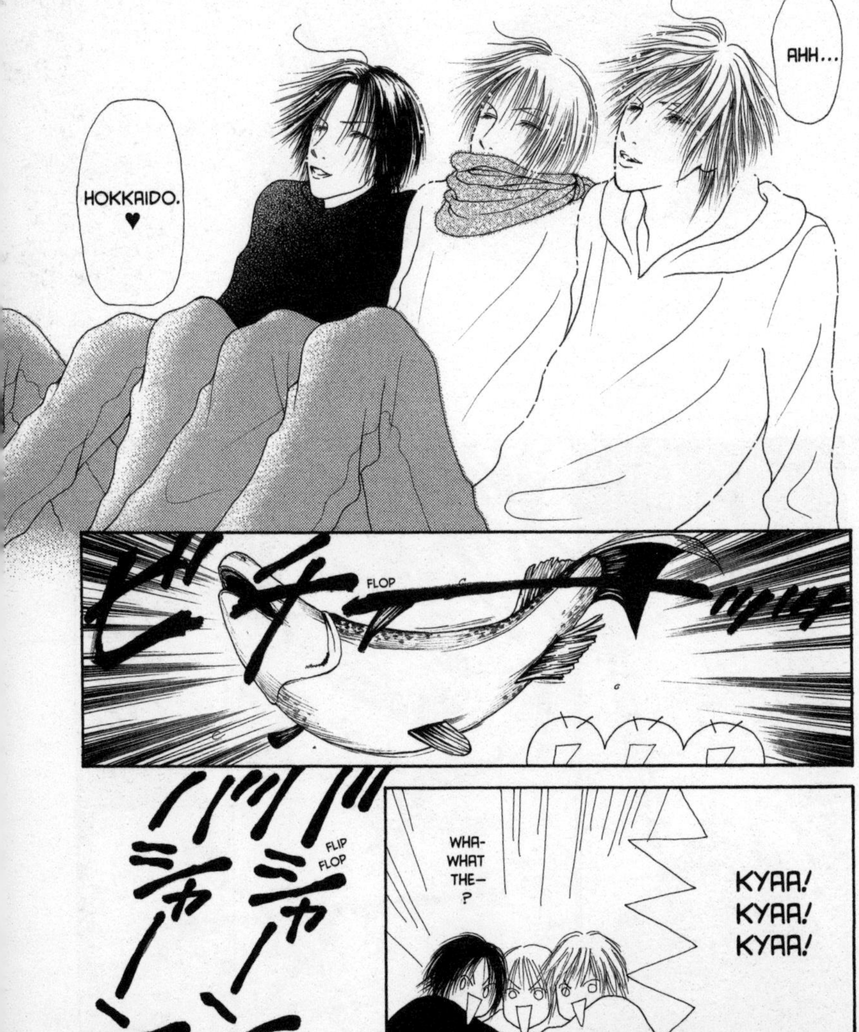
AHH...
HOKKAIDO. ♥
FLOP
KYAA! KYAA! KYAA!
WHA- WHAT THE—?
FLIP FLOP

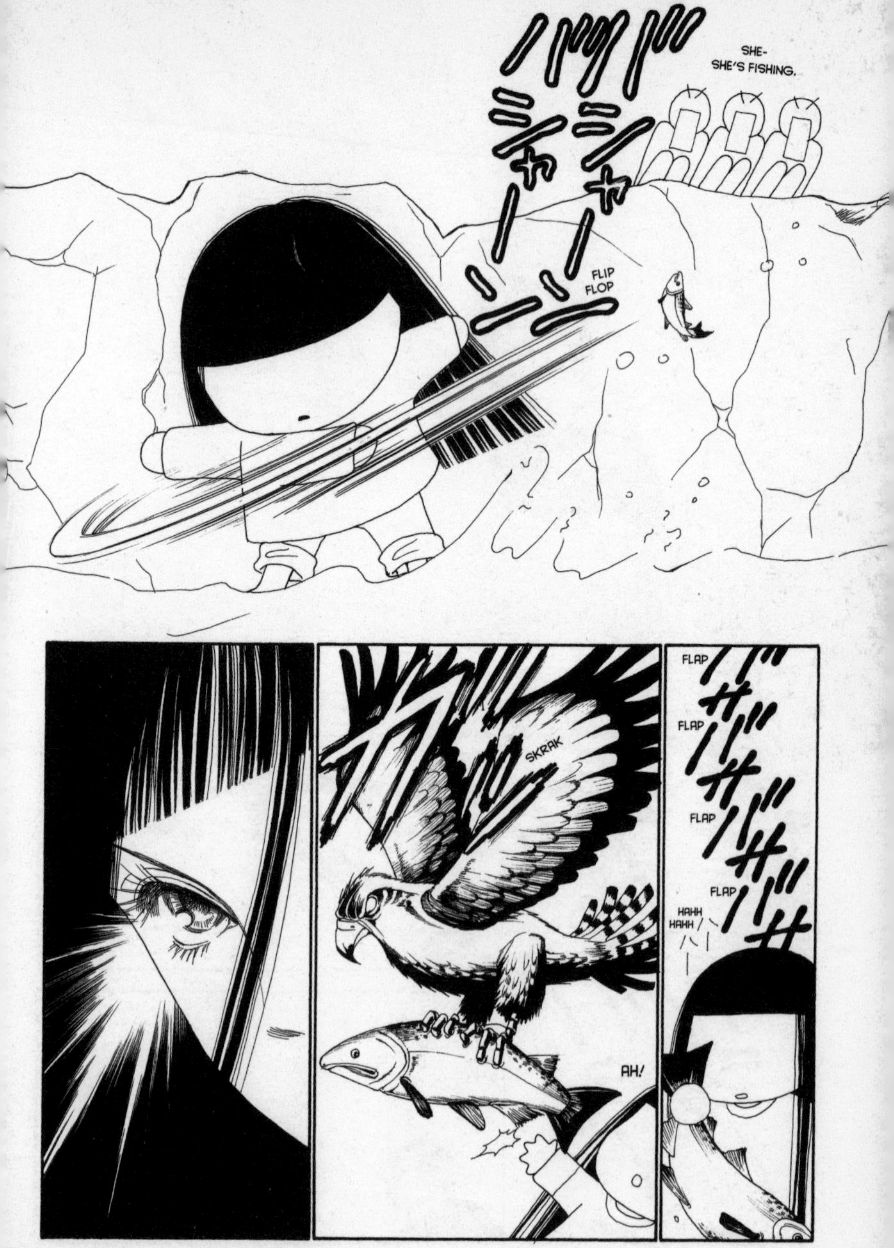
SHE-
SHE'S FISHING.
FLIP
FLOP
FLAP
FLAP
FLAP
FLAP
HAHH
HAHH
SKRAK
AH!

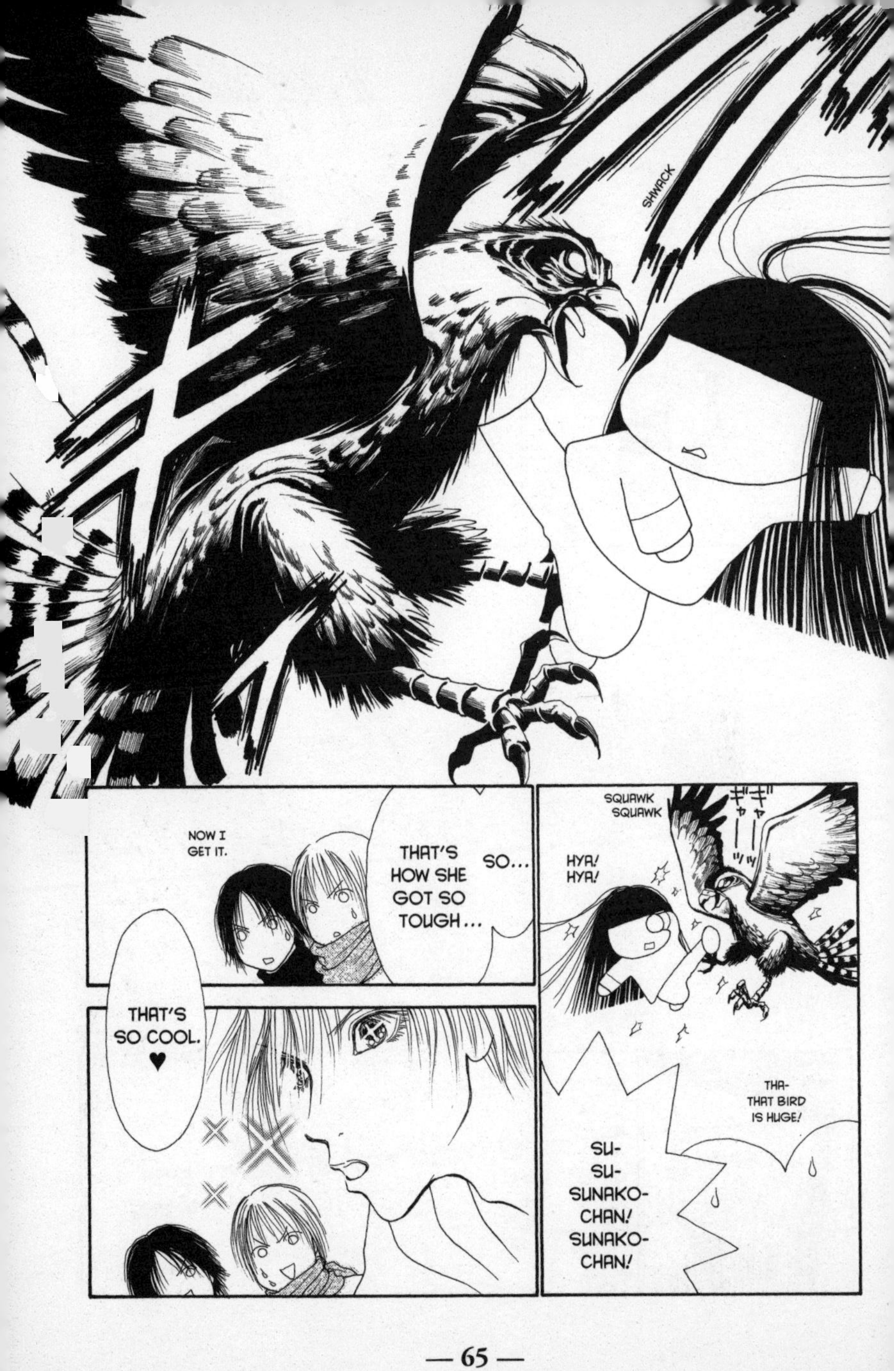
SHWACK
SQUAWK SQUAWK
ギャーギャー
HYA! HYA!
THA- THAT BIRD IS HUGE!
SU- SU- SUNAKO- CHAN! SUNAKO- CHAN!
SO...
THAT'S HOW SHE GOT SO TOUGH...
NOW I GET IT.
THAT'S SO COOL. ♥

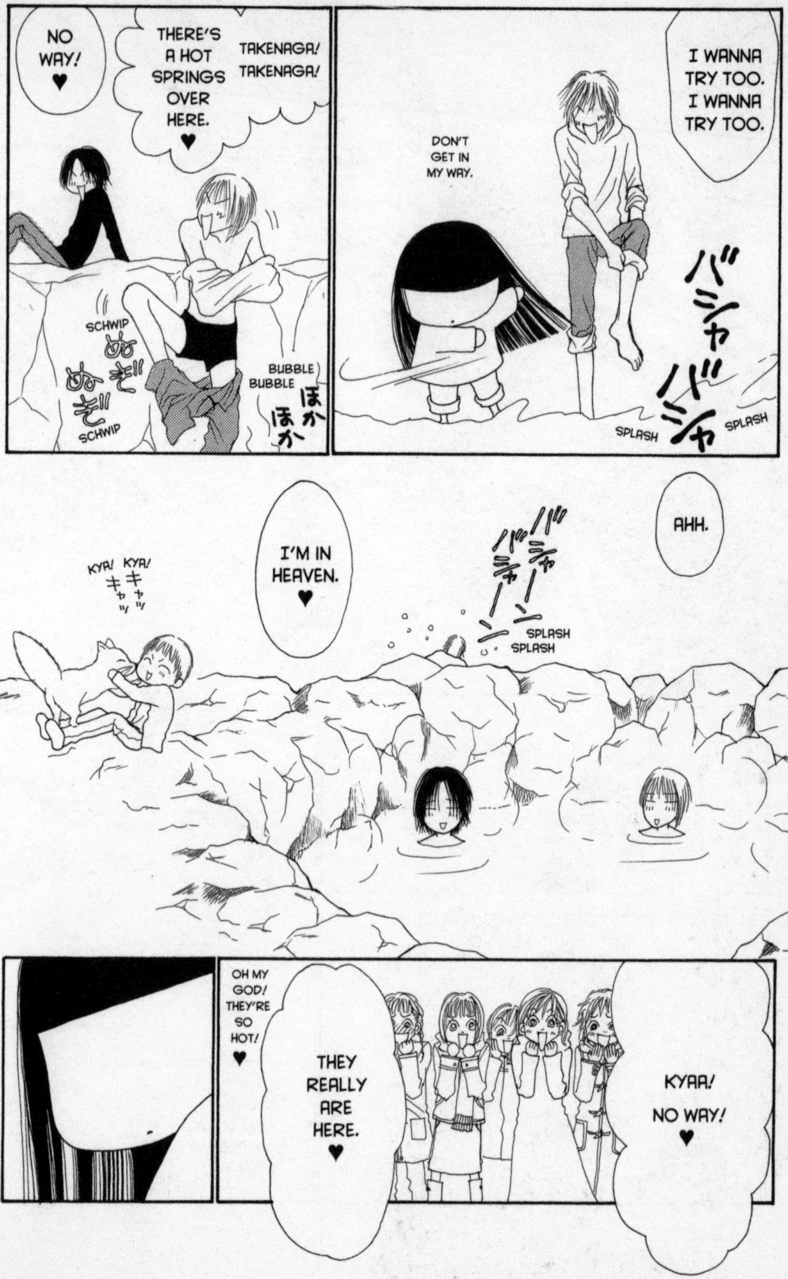

I WANNA TRY TOO. I WANNA TRY TOO.
DON'T GET IN MY WAY.
バシャバシャ
SPLASH SPLASH
TAKENAGA! TAKENAGA!
THERE'S A HOT SPRINGS OVER HERE. ♥
NO WAY! ♥
ぬぎぬぎ
SCHWIP SCHWIP
ほかほか
BUBBLE BUBBLE
AHH.
バシャーバシャーン
SPLASH SPLASH
I'M IN HEAVEN. ♥
キャッキャッ
KYA! KYA!
KYAA! NO WAY! ♥
THEY REALLY ARE HERE. ♥
OH MY GOD! THEY'RE SO HOT! ♥

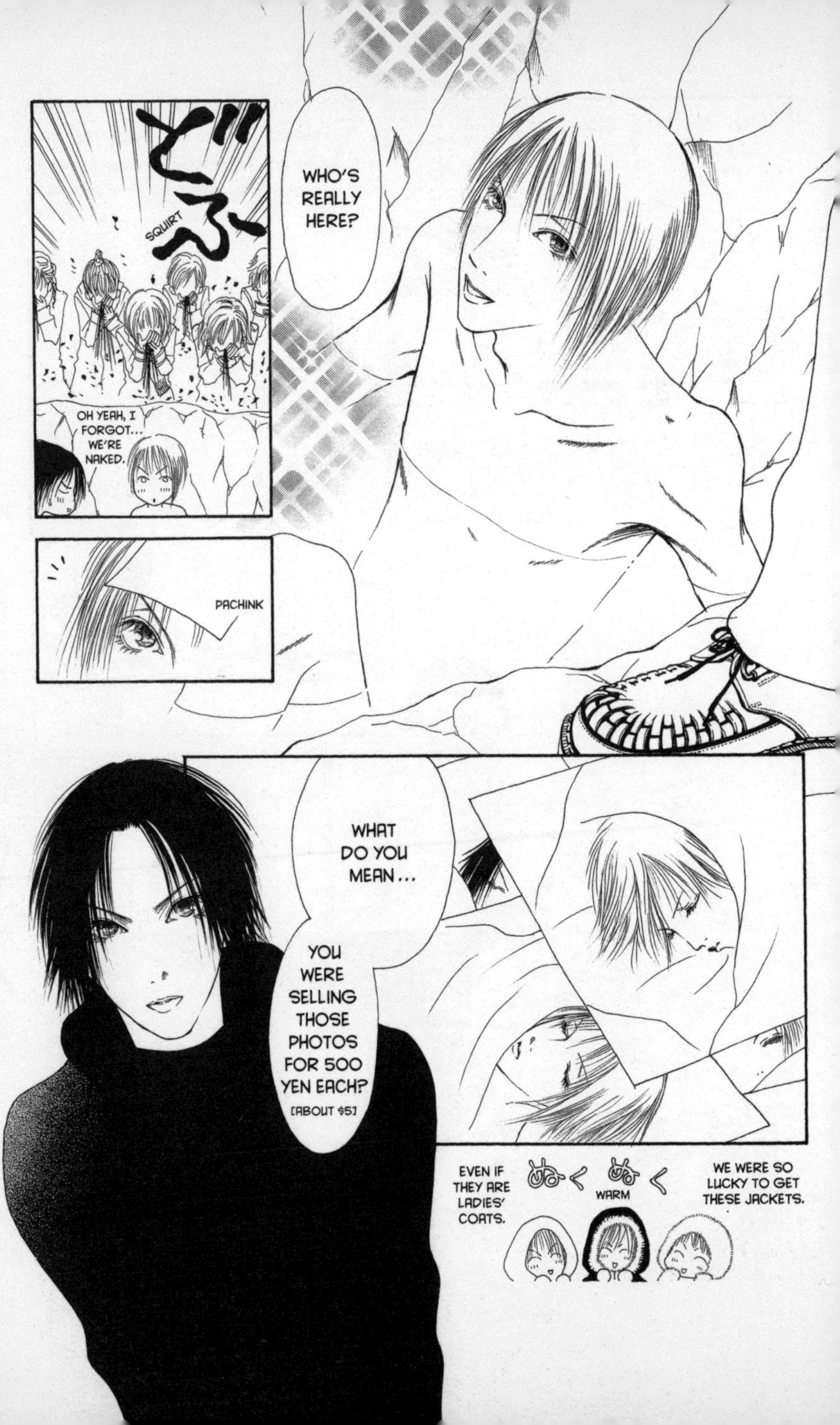
WHO'S REALLY HERE?
SQUIRT
OH YEAH, I FORGOT... WE'RE NAKED.
PACHINK
WHAT DO YOU MEAN...
YOU WERE SELLING THOSE PHOTOS FOR 500 YEN EACH?
[ABOUT $5]
WE WERE SO LUCKY TO GET THESE JACKETS.
ぬく ぬく
WARM
EVEN IF THEY ARE LADIES' COATS.

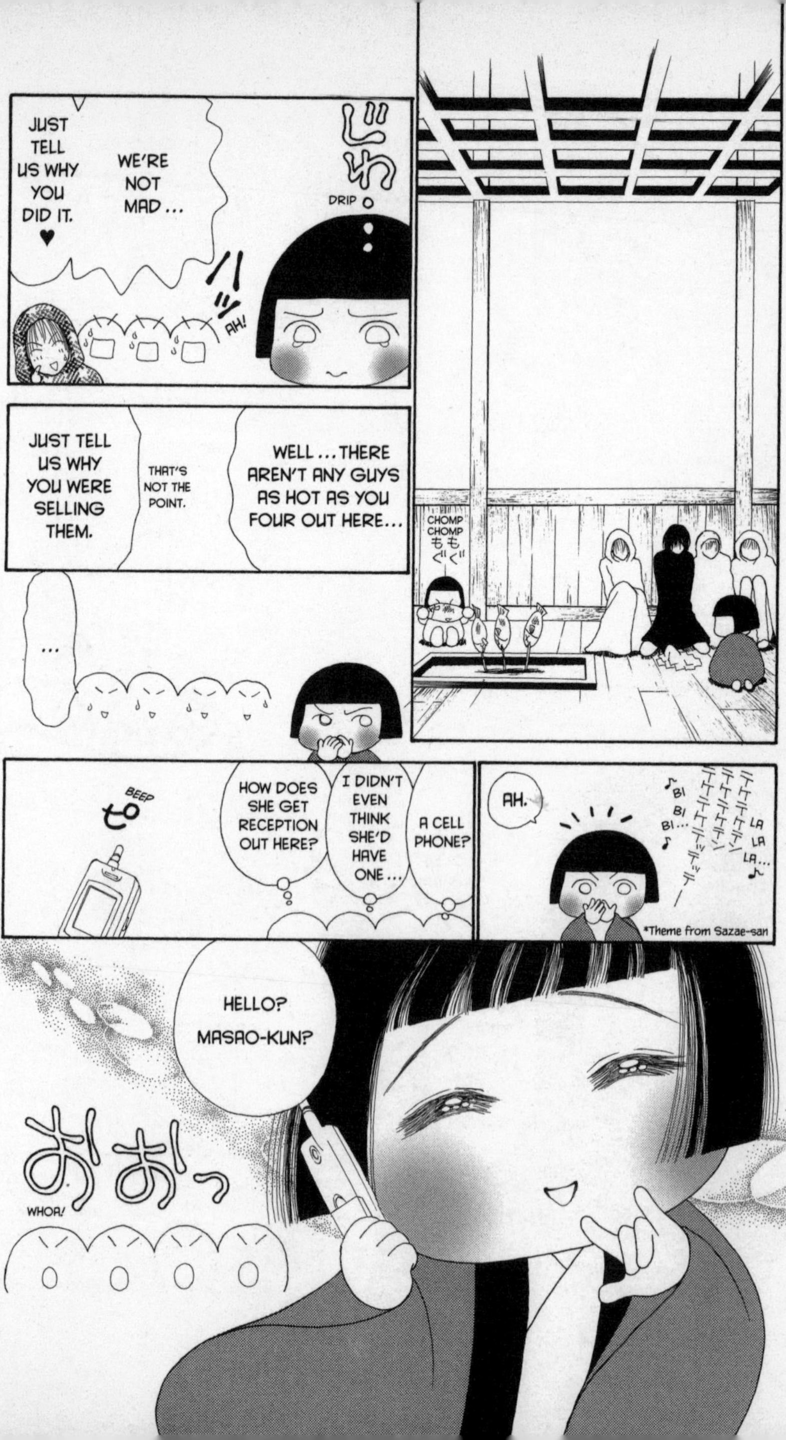
CHOMP CHOMP
もも
ぐぐ
じわ
DRIP
WE'RE NOT MAD...
JUST TELL US WHY YOU DID IT. ♥
ハッ
AH!
WELL... THERE AREN'T ANY GUYS AS HOT AS YOU FOUR OUT HERE...
THAT'S NOT THE POINT.
JUST TELL US WHY YOU WERE SELLING THEM.
...
テケテケテン
テケテケテン
テケテケテッテッテー
LA LA LA... ♪
♪ BI BI BI... ♪
AH.
*Theme from Sazae-san
A CELL PHONE?
I DIDN'T EVEN THINK SHE'D HAVE ONE...
HOW DOES SHE GET RECEPTION OUT HERE?
ピ
BEEP
HELLO? MASAO-KUN?
おおっ
WHOA!

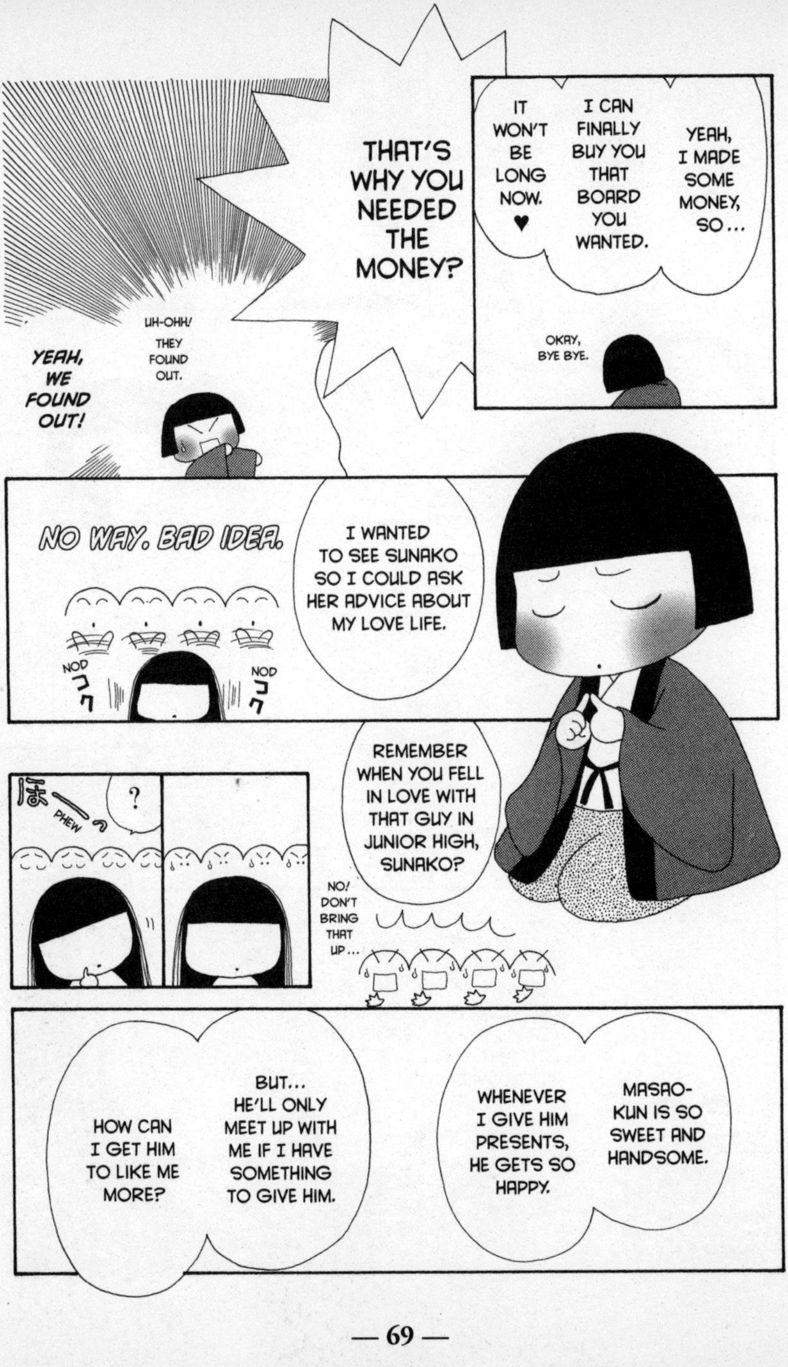
YEAH, I MADE SOME MONEY, SO...
I CAN FINALLY BUY YOU THAT BOARD YOU WANTED.
IT WON'T BE LONG NOW. ♥
OKAY, BYE BYE.
THAT'S WHY YOU NEEDED THE MONEY?
UH-OHH! THEY FOUND OUT.
YEAH, WE FOUND OUT!
I WANTED TO SEE SUNAKO SO I COULD ASK HER ADVICE ABOUT MY LOVE LIFE.
NO WAY. BAD IDEA.
NOD
NOD
REMEMBER WHEN YOU FELL IN LOVE WITH THAT GUY IN JUNIOR HIGH, SUNAKO?
NO! DON'T BRING THAT UP...
?
PHEW
MASAO-KUN IS SO SWEET AND HANDSOME.
WHENEVER I GIVE HIM PRESENTS, HE GETS SO HAPPY.
BUT... HE'LL ONLY MEET UP WITH ME IF I HAVE SOMETHING TO GIVE HIM.
HOW CAN I GET HIM TO LIKE ME MORE?

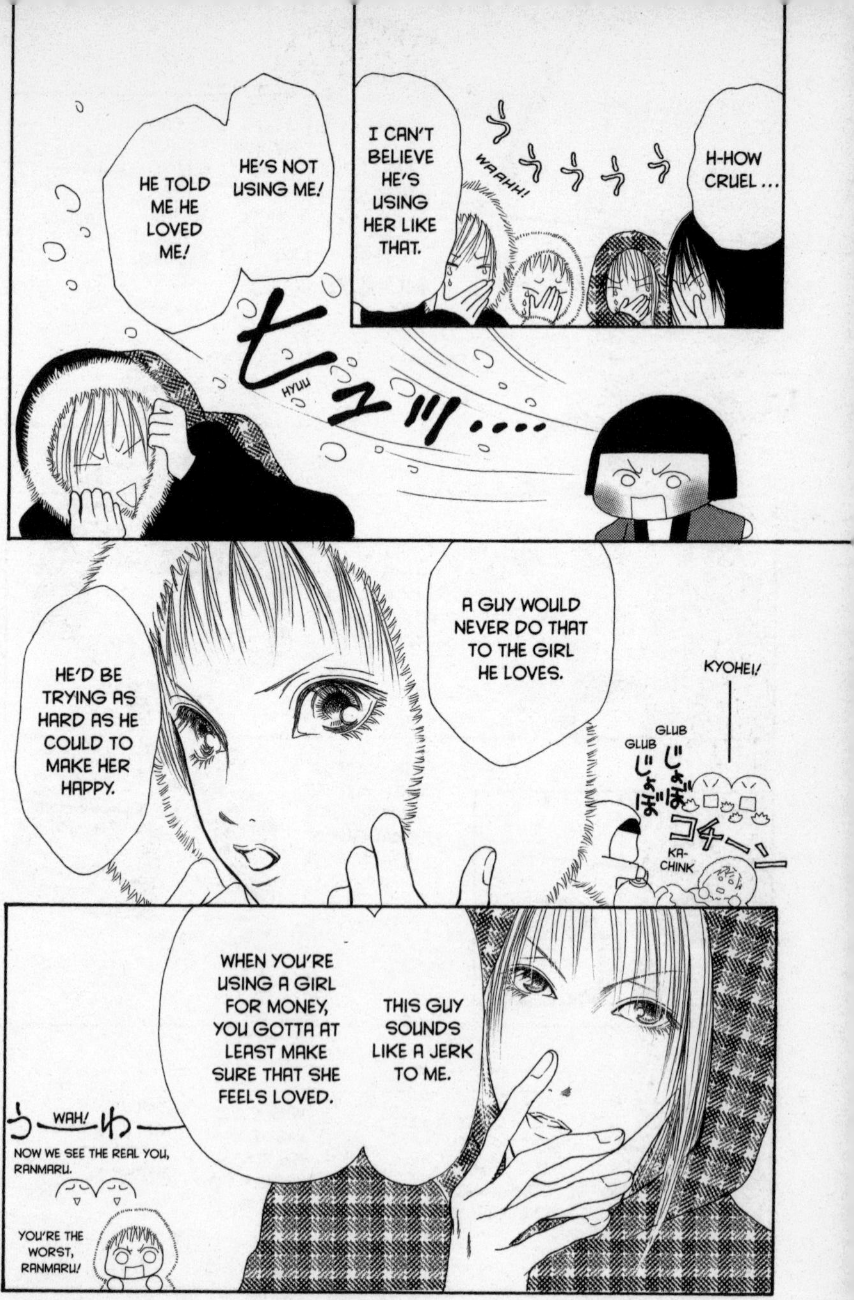
H-HOW CRUEL...
WAAHH!
I CAN'T BELIEVE HE'S USING HER LIKE THAT.
HE'S NOT USING ME!
HE TOLD ME HE LOVED ME!
HYUU
KYOHEI!
GLUB
GLUB
KA-CHINK
A GUY WOULD NEVER DO THAT TO THE GIRL HE LOVES.
HE'D BE TRYING AS HARD AS HE COULD TO MAKE HER HAPPY.
THIS GUY SOUNDS LIKE A JERK TO ME.
WHEN YOU'RE USING A GIRL FOR MONEY, YOU GOTTA AT LEAST MAKE SURE THAT SHE FEELS LOVED.
WAH!
NOW WE SEE THE REAL YOU, RANMARU.
YOU'RE THE WORST, RANMARU!

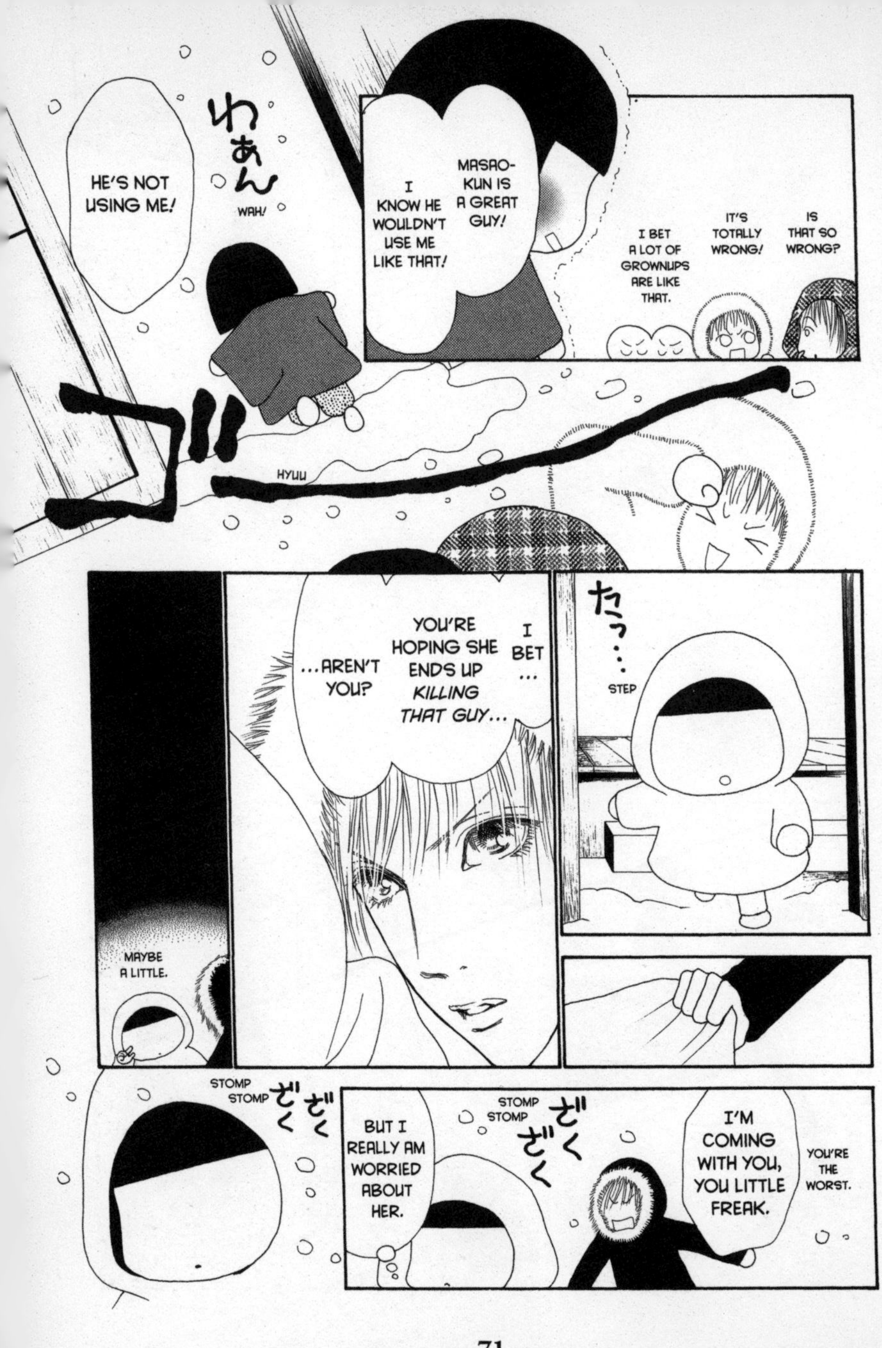
IS THAT SO WRONG?
IT'S TOTALLY WRONG!
I BET A LOT OF GROWNUPS ARE LIKE THAT.
MASAO-KUN IS A GREAT GUY!
I KNOW HE WOULDN'T USE ME LIKE THAT!
わあん
WAH!
HE'S NOT USING ME!
HYUU
たっ…
STEP
I BET…
YOU'RE HOPING SHE ENDS UP *KILLING THAT GUY*…
…AREN'T YOU?
MAYBE A LITTLE.
YOU'RE THE WORST.
I'M COMING WITH YOU, YOU LITTLE FREAK.
ざくざく
STOMP STOMP
BUT I REALLY AM WORRIED ABOUT HER.
ざくざく
STOMP STOMP

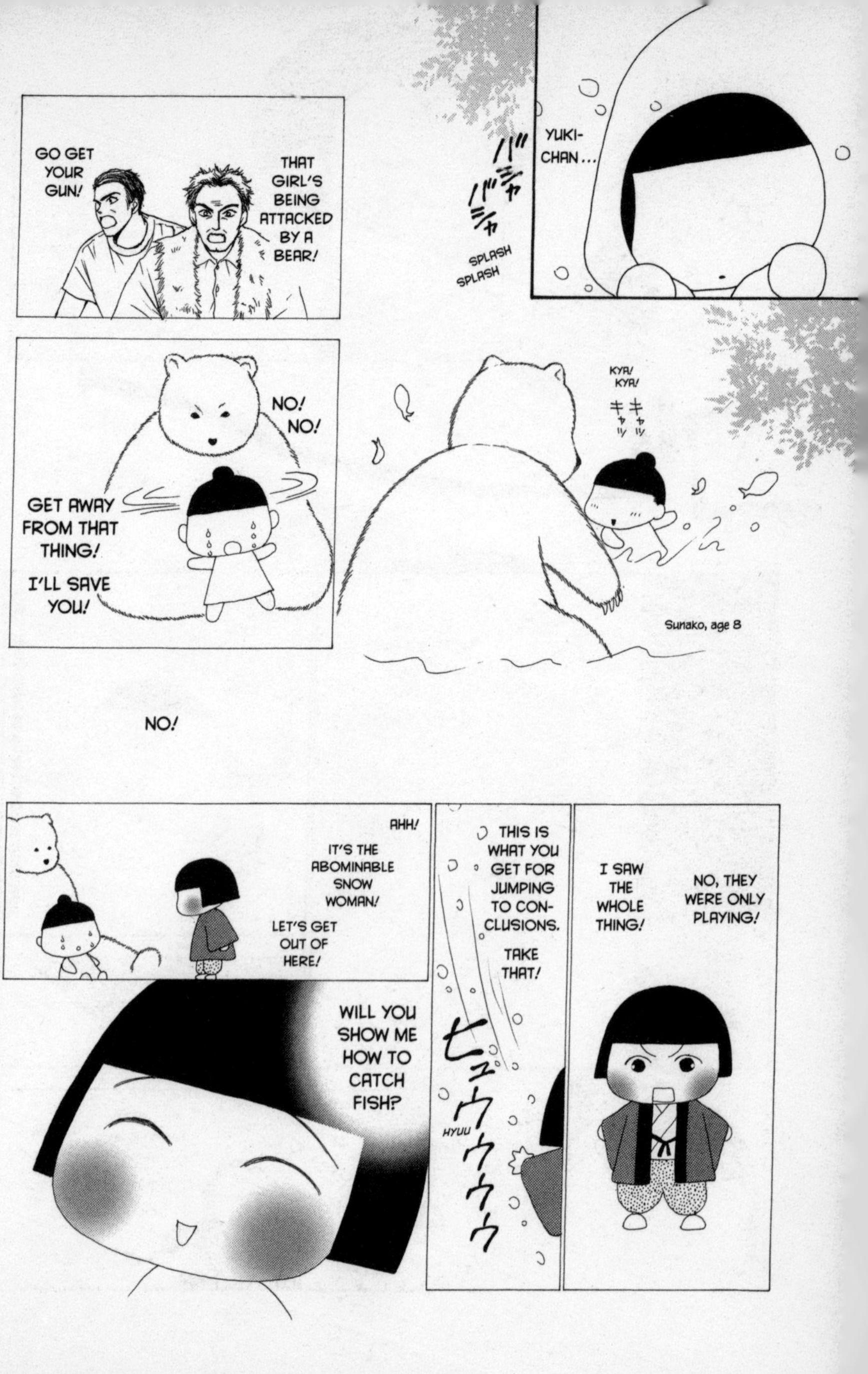
YUKI-CHAN...
バシャバシャ
SPLASH SPLASH
THAT GIRL'S BEING ATTACKED BY A BEAR!
GO GET YOUR GUN!
KYA! KYA!
キャキャ
Sunako, age 8
NO! NO!
GET AWAY FROM THAT THING!
I'LL SAVE YOU!
NO!
NO, THEY WERE ONLY PLAYING!
I SAW THE WHOLE THING!
THIS IS WHAT YOU GET FOR JUMPING TO CONCLUSIONS.
TAKE THAT!
ヒュウウウウ
HYUU
AHH!
IT'S THE ABOMINABLE SNOW WOMAN!
LET'S GET OUT OF HERE!
WILL YOU SHOW ME HOW TO CATCH FISH?

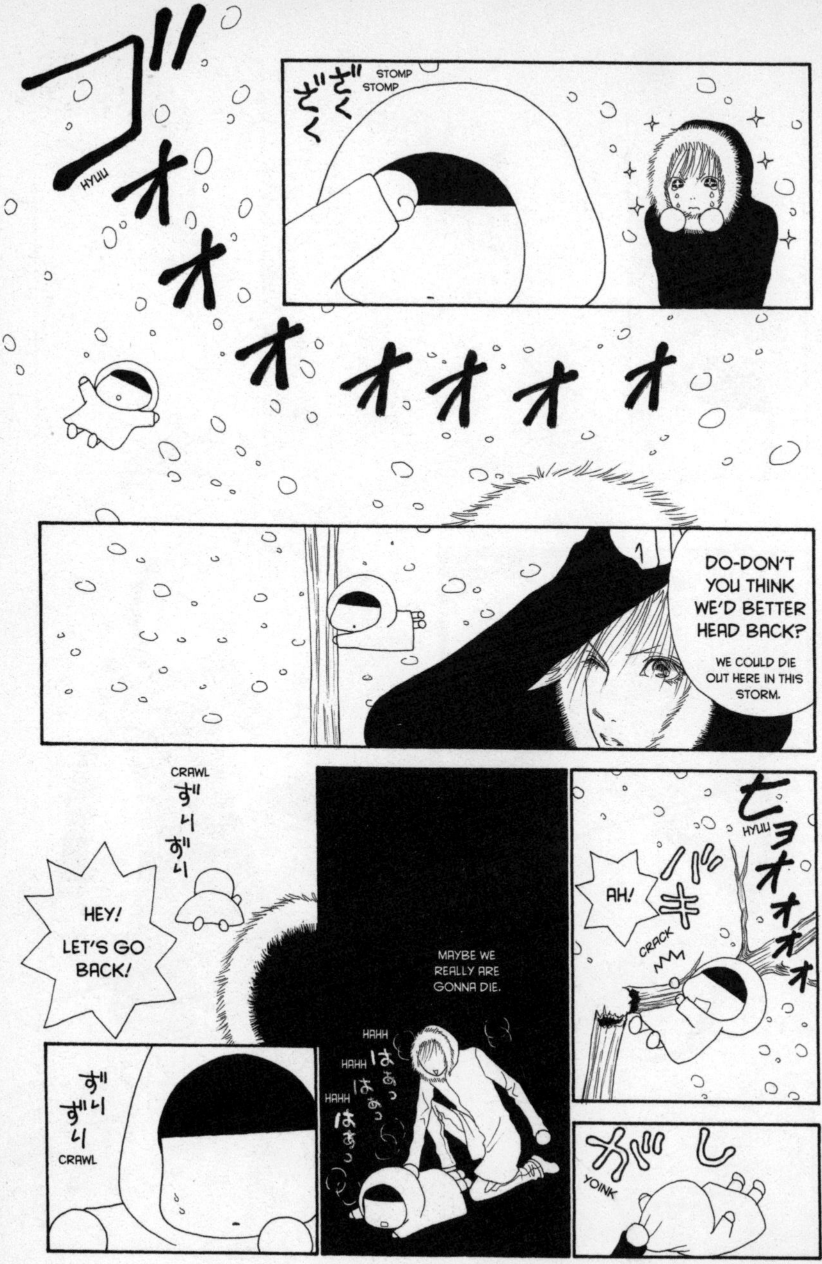
ざくざく
STOMP STOMP
ゴォォォォォォォォ
HYUU
DO-DON'T YOU THINK WE'D BETTER HEAD BACK?
WE COULD DIE OUT HERE IN THIS STORM.
ヒョオオオオオ
HYUU
バキ
CRACK
AH!
がし
YOINK
MAYBE WE REALLY ARE GONNA DIE.
はぁっ はぁっ はぁっ
HAHH HAHH HAHH
HEY! LET'S GO BACK!
ずりずり
CRAWL
ずりずり
CRAWL

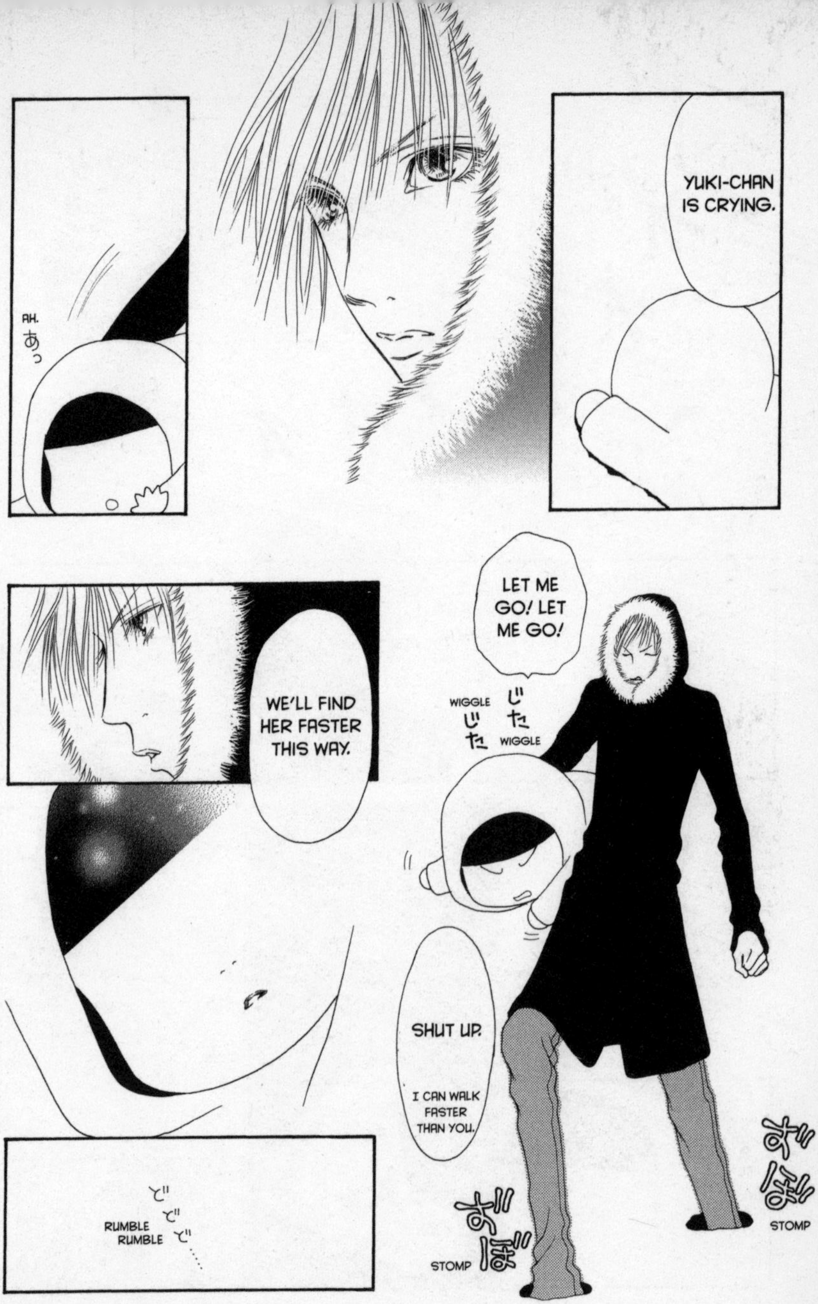
YUKI-CHAN IS CRYING.
AH.
あっ
LET ME GO! LET ME GO!
じた じた
WIGGLE WIGGLE
SHUT UP.
I CAN WALK FASTER THAN YOU.
ずぼ
STOMP
ずぼ
STOMP
WE'LL FIND HER FASTER THIS WAY.
どどど……
RUMBLE RUMBLE

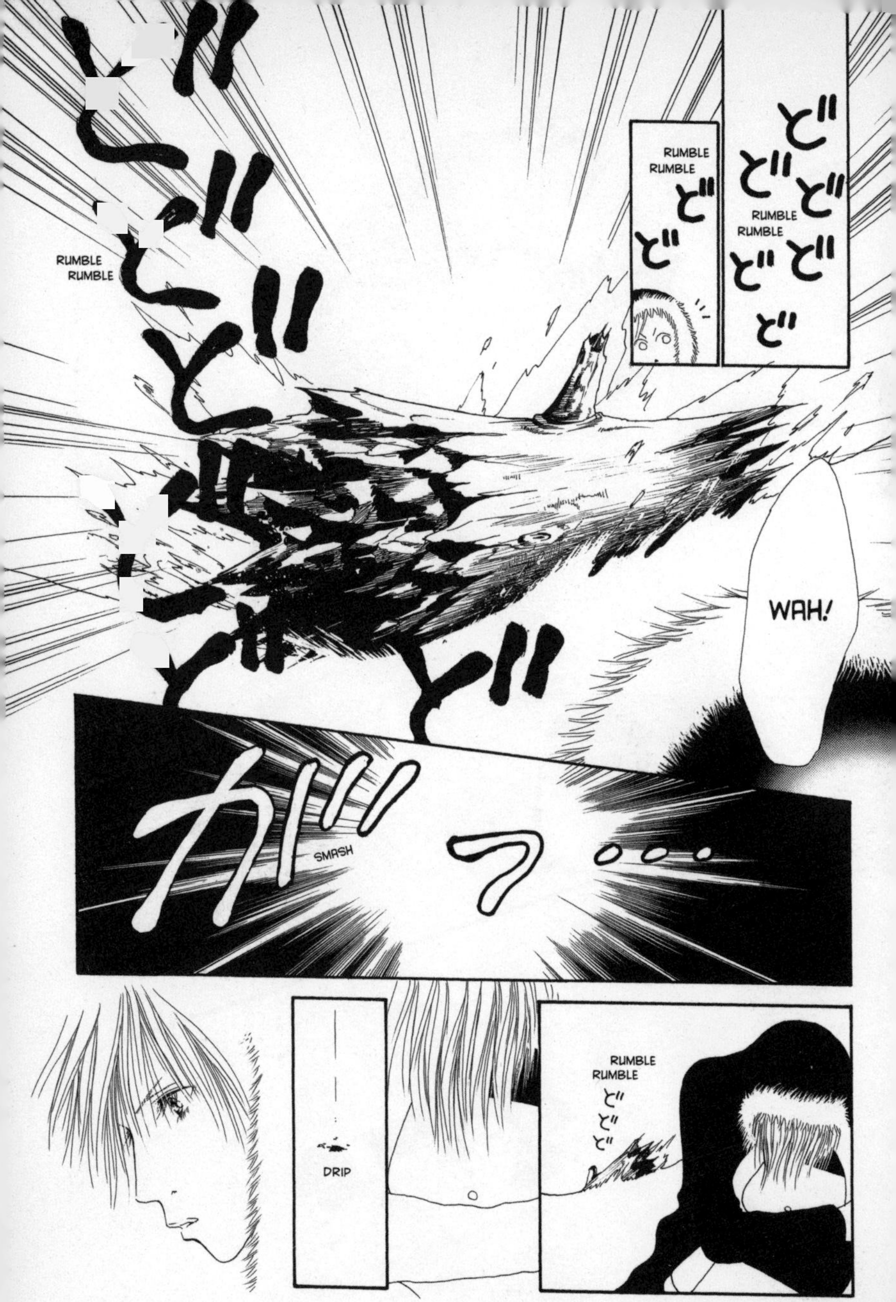
RUMBLE RUMBLE
RUMBLE RUMBLE
RUMBLE RUMBLE
WAH!
SMASH
RUMBLE RUMBLE
DRIP

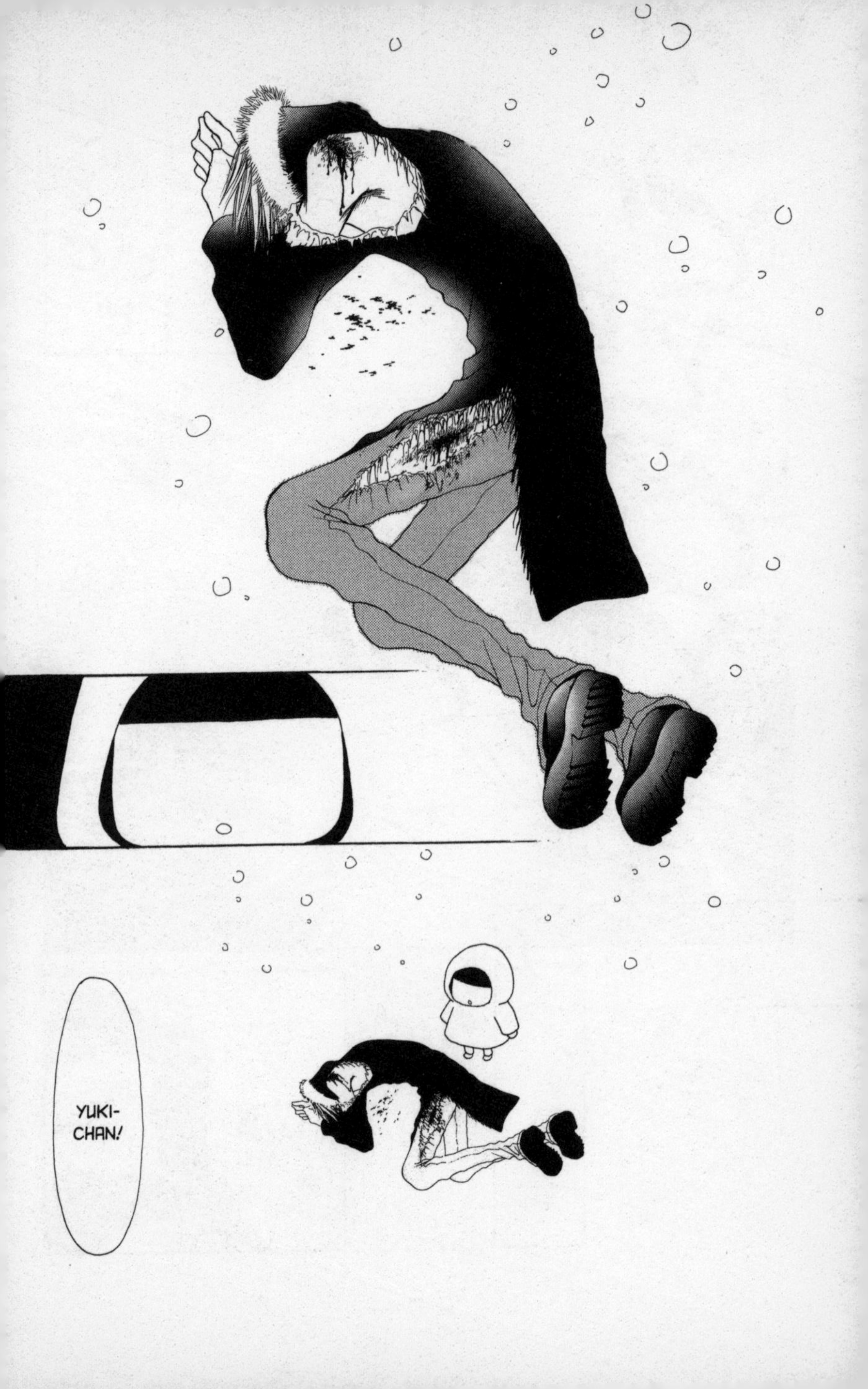
YUKI-CHAN!

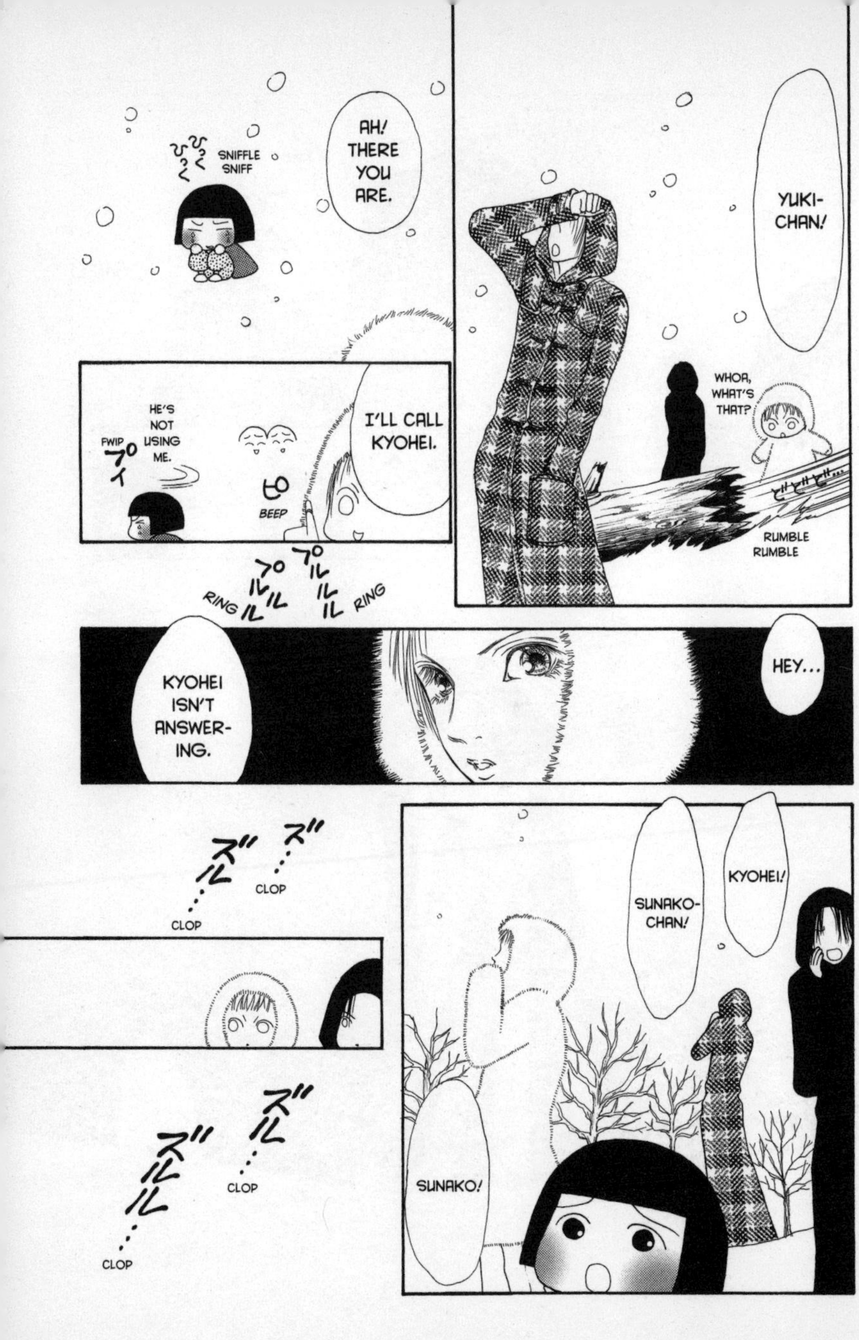
YUKI-CHAN!
WHOA, WHAT'S THAT?
RUMBLE RUMBLE
AH! THERE YOU ARE.
SNIFFLE SNIFF
I'LL CALL KYOHEI.
BEEP
HE'S NOT USING ME.
FWIP
RING RING
HEY...
KYOHEI ISN'T ANSWER-ING.
KYOHEI!
SUNAKO-CHAN!
SUNAKO!
CLOP
CLOP
CLOP
CLOP

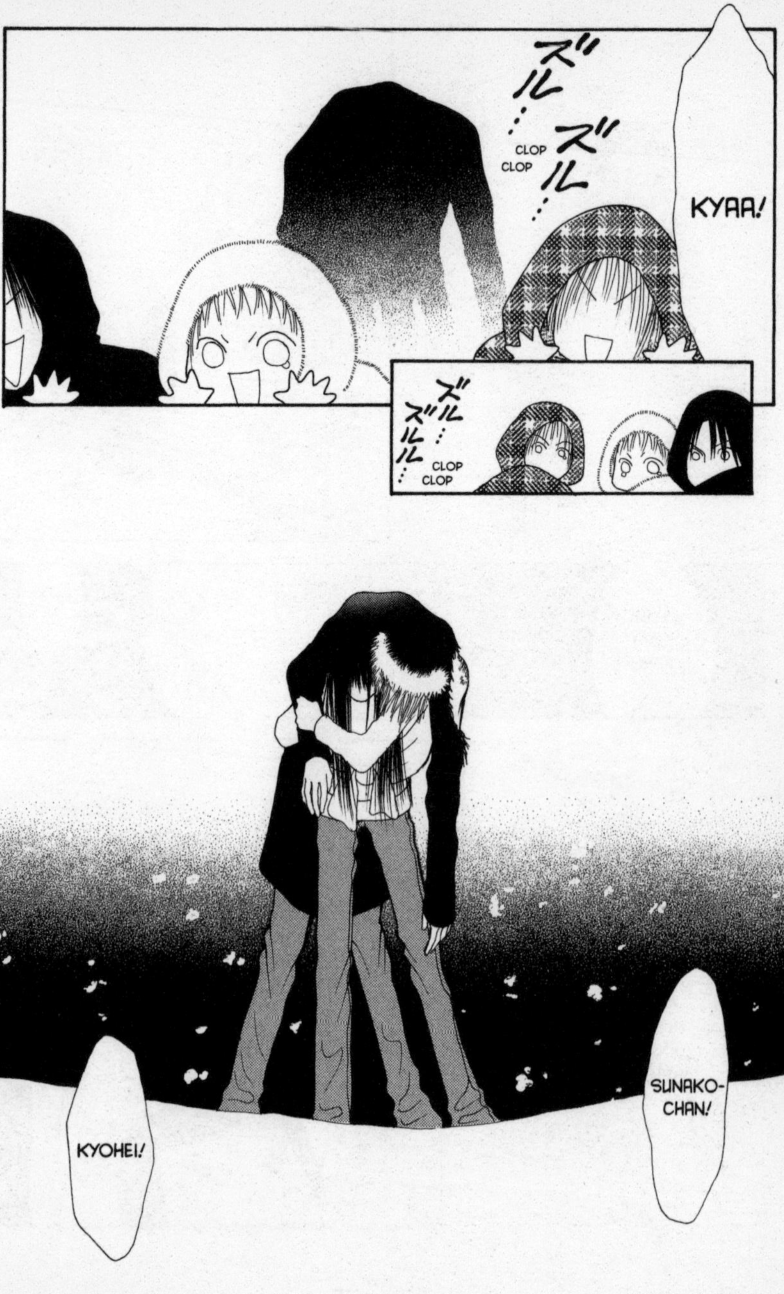
KYAA!
ズル… ズル…
CLOP CLOP
ズル… ズル…
CLOP CLOP
SUNAKO-CHAN!
KYOHEI!

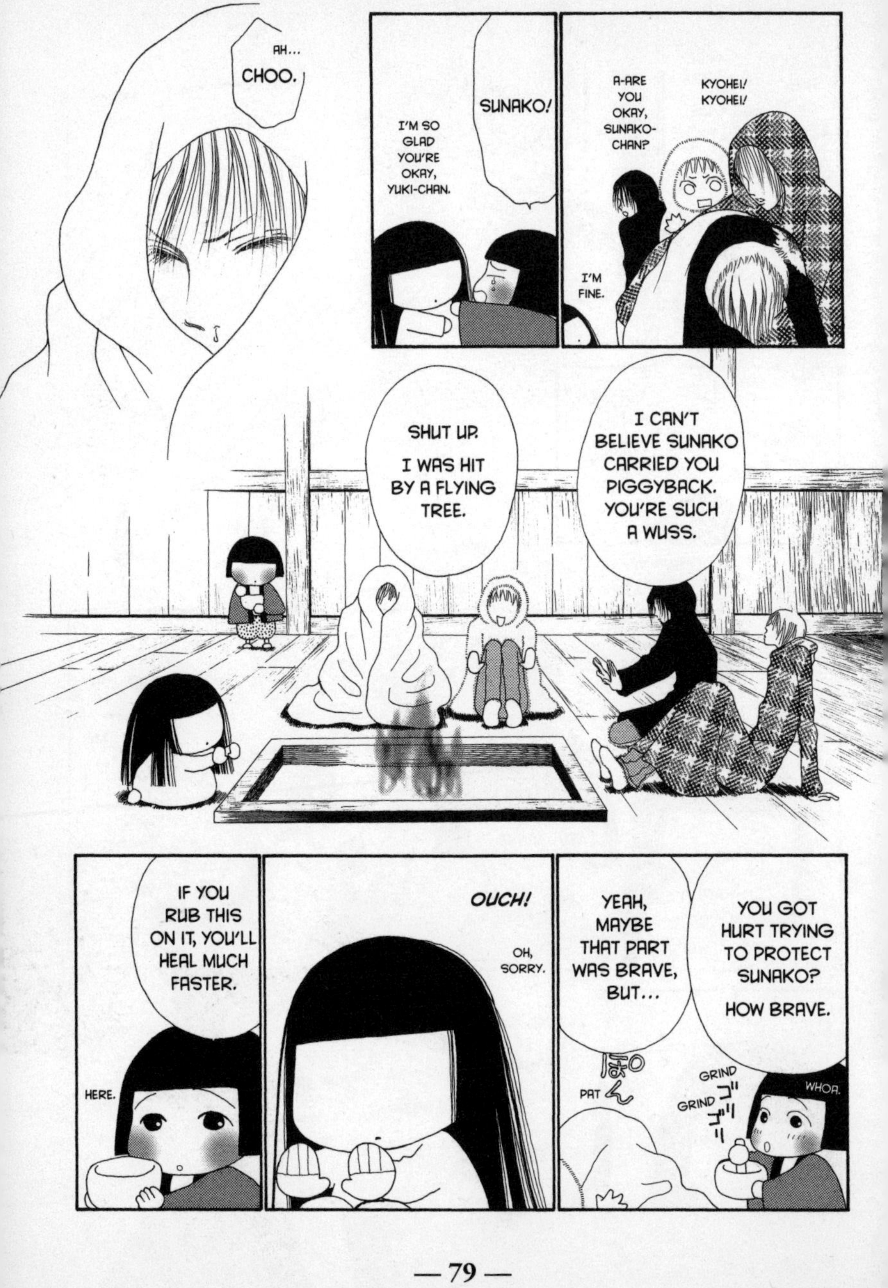
KYOHEI! KYOHEI!
A-ARE YOU OKAY, SUNAKO-CHAN?
I'M FINE.
SUNAKO!
I'M SO GLAD YOU'RE OKAY, YUKI-CHAN.
AH...
CHOO.
I CAN'T BELIEVE SUNAKO CARRIED YOU PIGGYBACK. YOU'RE SUCH A WUSS.
SHUT UP.
I WAS HIT BY A FLYING TREE.
YOU GOT HURT TRYING TO PROTECT SUNAKO?
HOW BRAVE.
YEAH, MAYBE THAT PART WAS BRAVE, BUT...
WHOA.
GRIND
ゴリ
GRIND
ゴリ
ぽん
PAT
OUCH!
OH, SORRY.
IF YOU RUB THIS ON IT, YOU'LL HEAL MUCH FASTER.
HERE.

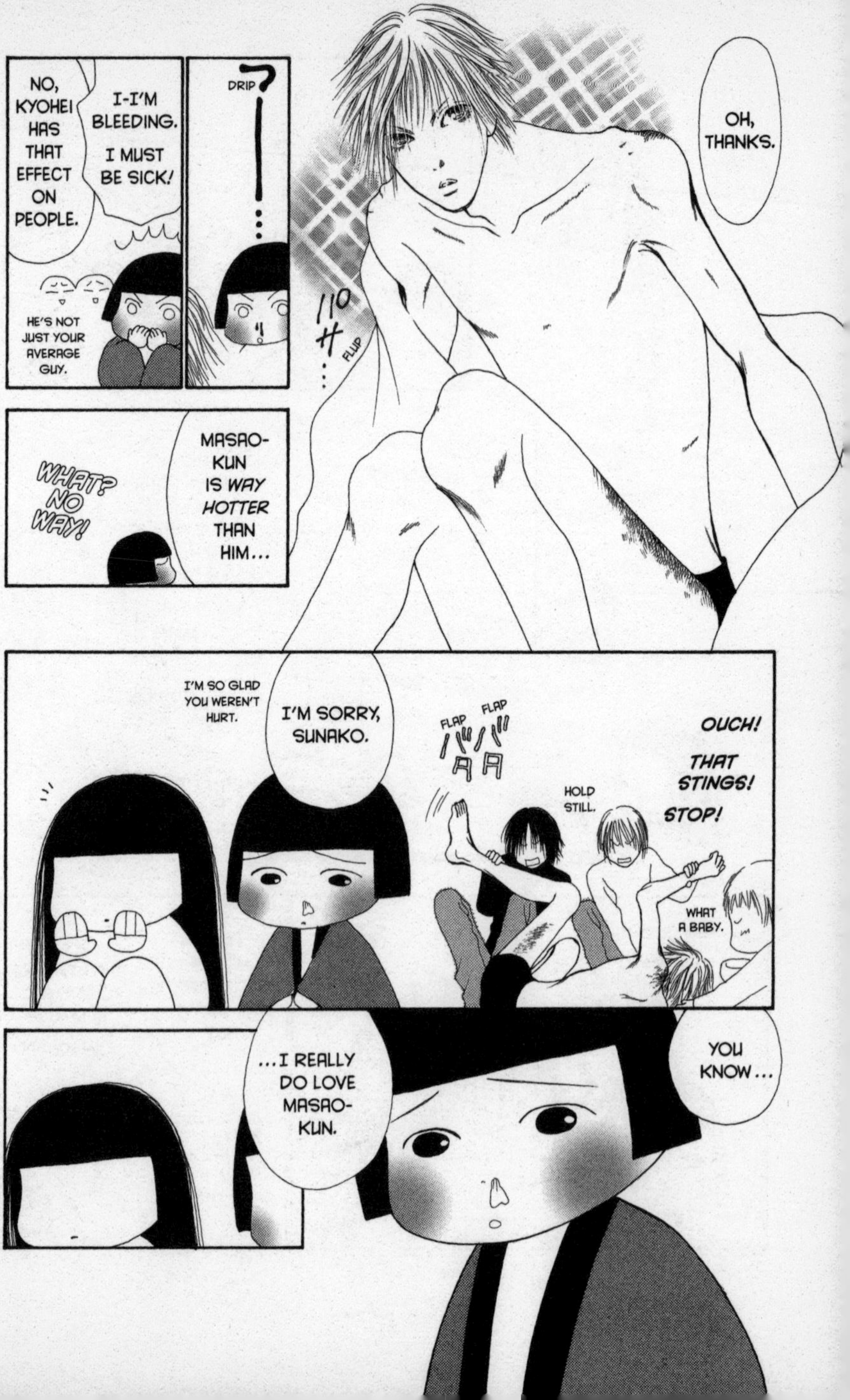
OH, THANKS.
FLAP
DRIP
I-I'M BLEEDING. I MUST BE SICK!
NO, KYOHEI HAS THAT EFFECT ON PEOPLE.
HE'S NOT JUST YOUR AVERAGE GUY.
MASAO-KUN IS WAY HOTTER THAN HIM...
WHAT? NO WAY!
OUCH! THAT STINGS! STOP!
WHAT A BABY.
HOLD STILL.
FLAP FLAP
I'M SORRY, SUNAKO.
I'M SO GLAD YOU WEREN'T HURT.
YOU KNOW...
...I REALLY DO LOVE MASAO-KUN.

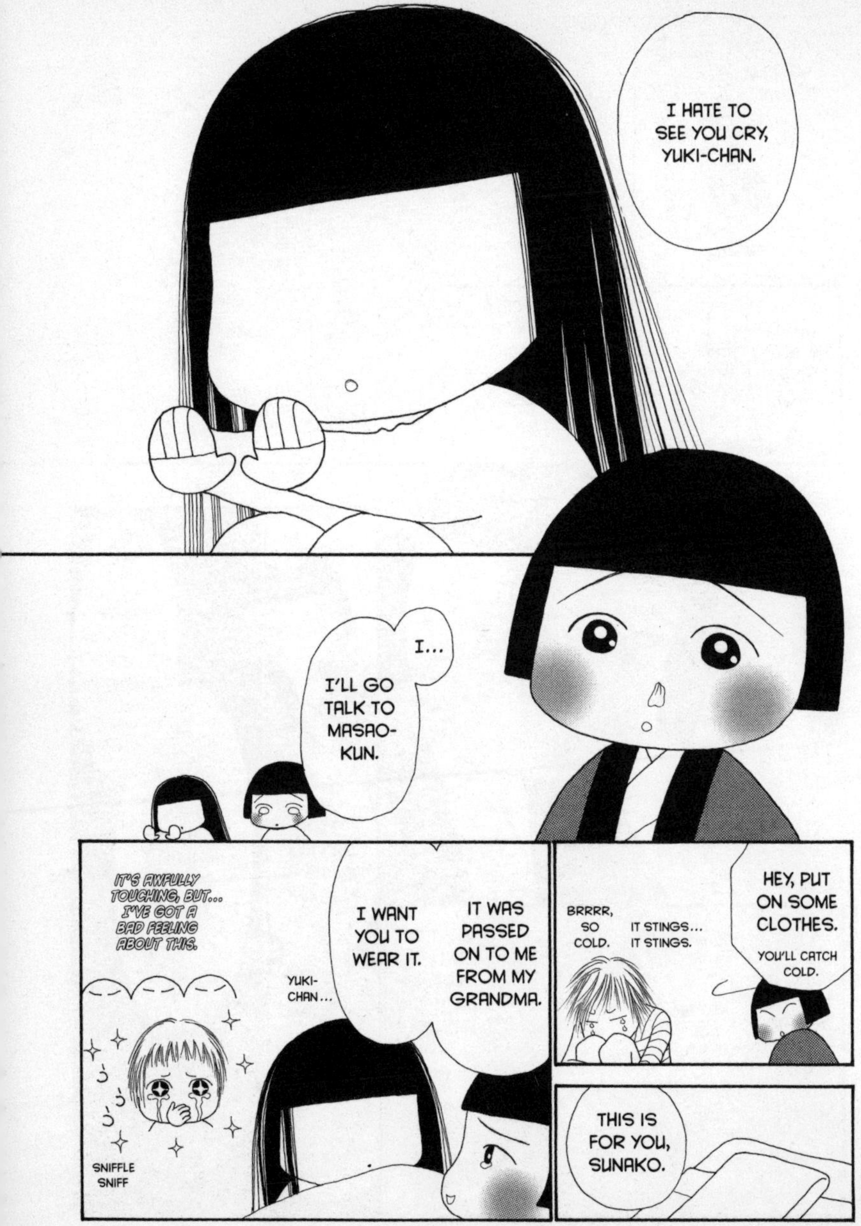
I HATE TO SEE YOU CRY, YUKI-CHAN.
I...
I'LL GO TALK TO MASAO-KUN.
HEY, PUT ON SOME CLOTHES.
YOU'LL CATCH COLD.
IT STINGS... IT STINGS.
BRRRR, SO COLD.
THIS IS FOR YOU, SUNAKO.
IT WAS PASSED ON TO ME FROM MY GRANDMA.
I WANT YOU TO WEAR IT.
YUKI-CHAN...
IT'S AWFULLY TOUCHING, BUT... I'VE GOT A BAD FEELING ABOUT THIS.
SNIFFLE SNIFF

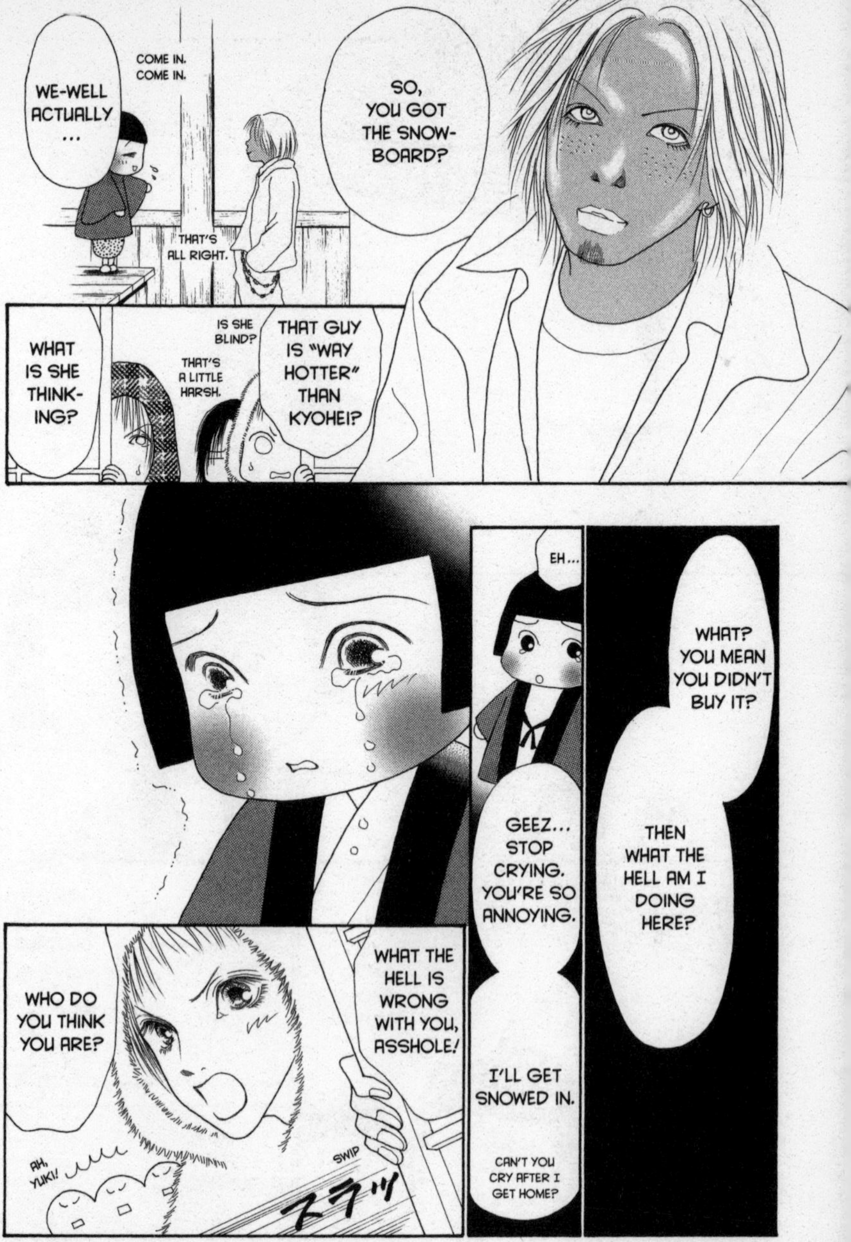
SO, YOU GOT THE SNOW-BOARD?
COME IN. COME IN.
WE-WELL ACTUALLY ...
THAT'S ALL RIGHT.
THAT GUY IS "WAY HOTTER" THAN KYOHEI?
IS SHE BLIND?
THAT'S A LITTLE HARSH.
WHAT IS SHE THINKING?
WHAT? YOU MEAN YOU DIDN'T BUY IT?
THEN WHAT THE HELL AM I DOING HERE?
EH...
GEEZ... STOP CRYING. YOU'RE SO ANNOYING.
I'LL GET SNOWED IN.
CAN'T YOU CRY AFTER I GET HOME?
WHAT THE HELL IS WRONG WITH YOU, ASSHOLE!
WHO DO YOU THINK YOU ARE?
SWIP
スラッ
AH, YUKI!

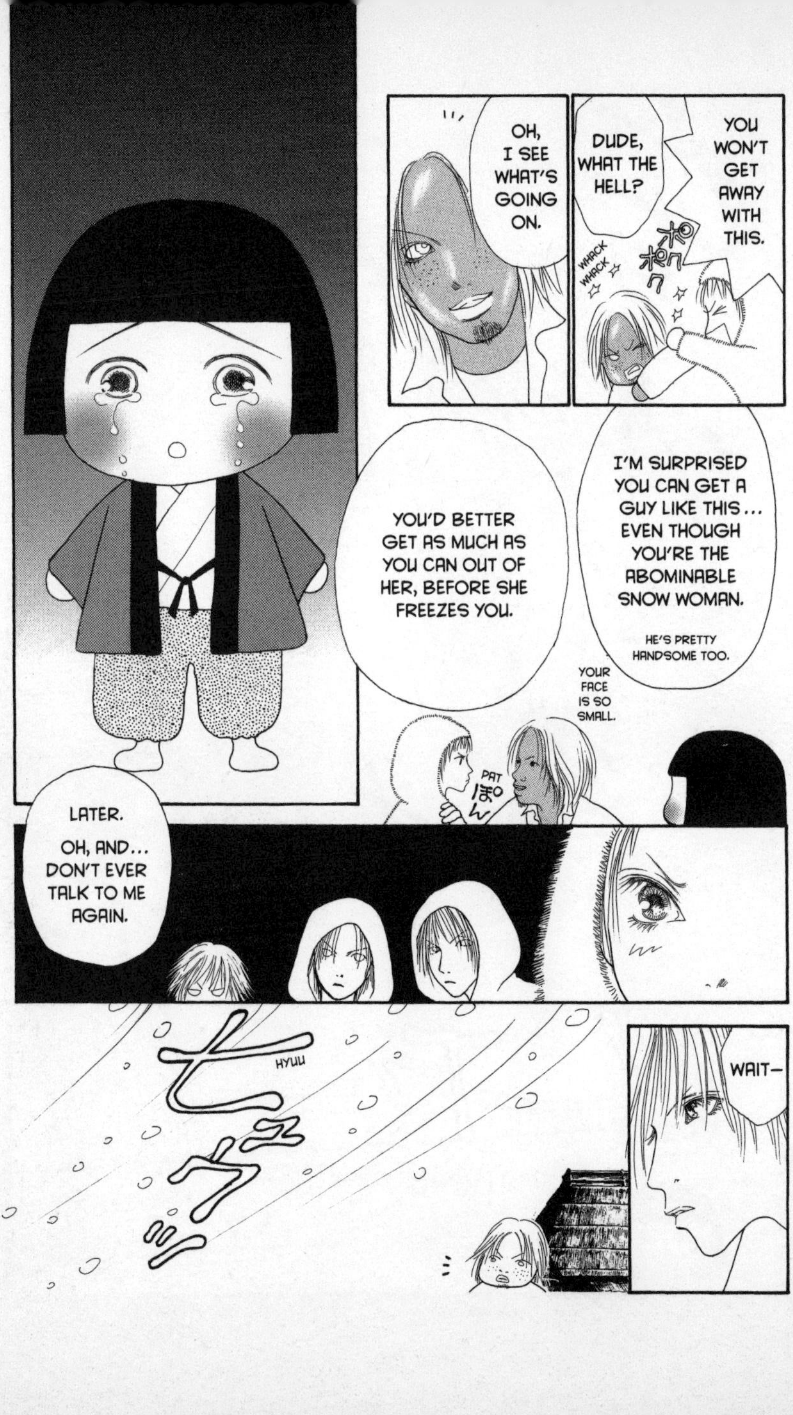
YOU WON'T GET AWAY WITH THIS.
DUDE, WHAT THE HELL?
WHACK WHACK
OH, I SEE WHAT'S GOING ON.
I'M SURPRISED YOU CAN GET A GUY LIKE THIS... EVEN THOUGH YOU'RE THE ABOMINABLE SNOW WOMAN.
HE'S PRETTY HANDSOME TOO.
YOUR FACE IS SO SMALL.
YOU'D BETTER GET AS MUCH AS YOU CAN OUT OF HER, BEFORE SHE FREEZES YOU.
PAT
LATER.
OH, AND... DON'T EVER TALK TO ME AGAIN.
WAIT—
HYUU

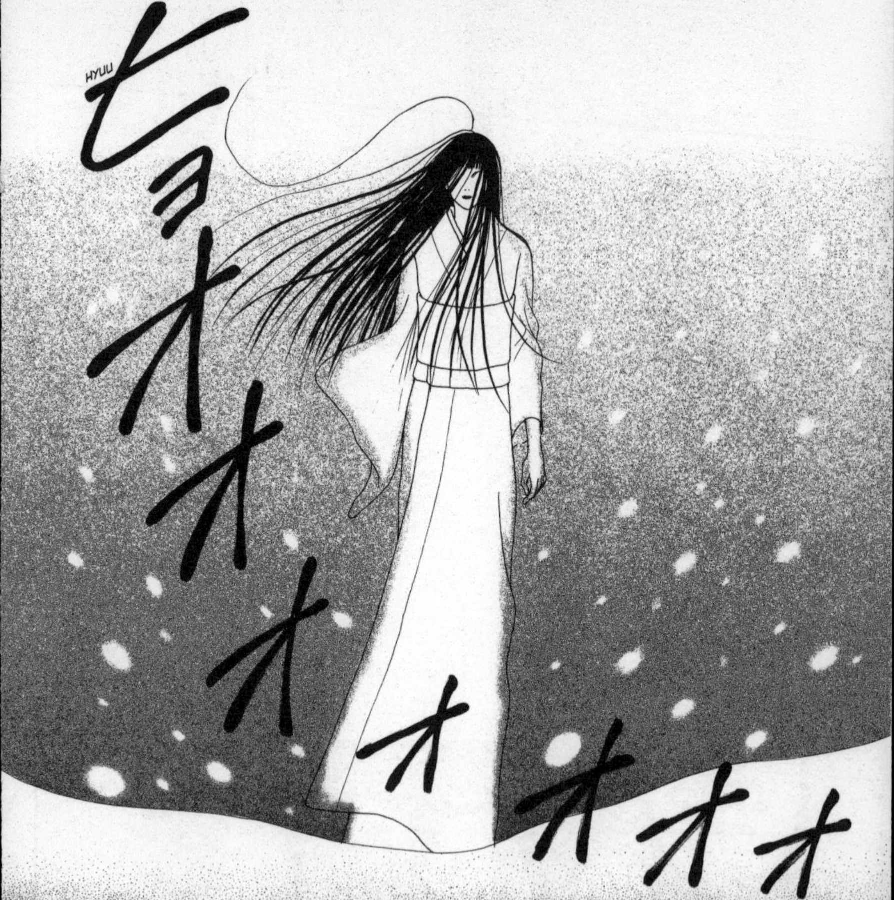

ヒョオオオオオオオ
HYUU

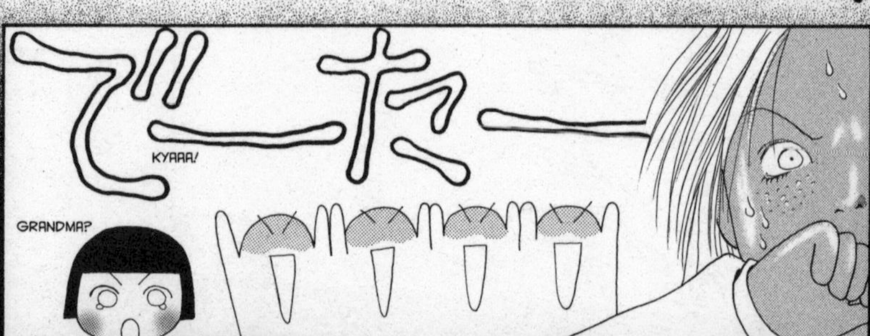

でーたー
KYAAA!
GRANDMA?

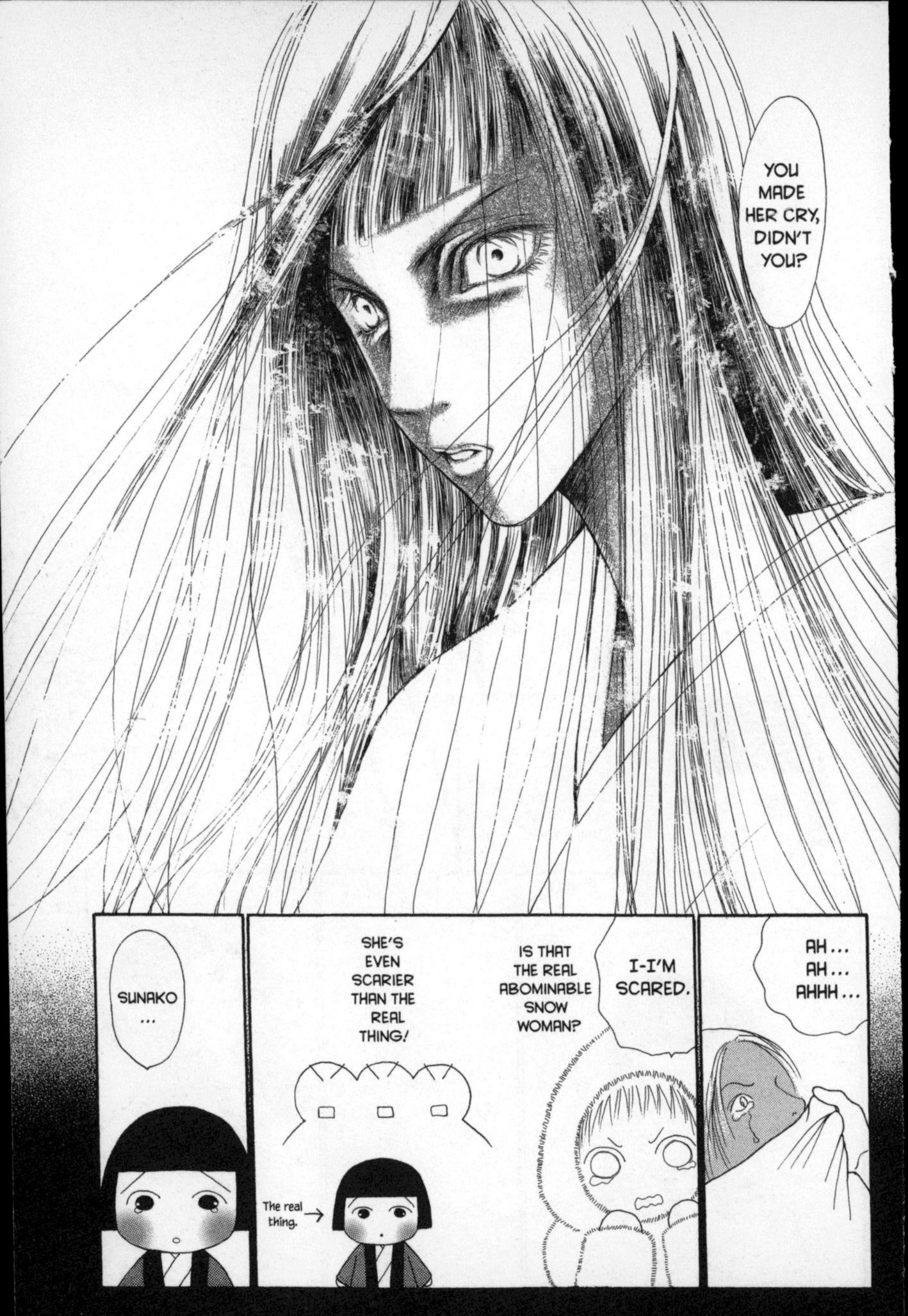
YOU MADE HER CRY, DIDN'T YOU?
AH... AH... AHHH...
I-I'M SCARED.
IS THAT THE REAL ABOMINABLE SNOW WOMAN?
SHE'S EVEN SCARIER THAN THE REAL THING!
The real thing.
SUNAKO ...

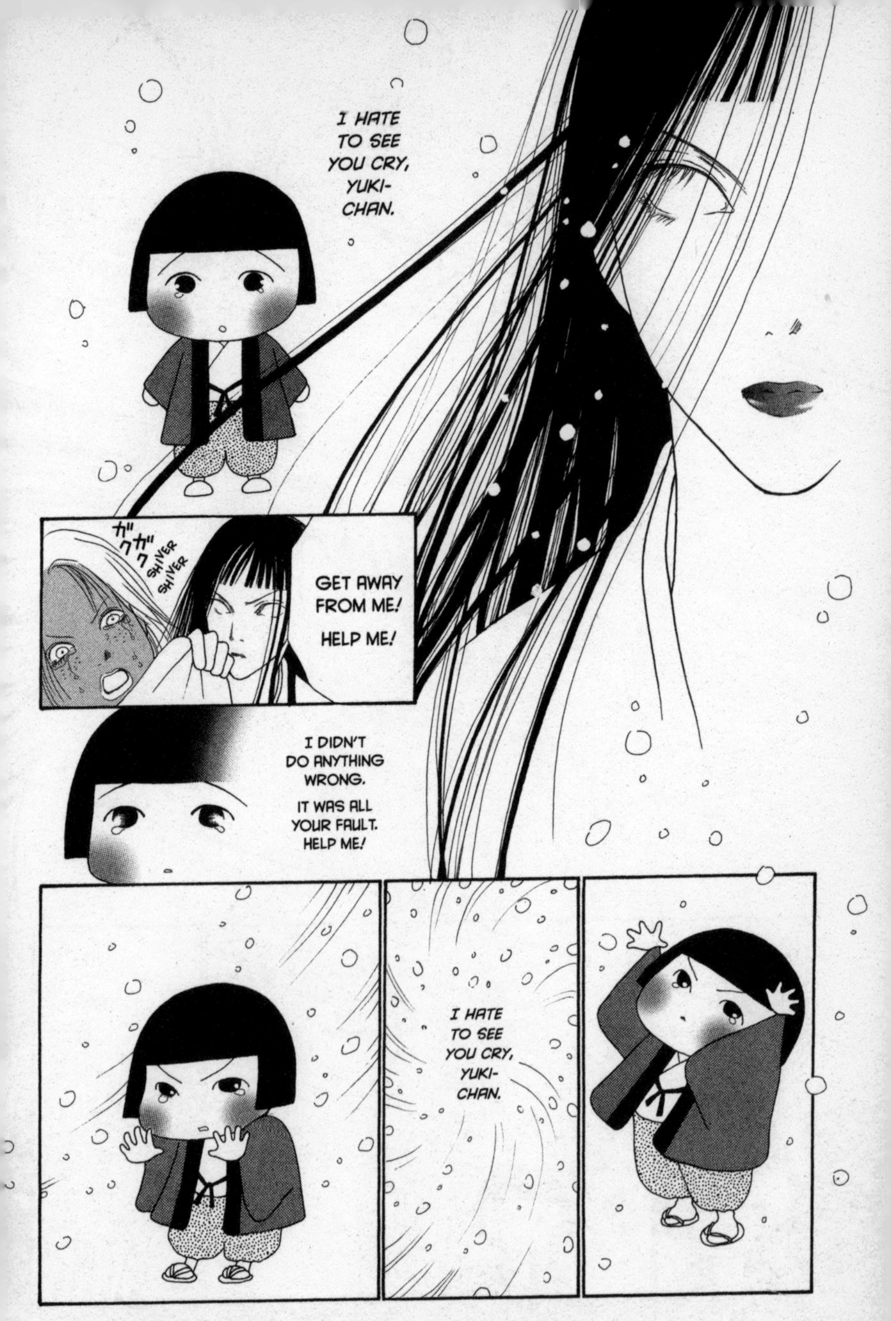
I HATE TO SEE YOU CRY, YUKI-CHAN.
GET AWAY FROM ME!
HELP ME!
ガクガク SHIVER SHIVER
I DIDN'T DO ANYTHING WRONG.
IT WAS ALL YOUR FAULT. HELP ME!
I HATE TO SEE YOU CRY, YUKI-CHAN.

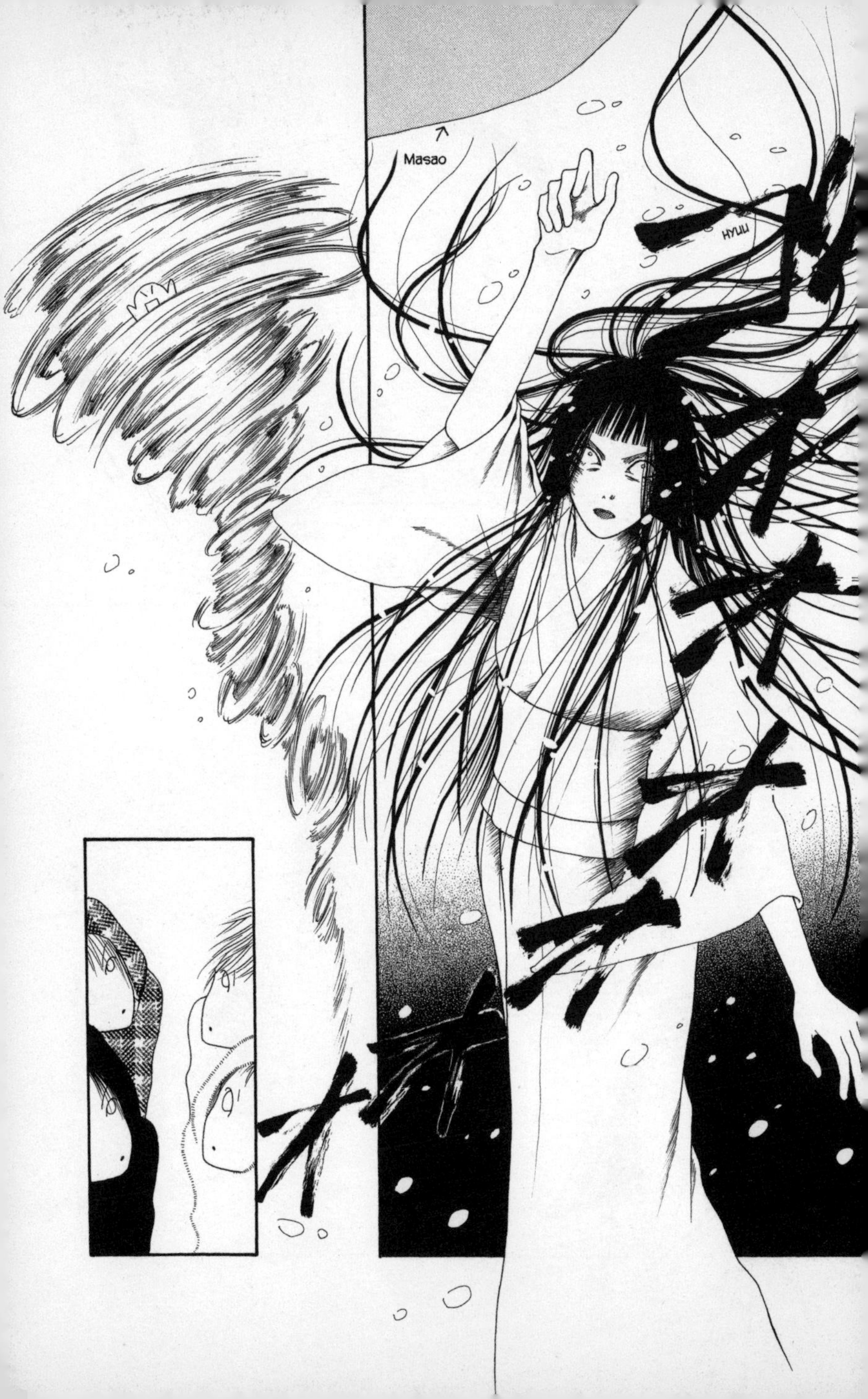
Masao
HYUU

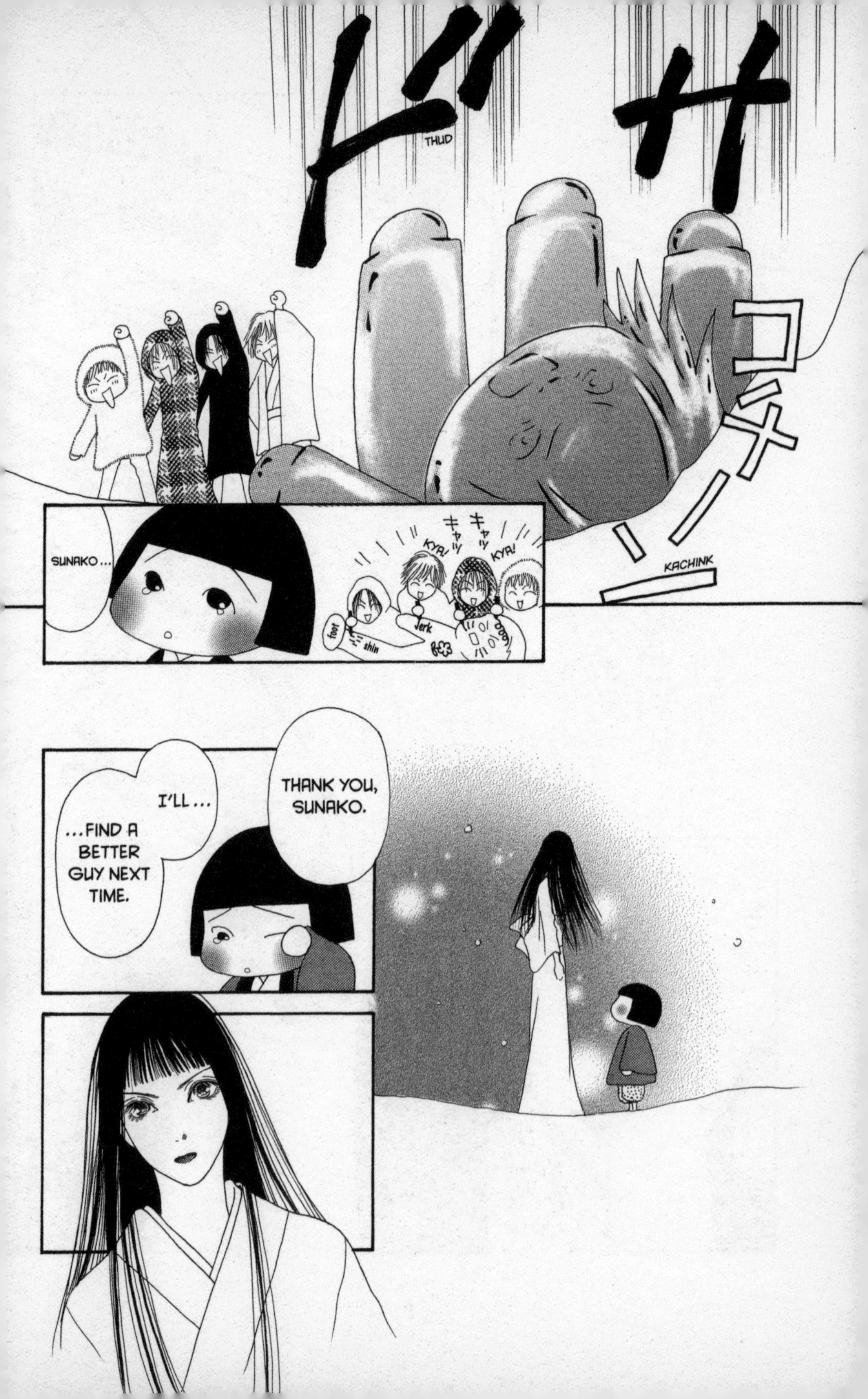
THUD
KACHINK
KYA!
KYA!
Jerk
foot
shin
SUNAKO...
THANK YOU, SUNAKO.
I'LL...
...FIND A BETTER GUY NEXT TIME.

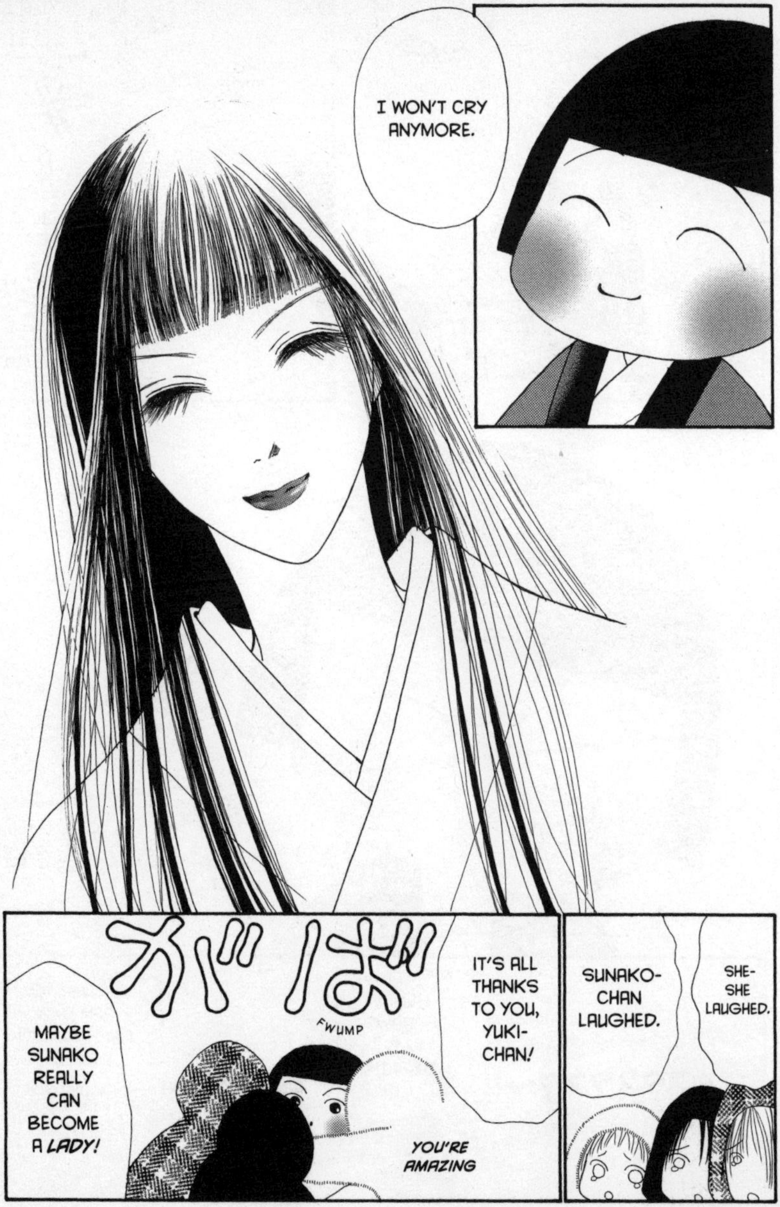
I WON'T CRY ANYMORE.
SHE-SHE LAUGHED.
SUNAKO-CHAN LAUGHED.
ガば
FWUMP
IT'S ALL THANKS TO YOU, YUKI-CHAN!
YOU'RE AMAZING
MAYBE SUNAKO REALLY CAN BECOME A LADY!

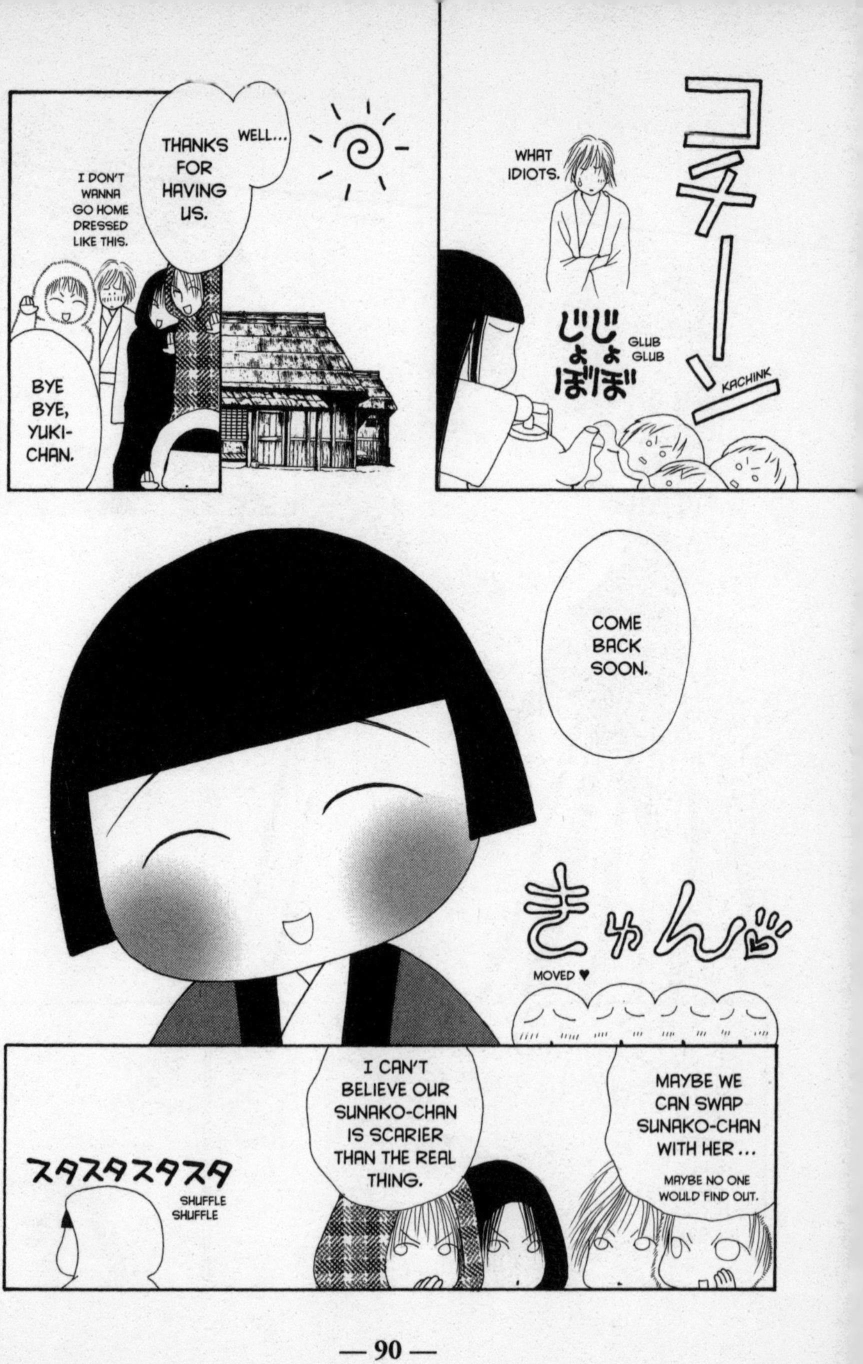
コチーン
KACHINK
WHAT IDIOTS.
じょぼじょぼ
GLUB GLUB
WELL...
THANKS FOR HAVING US.
I DON'T WANNA GO HOME DRESSED LIKE THIS.
BYE BYE, YUKI-CHAN.
COME BACK SOON.
きゅん
MOVED ♥
MAYBE WE CAN SWAP SUNAKO-CHAN WITH HER...
MAYBE NO ONE WOULD FIND OUT.
I CAN'T BELIEVE OUR SUNAKO-CHAN IS SCARIER THAN THE REAL THING.
スタスタスタスタ
SHUFFLE SHUFFLE

Chapter 25
You're More Beautiful Than a Rose

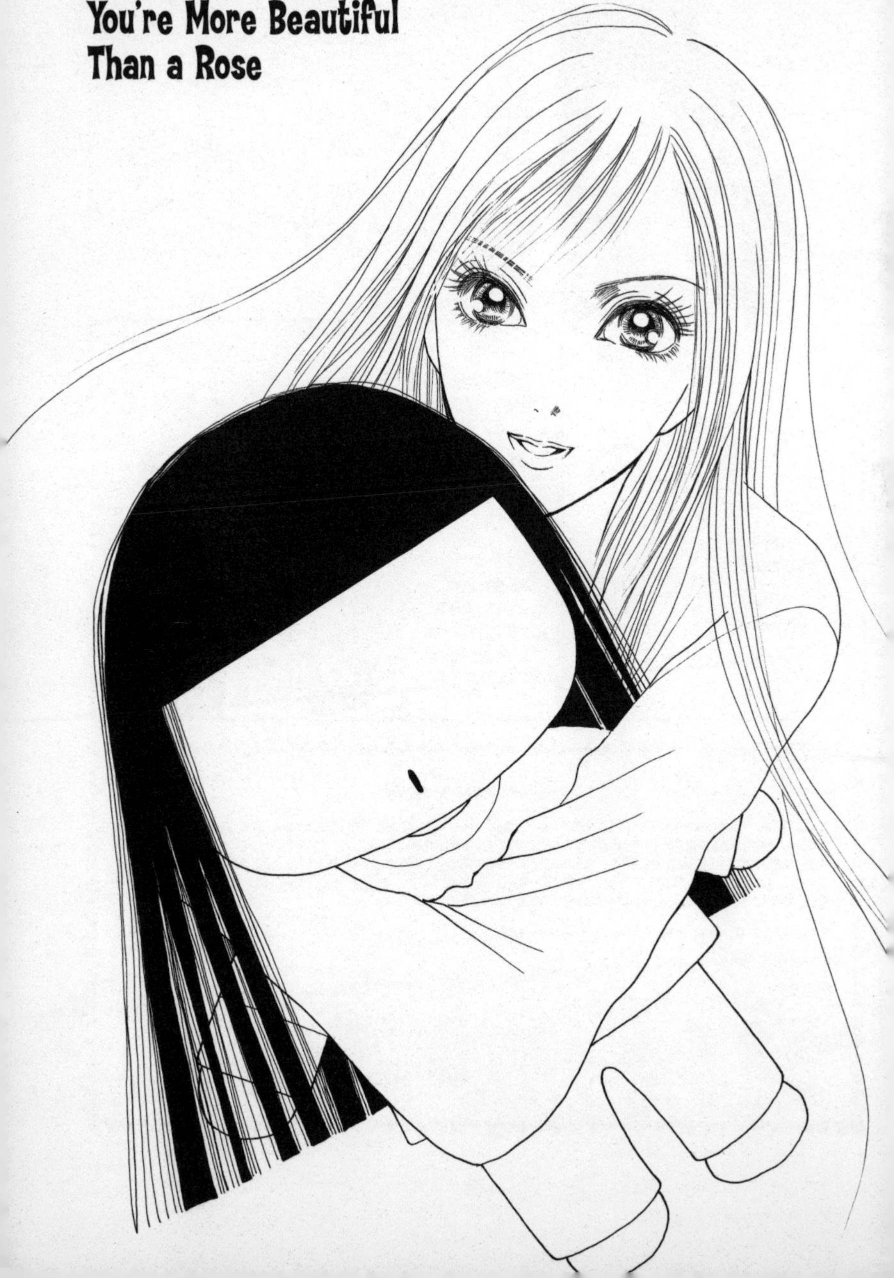

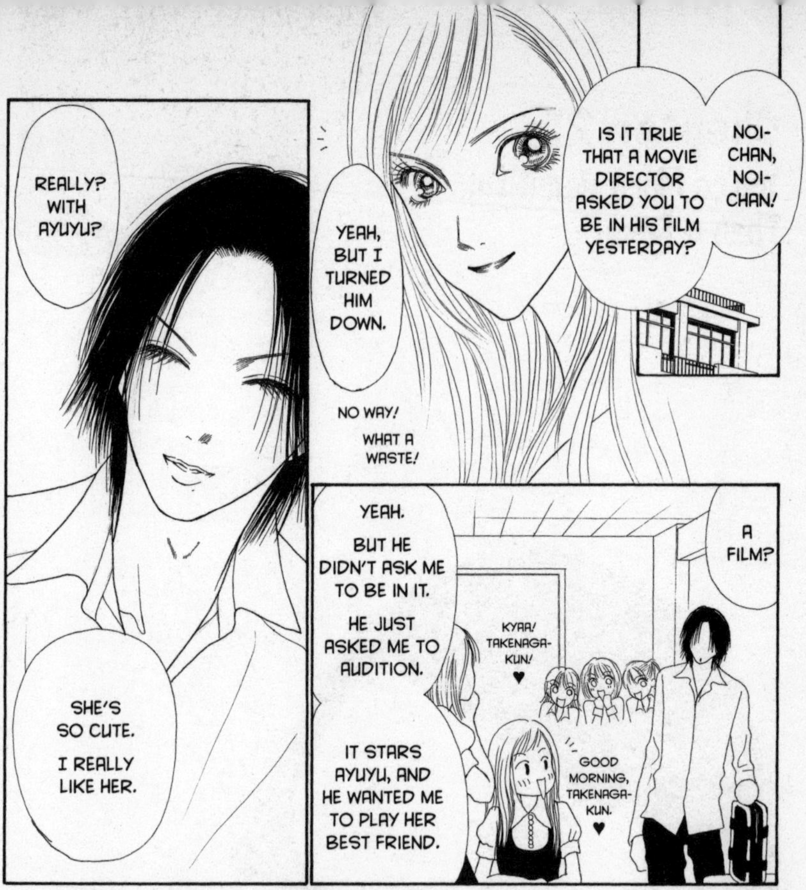
NOI-CHAN, NOI-CHAN!
IS IT TRUE THAT A MOVIE DIRECTOR ASKED YOU TO BE IN HIS FILM YESTERDAY?
YEAH, BUT I TURNED HIM DOWN.
NO WAY!
WHAT A WASTE!
A FILM?
GOOD MORNING, TAKENAGA-KUN. ♥
KYAA! TAKENAGA-KUN! ♥
YEAH.
BUT HE DIDN'T ASK ME TO BE IN IT.
HE JUST ASKED ME TO AUDITION.
IT STARS AYUYU, AND HE WANTED ME TO PLAY HER BEST FRIEND.
REALLY? WITH AYUYU?
SHE'S SO CUTE.
I REALLY LIKE HER.

BEHIND THE SCENES

I JUST GOT A NEW "SUPER"(?) ASSISTANT. (BUT THIS MIGHT BE THE ONLY TIME SHE HELPS ME OUT.) WHEN I WAS FINISHING UP ONE DAY, A FRIEND OF MINE (YUKO OGAWA—OFFICE WORKER) CAME TO HANG OUT AND HELPED ME WITH THE INKING. SHE'S REALLY GOOD AT INKING AND COLORING! I WAS AMAZED! ON TOP OF THAT, SHE CLEANED UP THE ROOM TILL IT SPARKLED, AND MADE COFFEE TOO. ♥

↖ SHE WAS TAUGHT BY IYU KOZAKURA (BEKKAN FRIEND).

I PROPOSED TO HER SEVERAL TIMES THAT DAY.

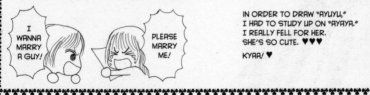

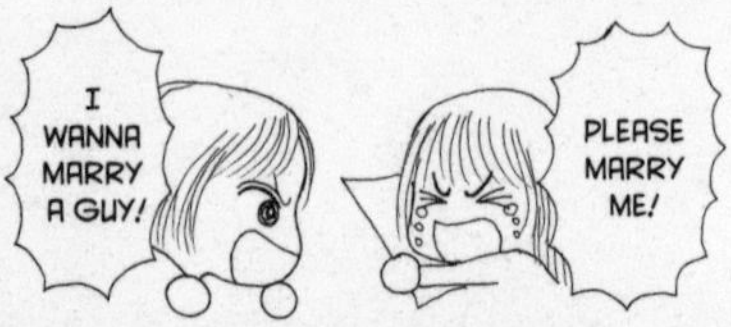
PLEASE MARRY ME!
I WANNA MARRY A GUY!

IN ORDER TO DRAW "AYUYU," I HAD TO STUDY UP ON "AYAYA." I REALLY FELL FOR HER. SHE'S SO CUTE. ♥♥♥

KYAA! ♥

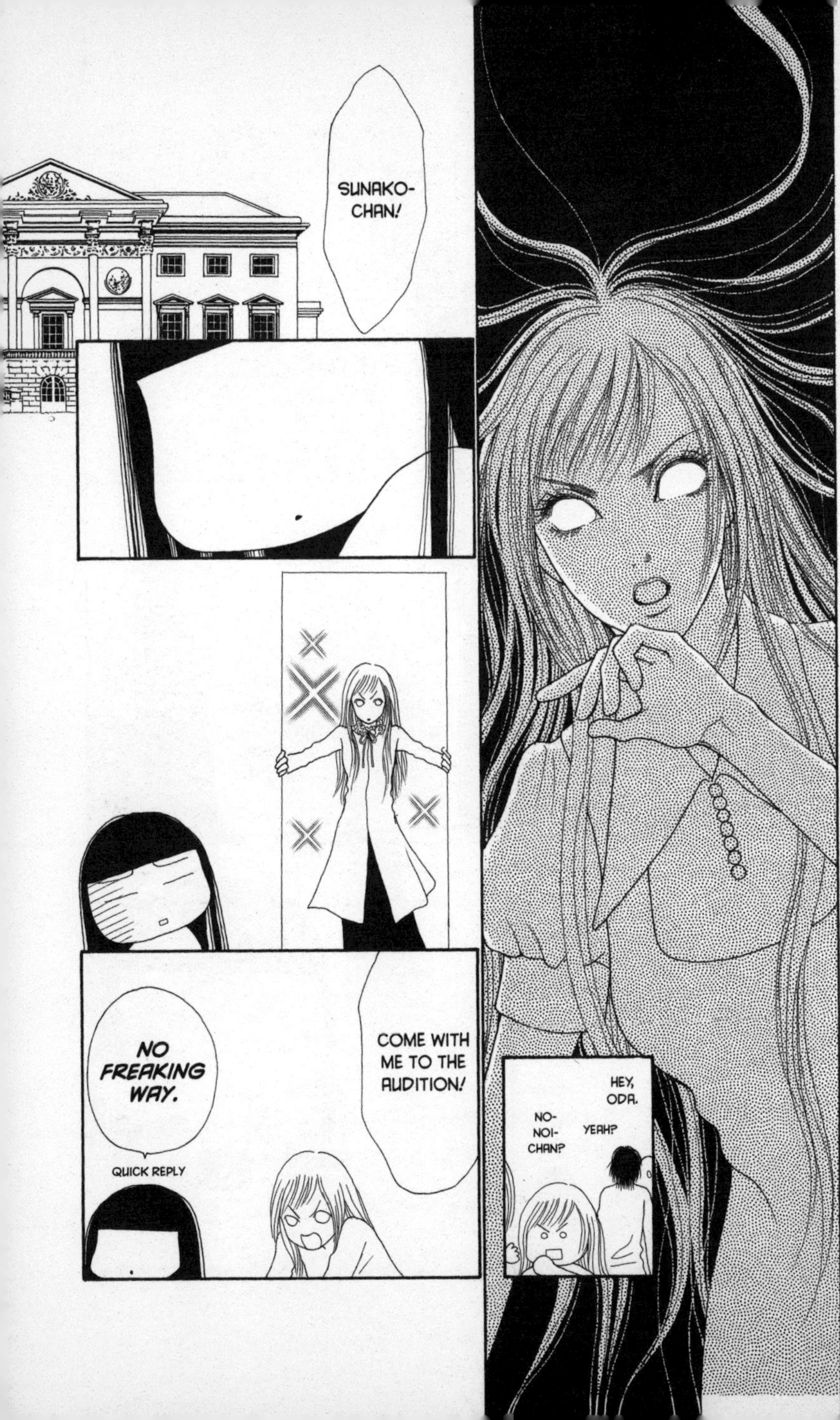
HEY, ODA.
YEAH?
NO-NOI-CHAN?
SUNAKO-CHAN!
COME WITH ME TO THE AUDITION!
NO FREAKING WAY.
QUICK REPLY

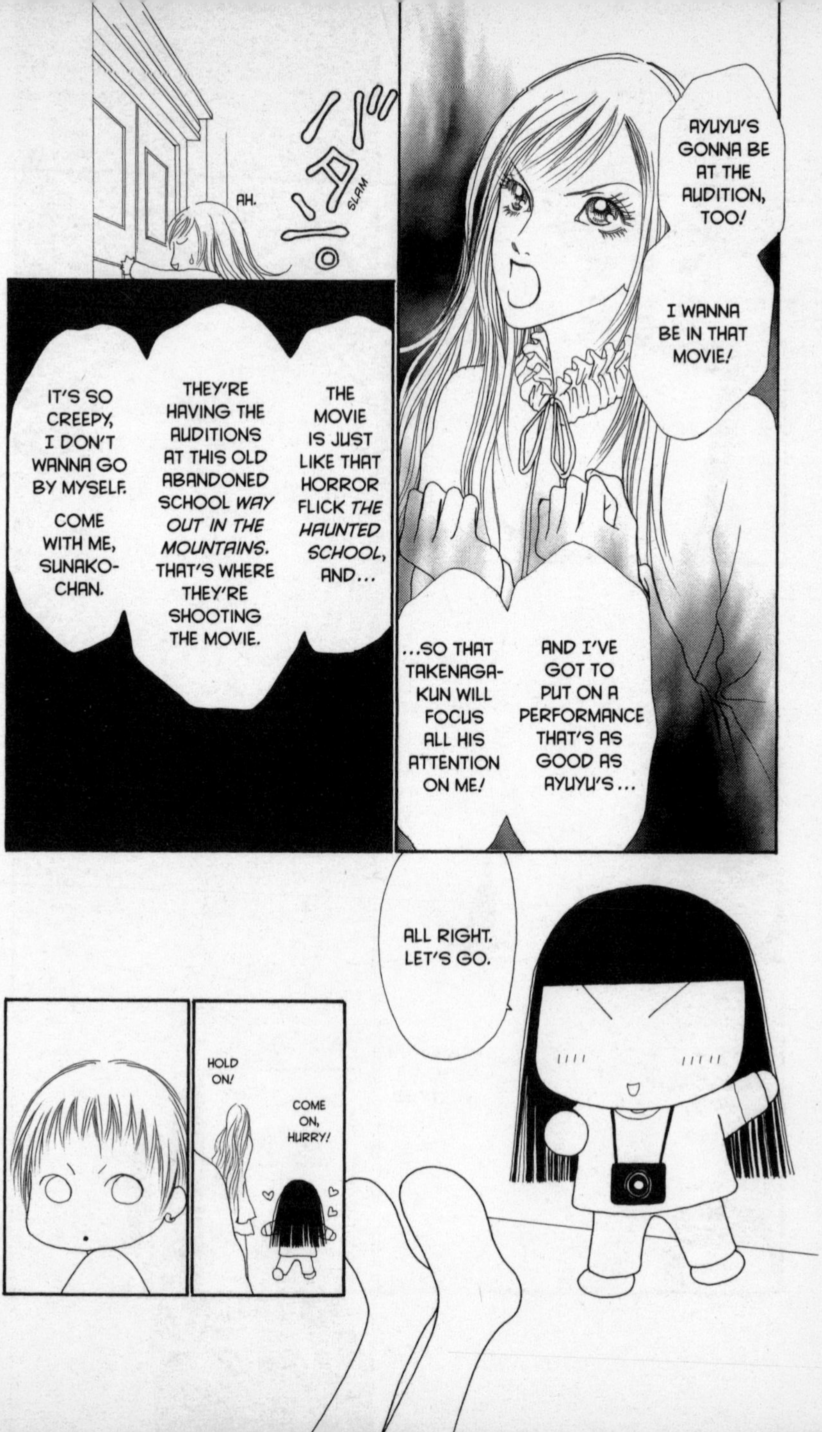
AYUYU'S GONNA BE AT THE AUDITION, TOO!
I WANNA BE IN THAT MOVIE!
AND I'VE GOT TO PUT ON A PERFORMANCE THAT'S AS GOOD AS AYUYU'S...
...SO THAT TAKENAGA-KUN WILL FOCUS ALL HIS ATTENTION ON ME!
SLAM
AH.
THE MOVIE IS JUST LIKE THAT HORROR FLICK *THE HAUNTED SCHOOL*, AND...
THEY'RE HAVING THE AUDITIONS AT THIS OLD ABANDONED SCHOOL *WAY OUT IN THE MOUNTAINS*. THAT'S WHERE THEY'RE SHOOTING THE MOVIE.
IT'S SO CREEPY, I DON'T WANNA GO BY MYSELF.
COME WITH ME, SUNAKO-CHAN.
ALL RIGHT. LET'S GO.
HOLD ON!
COME ON, HURRY!

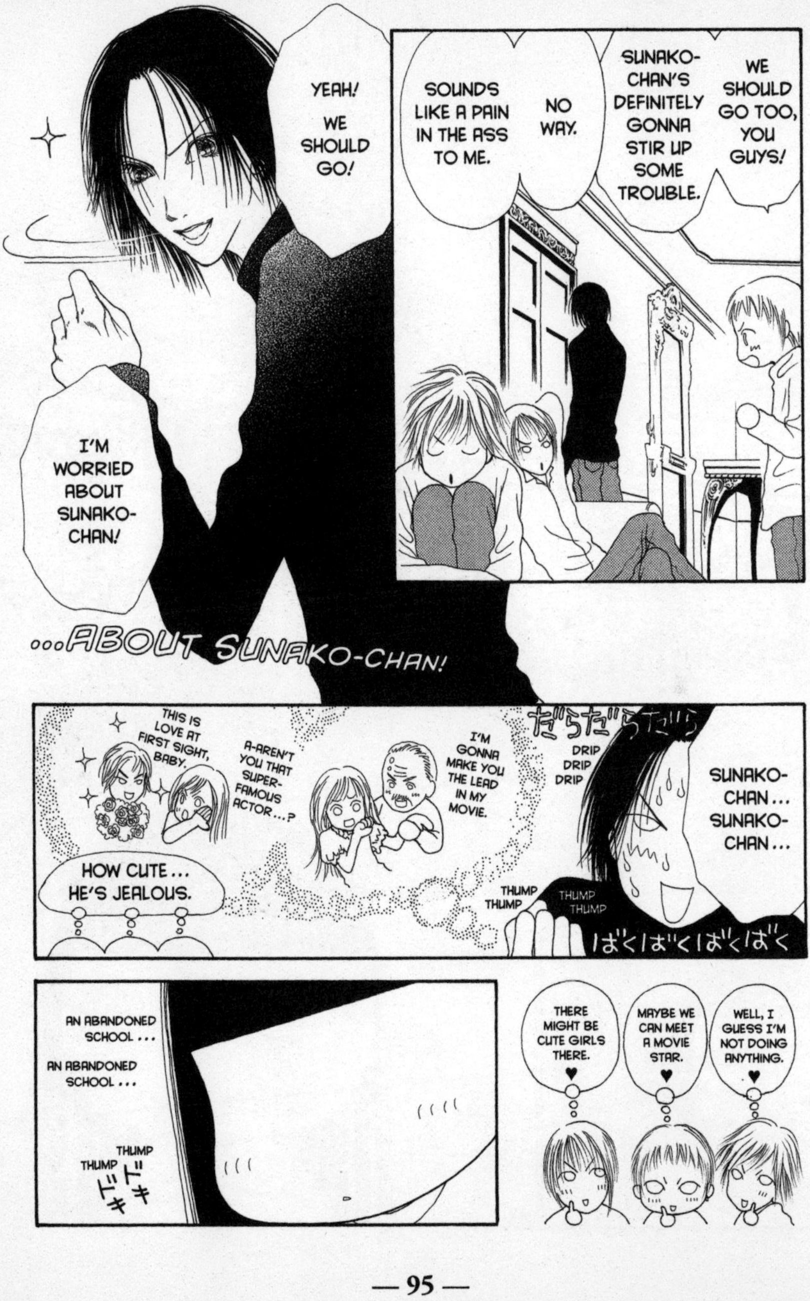
WE SHOULD GO TOO, YOU GUYS!
SUNAKO-CHAN'S DEFINITELY GONNA STIR UP SOME TROUBLE.
NO WAY.
SOUNDS LIKE A PAIN IN THE ASS TO ME.
YEAH! WE SHOULD GO!
I'M WORRIED ABOUT SUNAKO-CHAN!
...ABOUT SUNAKO-CHAN!
SUNAKO-CHAN... SUNAKO-CHAN...
だらだらだら
DRIP DRIP DRIP
ばくばくばくばく
THUMP THUMP
THUMP THUMP
I'M GONNA MAKE YOU THE LEAD IN MY MOVIE.
A-AREN'T YOU THAT SUPER-FAMOUS ACTOR...?
THIS IS LOVE AT FIRST SIGHT, BABY.
HOW CUTE... HE'S JEALOUS.
WELL, I GUESS I'M NOT DOING ANYTHING. ♥
MAYBE WE CAN MEET A MOVIE STAR. ♥
THERE MIGHT BE CUTE GIRLS THERE. ♥
AN ABANDONED SCHOOL...
AN ABANDONED SCHOOL...
THUMP THUMP
ドキドキ

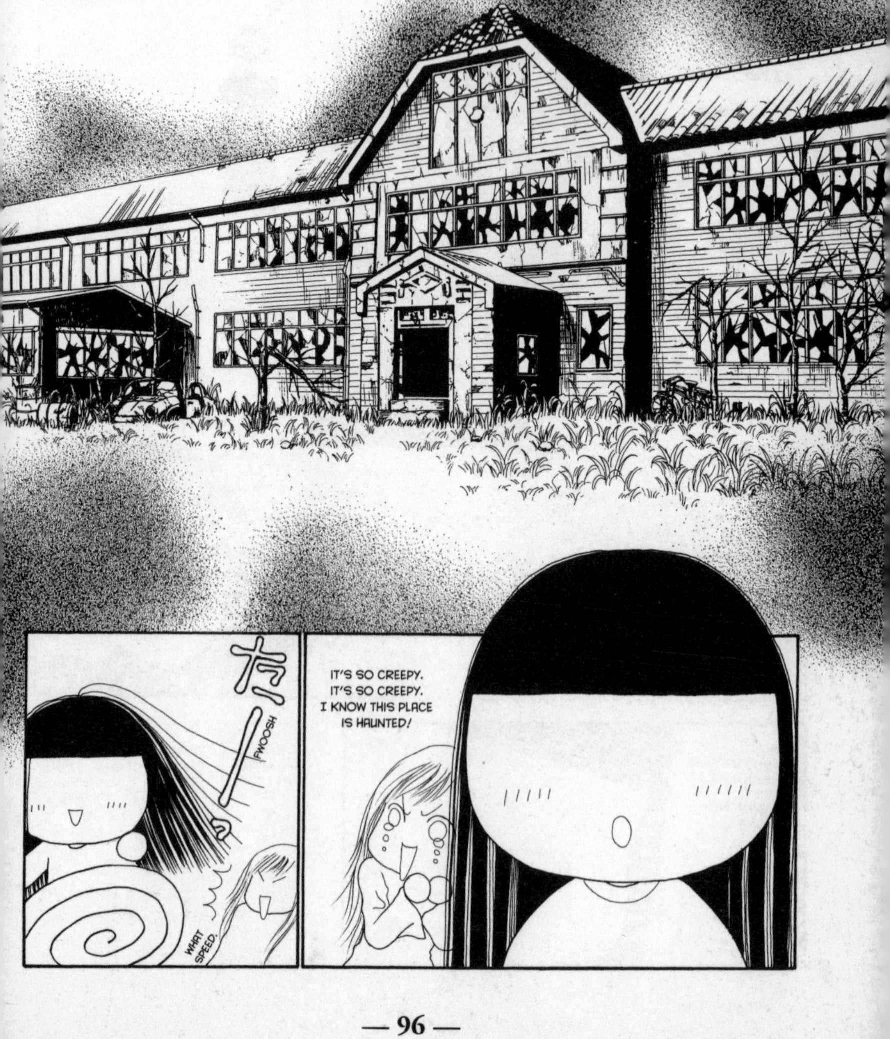
IT'S SO CREEPY.
IT'S SO CREEPY.
I KNOW THIS PLACE
IS HAUNTED!
たー
FWOOSH
WHAT SPEED.

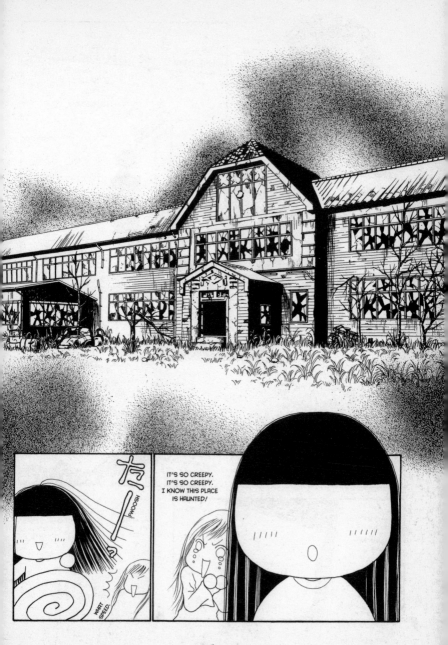

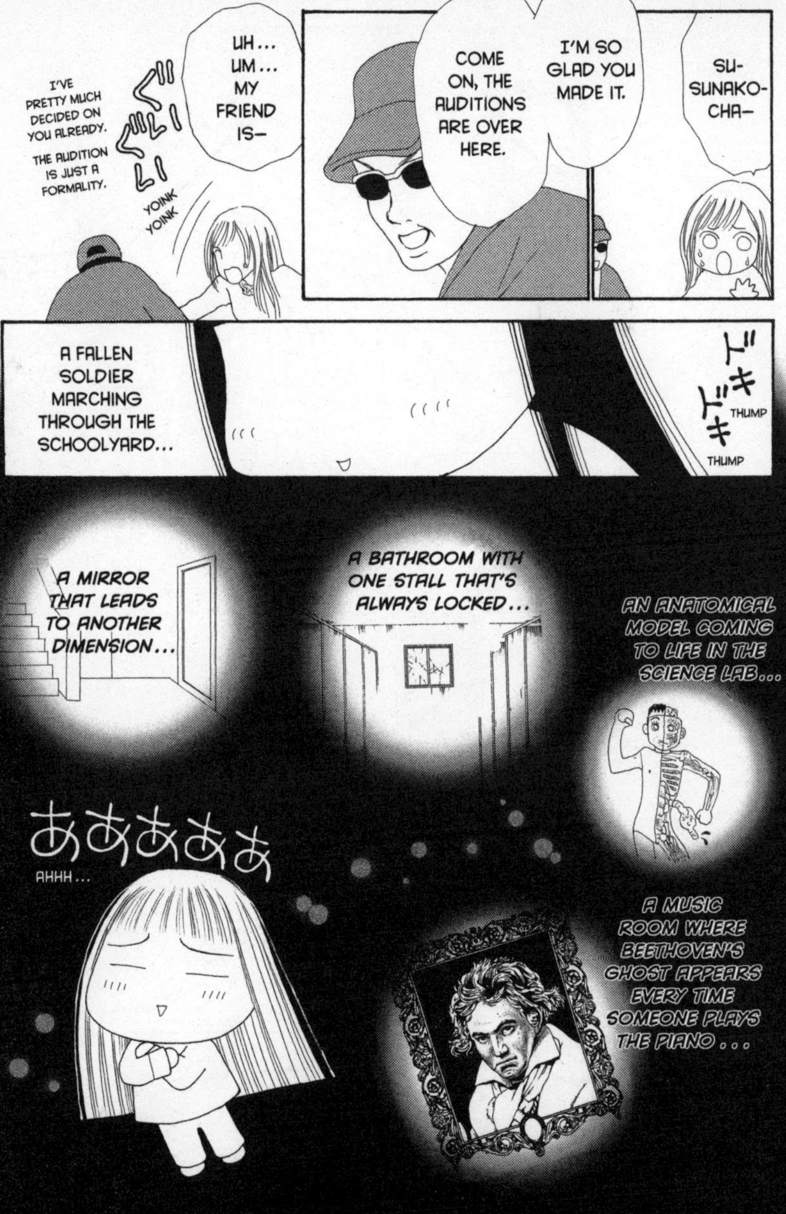
SU-SUNAKO-CHA—
I'M SO GLAD YOU MADE IT.
COME ON, THE AUDITIONS ARE OVER HERE.
UH... UM... MY FRIEND IS—
ぐいぐいぐい
YOINK YOINK
I'VE PRETTY MUCH DECIDED ON YOU ALREADY.
THE AUDITION IS JUST A FORMALITY.
ドキドキ
THUMP THUMP
A FALLEN SOLDIER MARCHING THROUGH THE SCHOOLYARD...
A BATHROOM WITH ONE STALL THAT'S ALWAYS LOCKED...
A MIRROR THAT LEADS TO ANOTHER DIMENSION...
AN ANATOMICAL MODEL COMING TO LIFE IN THE SCIENCE LAB...
A MUSIC ROOM WHERE BEETHOVEN'S GHOST APPEARS EVERY TIME SOMEONE PLAYS THE PIANO...
ああああああ
AHHH...

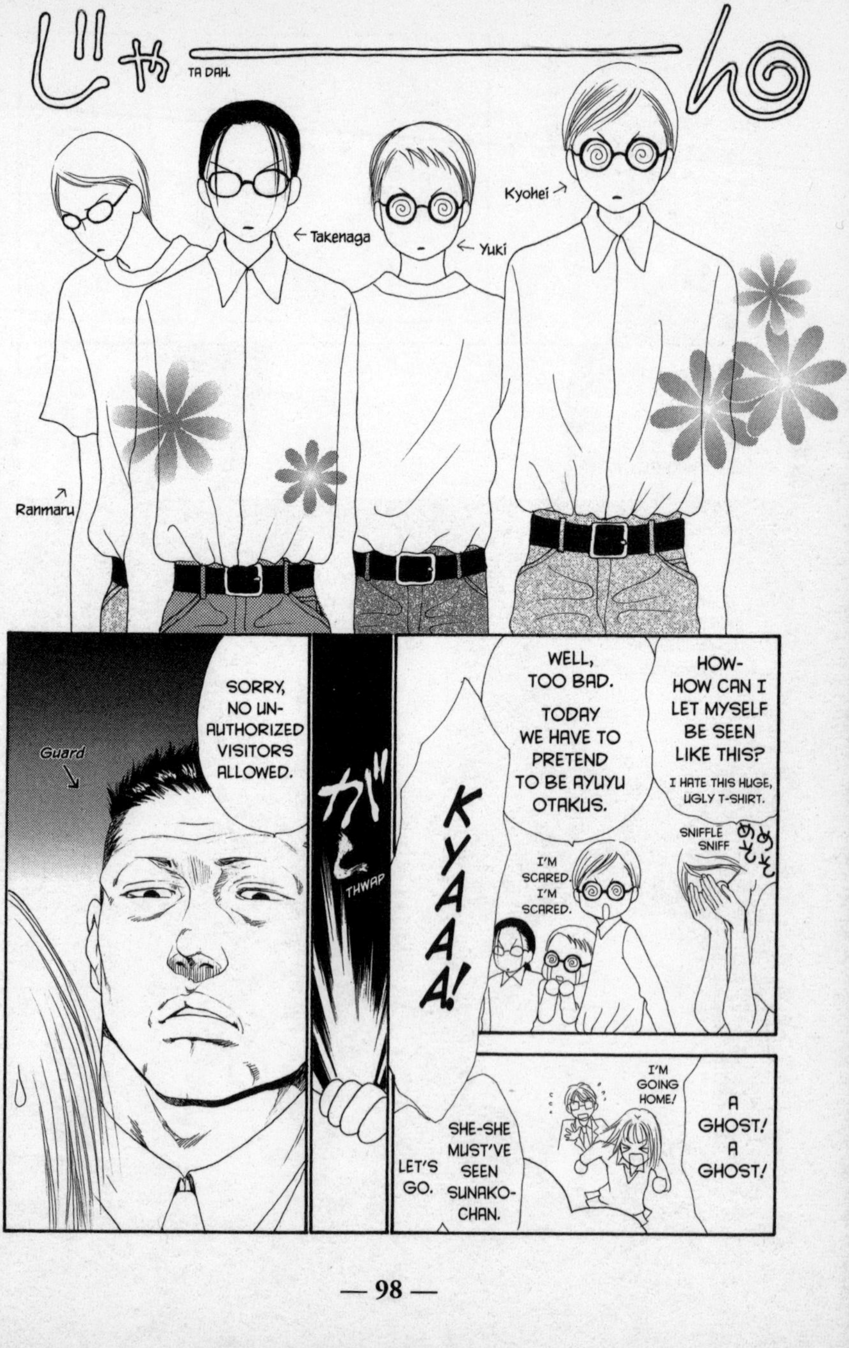
じゃ——ん
TA DAH.
Kyohei
Yuki
Takenaga
Ranmaru
HOW-HOW CAN I LET MYSELF BE SEEN LIKE THIS?
I HATE THIS HUGE, UGLY T-SHIRT.
めそめそ
SNIFFLE SNIFF
WELL, TOO BAD.
TODAY WE HAVE TO PRETEND TO BE AYUYU OTAKUS.
I'M SCARED. I'M SCARED.
A GHOST! A GHOST!
I'M GOING HOME!
SHE-SHE MUST'VE SEEN SUNAKO-CHAN.
LET'S GO.
KYAAAA!
がし
THWAP
SORRY, NO UN-AUTHORIZED VISITORS ALLOWED.
Guard

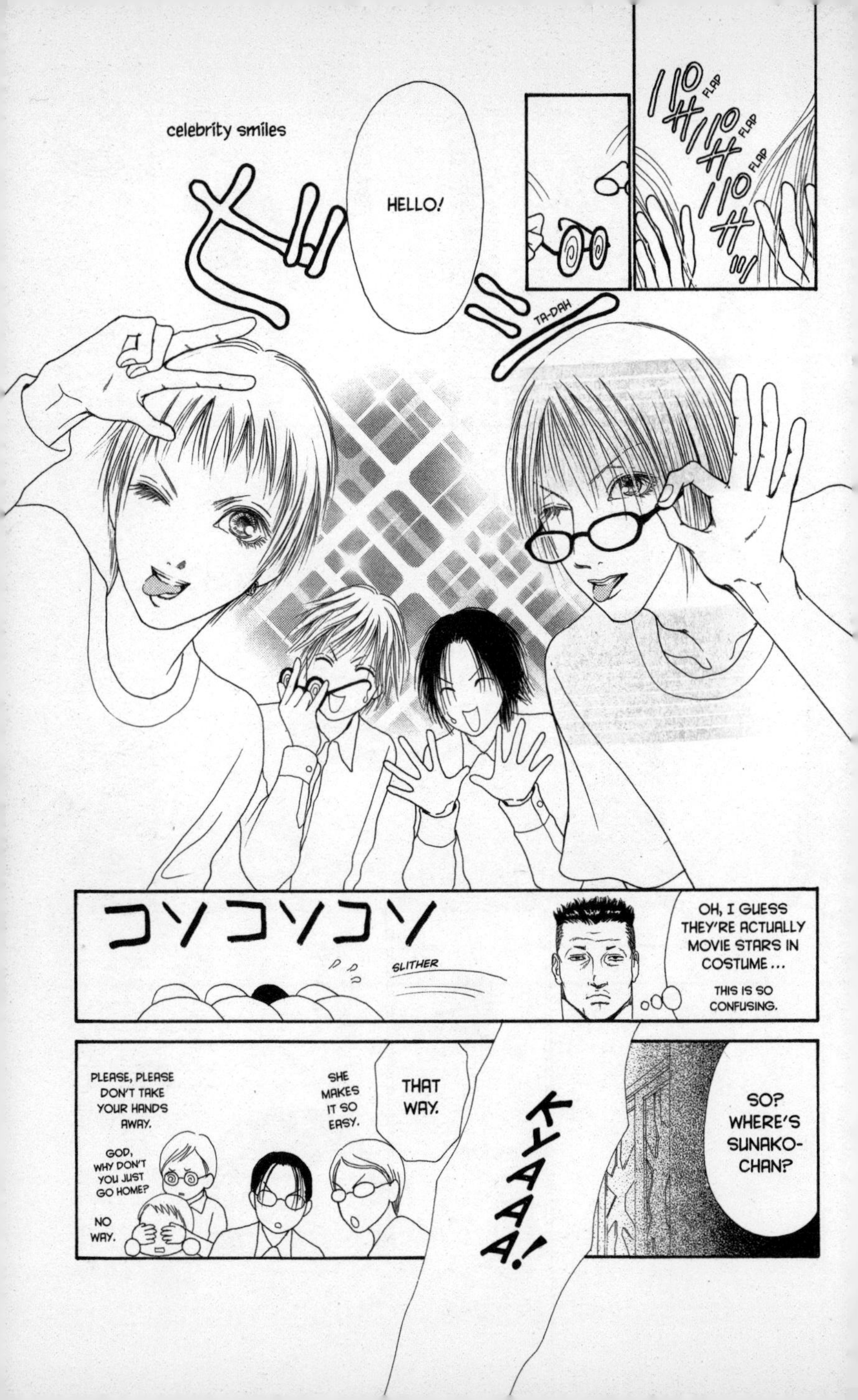

FLAP
FLAP
FLAP
TA-DAH
HELLO!
celebrity smiles
OH, I GUESS THEY'RE ACTUALLY MOVIE STARS IN COSTUME ...
THIS IS SO CONFUSING.
コソコソコソ
SLITHER
SO? WHERE'S SUNAKO-CHAN?
KYAAAA!
THAT WAY.
SHE MAKES IT SO EASY.
PLEASE, PLEASE DON'T TAKE YOUR HANDS AWAY.
GOD, WHY DON'T YOU JUST GO HOME?
NO WAY.

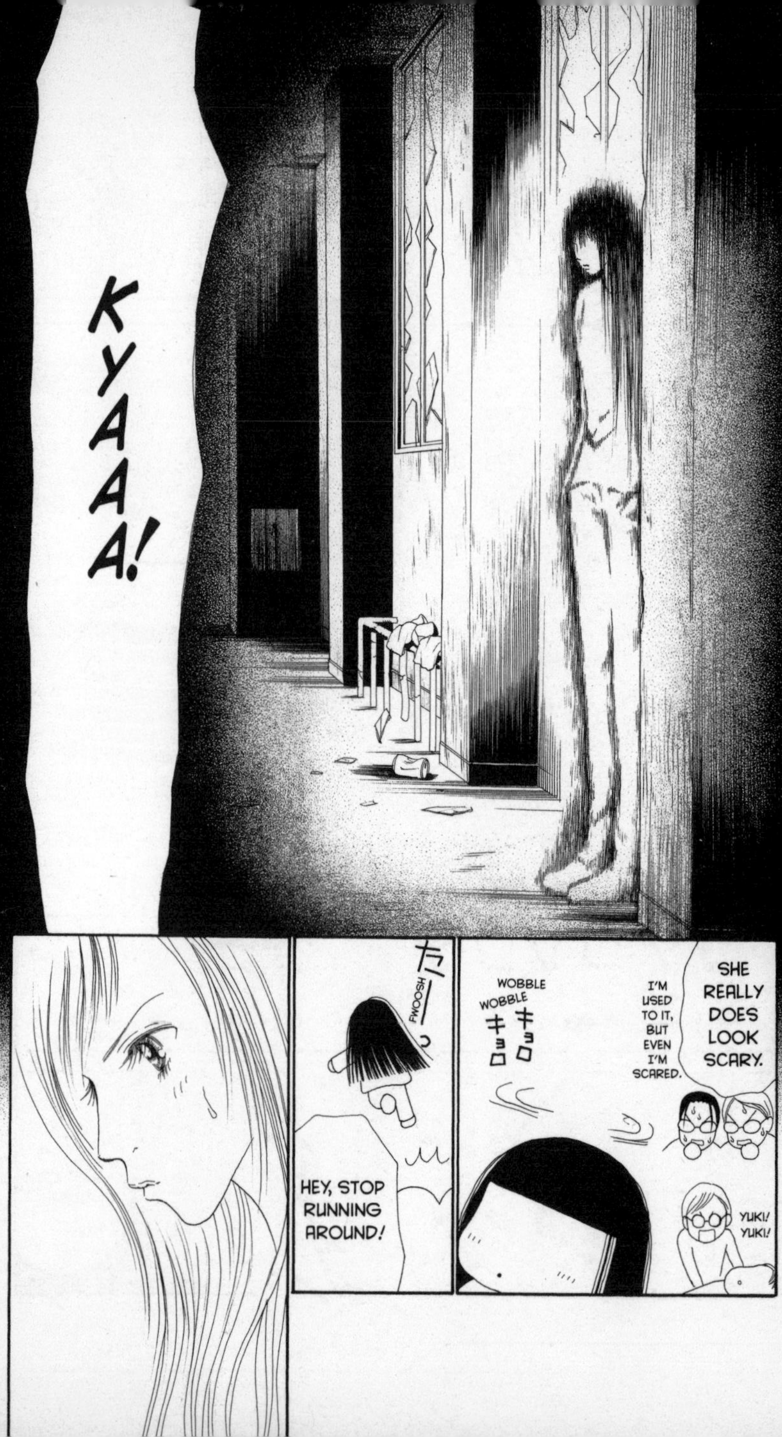
KYAAAA!
SHE REALLY DOES LOOK SCARY.
I'M USED TO IT, BUT EVEN I'M SCARED.
WOBBLE WOBBLE
キョロキョロ
YUKI! YUKI!
たーっ
FWOOSH
HEY, STOP RUNNING AROUND!

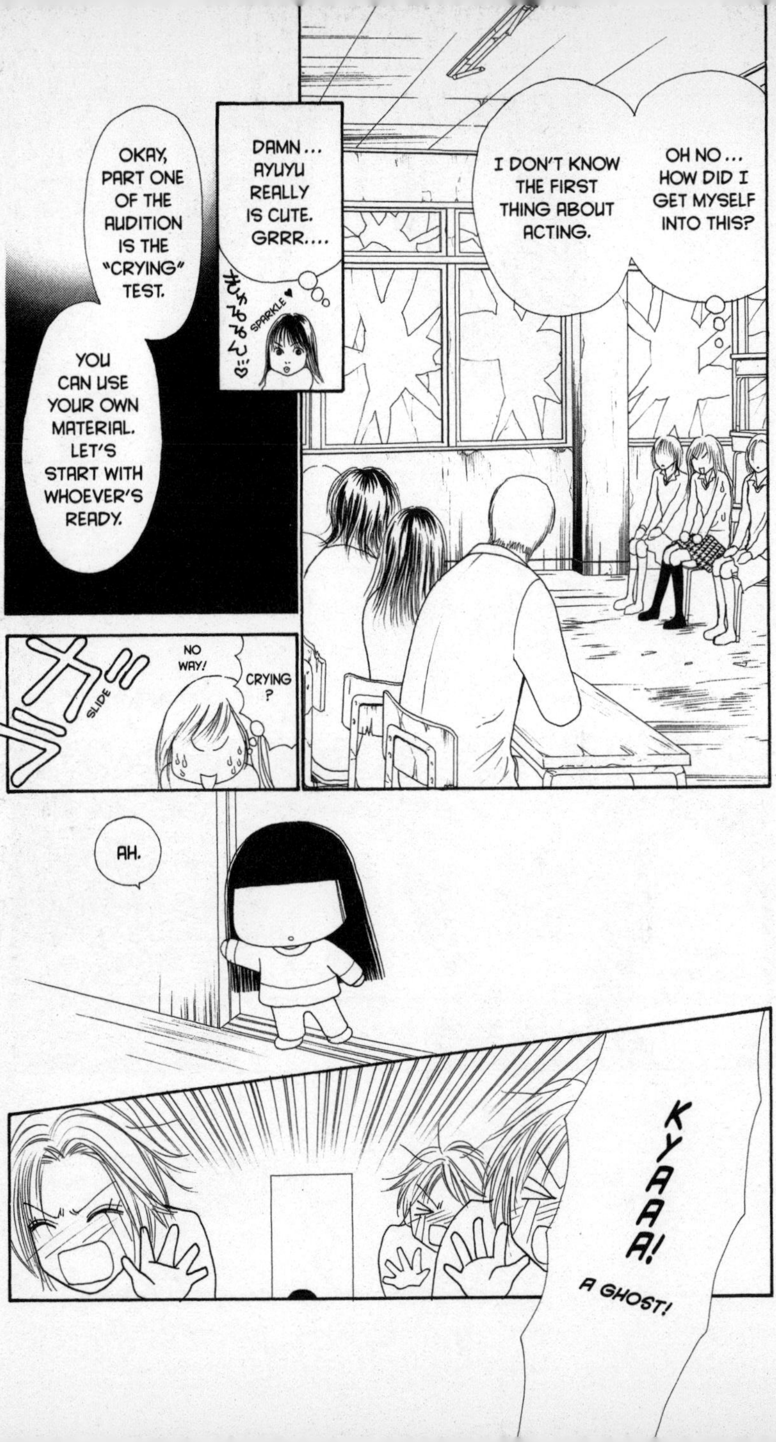
OH NO... HOW DID I GET MYSELF INTO THIS?
I DON'T KNOW THE FIRST THING ABOUT ACTING.
DAMN... AYUYU REALLY IS CUTE. GRRR....
SPARKLE
OKAY, PART ONE OF THE AUDITION IS THE "CRYING" TEST.
YOU CAN USE YOUR OWN MATERIAL. LET'S START WITH WHOEVER'S READY.
CRYING?
NO WAY!
SLIDE
AH.
KYAAAA!
A GHOST!

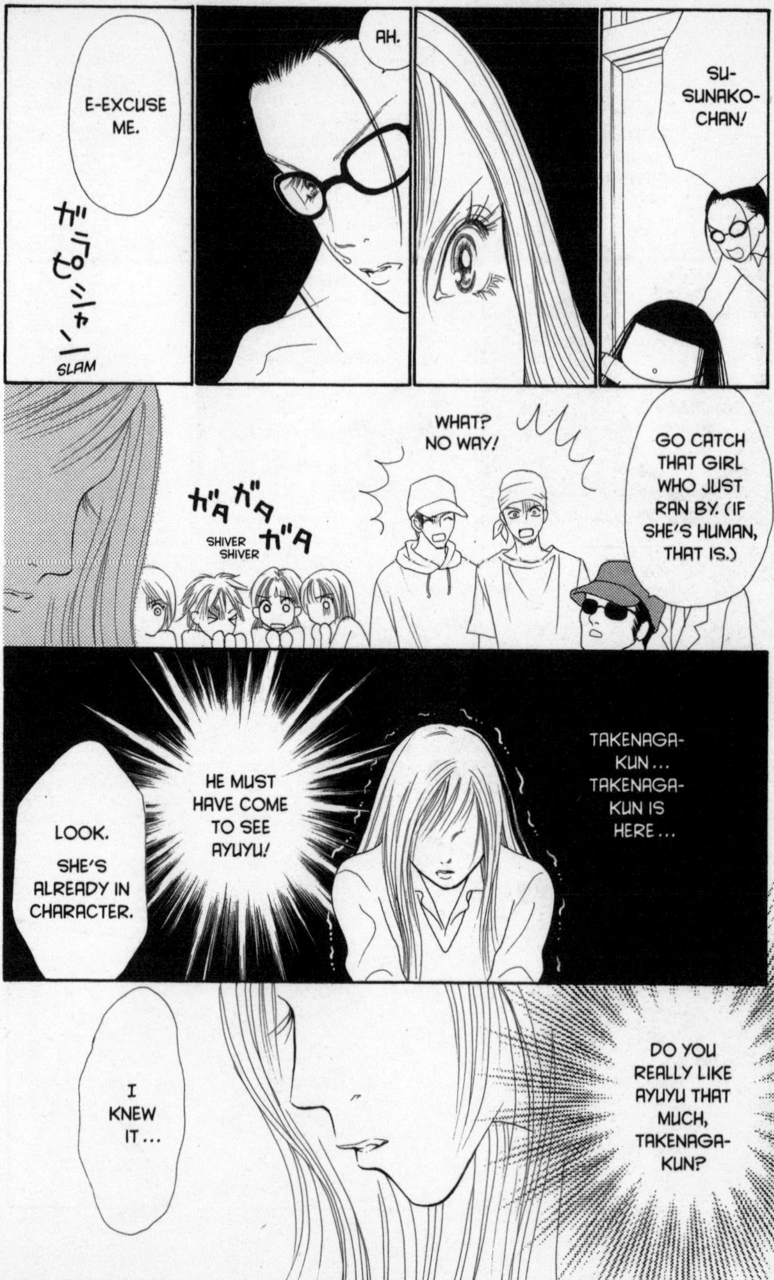
SU-SUNAKO-CHAN!
AH.
E-EXCUSE ME.
ガラピシャン
SLAM
GO CATCH THAT GIRL WHO JUST RAN BY. (IF SHE'S HUMAN, THAT IS.)
WHAT? NO WAY!
ガタガタガタ
SHIVER SHIVER
TAKENAGA-KUN... TAKENAGA-KUN IS HERE...
HE MUST HAVE COME TO SEE AYUYU!
LOOK. SHE'S ALREADY IN CHARACTER.
DO YOU REALLY LIKE AYUYU THAT MUCH, TAKENAGA-KUN?
I KNEW IT...

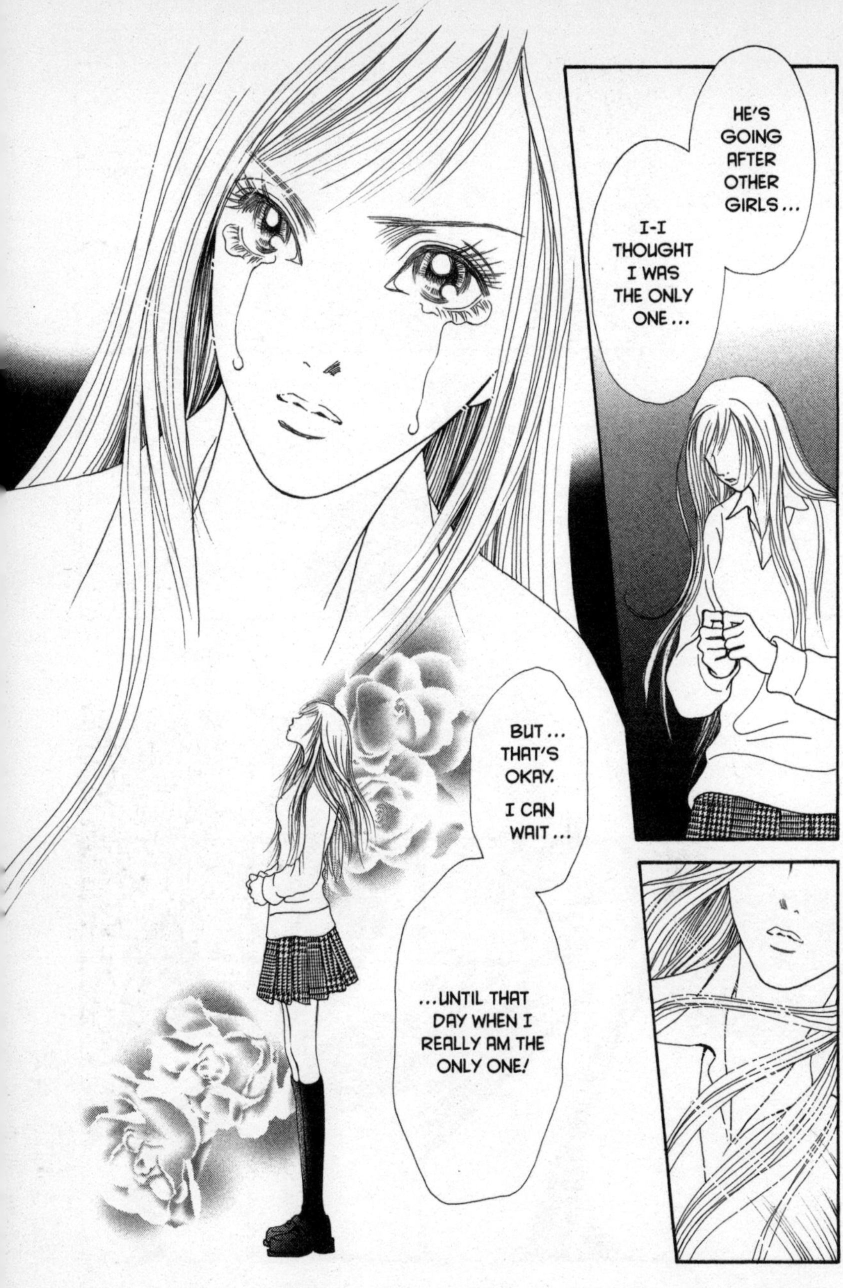
HE'S GOING AFTER OTHER GIRLS...
I-I THOUGHT I WAS THE ONLY ONE...
BUT... THAT'S OKAY.
I CAN WAIT...
...UNTIL THAT DAY WHEN I REALLY AM THE ONLY ONE!

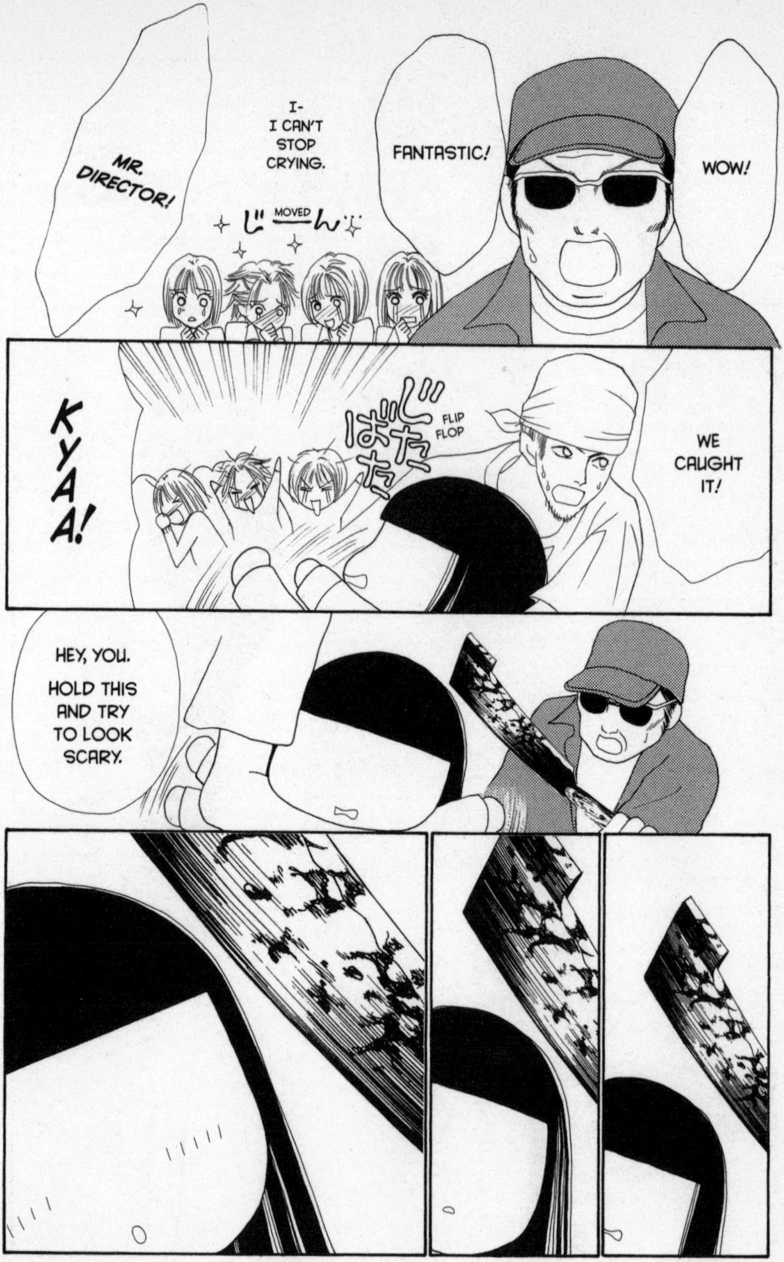
WOW!
FANTASTIC!
I- I CAN'T STOP CRYING.
MR. DIRECTOR!
MOVED
WE CAUGHT IT!
FLIP FLOP
KYAA!
HEY, YOU.
HOLD THIS AND TRY TO LOOK SCARY.

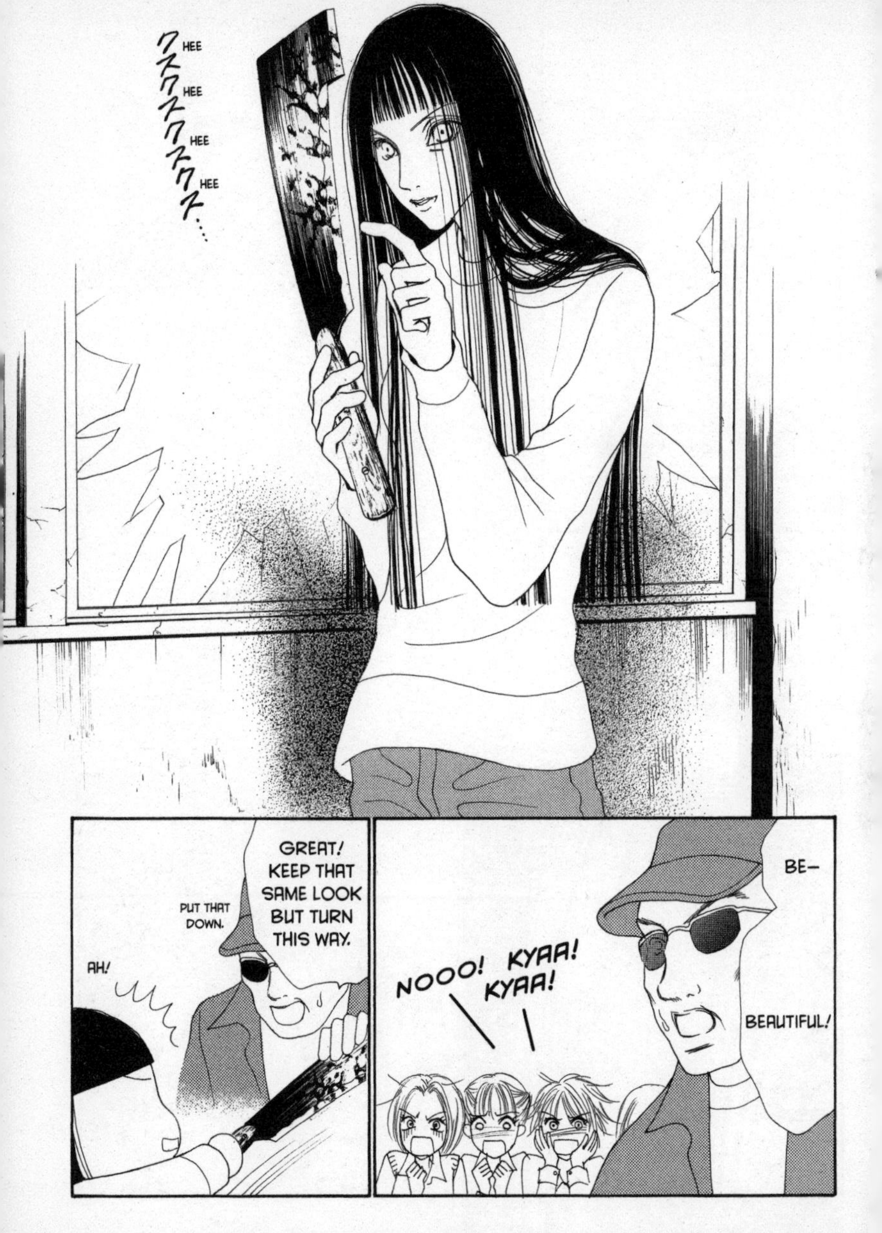
クスクスクスクス…
HEE
HEE
HEE
HEE
BE—
BEAUTIFUL!
NOOO!
KYAA!
KYAA!
GREAT! KEEP THAT SAME LOOK BUT TURN THIS WAY.
PUT THAT DOWN.
AH!

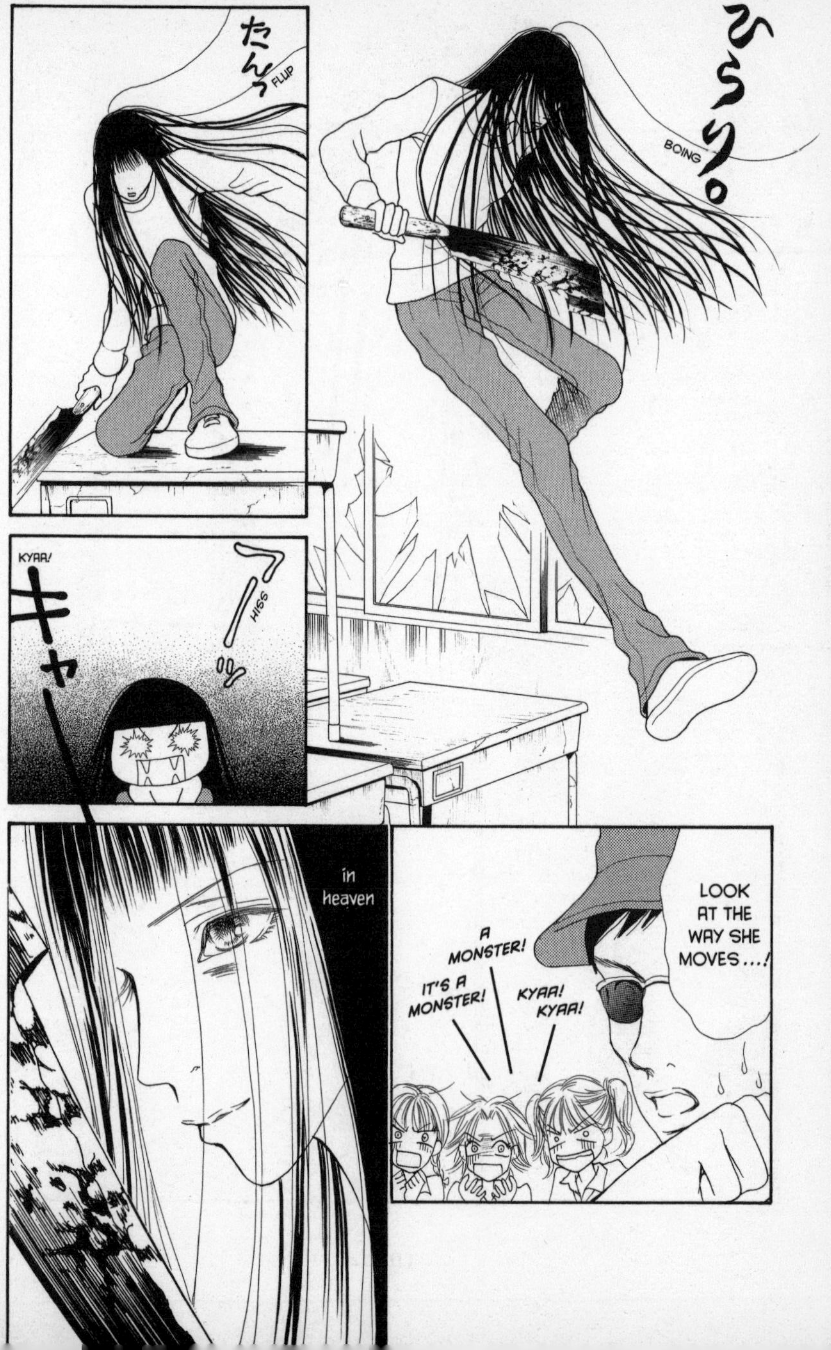
ひらり。
BOING
たんっ
FLUP
フーッ
HISS
キャー
KYAA!
LOOK AT THE WAY SHE MOVES...!
A MONSTER!
KYAA! KYAA!
IT'S A MONSTER!
in heaven

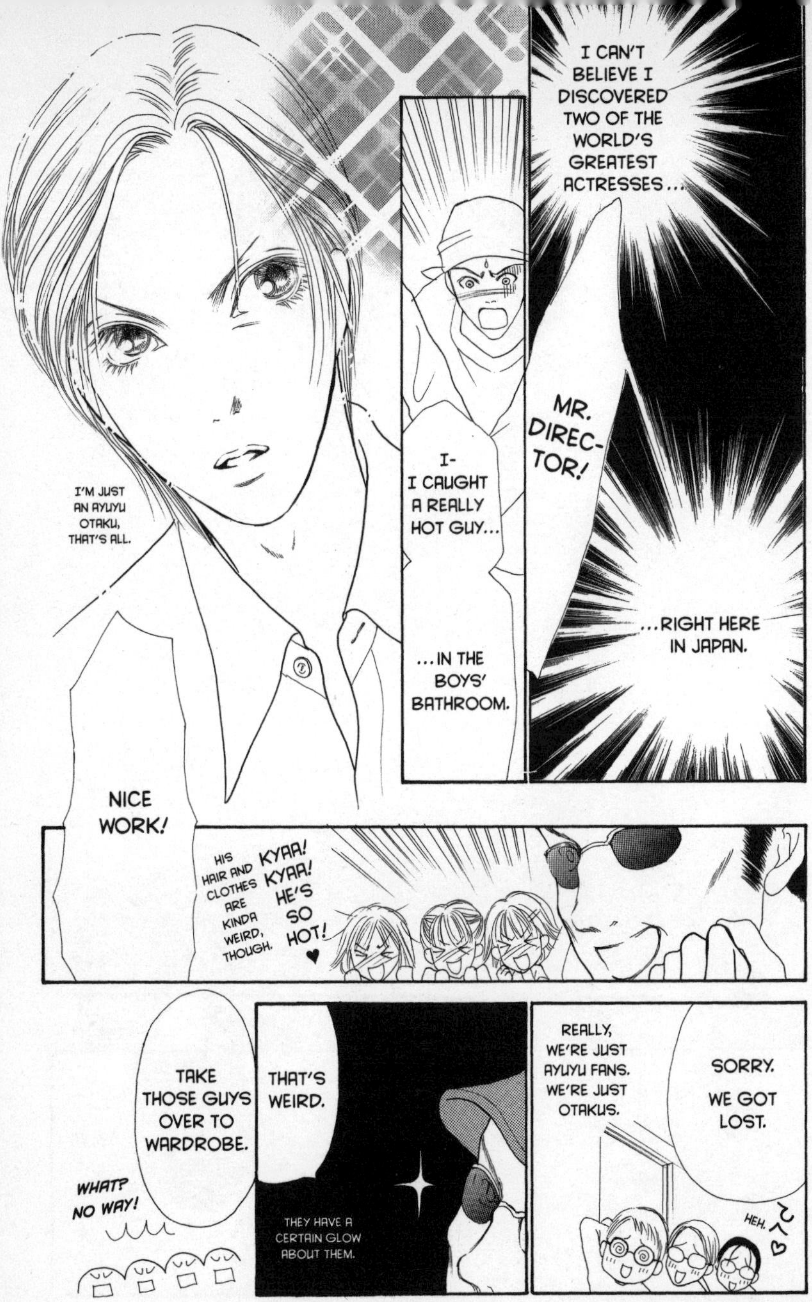

I CAN'T BELIEVE I DISCOVERED TWO OF THE WORLD'S GREATEST ACTRESSES...
MR. DIRECTOR!
...RIGHT HERE IN JAPAN.
I- I CAUGHT A REALLY HOT GUY...
...IN THE BOYS' BATHROOM.
I'M JUST AN AYUYU OTAKU, THAT'S ALL.
NICE WORK!
KYAA! KYAA! HE'S SO HOT! ♥
HIS HAIR AND CLOTHES ARE KINDA WEIRD, THOUGH.
SORRY. WE GOT LOST.
REALLY, WE'RE JUST AYUYU FANS. WE'RE JUST OTAKUS.
HEH. ♡
THAT'S WEIRD.
THEY HAVE A CERTAIN GLOW ABOUT THEM.
TAKE THOSE GUYS OVER TO WARDROBE.
WHAT? NO WAY!

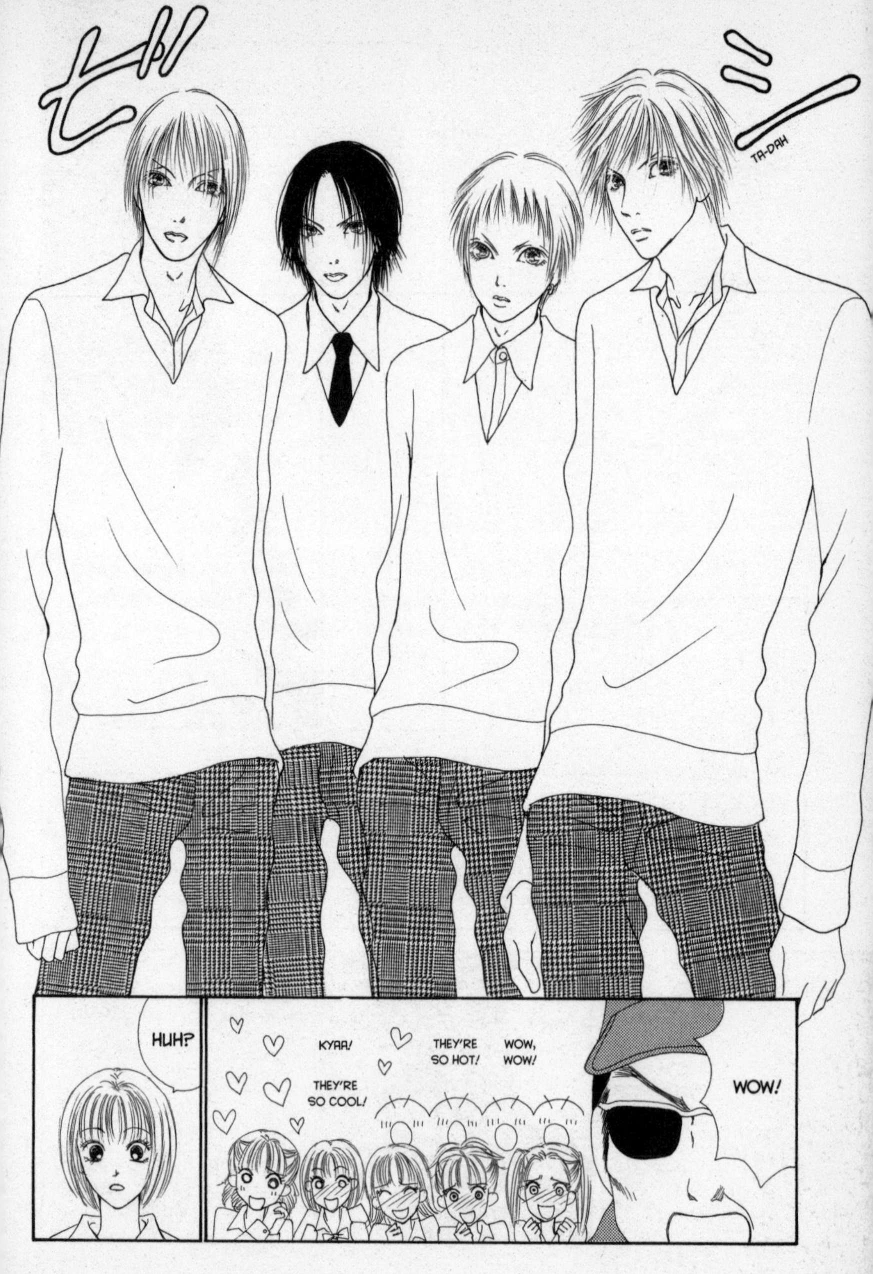
TA-DAH
WOW!
WOW, WOW!
THEY'RE SO HOT!
KYAA!
THEY'RE SO COOL!
HUH?

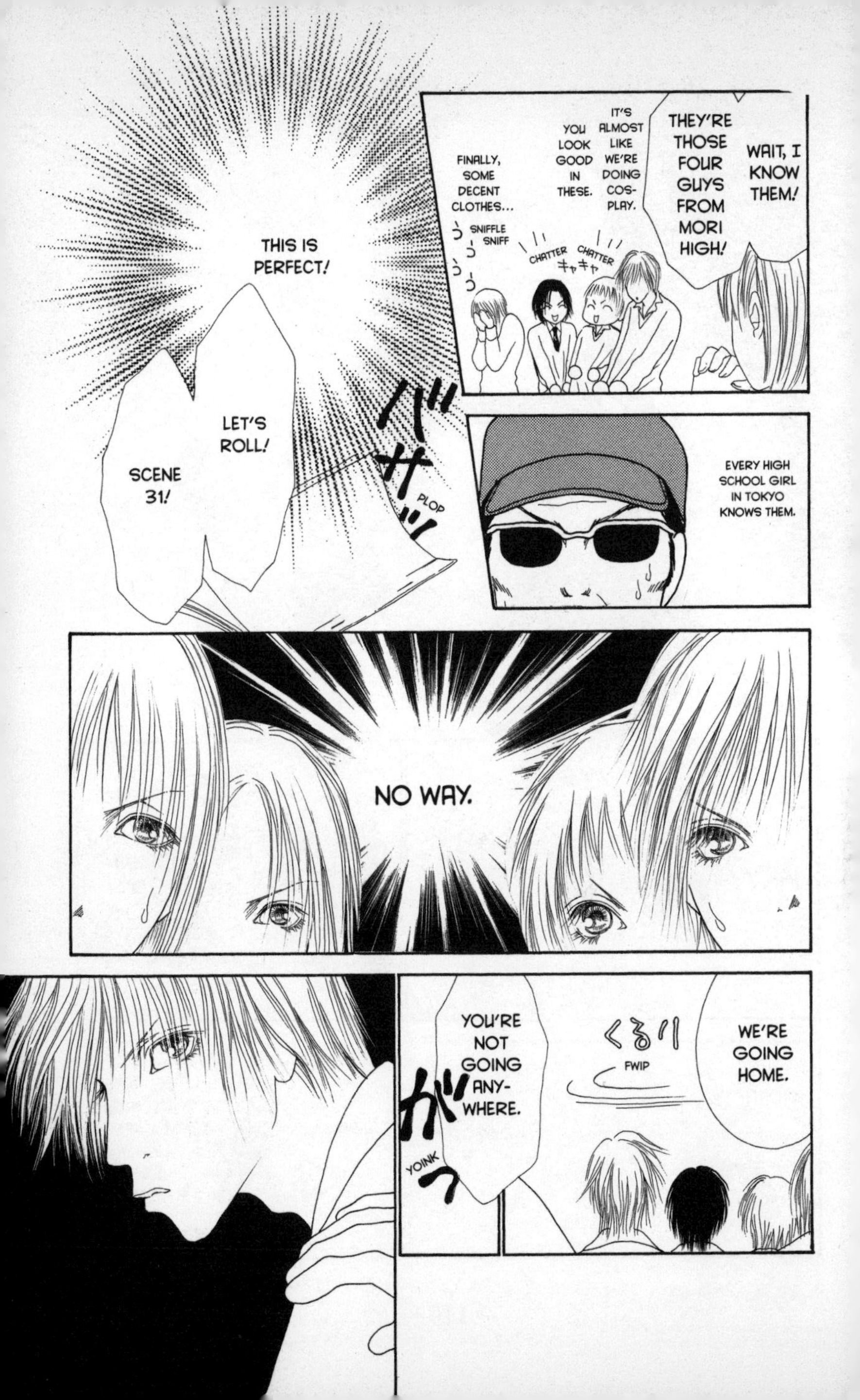
WAIT, I KNOW THEM!
THEY'RE THOSE FOUR GUYS FROM MORI HIGH!
IT'S ALMOST LIKE WE'RE DOING COS-PLAY.
YOU LOOK GOOD IN THESE.
CHATTER CHATTER
FINALLY, SOME DECENT CLOTHES...
SNIFFLE SNIFF
EVERY HIGH SCHOOL GIRL IN TOKYO KNOWS THEM.
THIS IS PERFECT!
LET'S ROLL!
SCENE 31!
PLOP
NO WAY.
WE'RE GOING HOME.
FWIP
YOU'RE NOT GOING ANY-WHERE.
YOINK

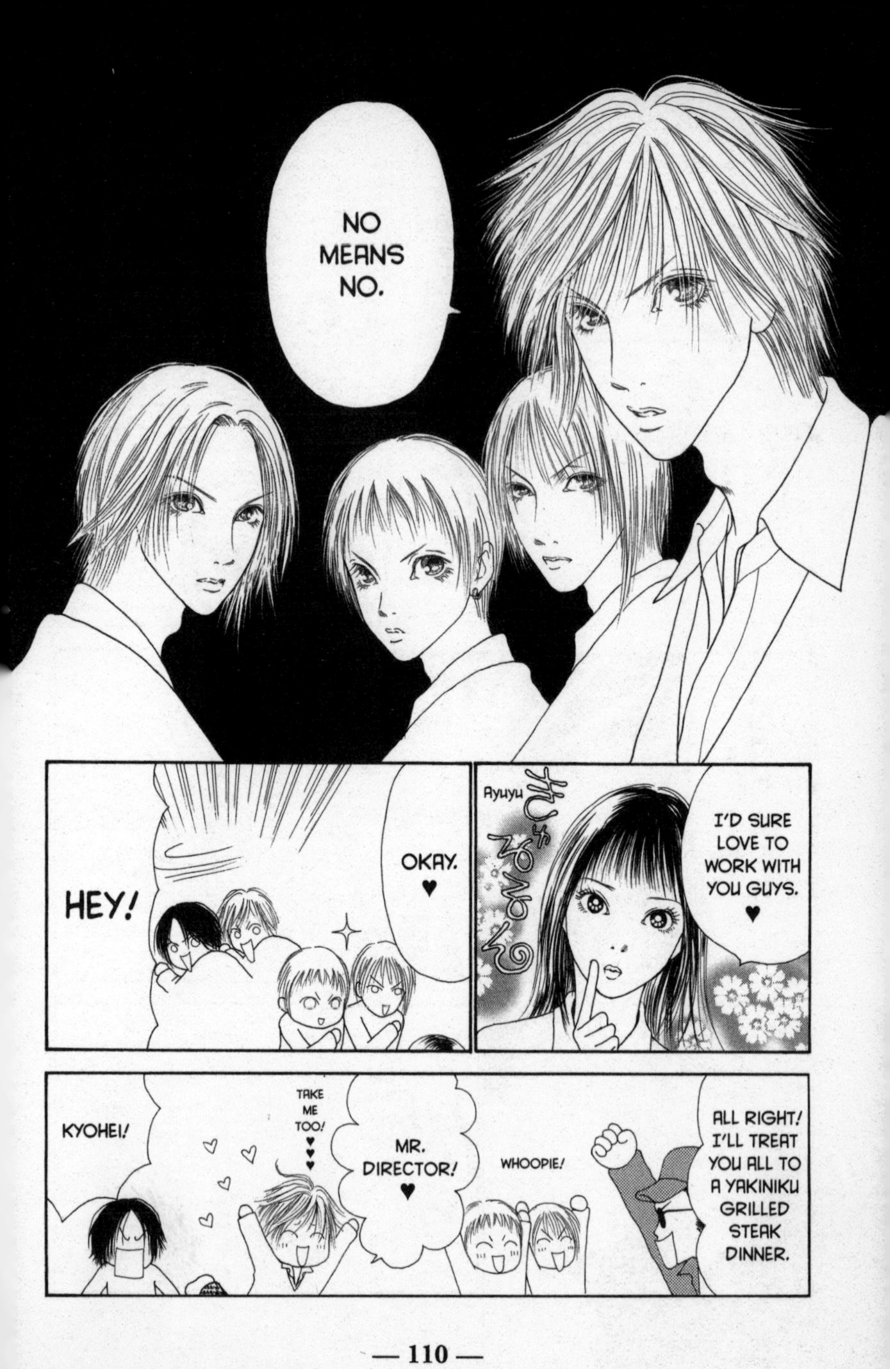
NO MEANS NO.
Ayuyu
I'D SURE LOVE TO WORK WITH YOU GUYS. ♥
OKAY. ♥
HEY!
ALL RIGHT! I'LL TREAT YOU ALL TO A YAKINIKU GRILLED STEAK DINNER.
WHOOPIE!
MR. DIRECTOR! ♥
TAKE ME TOO! ♥♥♥
KYOHEI!

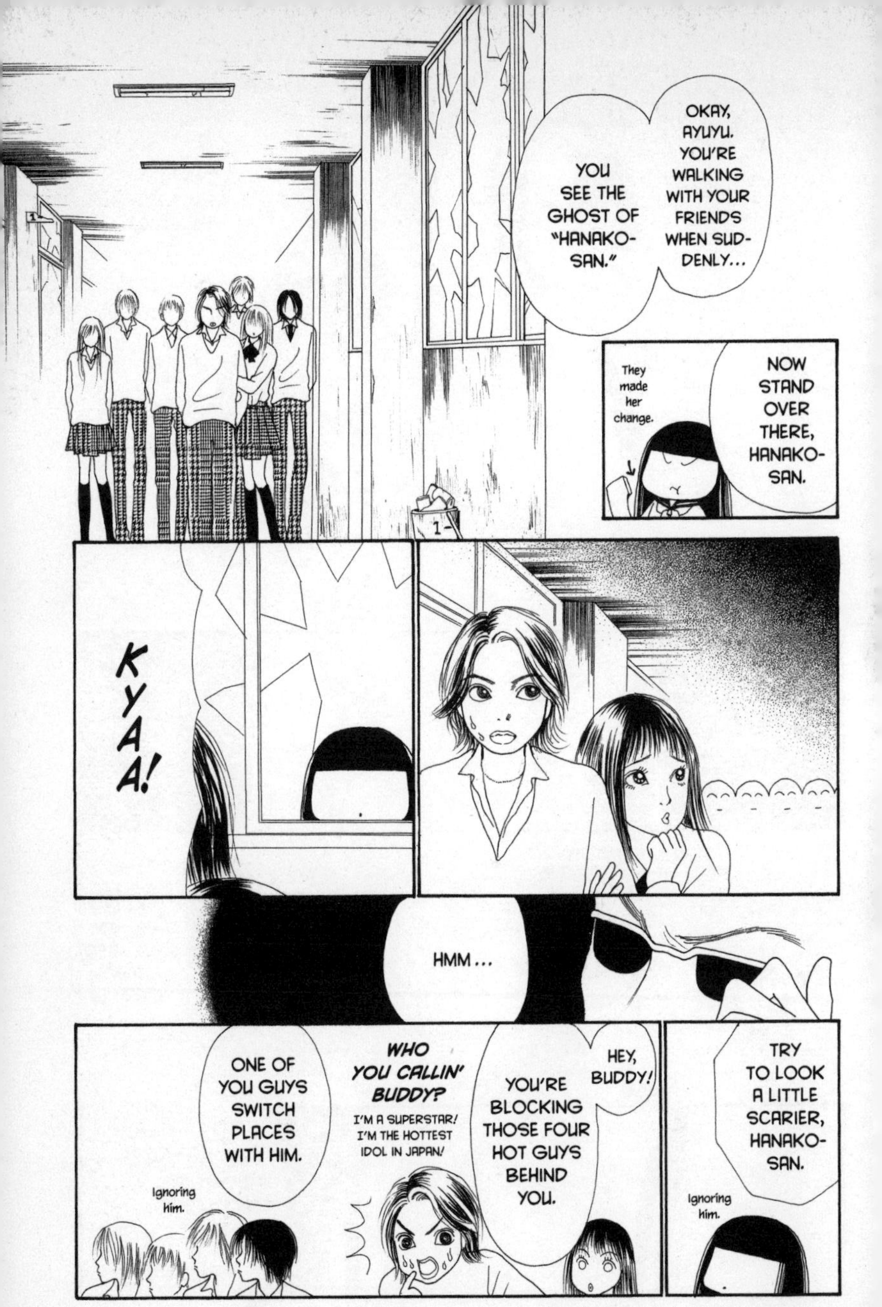
OKAY, AYUYU. YOU'RE WALKING WITH YOUR FRIENDS WHEN SUD-DENLY...
YOU SEE THE GHOST OF "HANAKO-SAN."
NOW STAND OVER THERE, HANAKO-SAN.
They made her change.
KYAA!
HMM...
TRY TO LOOK A LITTLE SCARIER, HANAKO-SAN.
Ignoring him.
HEY, BUDDY!
YOU'RE BLOCKING THOSE FOUR HOT GUYS BEHIND YOU.
WHO YOU CALLIN' BUDDY?
I'M A SUPERSTAR! I'M THE HOTTEST IDOL IN JAPAN!
ONE OF YOU GUYS SWITCH PLACES WITH HIM.
Ignoring him.

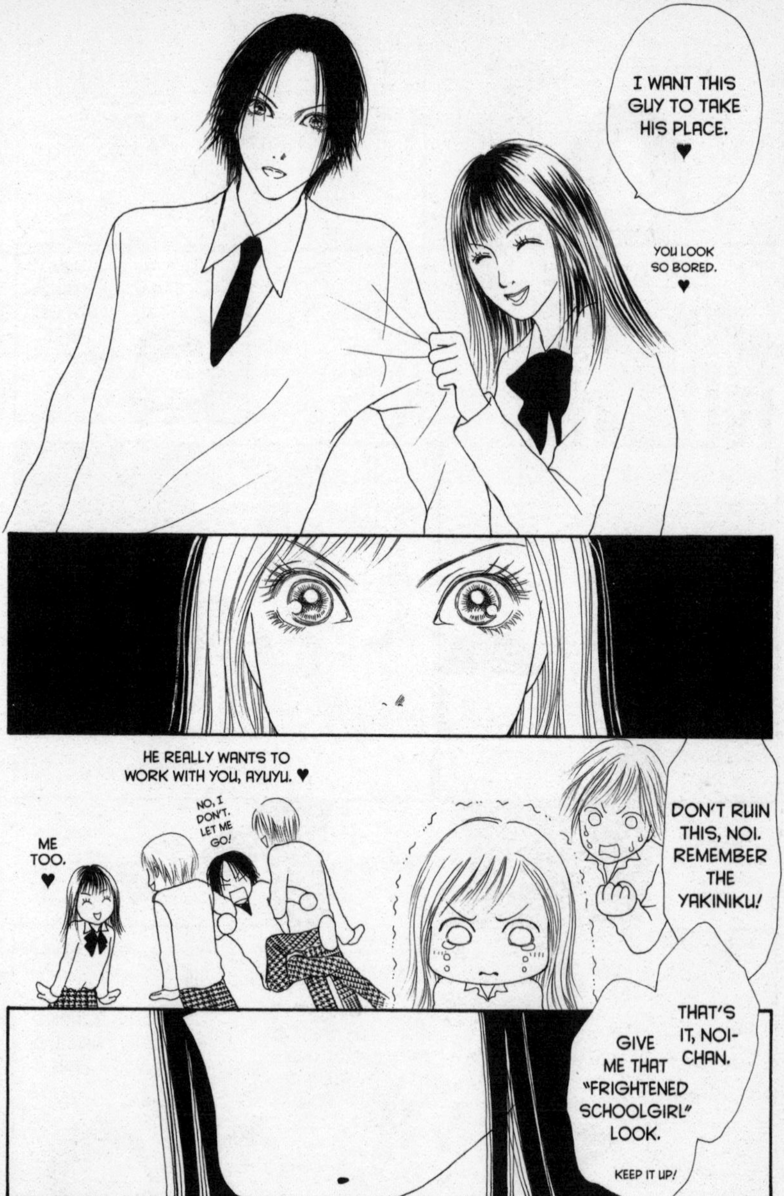
I WANT THIS GUY TO TAKE HIS PLACE. ♥
YOU LOOK SO BORED. ♥
DON'T RUIN THIS, NOI. REMEMBER THE YAKINIKU!
HE REALLY WANTS TO WORK WITH YOU, AYUYU. ♥
NO, I DON'T. LET ME GO!
ME TOO. ♥
THAT'S IT, NOI-CHAN.
GIVE ME THAT "FRIGHTENED SCHOOLGIRL" LOOK.
KEEP IT UP!

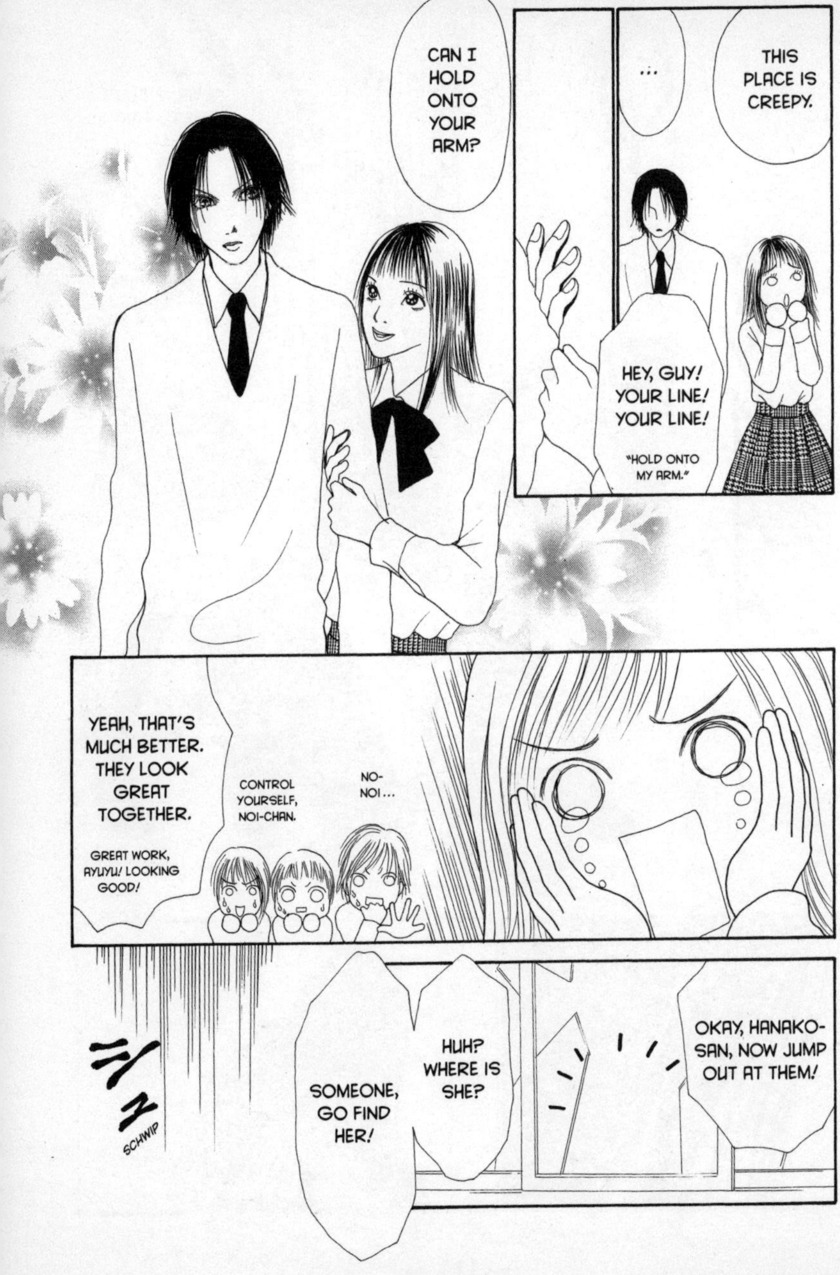

THIS PLACE IS CREEPY.
...
HEY, GUY! YOUR LINE! YOUR LINE!
"HOLD ONTO MY ARM."
CAN I HOLD ONTO YOUR ARM?
NO-NOI...
CONTROL YOURSELF, NOI-CHAN.
YEAH, THAT'S MUCH BETTER. THEY LOOK GREAT TOGETHER.
GREAT WORK, AYUYU! LOOKING GOOD!
OKAY, HANAKO-SAN, NOW JUMP OUT AT THEM!
HUH? WHERE IS SHE?
SOMEONE, GO FIND HER!
SCHWIP

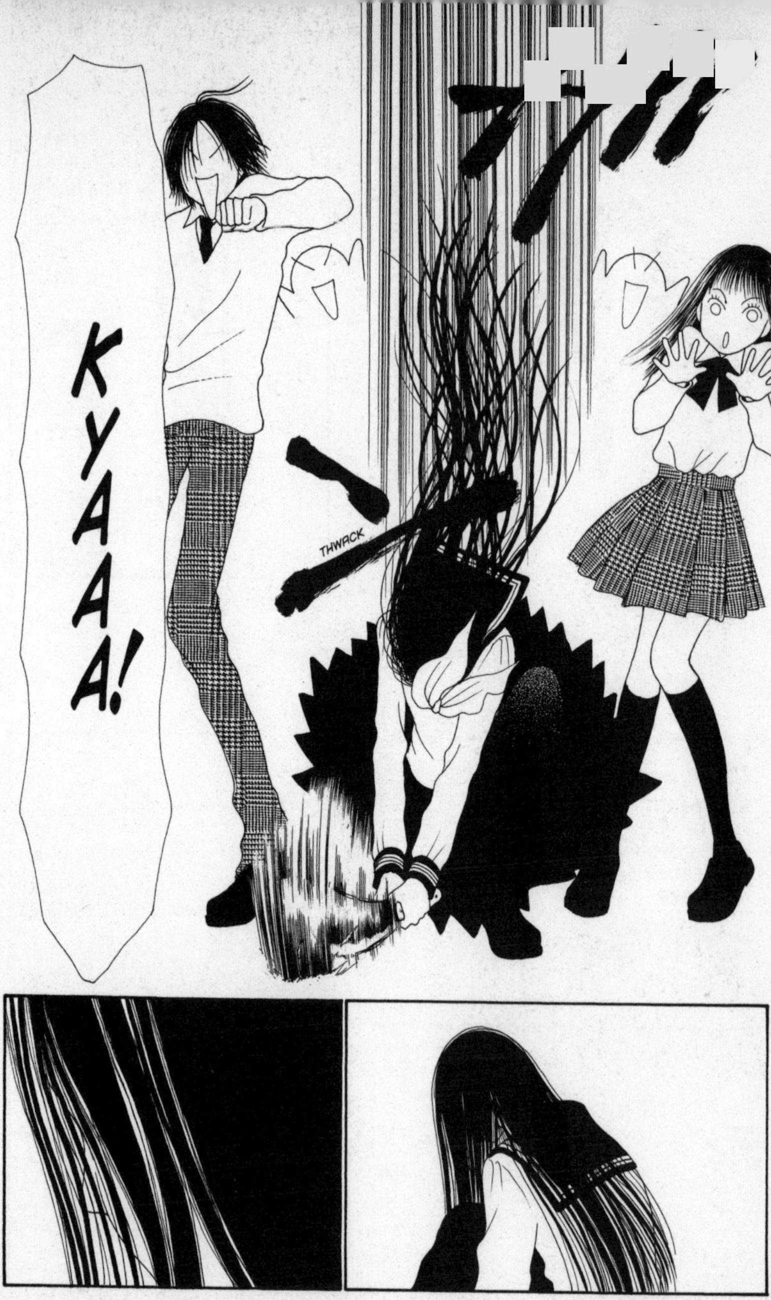
THWACK
KYAAA!

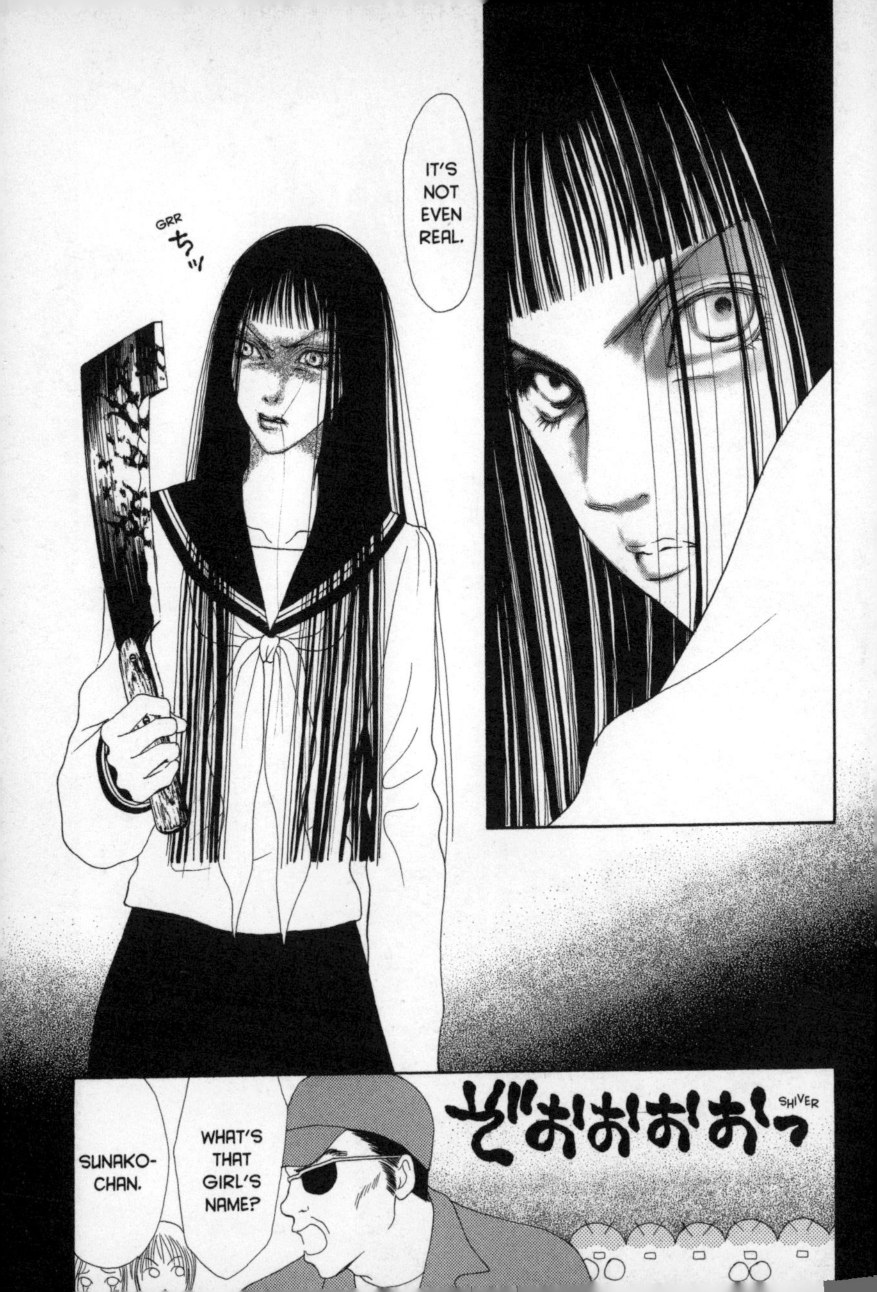
IT'S NOT EVEN REAL.
GRR
ちッ
ぞおおおおっ
SHIVER
WHAT'S THAT GIRL'S NAME?
SUNAKO-CHAN.

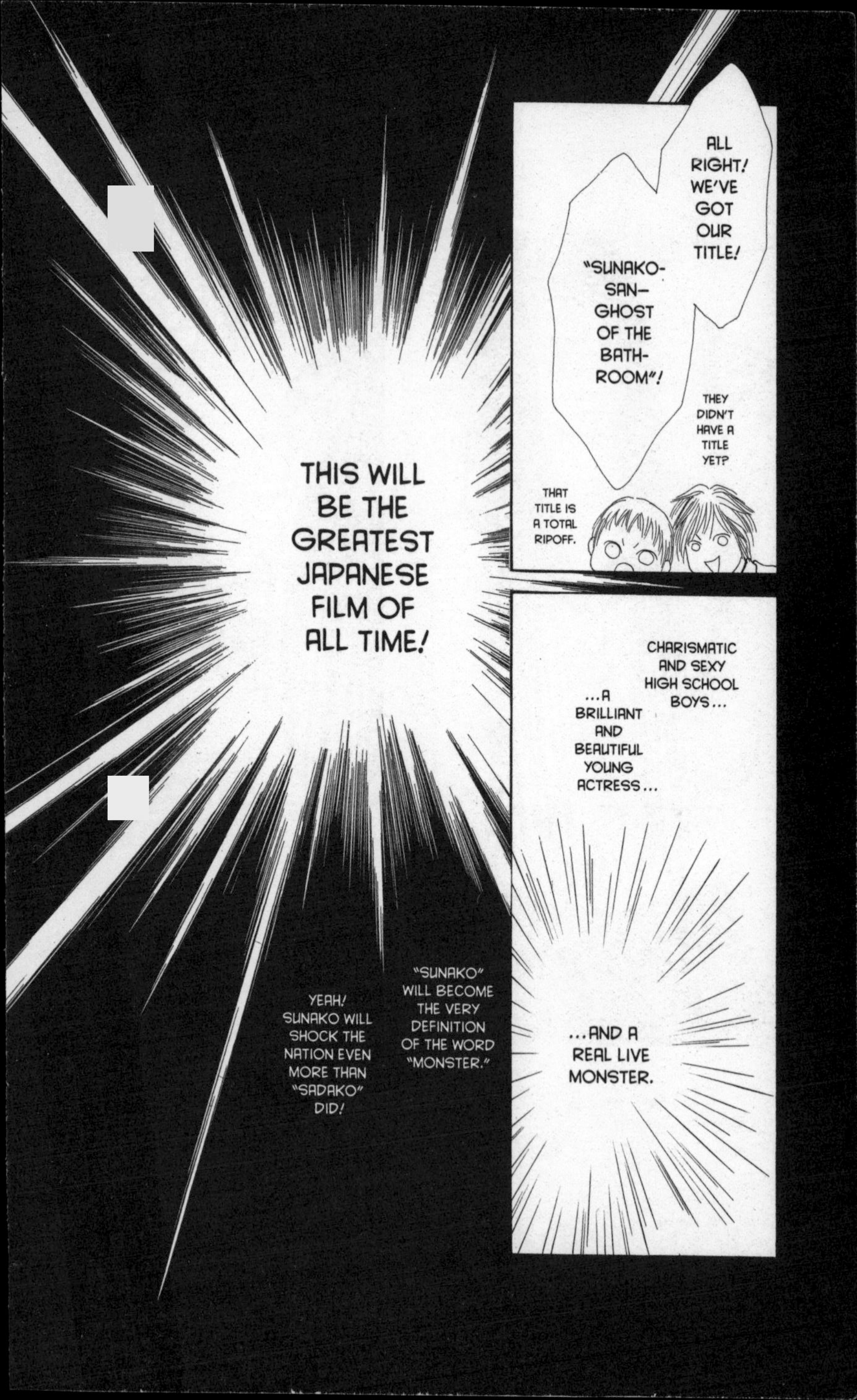
ALL RIGHT! WE'VE GOT OUR TITLE!
"SUNAKO-SAN—GHOST OF THE BATHROOM"!
THEY DIDN'T HAVE A TITLE YET?
THAT TITLE IS A TOTAL RIPOFF.
CHARISMATIC AND SEXY HIGH SCHOOL BOYS...
...A BRILLIANT AND BEAUTIFUL YOUNG ACTRESS...
...AND A REAL LIVE MONSTER.
THIS WILL BE THE GREATEST JAPANESE FILM OF ALL TIME!
"SUNAKO" WILL BECOME THE VERY DEFINITION OF THE WORD "MONSTER."
YEAH! SUNAKO WILL SHOCK THE NATION EVEN MORE THAN "SADAKO" DID!

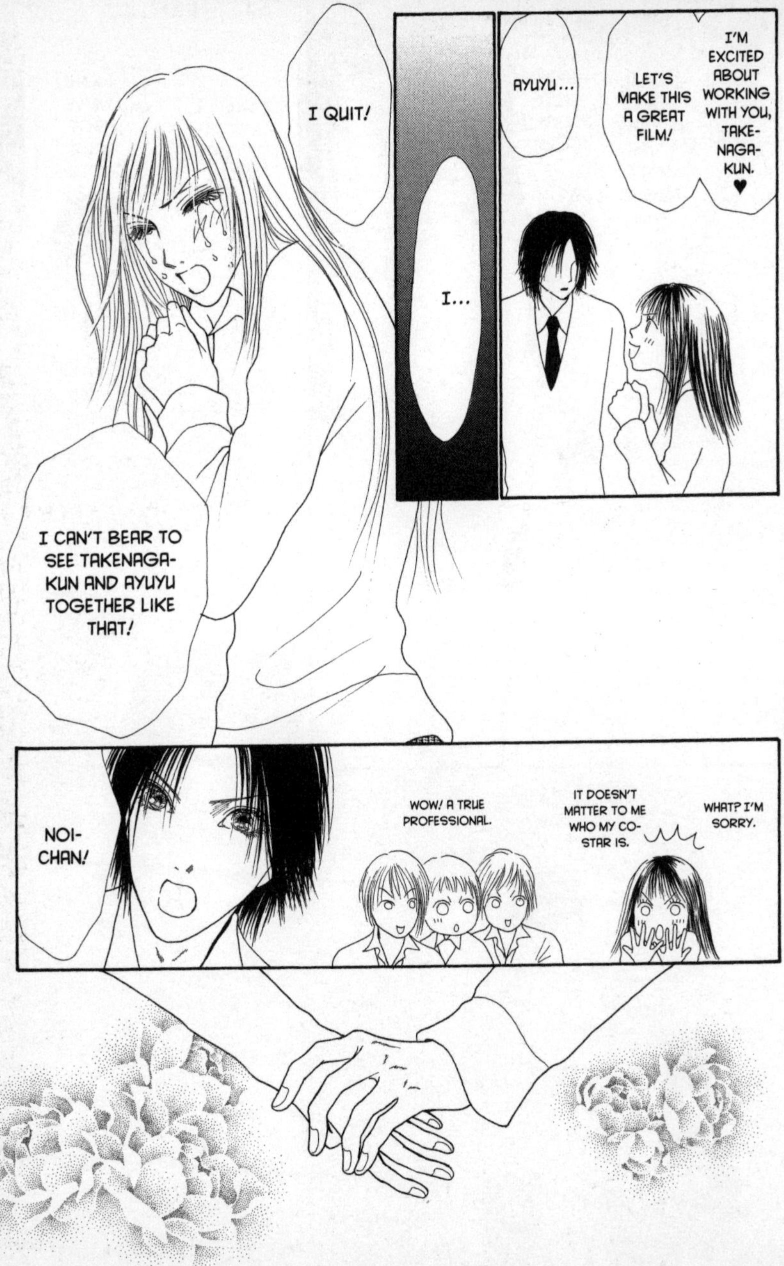
I'M EXCITED ABOUT WORKING WITH YOU, TAKE-NAGA-KUN. ♥
LET'S MAKE THIS A GREAT FILM!
AYUYU...
I...
I QUIT!
I CAN'T BEAR TO SEE TAKENAGA-KUN AND AYUYU TOGETHER LIKE THAT!
WHAT? I'M SORRY.
IT DOESN'T MATTER TO ME WHO MY CO-STAR IS.
WOW! A TRUE PROFESSIONAL.
NOI-CHAN!

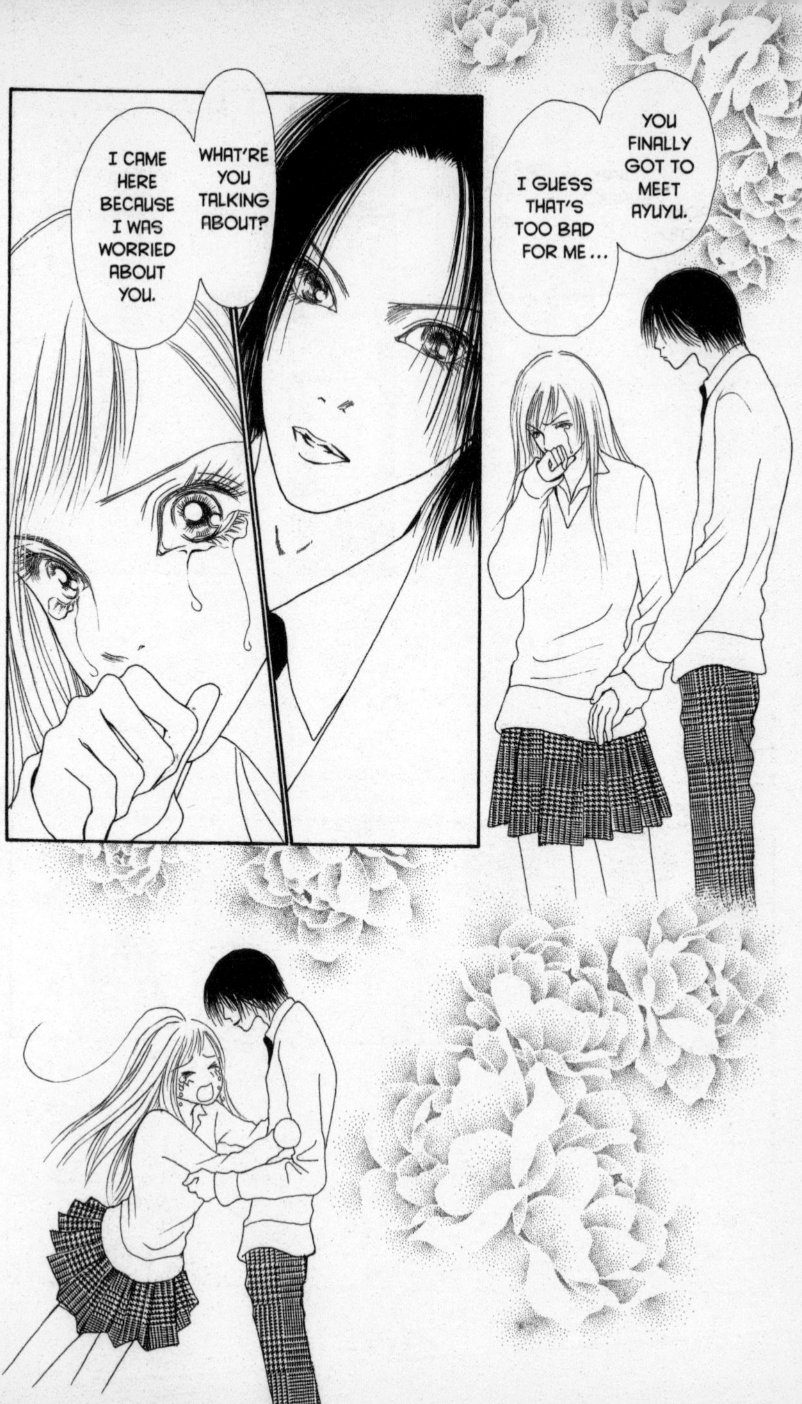
YOU FINALLY GOT TO MEET AYUYU.
I GUESS THAT'S TOO BAD FOR ME...
WHAT'RE YOU TALKING ABOUT?
I CAME HERE BECAUSE I WAS WORRIED ABOUT YOU.

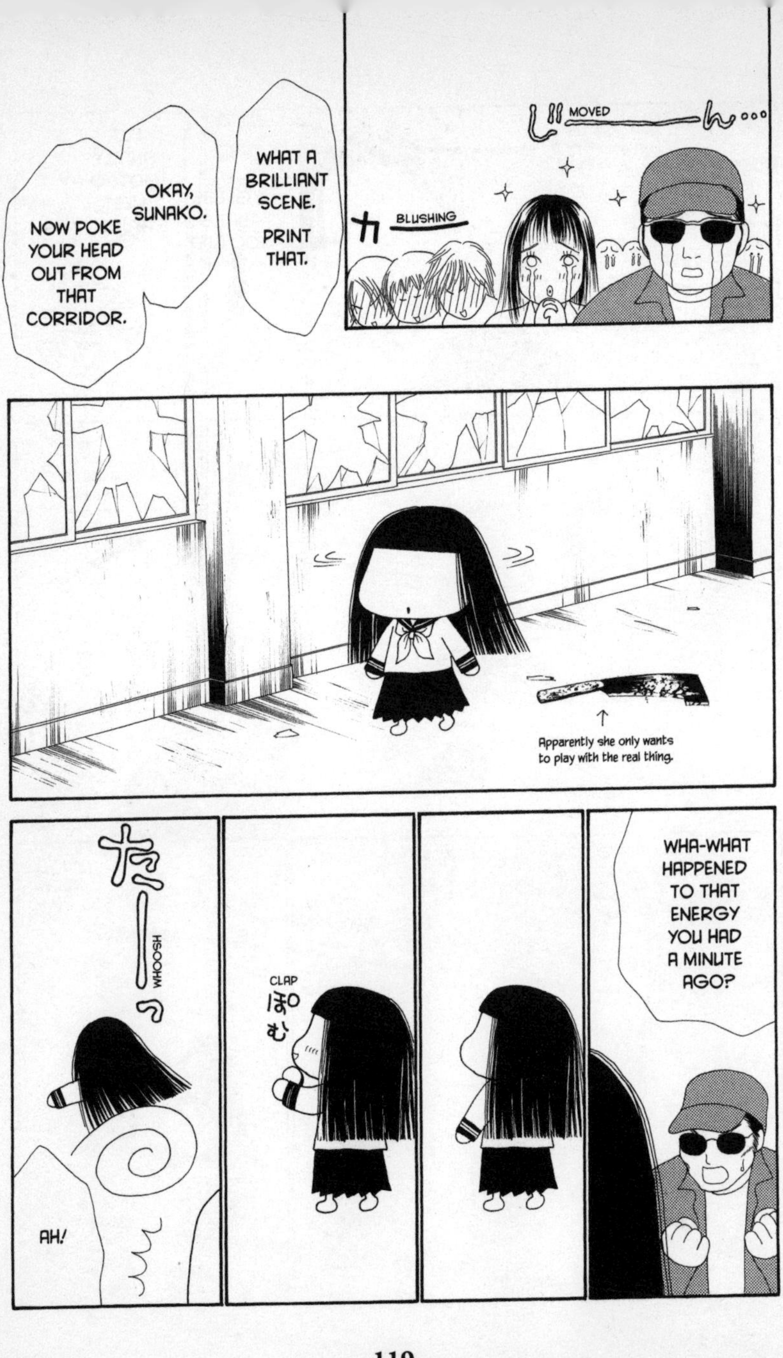
じ〜〜ん…
MOVED
カ
BLUSHING
WHAT A BRILLIANT SCENE.
PRINT THAT.
OKAY, SUNAKO.
NOW POKE YOUR HEAD OUT FROM THAT CORRIDOR.
Apparently she only wants to play with the real thing.
WHA-WHAT HAPPENED TO THAT ENERGY YOU HAD A MINUTE AGO?
ぽむ
CLAP
たーっ
WHOOSH
AH!

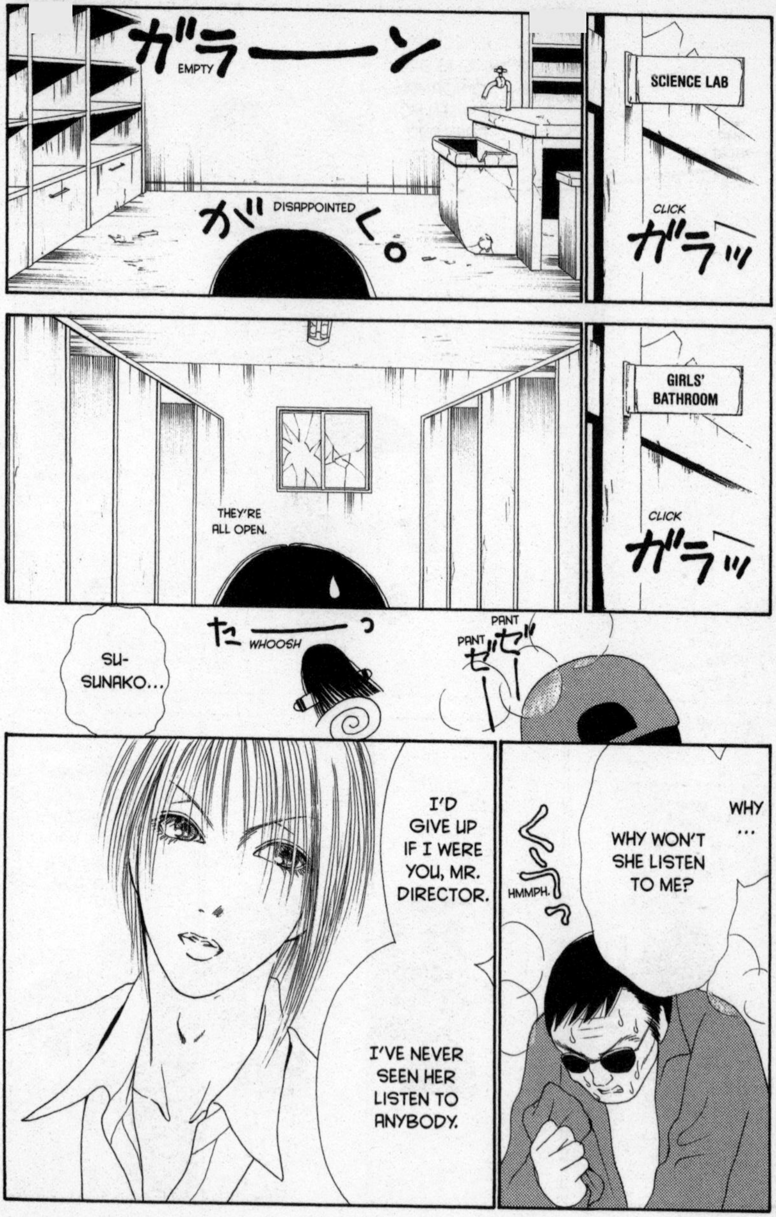
SCIENCE LAB
CLICK
ガラッ
ガラーン
EMPTY
がく。
DISAPPOINTED
GIRLS' BATHROOM
CLICK
ガラッ
THEY'RE ALL OPEN.
PANT
PANT
ぜーぜー
たーっ
WHOOSH
SU- SUNAKO...
WHY ...
WHY WON'T SHE LISTEN TO ME?
くぅ
HMMPH.
I'D GIVE UP IF I WERE YOU, MR. DIRECTOR.
I'VE NEVER SEEN HER LISTEN TO ANYBODY.

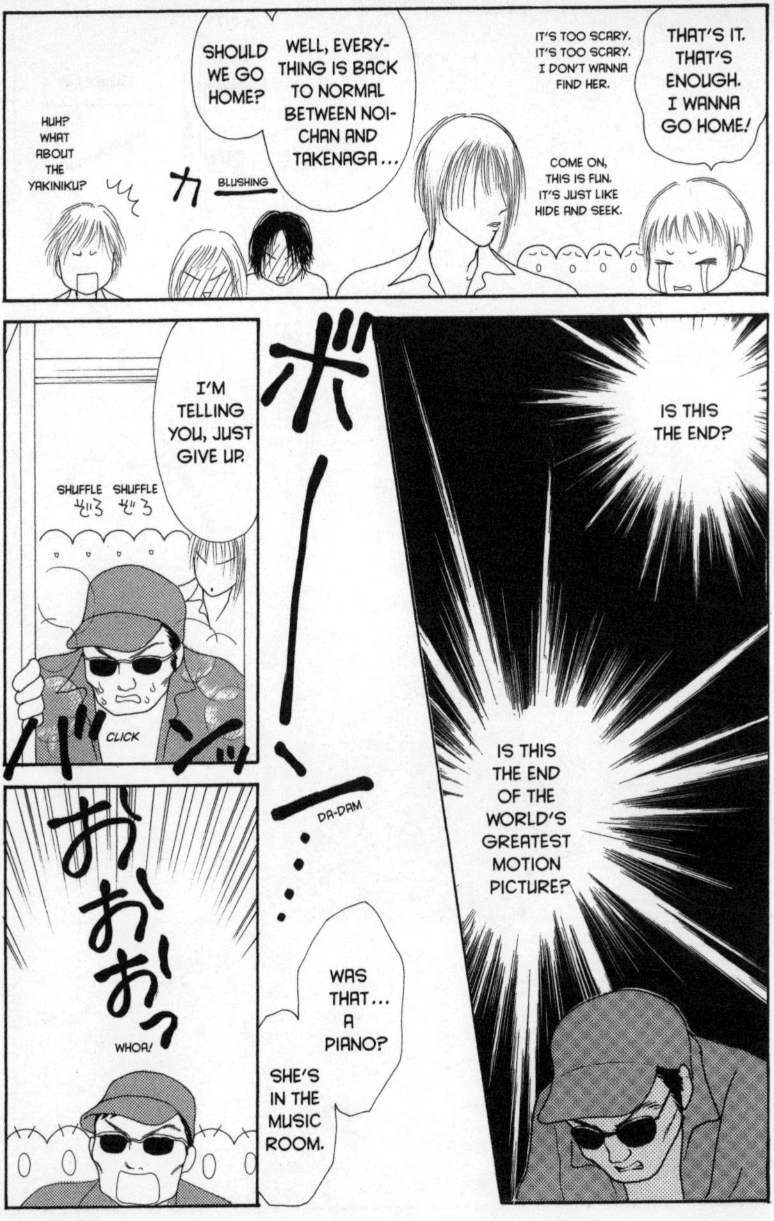
THAT'S IT. THAT'S ENOUGH. I WANNA GO HOME!
IT'S TOO SCARY. IT'S TOO SCARY. I DON'T WANNA FIND HER.
COME ON, THIS IS FUN. IT'S JUST LIKE HIDE AND SEEK.
WELL, EVERY-THING IS BACK TO NORMAL BETWEEN NOI-CHAN AND TAKENAGA...
SHOULD WE GO HOME?
カ
BLUSHING
HUH? WHAT ABOUT THE YAKINIKU?
IS THIS THE END?
IS THIS THE END OF THE WORLD'S GREATEST MOTION PICTURE?
I'M TELLING YOU, JUST GIVE UP.
SHUFFLE SHUFFLE
ぞろぞろ
バンッ
CLICK
ボーン…
DA-DAM
おおおっ
WHOA!
WAS THAT... A PIANO?
SHE'S IN THE MUSIC ROOM.

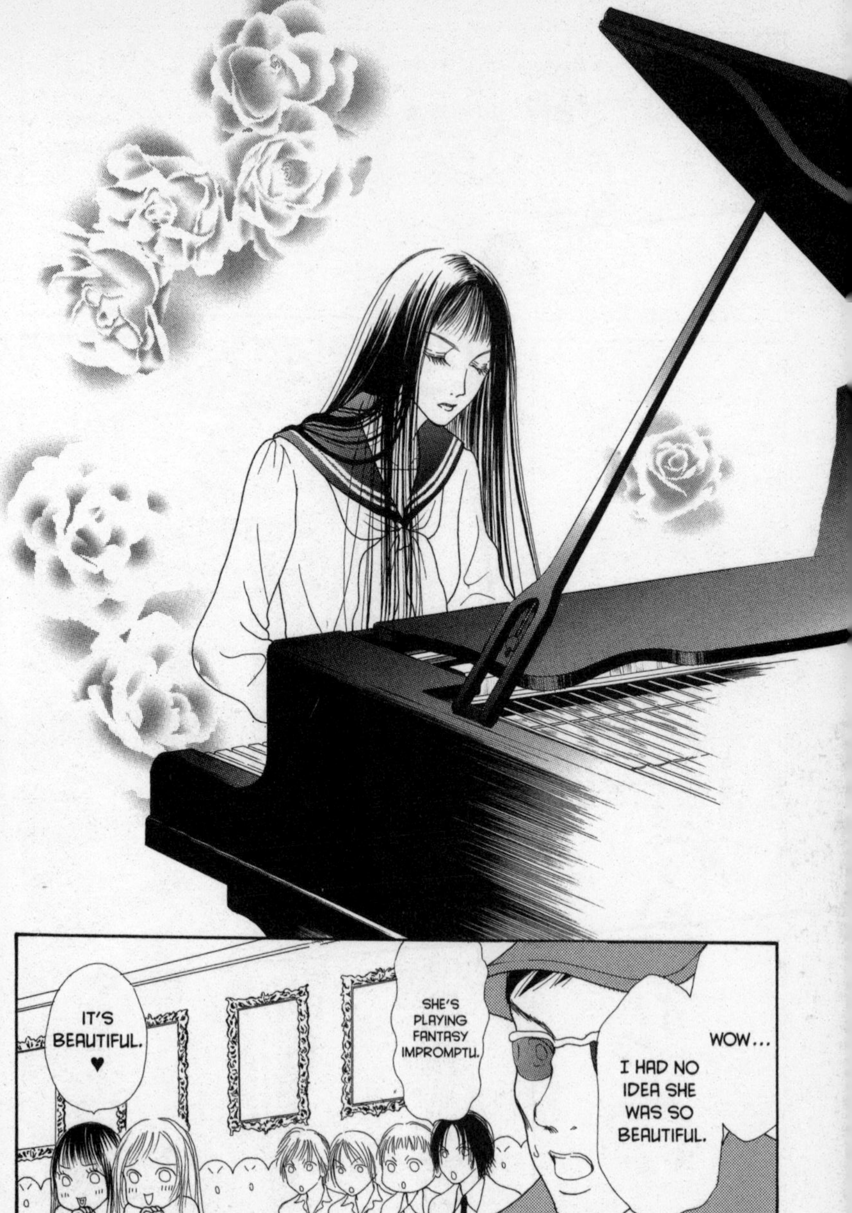
WOW...
I HAD NO IDEA SHE WAS SO BEAUTIFUL.
SHE'S PLAYING FANTASY IMPROMPTU.
IT'S BEAUTIFUL. ♥

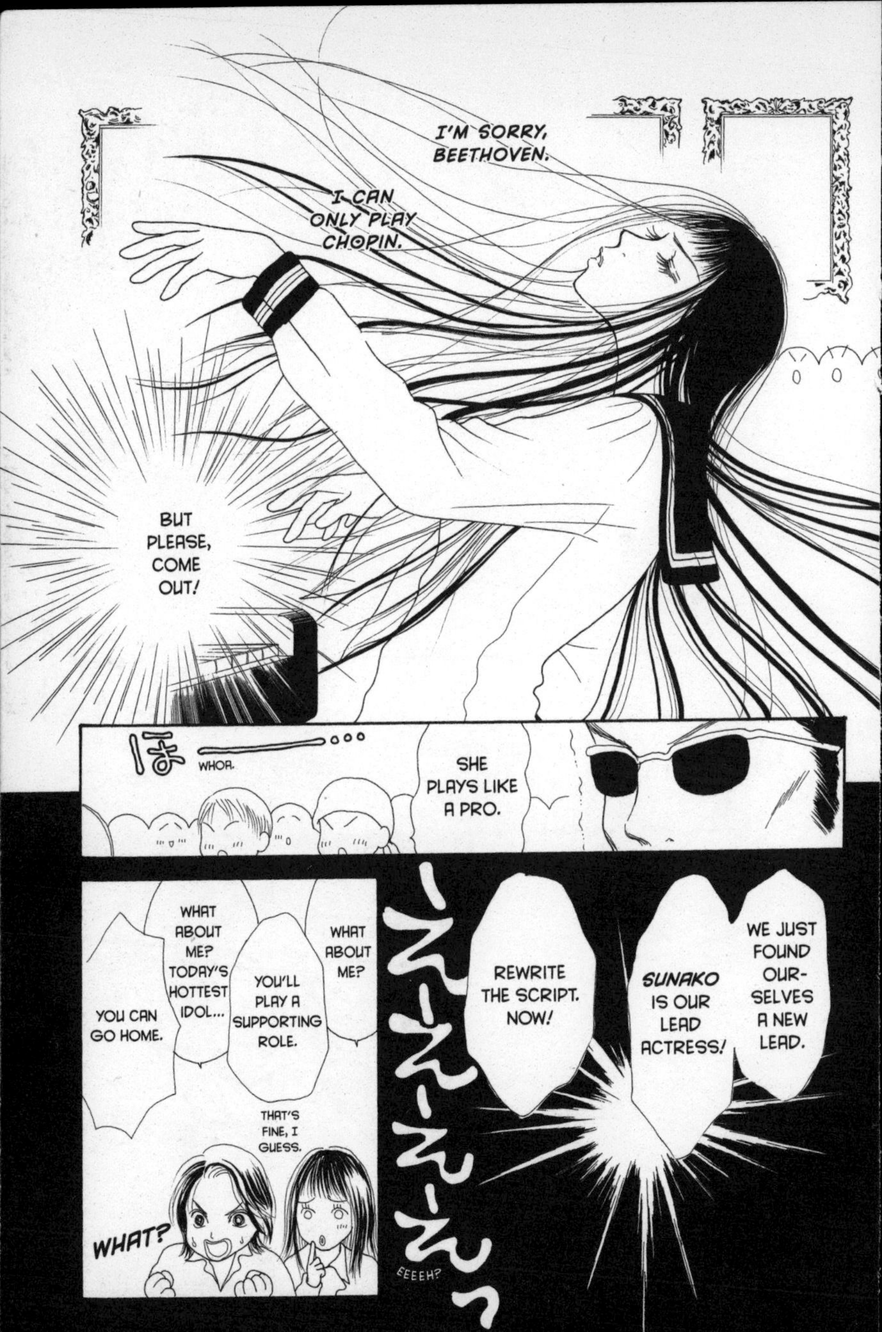
I'M SORRY, BEETHOVEN.
I CAN ONLY PLAY CHOPIN.
BUT PLEASE, COME OUT!
SHE PLAYS LIKE A PRO.
ほ———ooo
WHOA.
WE JUST FOUND OURSELVES A NEW LEAD.
SUNAKO IS OUR LEAD ACTRESS!
REWRITE THE SCRIPT. NOW!
EEEEH?
WHAT ABOUT ME?
YOU'LL PLAY A SUPPORTING ROLE.
WHAT ABOUT ME? TODAY'S HOTTEST IDOL...
YOU CAN GO HOME.
THAT'S FINE, I GUESS.
WHAT?

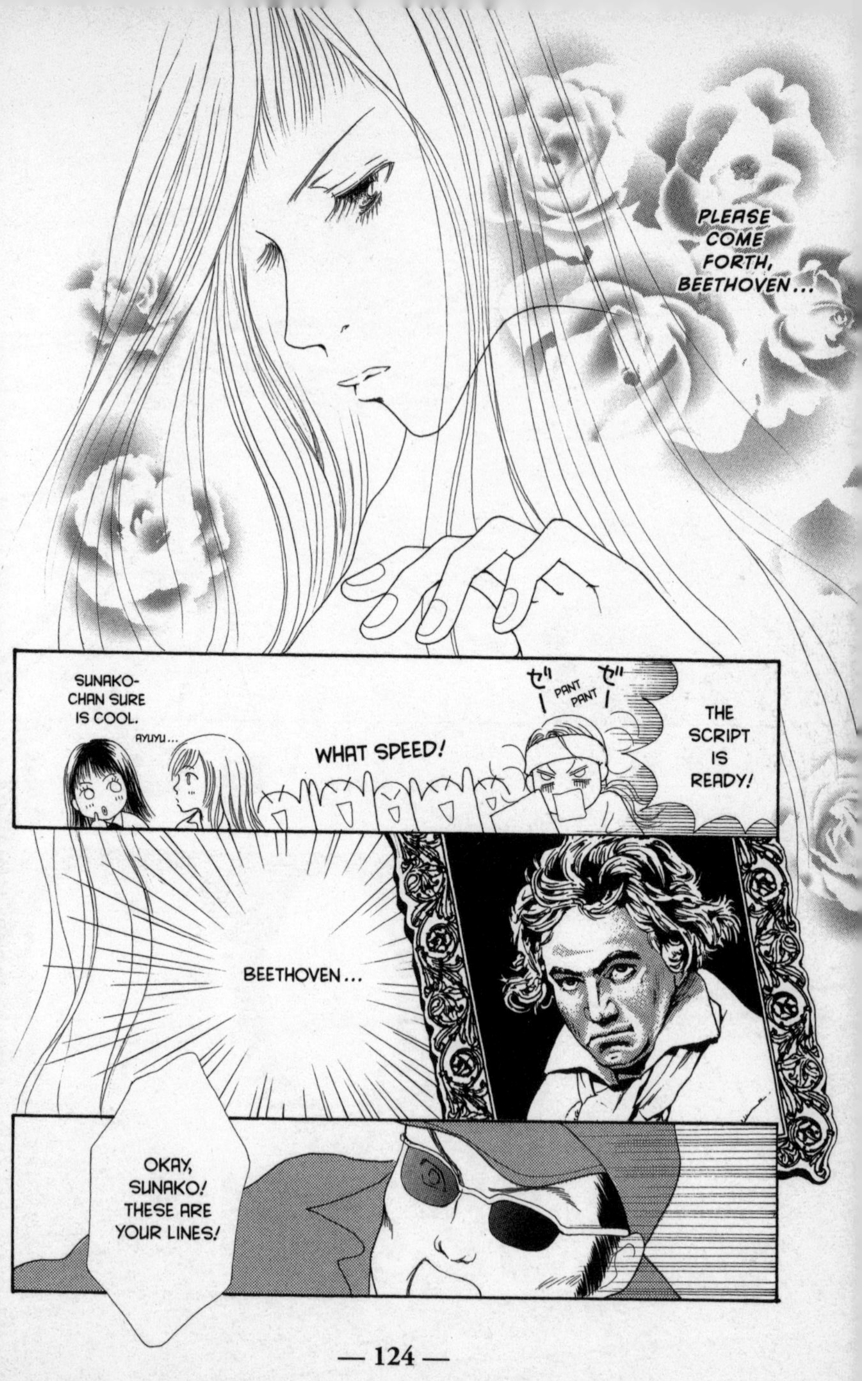
PLEASE COME FORTH, BEETHOVEN...
THE SCRIPT IS READY!
ゼー
PANT PANT
ゼー
WHAT SPEED!
AYUYU...
SUNAKO-CHAN SURE IS COOL.
BEETHOVEN...
OKAY, SUNAKO! THESE ARE YOUR LINES!

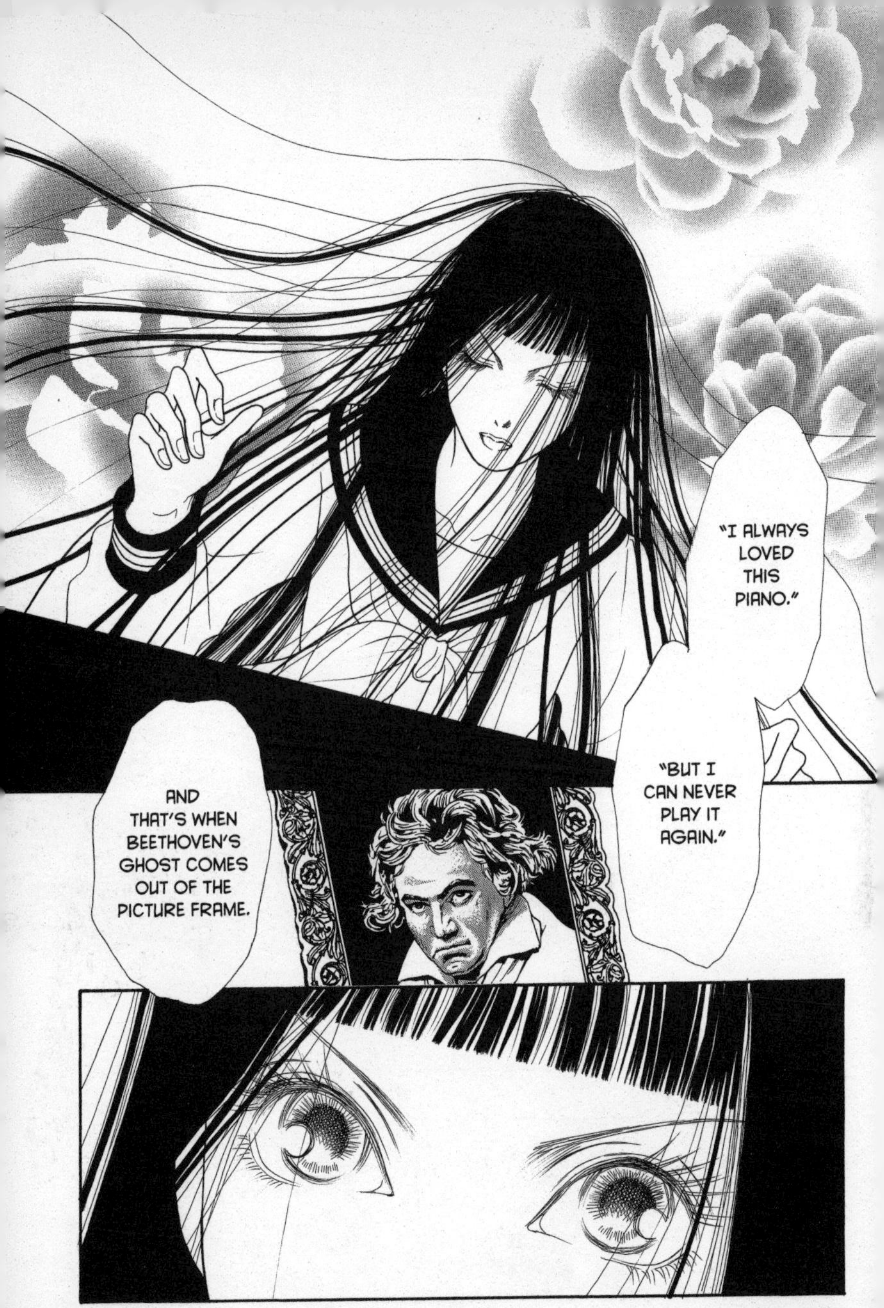
"I ALWAYS LOVED THIS PIANO."
"BUT I CAN NEVER PLAY IT AGAIN."
AND THAT'S WHEN BEETHOVEN'S GHOST COMES OUT OF THE PICTURE FRAME.

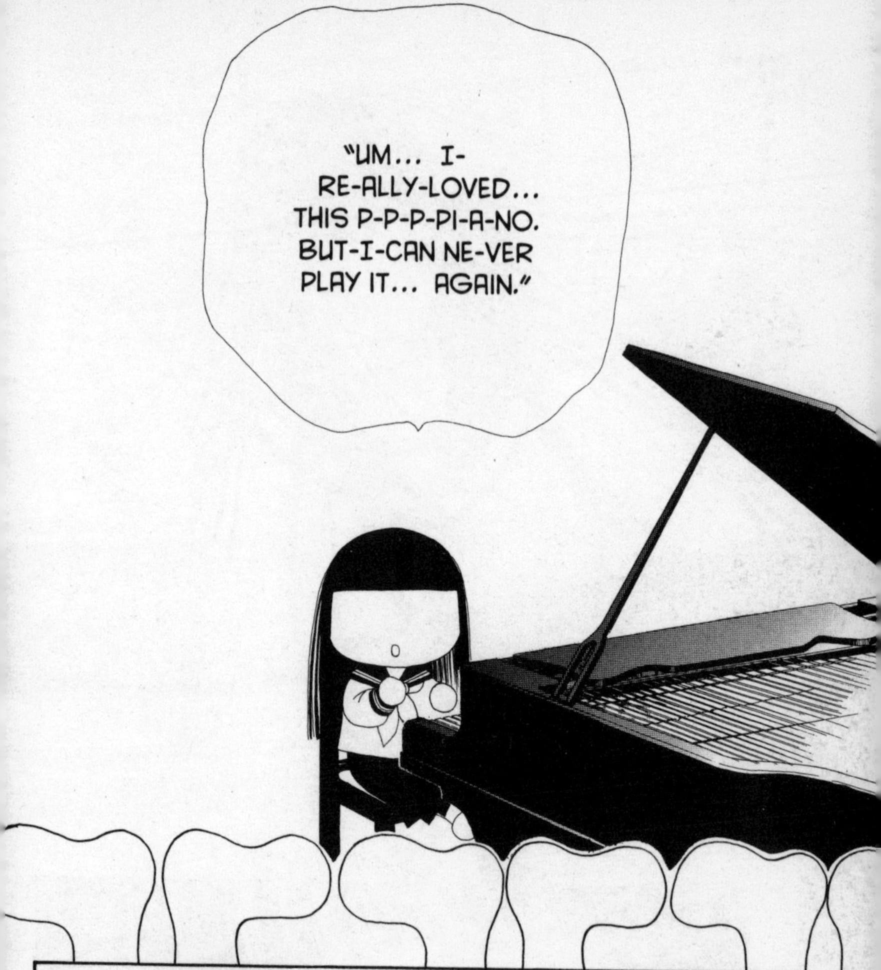
"UM... I-
RE-ALLY-LOVED...
THIS P-P-P-PI-A-NO.
BUT-I-CAN NE-VER
PLAY IT... AGAIN."

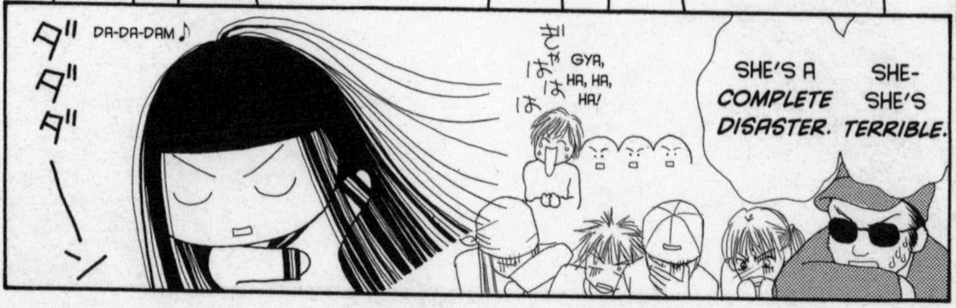
SHE-SHE'S TERRIBLE.
SHE'S A COMPLETE DISASTER.
ぎゃははは
GYA, HA, HA, HA!
ダダダーン
DA-DA-DAM♪

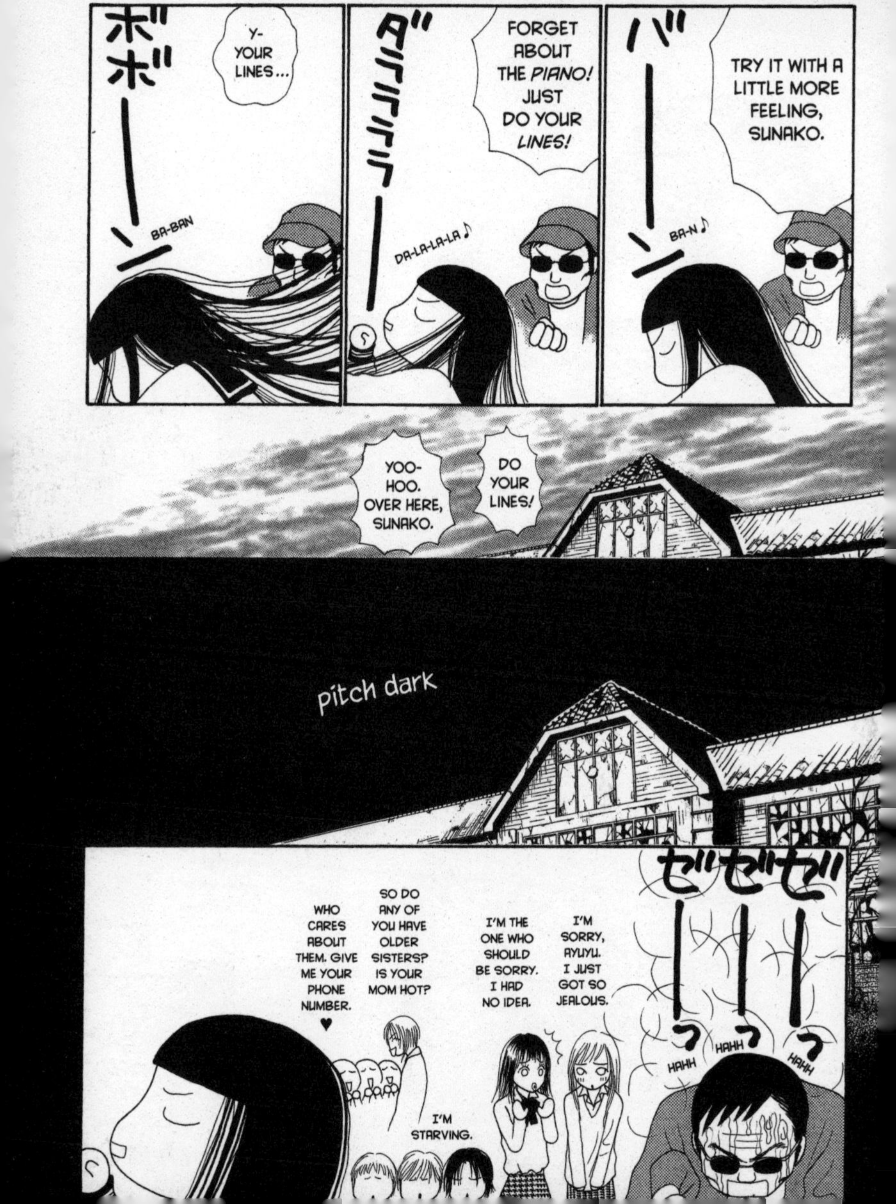
TRY IT WITH A LITTLE MORE FEELING, SUNAKO.
BA-N♪
FORGET ABOUT THE PIANO! JUST DO YOUR LINES!
DA-LA-LA-LA♪
Y- YOUR LINES...
BA-BAN
DO YOUR LINES!
YOO-HOO. OVER HERE, SUNAKO.
pitch dark
HAHH
HAHH
HAHH
I'M SORRY, AYUYU. I JUST GOT SO JEALOUS.
I'M THE ONE WHO SHOULD BE SORRY. I HAD NO IDEA.
SO DO ANY OF YOU HAVE OLDER SISTERS? IS YOUR MOM HOT?
WHO CARES ABOUT THEM. GIVE ME YOUR PHONE NUMBER. ♥
I'M STARVING.

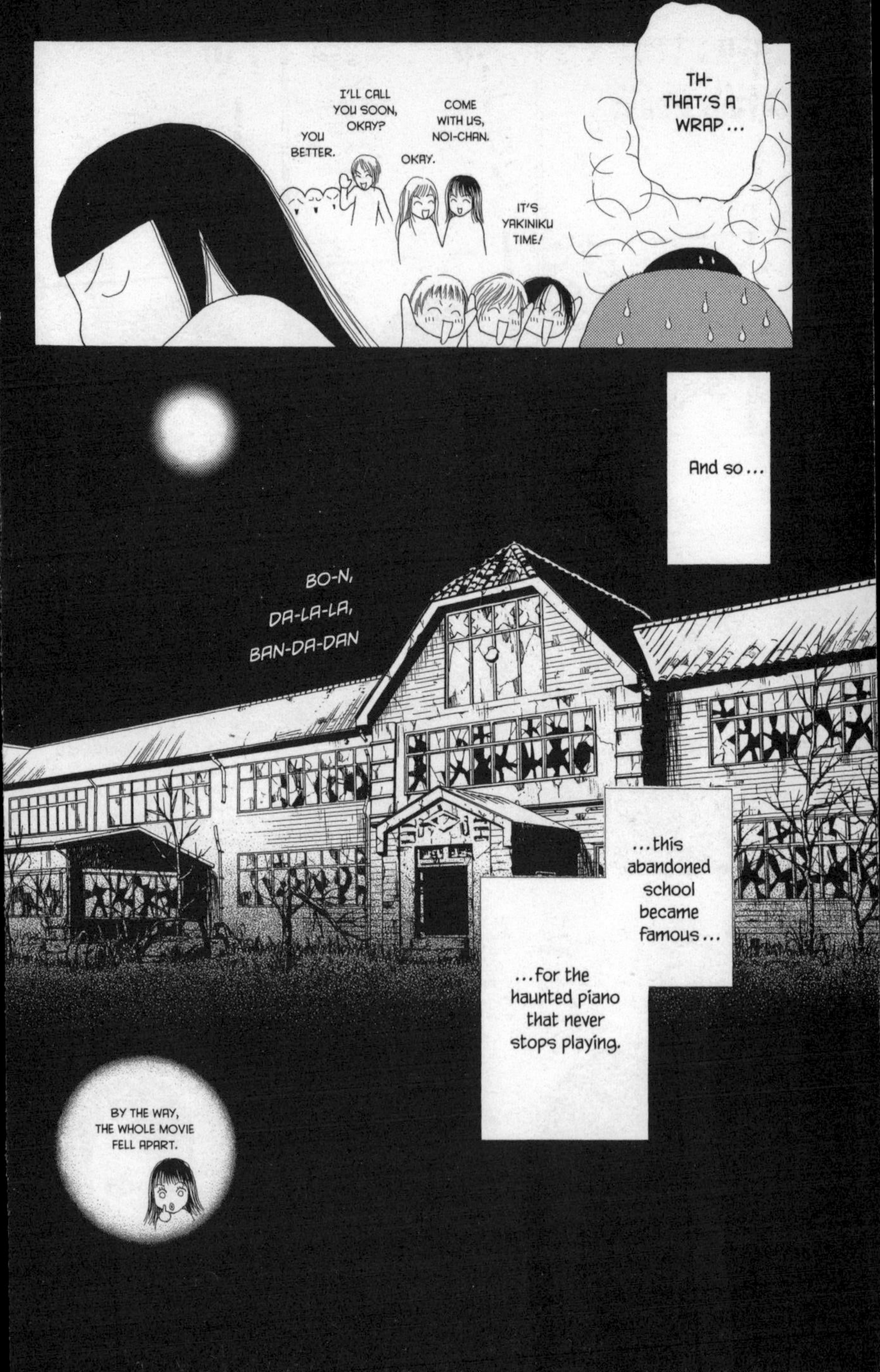
TH- THAT'S A WRAP...
IT'S YAKINIKU TIME!
COME WITH US, NOI-CHAN.
OKAY.
I'LL CALL YOU SOON, OKAY?
YOU BETTER.
And so...
BO-N, DA-LA-LA, BAN-DA-DAN
...this abandoned school became famous...
...for the haunted piano that never stops playing.
BY THE WAY, THE WHOLE MOVIE FELL APART.

Chapter 26
Diving Panic

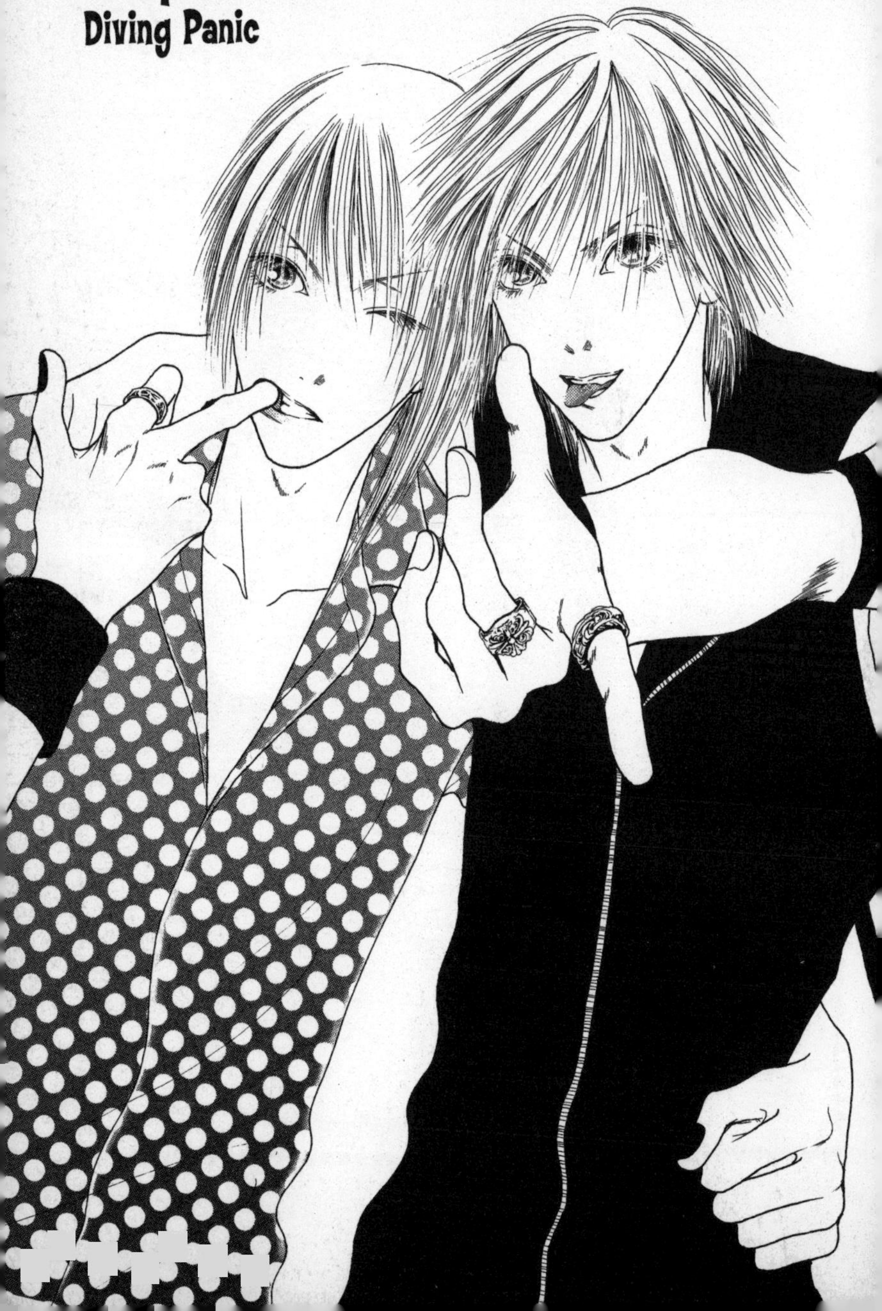

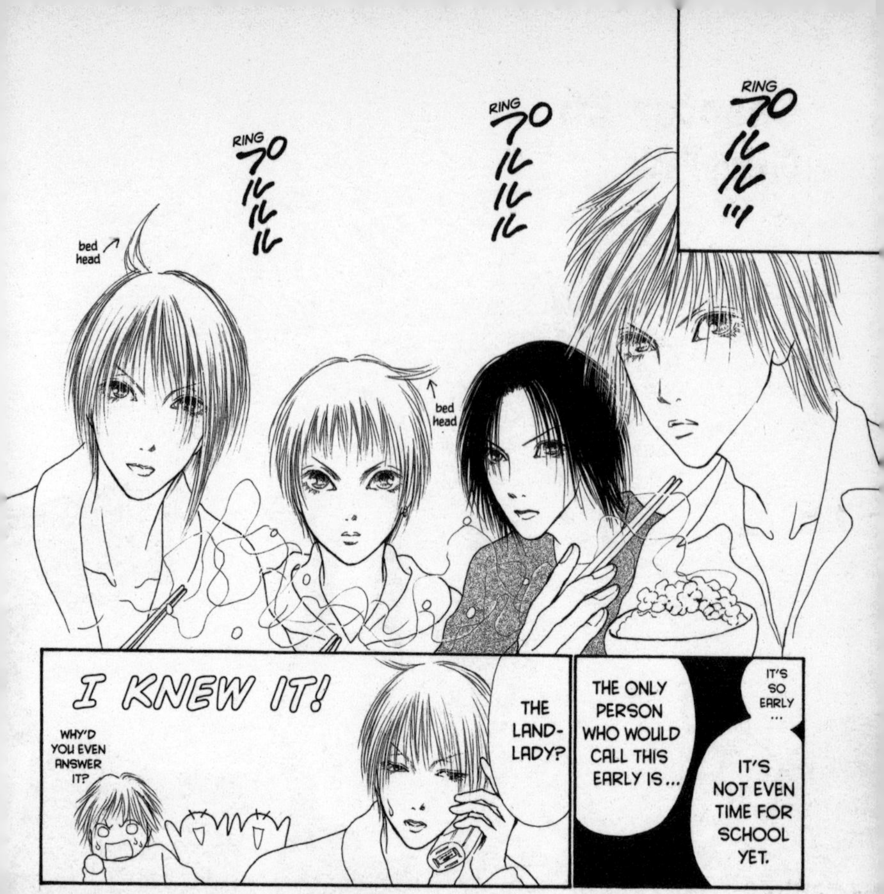
RING
プルルッ
RING
プルルル
RING
プルルル
bed head
bed head
IT'S SO EARLY...
IT'S NOT EVEN TIME FOR SCHOOL YET.
THE ONLY PERSON WHO WOULD CALL THIS EARLY IS...
THE LAND-LADY?
I KNEW IT!
WHY'D YOU EVEN ANSWER IT?

BEHIND THE SCENES

AYUAYU WATANABE AND ATSUKO NAMBA-CHAN HELPED ME ON THIS. ♥
TWO HOT GIRLS TOGETHER AGAIN. ♥

BUT WHILE SHE WAS HELPING ME, NAMBA-CHAN CAUGHT A COLD, AND HER NOSE STARTED RUNNING LIKE A FAUCET. WHEN I TURNED TO LOOK BACK AT NAMBA-CHAN...

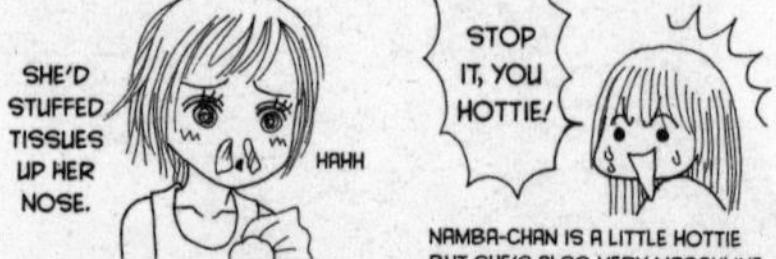
SHE'D STUFFED TISSUES UP HER NOSE.
HAHH
STOP IT, YOU HOTTIE!
NAMBA-CHAN IS A LITTLE HOTTIE BUT SHE'S ALSO VERY MASCULINE.

IT'S SO FUN DRAWING NAKED BOYS.

I DEFINITELY WANT YOU GUYS TO SEND ME PICTURES OF HOT NAKED GUYS (WITH PANTS ON).

I DON'T WANNA HAVE TO KEEP USING MY ANATOMY TEXT BOOK.

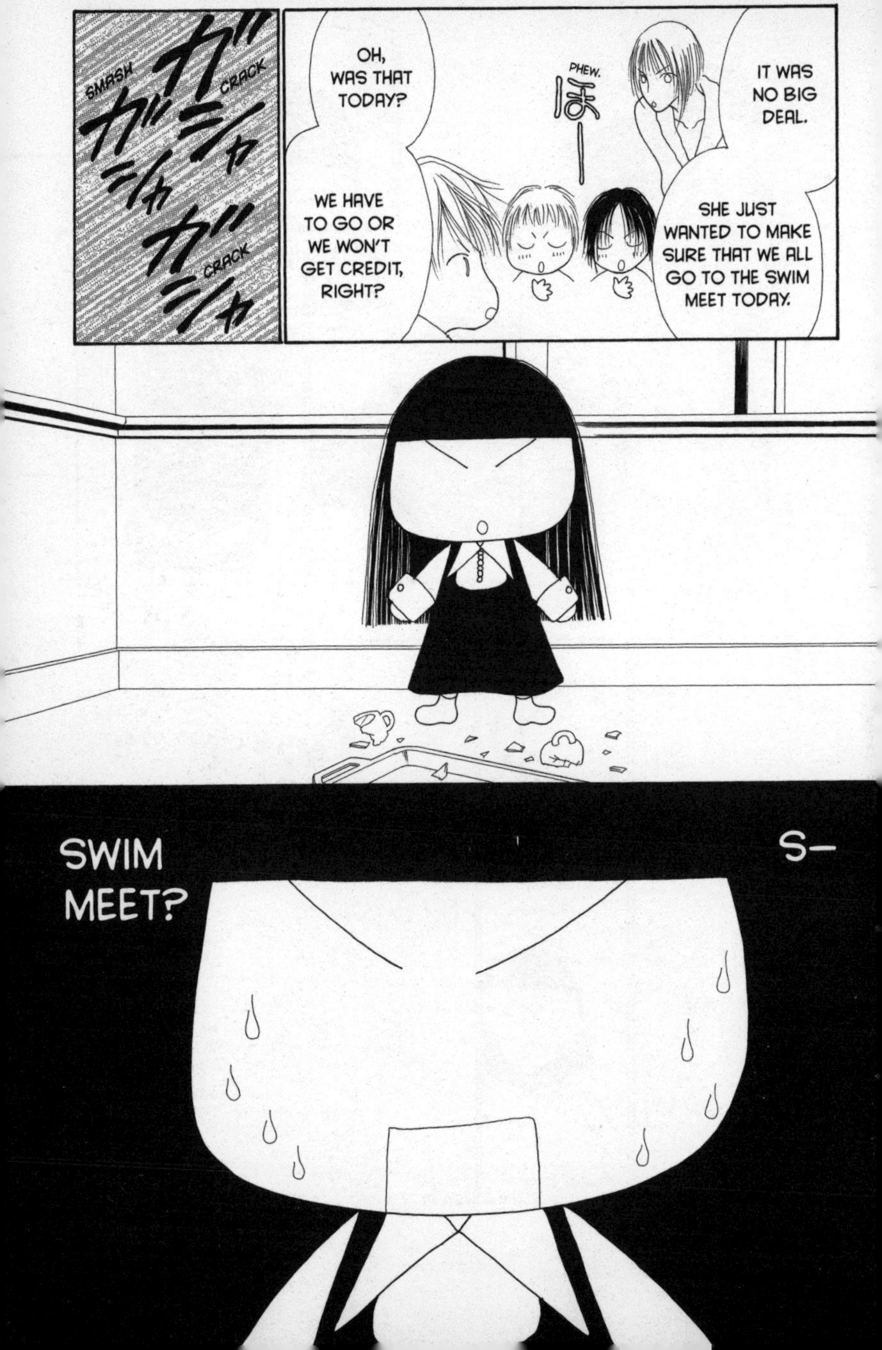
IT WAS NO BIG DEAL.
SHE JUST WANTED TO MAKE SURE THAT WE ALL GO TO THE SWIM MEET TODAY.
PHEW.
ほー
OH, WAS THAT TODAY?
WE HAVE TO GO OR WE WON'T GET CREDIT, RIGHT?
SMASH
CRACK
CRACK
S—
SWIM MEET?

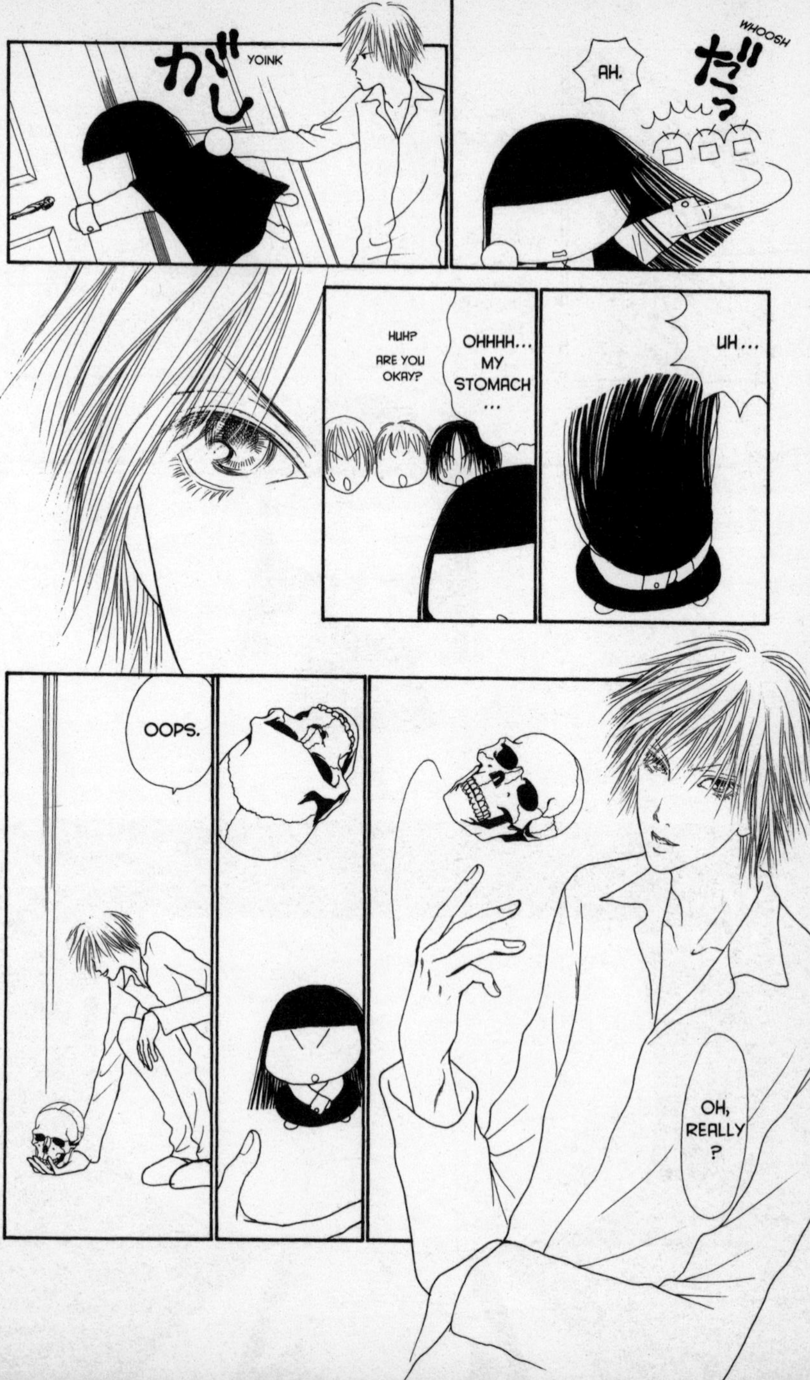
AH.
だっ
WHOOSH
がし
YOINK
UH...
OHHHH... MY STOMACH ...
HUH? ARE YOU OKAY?
OH, REALLY ?
OOPS.

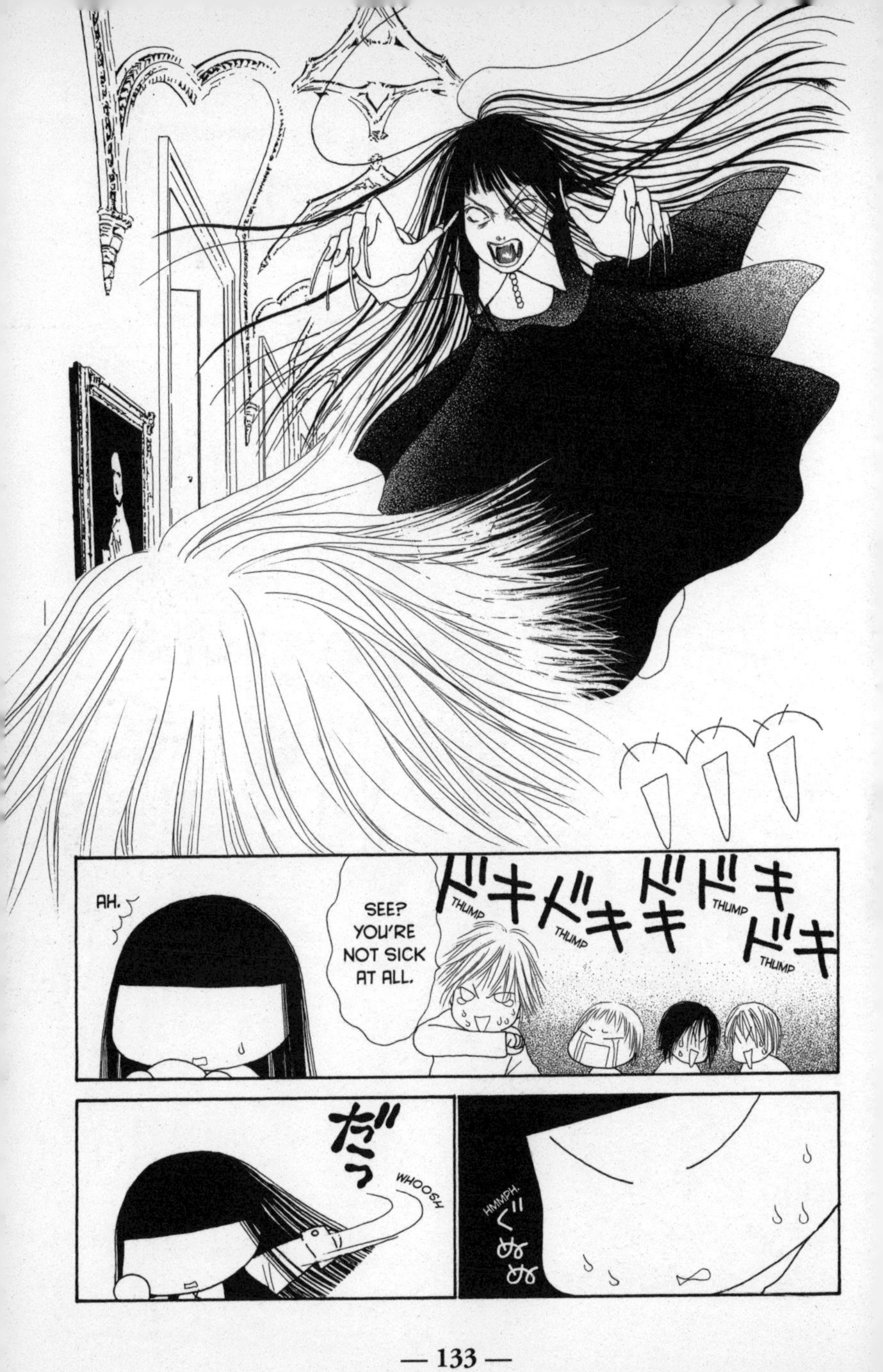
ドキドキドキドキドキ
THUMP
THUMP
THUMP
THUMP
SEE? YOU'RE NOT SICK AT ALL.
AH.
ぐぬぬ
HMMPH.
だっ
WHOOSH

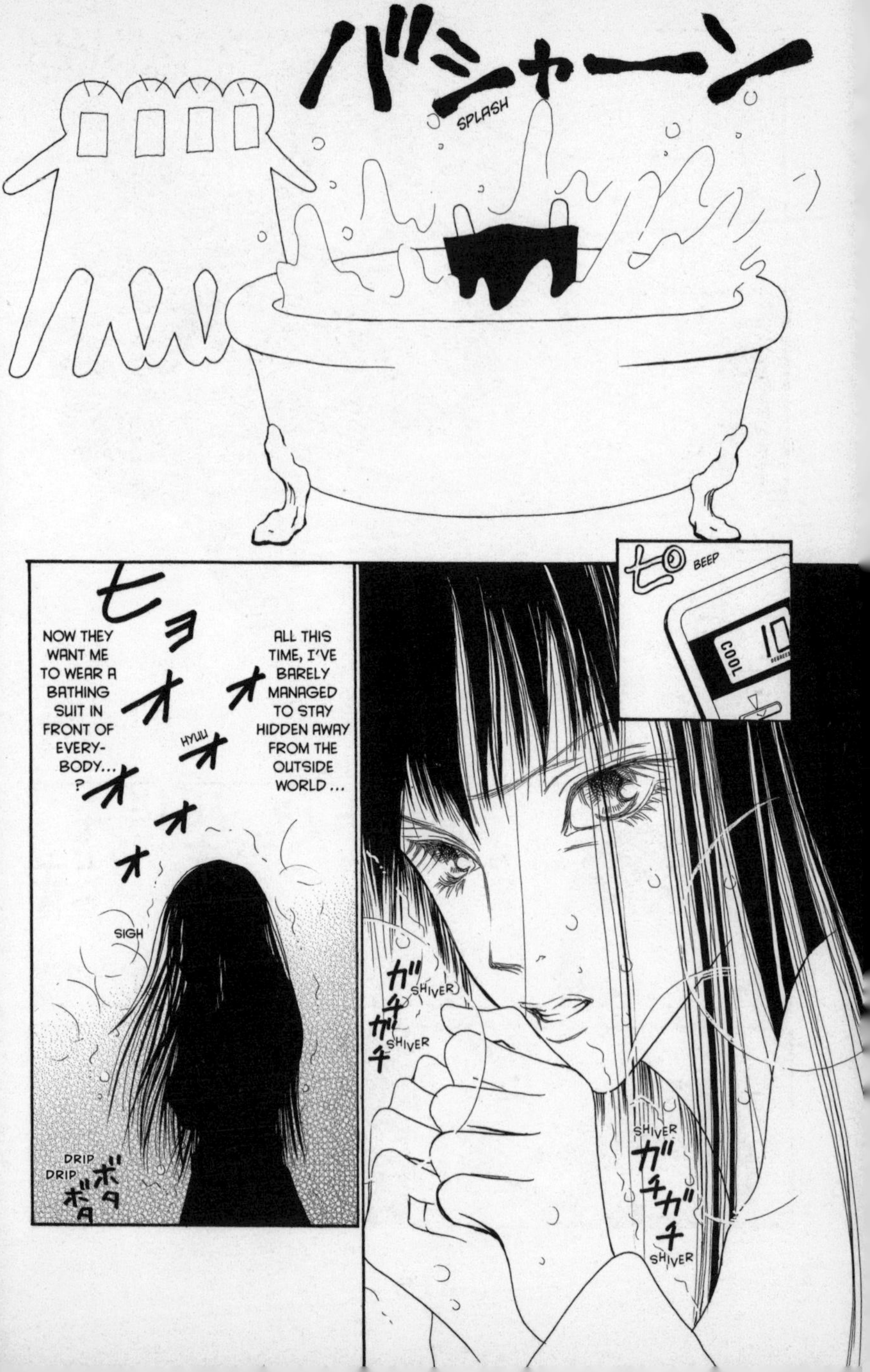
バシャーン
SPLASH
ピ
BEEP
COOL
10
ガチガチ
SHIVER
SHIVER
SHIVER
ガチガチ
SHIVER
ヒョオオオオオオ
HYUU
ALL THIS TIME, I'VE BARELY MANAGED TO STAY HIDDEN AWAY FROM THE OUTSIDE WORLD...
NOW THEY WANT ME TO WEAR A BATHING SUIT IN FRONT OF EVERYBODY...?
SIGH
DRIP DRIP
ボタボタ

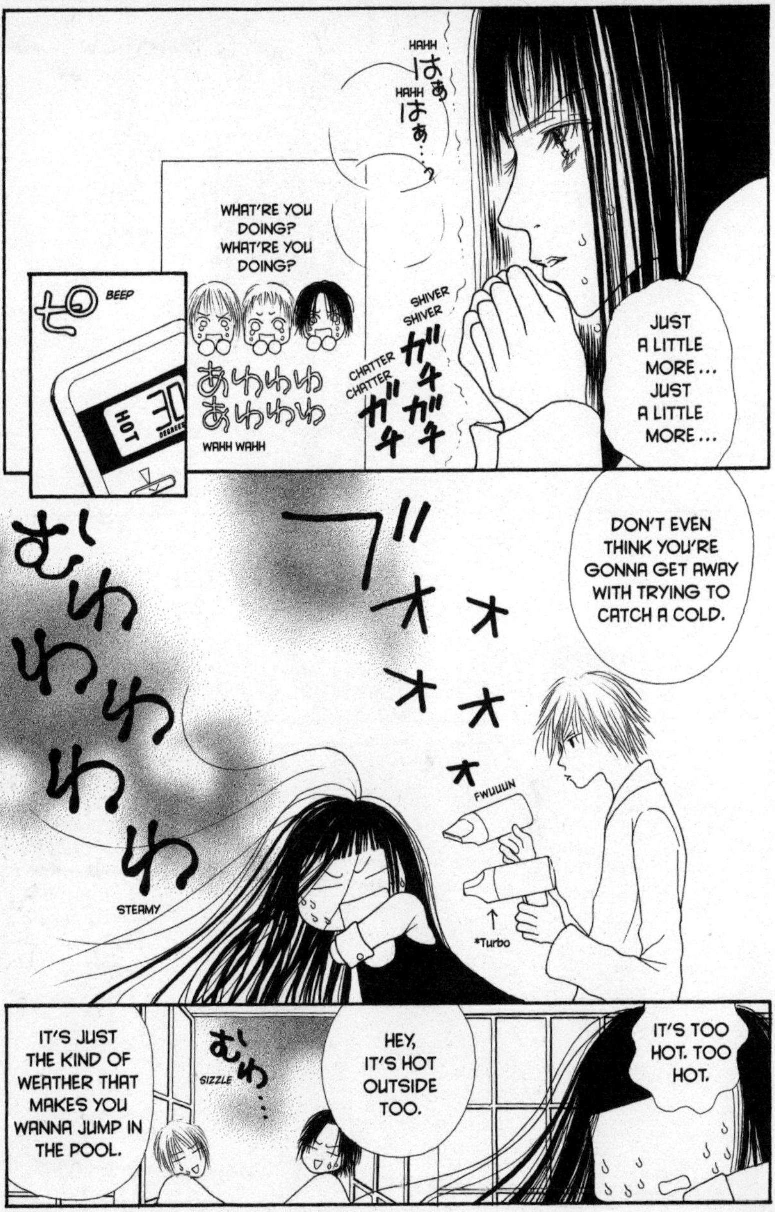
JUST A LITTLE MORE… JUST A LITTLE MORE…
はぁはぁ…
HAHH HAHH
ガチガチ
SHIVER SHIVER
CHATTER CHATTER
WHAT'RE YOU DOING? WHAT'RE YOU DOING?
あわわわ あわわわ
WAHH WAHH
ぴ
BEEP
HOT 30 DEGREES
DON'T EVEN THINK YOU'RE GONNA GET AWAY WITH TRYING TO CATCH A COLD.
ブオオオオオ
FWUUUN
*Turbo
むわわわわわ
STEAMY
IT'S TOO HOT. TOO HOT.
HEY, IT'S HOT OUTSIDE TOO.
むわ…
SIZZLE
IT'S JUST THE KIND OF WEATHER THAT MAKES YOU WANNA JUMP IN THE POOL.

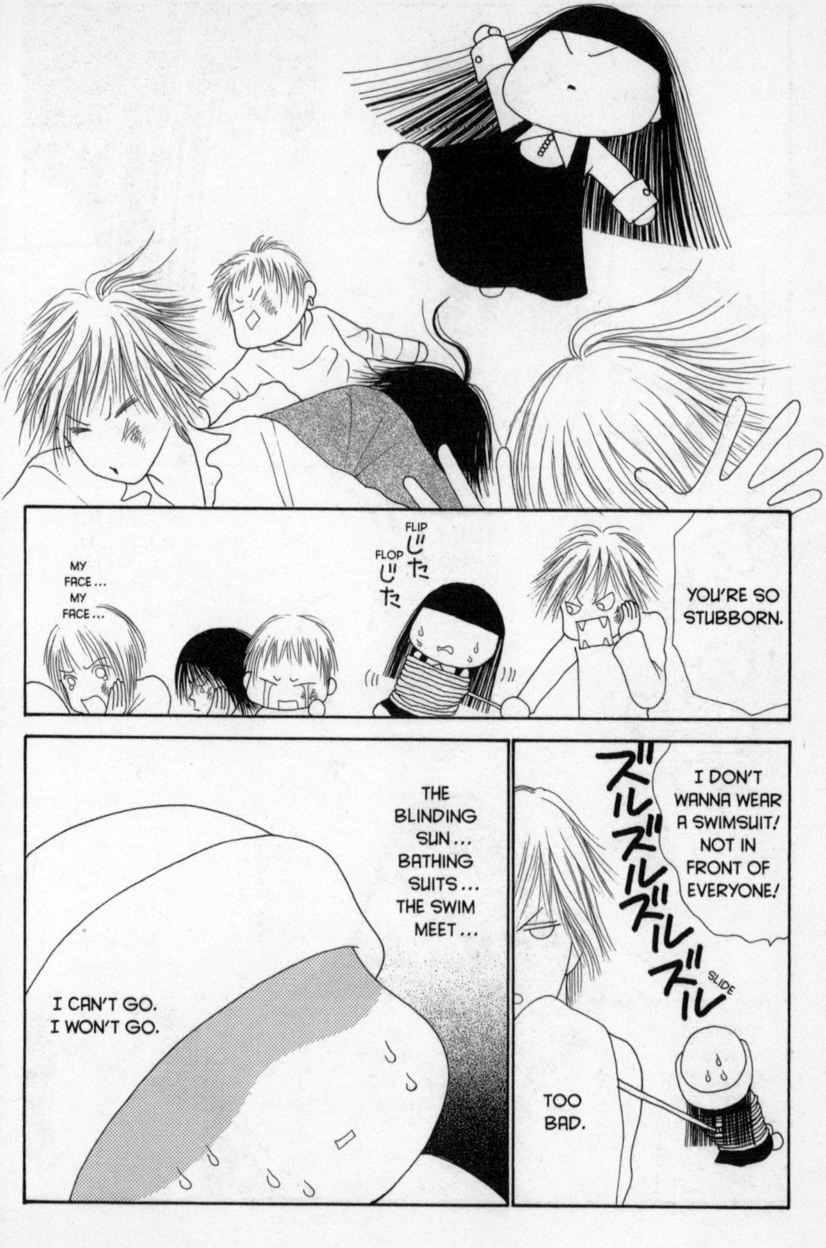
YOU'RE SO STUBBORN.
FLIP じた
FLOP じた
MY FACE... MY FACE...
I DON'T WANNA WEAR A SWIMSUIT! NOT IN FRONT OF EVERYONE!
ズルズルズルズル
SLIDE
TOO BAD.
THE BLINDING SUN... BATHING SUITS... THE SWIM MEET...
I CAN'T GO. I WON'T GO.

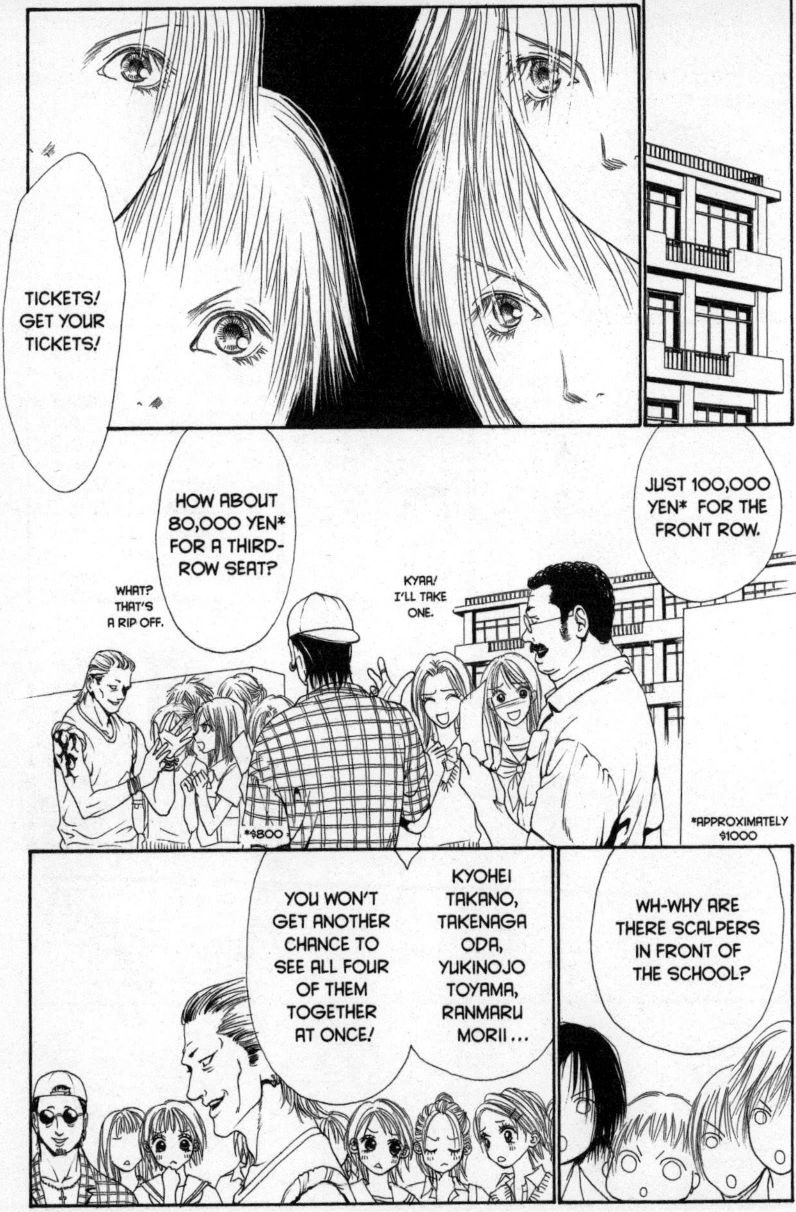
TICKETS! GET YOUR TICKETS!
JUST 100,000 YEN* FOR THE FRONT ROW.
KYAA! I'LL TAKE ONE.
HOW ABOUT 80,000 YEN* FOR A THIRD-ROW SEAT?
WHAT? THAT'S A RIP OFF.
*APPROXIMATELY $1000
*$800
WH-WHY ARE THERE SCALPERS IN FRONT OF THE SCHOOL?
KYOHEI TAKANO, TAKENAGA ODA, YUKINOJO TOYAMA, RANMARU MORII ...
YOU WON'T GET ANOTHER CHANCE TO SEE ALL FOUR OF THEM TOGETHER AT ONCE!

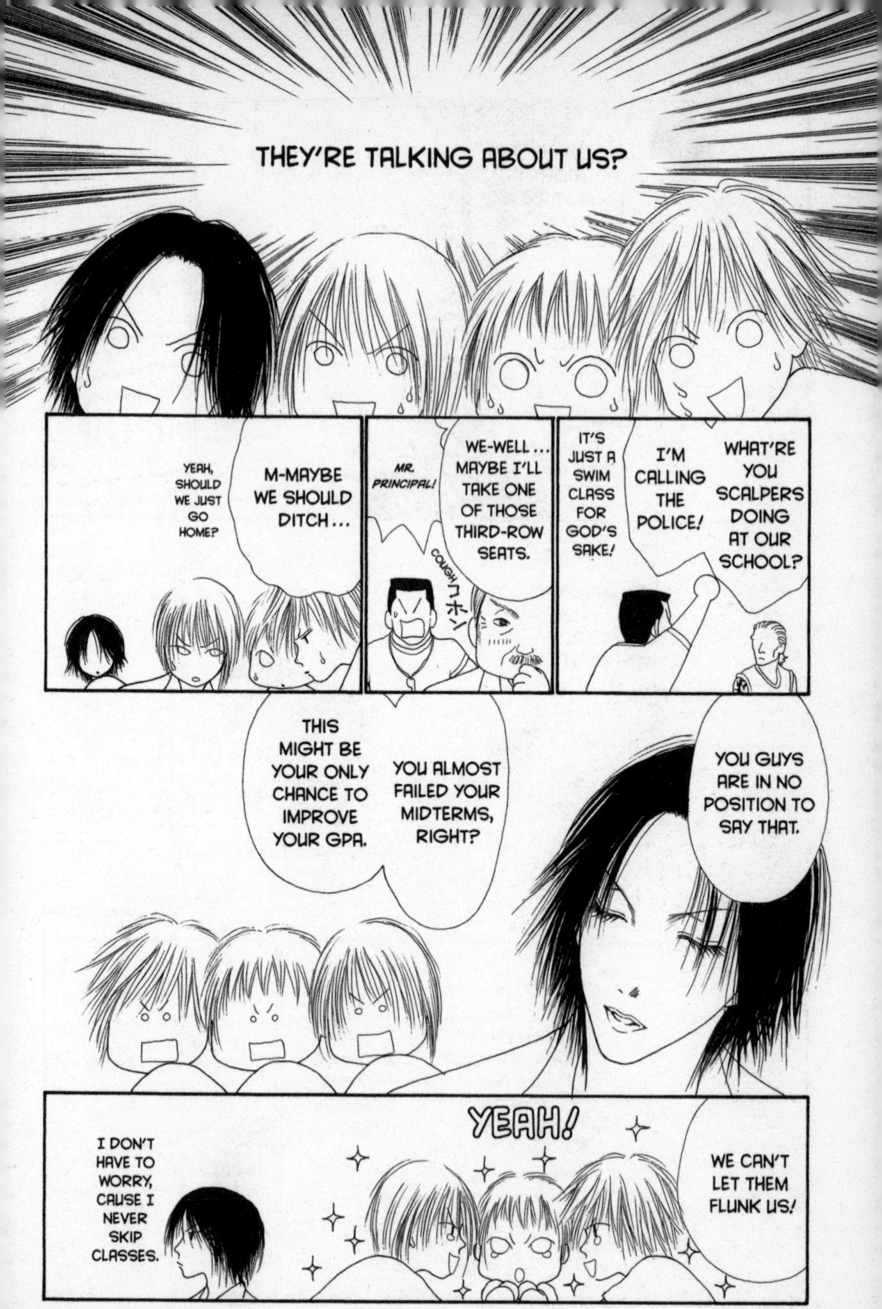
THEY'RE TALKING ABOUT US?
WHAT'RE YOU SCALPERS DOING AT OUR SCHOOL?
I'M CALLING THE POLICE!
IT'S JUST A SWIM CLASS FOR GOD'S SAKE!
WE-WELL... MAYBE I'LL TAKE ONE OF THOSE THIRD-ROW SEATS.
MR. PRINCIPAL!
COUGH コホン
M-MAYBE WE SHOULD DITCH...
YEAH, SHOULD WE JUST GO HOME?
YOU GUYS ARE IN NO POSITION TO SAY THAT.
YOU ALMOST FAILED YOUR MIDTERMS, RIGHT?
THIS MIGHT BE YOUR ONLY CHANCE TO IMPROVE YOUR GPA.
WE CAN'T LET THEM FLUNK US!
YEAH!
I DON'T HAVE TO WORRY, CAUSE I NEVER SKIP CLASSES.

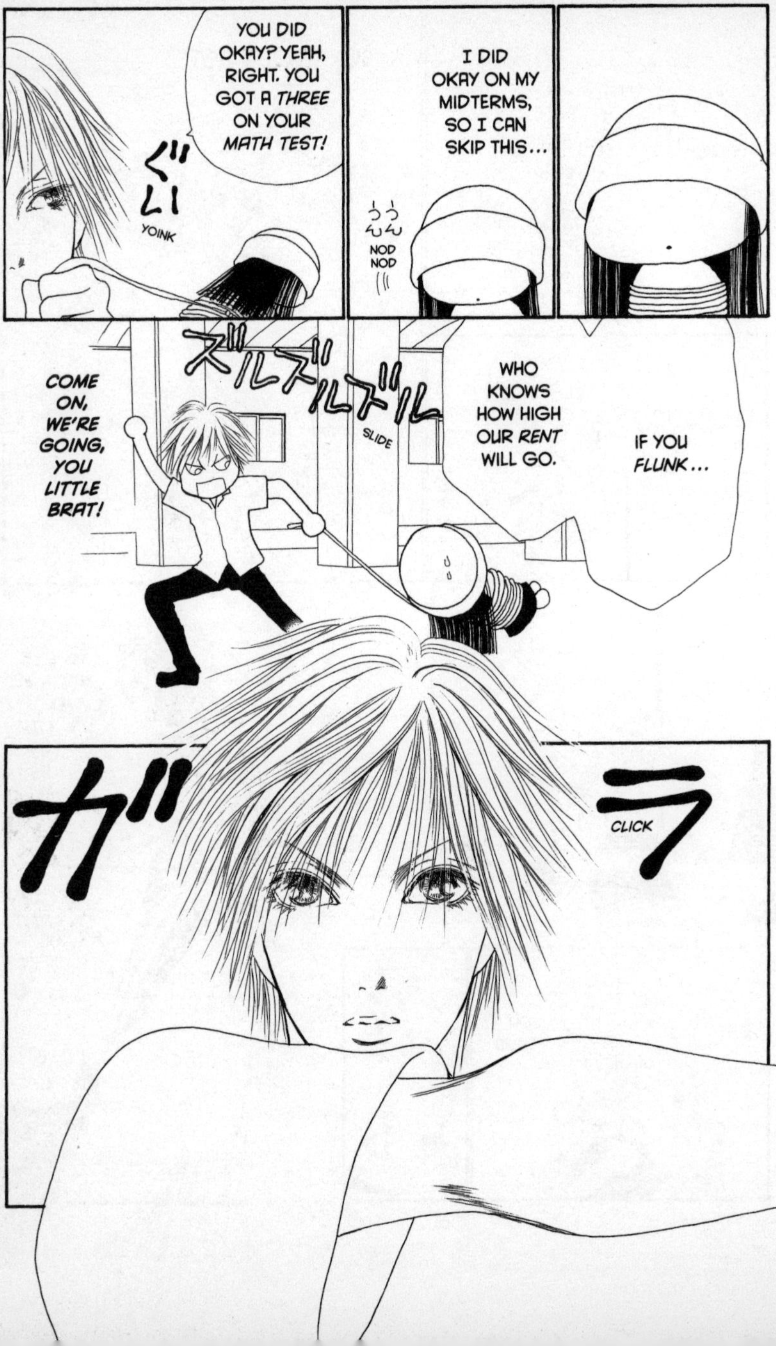
I DID OKAY ON MY MIDTERMS, SO I CAN SKIP THIS…
うんうん
NOD NOD
YOU DID OKAY? YEAH, RIGHT. YOU GOT A *THREE* ON YOUR *MATH TEST!*
ぐい
YOINK
IF YOU *FLUNK*…
WHO KNOWS HOW HIGH OUR *RENT* WILL GO.
ズルズルズル
SLIDE
COME ON, WE'RE GOING, YOU LITTLE BRAT!
ガラ
CLICK

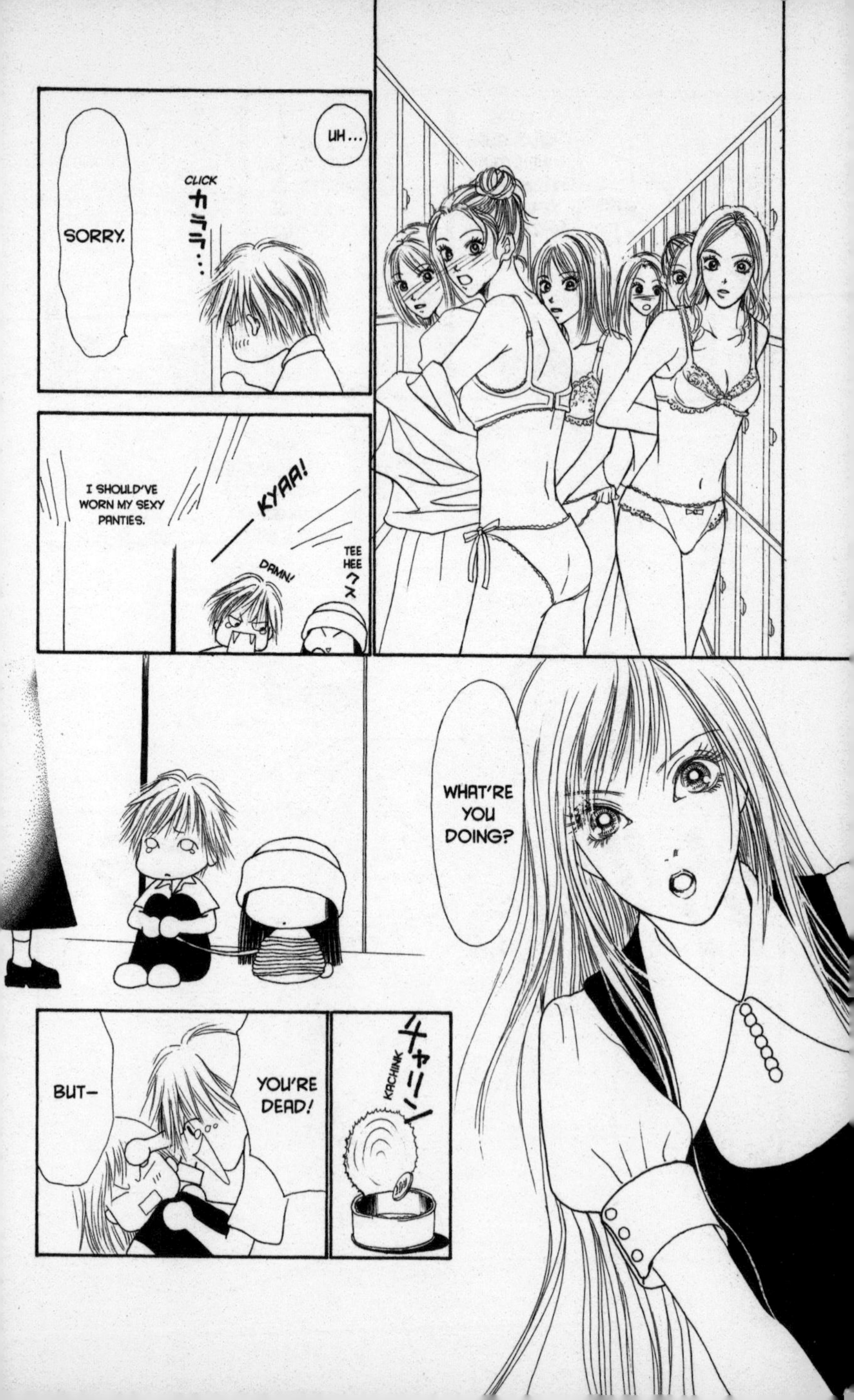
UH...
CLICK
カララ...
SORRY.
KYAA!
TEE HEE
クス
DAMN!
I SHOULD'VE WORN MY SEXY PANTIES.
WHAT'RE YOU DOING?
KACHINK
チャリン!
YOU'RE DEAD!
BUT–

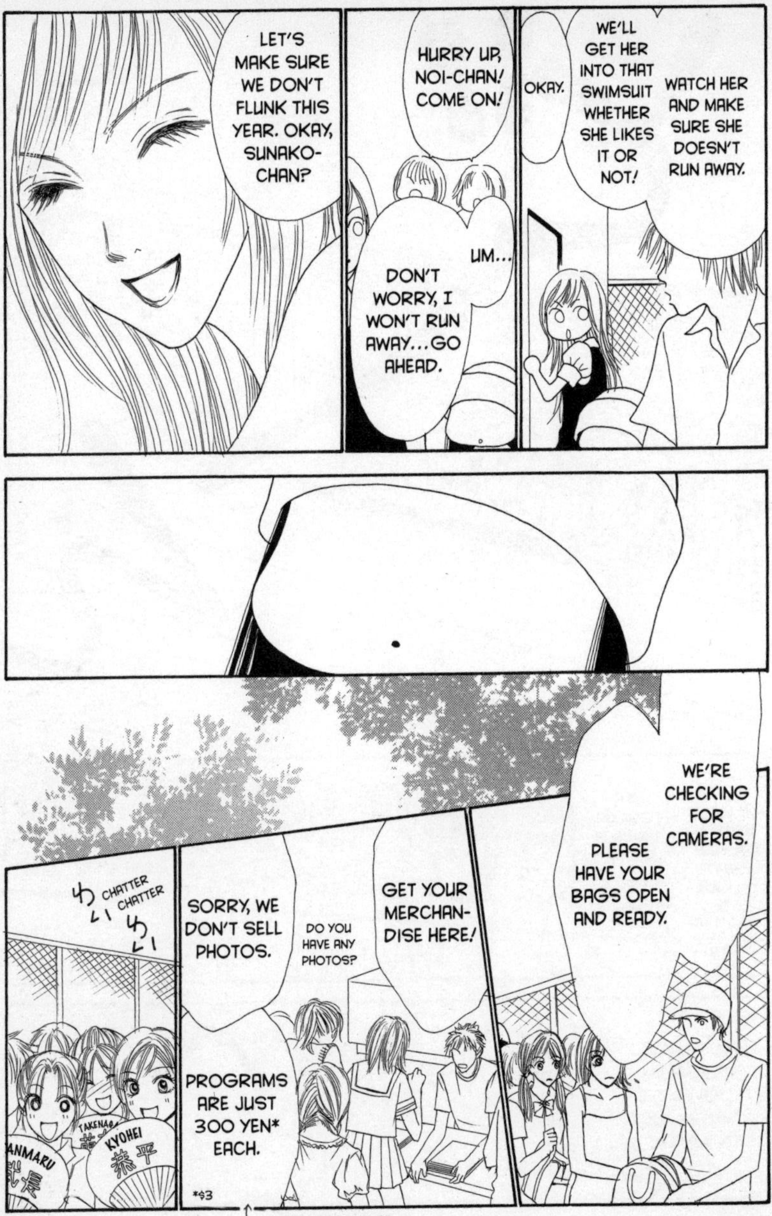
WATCH HER AND MAKE SURE SHE DOESN'T RUN AWAY.
WE'LL GET HER INTO THAT SWIMSUIT WHETHER SHE LIKES IT OR NOT!
OKAY.
HURRY UP, NOI-CHAN! COME ON!
UM...
DON'T WORRY, I WON'T RUN AWAY...GO AHEAD.
LET'S MAKE SURE WE DON'T FLUNK THIS YEAR. OKAY, SUNAKO-CHAN?
WE'RE CHECKING FOR CAMERAS.
PLEASE HAVE YOUR BAGS OPEN AND READY.
GET YOUR MERCHAN-DISE HERE!
DO YOU HAVE ANY PHOTOS?
SORRY, WE DON'T SELL PHOTOS.
PROGRAMS ARE JUST 300 YEN* EACH.
*$3
わいわい CHATTER CHATTER
KYOHEI 恭平

JUST A LIST OF NAMES.

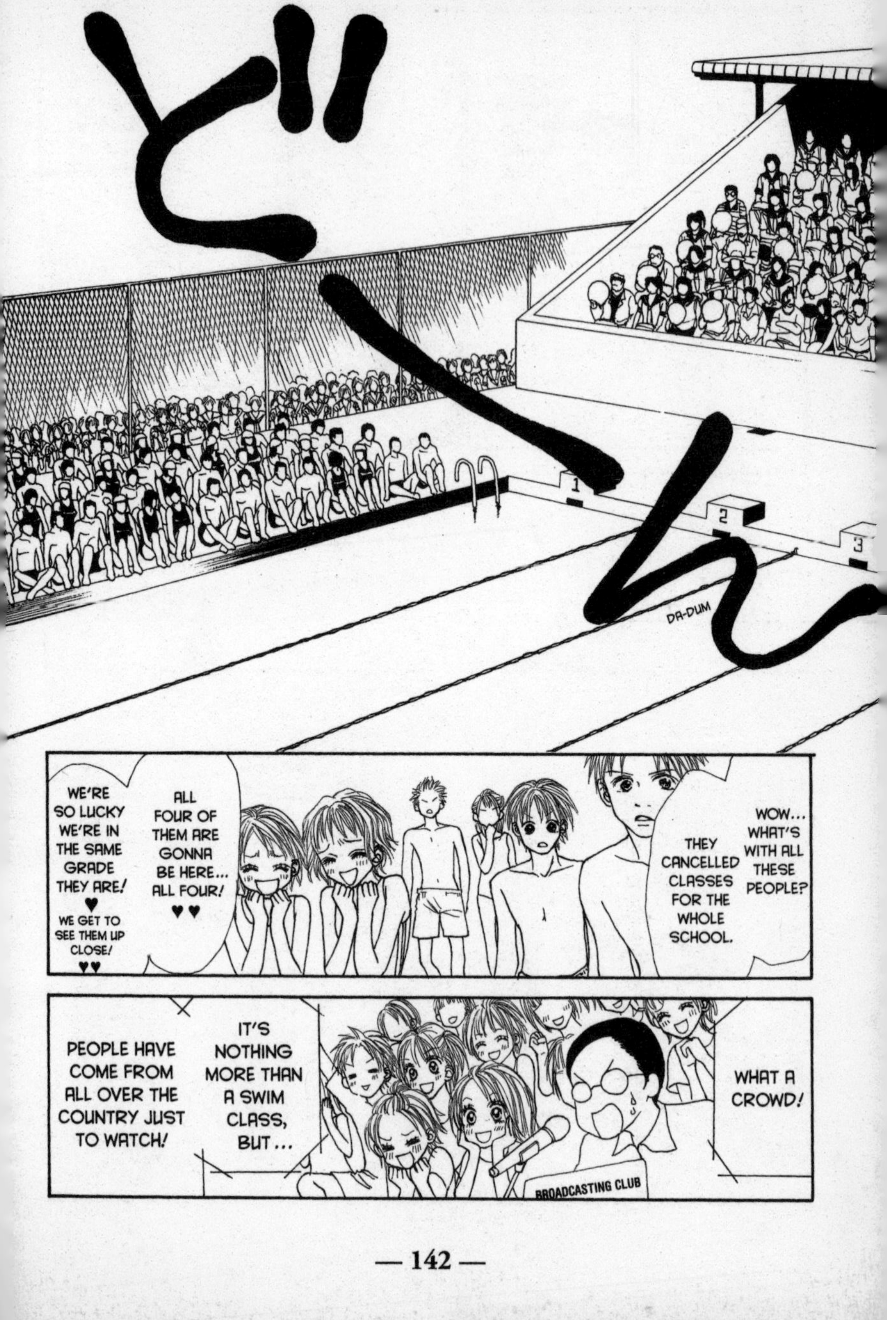
どーん
DA-DUM
WOW... WHAT'S WITH ALL THESE PEOPLE?
THEY CANCELLED CLASSES FOR THE WHOLE SCHOOL.
ALL FOUR OF THEM ARE GONNA BE HERE... ALL FOUR! ♥♥
WE'RE SO LUCKY WE'RE IN THE SAME GRADE THEY ARE! ♥
WE GET TO SEE THEM UP CLOSE! ♥♥
WHAT A CROWD!
BROADCASTING CLUB
IT'S NOTHING MORE THAN A SWIM CLASS, BUT...
PEOPLE HAVE COME FROM ALL OVER THE COUNTRY JUST TO WATCH!

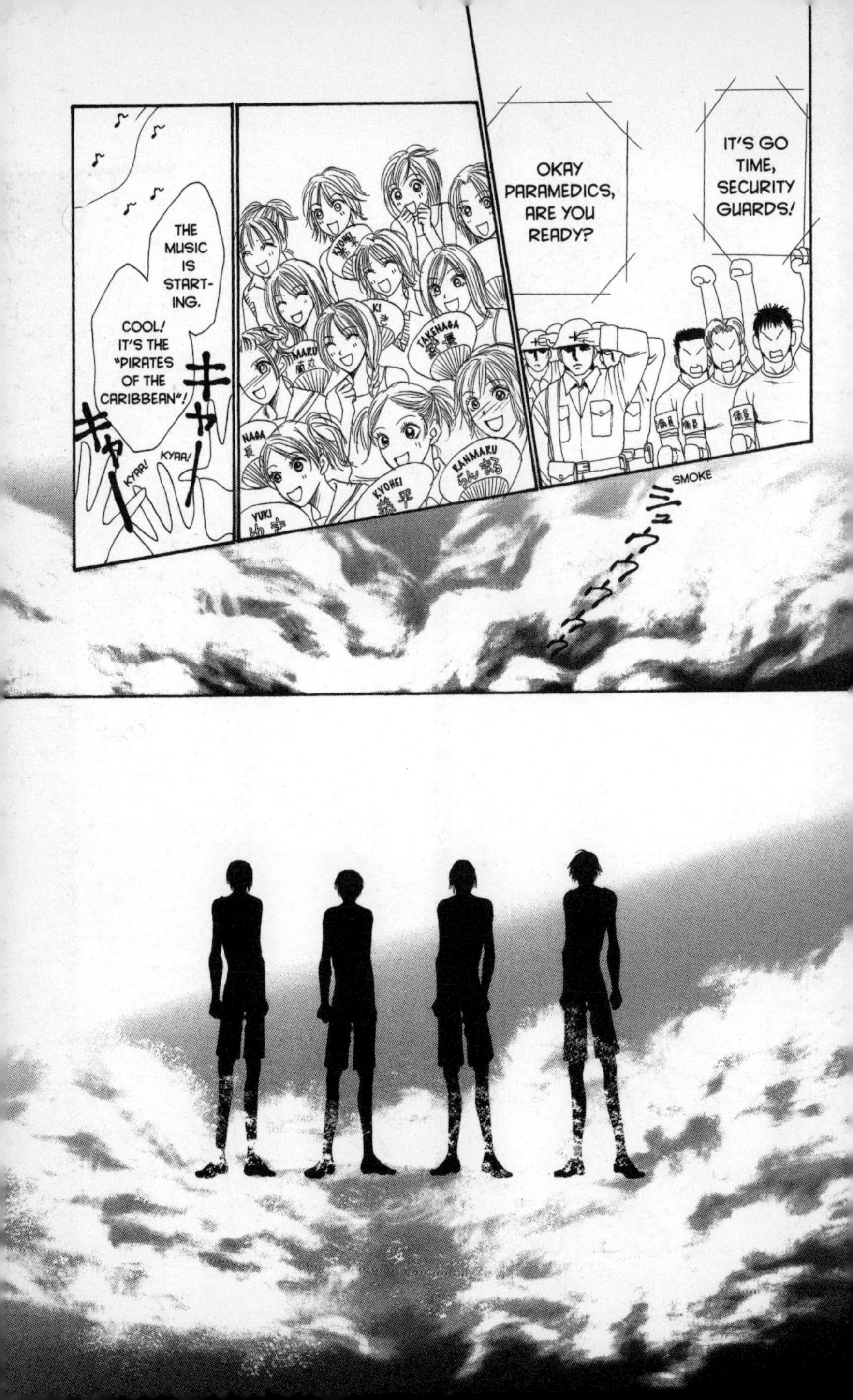
IT'S GO TIME, SECURITY GUARDS!
OKAY PARAMEDICS, ARE YOU READY?
KYOHEI
KI
TAKENAGA
MARU
NAGA
RANMARU
KYOHEI
YUKI
THE MUSIC IS STARTING.
COOL! IT'S THE "PIRATES OF THE CARIBBEAN"!
KYAA!
KYAA!
SMOKE

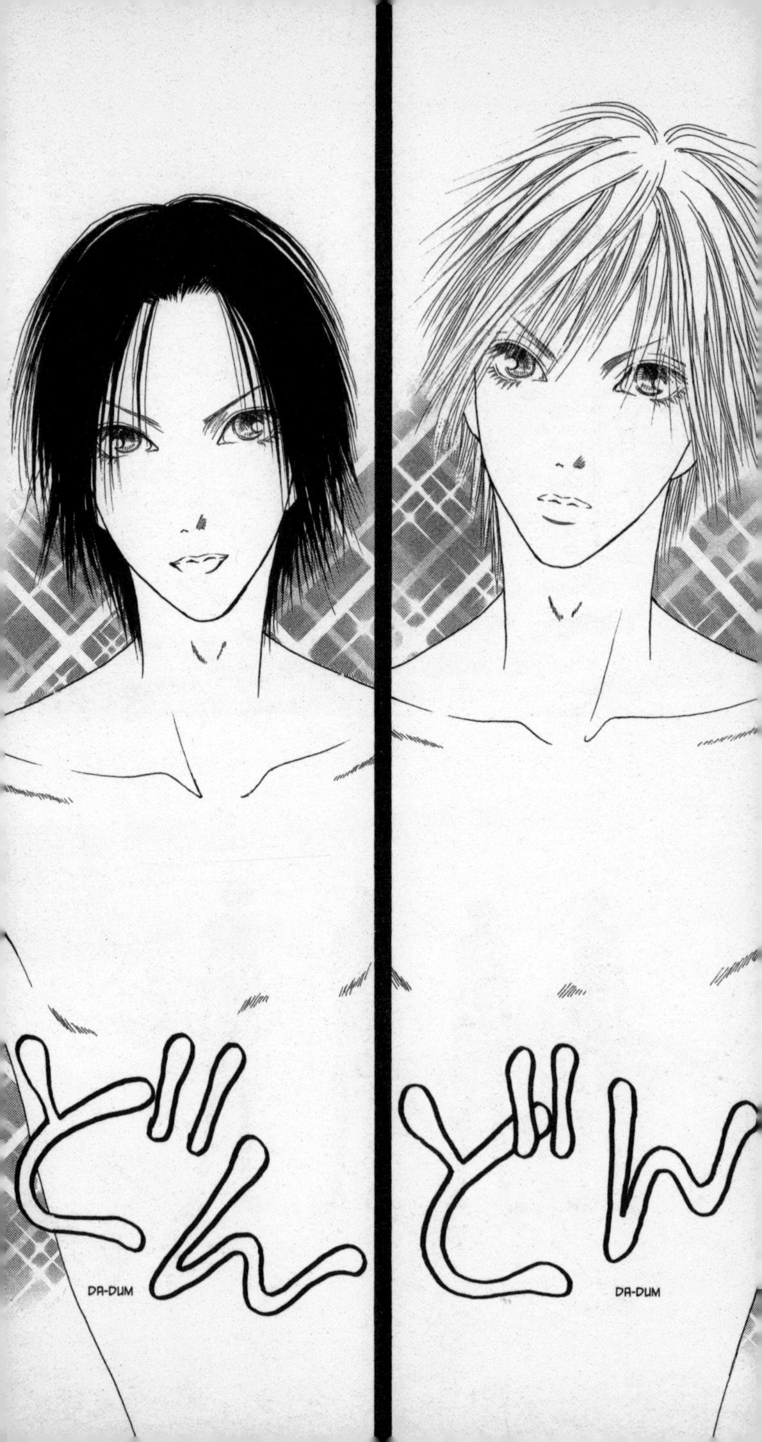
どん
DA-DUM
どん
DA-DUM

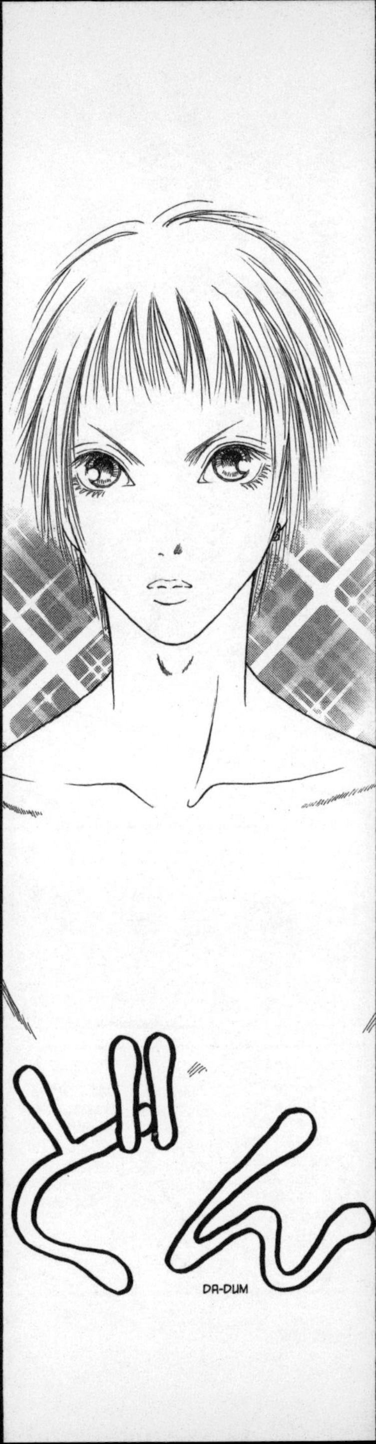
どん
DA-DUM
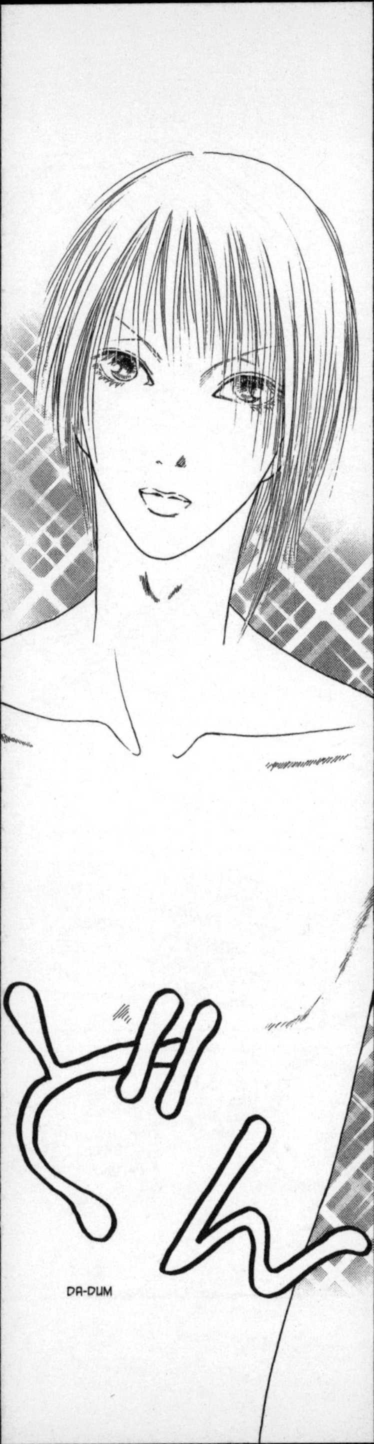
どん
DA-DUM

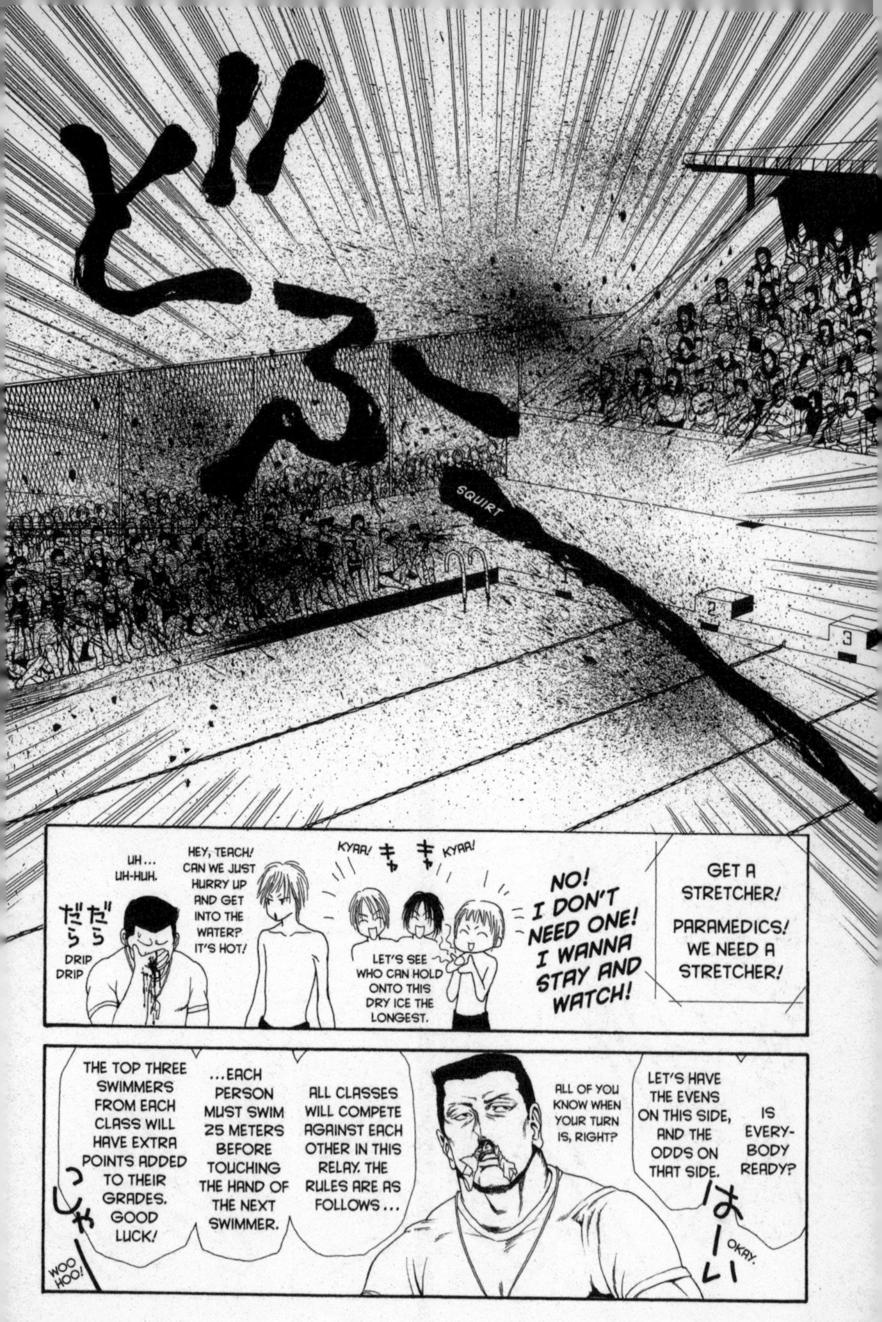
SQUIRT
GET A STRETCHER!
PARAMEDICS! WE NEED A STRETCHER!
NO! I DON'T NEED ONE! I WANNA STAY AND WATCH!
KYAA! KYAA!
LET'S SEE WHO CAN HOLD ONTO THIS DRY ICE THE LONGEST.
HEY, TEACH! CAN WE JUST HURRY UP AND GET INTO THE WATER? IT'S HOT!
UH... UH-HUH.
だらだら
DRIP DRIP
IS EVERY-BODY READY?
はーい
OKAY.
LET'S HAVE THE EVENS ON THIS SIDE, AND THE ODDS ON THAT SIDE.
ALL OF YOU KNOW WHEN YOUR TURN IS, RIGHT?
ALL CLASSES WILL COMPETE AGAINST EACH OTHER IN THIS RELAY. THE RULES ARE AS FOLLOWS...
...EACH PERSON MUST SWIM 25 METERS BEFORE TOUCHING THE HAND OF THE NEXT SWIMMER.
THE TOP THREE SWIMMERS FROM EACH CLASS WILL HAVE EXTRA POINTS ADDED TO THEIR GRADES. GOOD LUCK!
WOO HOO!

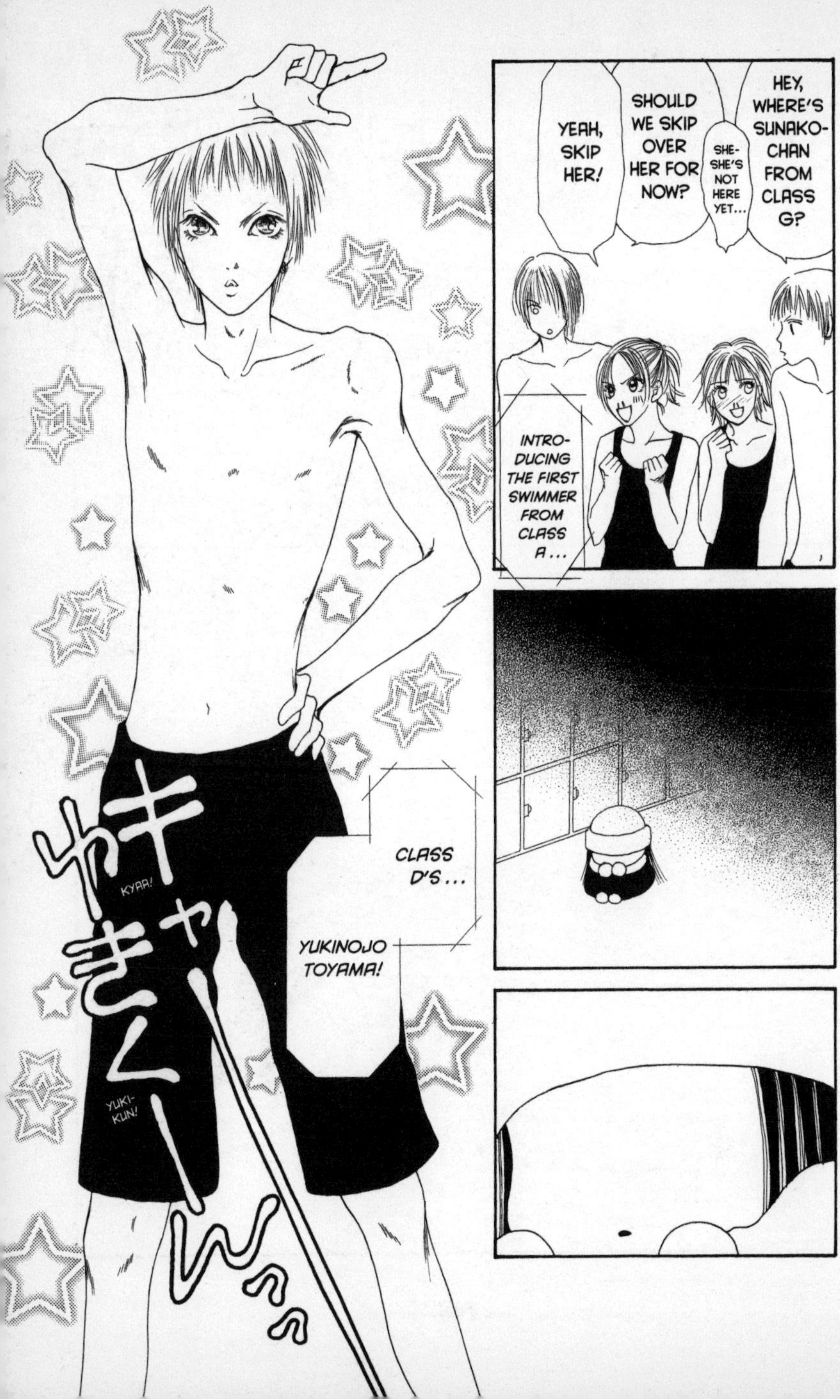
HEY, WHERE'S SUNAKO-CHAN FROM CLASS G?
SHE-SHE'S NOT HERE YET...
SHOULD WE SKIP OVER HER FOR NOW?
YEAH, SKIP HER!
INTRODUCING THE FIRST SWIMMER FROM CLASS A...
CLASS D'S...
YUKINOJO TOYAMA!
キャー
KYAA!
ゆきくーん
YUKI-KUN!

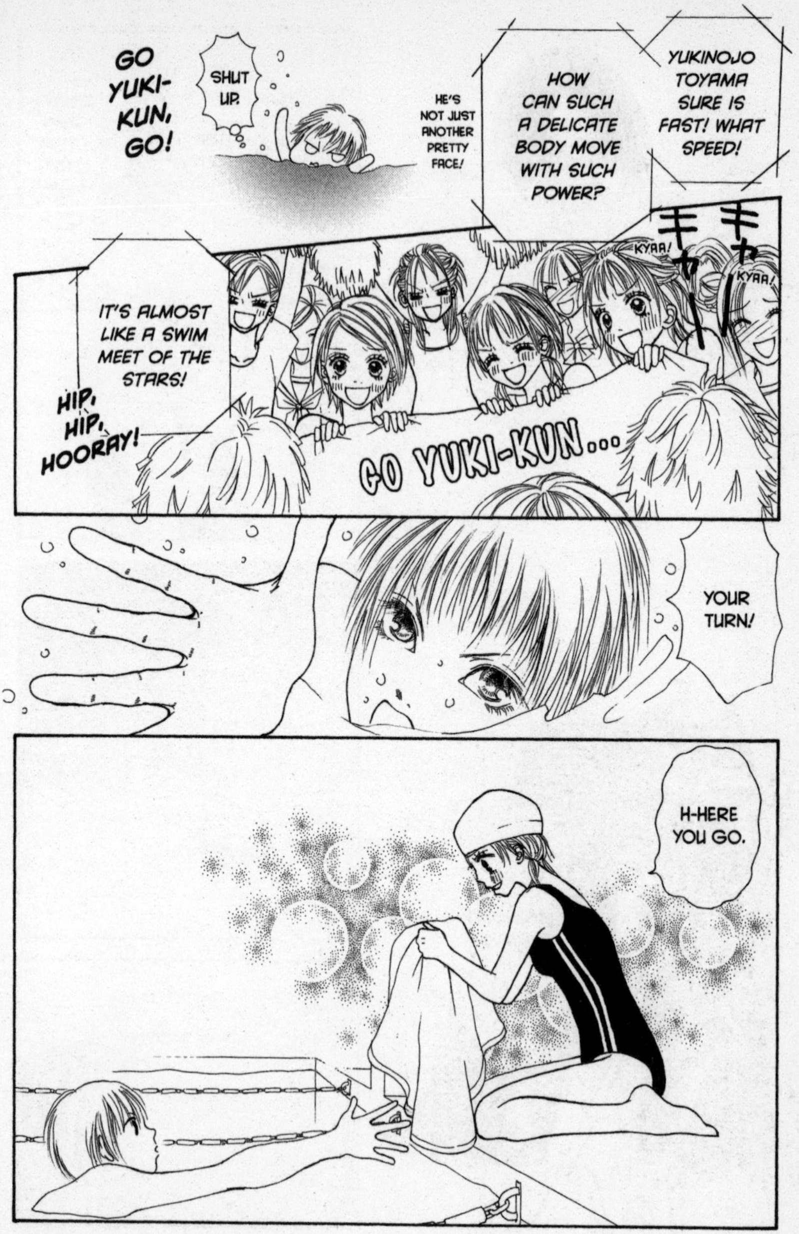
YUKINOJO TOYAMA SURE IS FAST! WHAT SPEED!
HOW CAN SUCH A DELICATE BODY MOVE WITH SUCH POWER?
HE'S NOT JUST ANOTHER PRETTY FACE!
SHUT UP.
GO YUKI-KUN, GO!
キャー
キャー
KYAA!
KYAA!
IT'S ALMOST LIKE A SWIM MEET OF THE STARS!
HIP, HIP, HOORAY!
GO YUKI-KUN...
YOUR TURN!
H-HERE YOU GO.

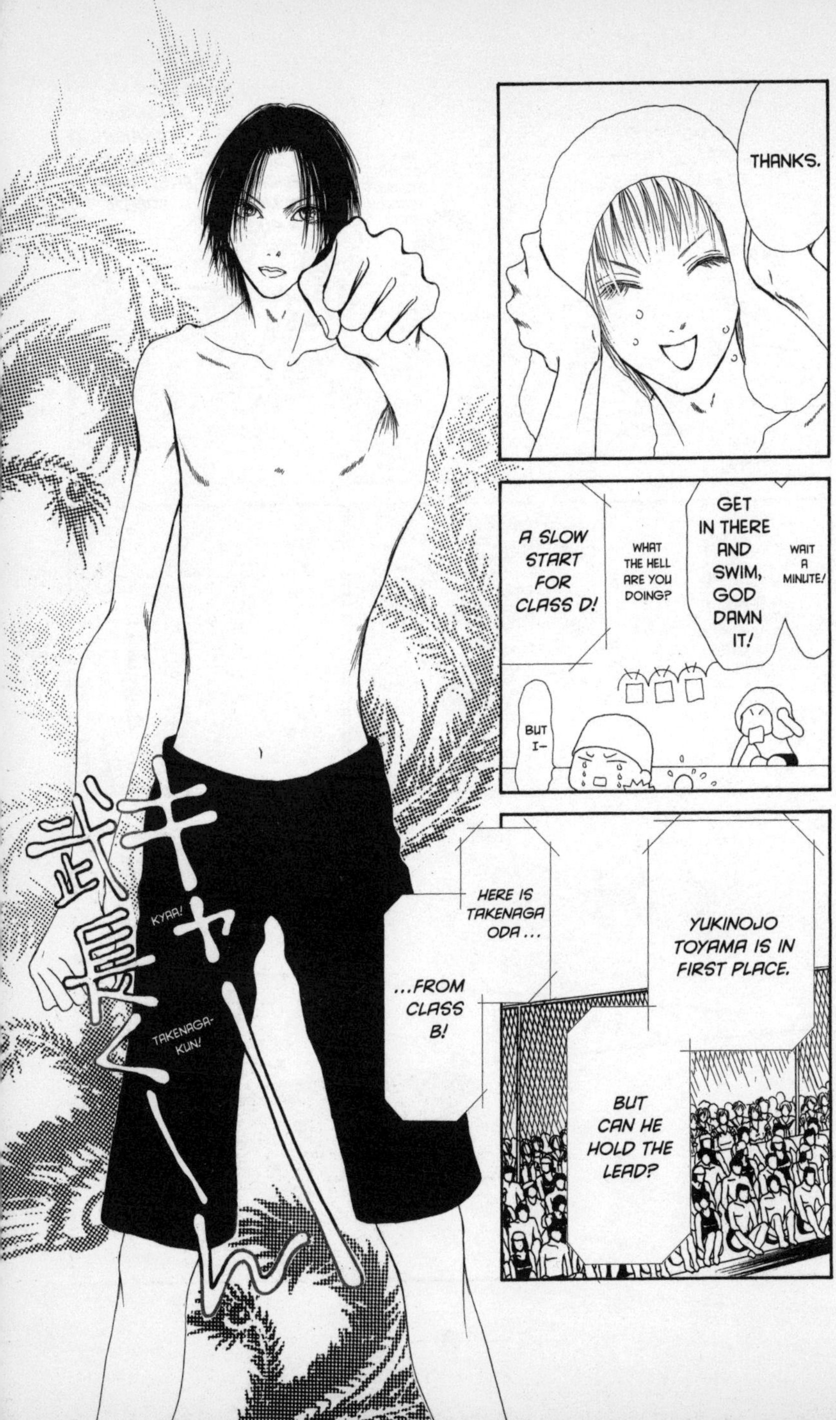
THANKS.
WAIT A MINUTE!
GET IN THERE AND SWIM, GOD DAMN IT!
WHAT THE HELL ARE YOU DOING?
A SLOW START FOR CLASS D!
BUT I–
YUKINOJO TOYAMA IS IN FIRST PLACE.
BUT CAN HE HOLD THE LEAD?
HERE IS TAKENAGA ODA...
...FROM CLASS B!
キャ〜
武長くん
KYAA!
TAKENAGA-KUN!

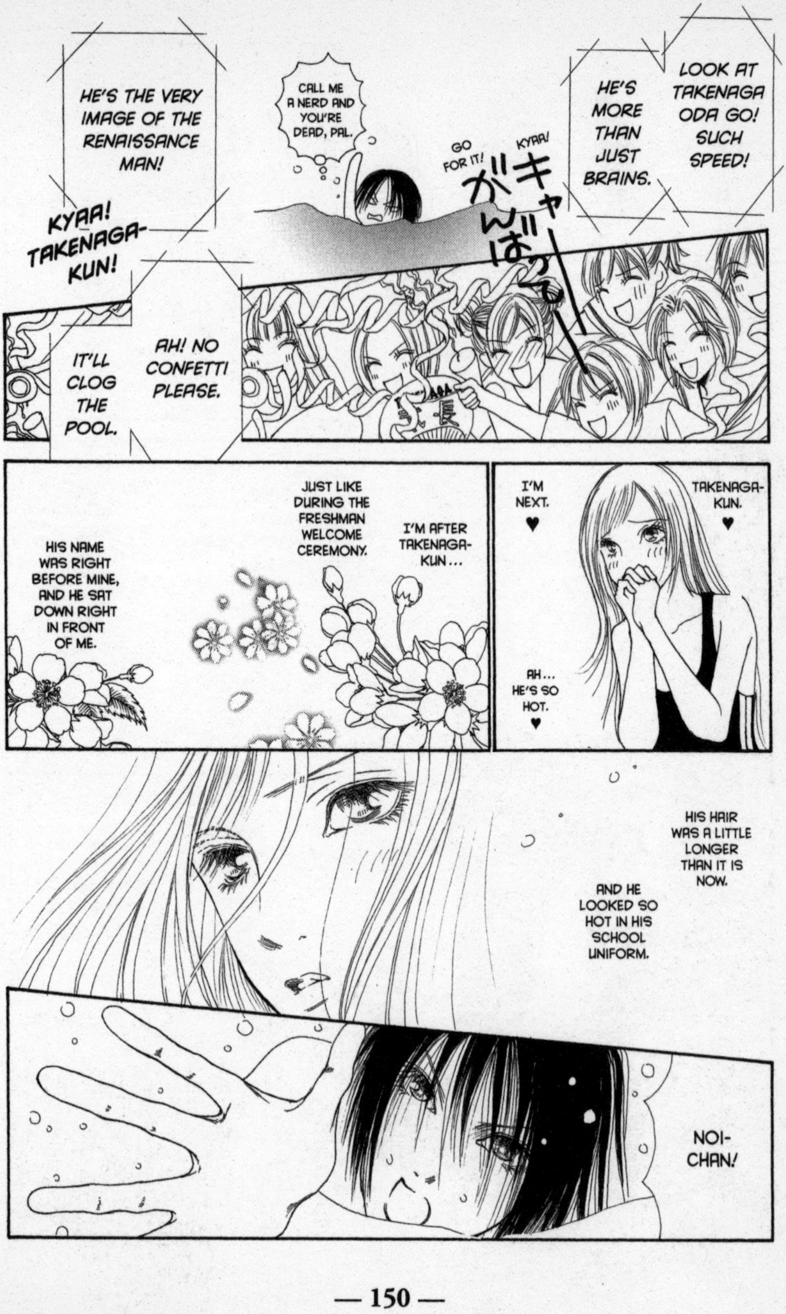
LOOK AT TAKENAGA ODA GO! SUCH SPEED!
HE'S MORE THAN JUST BRAINS.
KYAA!
キャー
GO FOR IT!
がんばって
CALL ME A NERD AND YOU'RE DEAD, PAL.
HE'S THE VERY IMAGE OF THE RENAISSANCE MAN!
KYAA! TAKENAGA-KUN!
AH! NO CONFETTI PLEASE.
IT'LL CLOG THE POOL.
TAKENAGA-KUN. ♥
I'M NEXT. ♥
AH... HE'S SO HOT. ♥
I'M AFTER TAKENAGA-KUN...
JUST LIKE DURING THE FRESHMAN WELCOME CEREMONY.
HIS NAME WAS RIGHT BEFORE MINE, AND HE SAT DOWN RIGHT IN FRONT OF ME.
HIS HAIR WAS A LITTLE LONGER THAN IT IS NOW.
AND HE LOOKED SO HOT IN HIS SCHOOL UNIFORM.
NOI-CHAN!

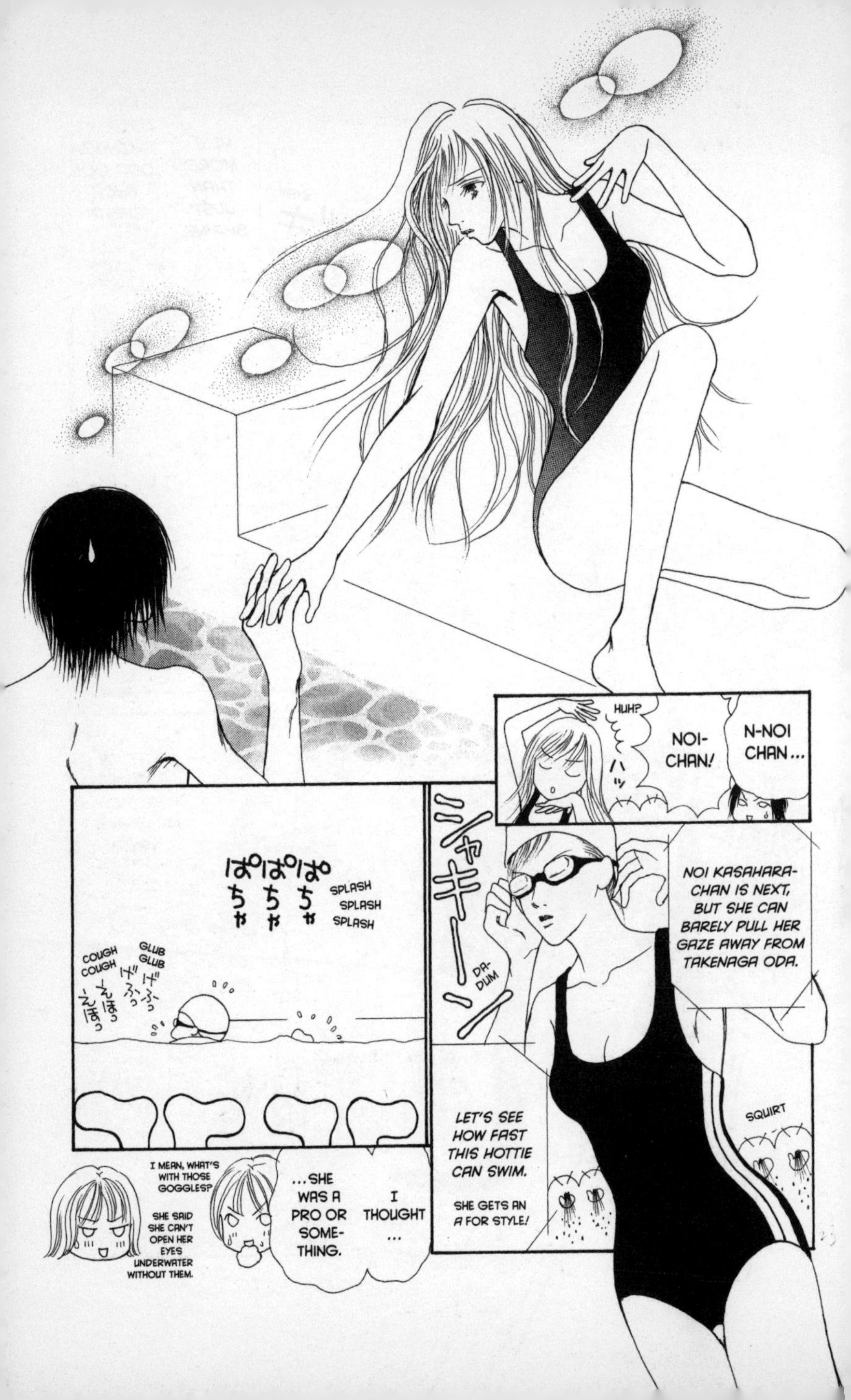
N-NOI CHAN...
NOI-CHAN!
HUH?
ハッ
シャキーン
NOI KASAHARA-CHAN IS NEXT, BUT SHE CAN BARELY PULL HER GAZE AWAY FROM TAKENAGA ODA.
DA-DUM
SQUIRT
LET'S SEE HOW FAST THIS HOTTIE CAN SWIM.
SHE GETS AN A FOR STYLE!
ぱちゃぱちゃぱちゃ
SPLASH SPLASH SPLASH
ガぶっ ガぶっ
GLUB GLUB
えほっ えほっ
COUGH COUGH
I THOUGHT ...
...SHE WAS A PRO OR SOME-THING.
I MEAN, WHAT'S WITH THOSE GOGGLES?
SHE SAID SHE CAN'T OPEN HER EYES UNDERWATER WITHOUT THEM.

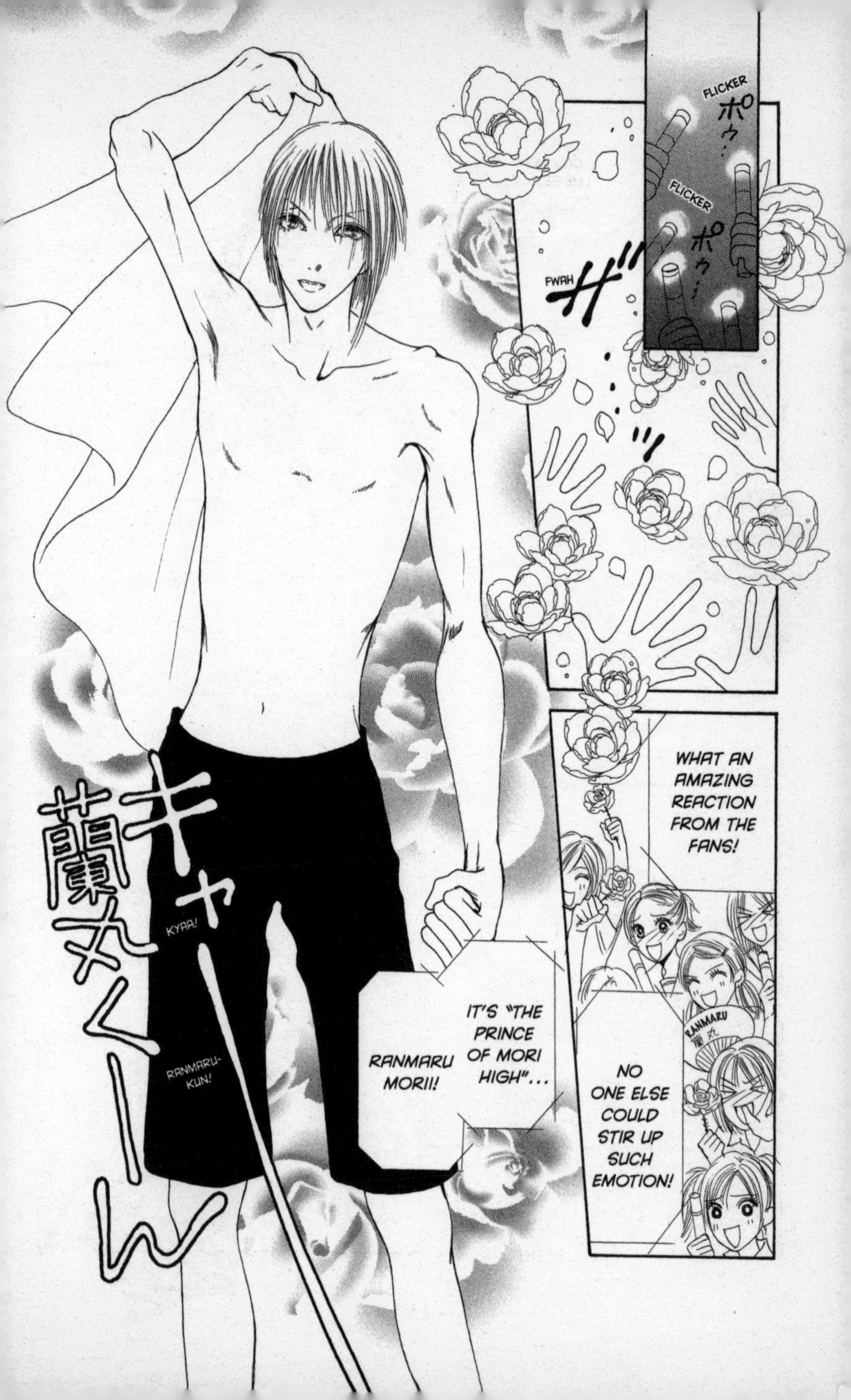
FLICKER
ポウ…
FLICKER
ポウ…
FWAH
ザッ
WHAT AN AMAZING REACTION FROM THE FANS!
RANMARU
蘭丸
NO ONE ELSE COULD STIR UP SUCH EMOTION!
IT'S "THE PRINCE OF MORI HIGH"...
RANMARU MORII!
キャー
KYAA!
蘭丸くーん
RANMARU-KUN!

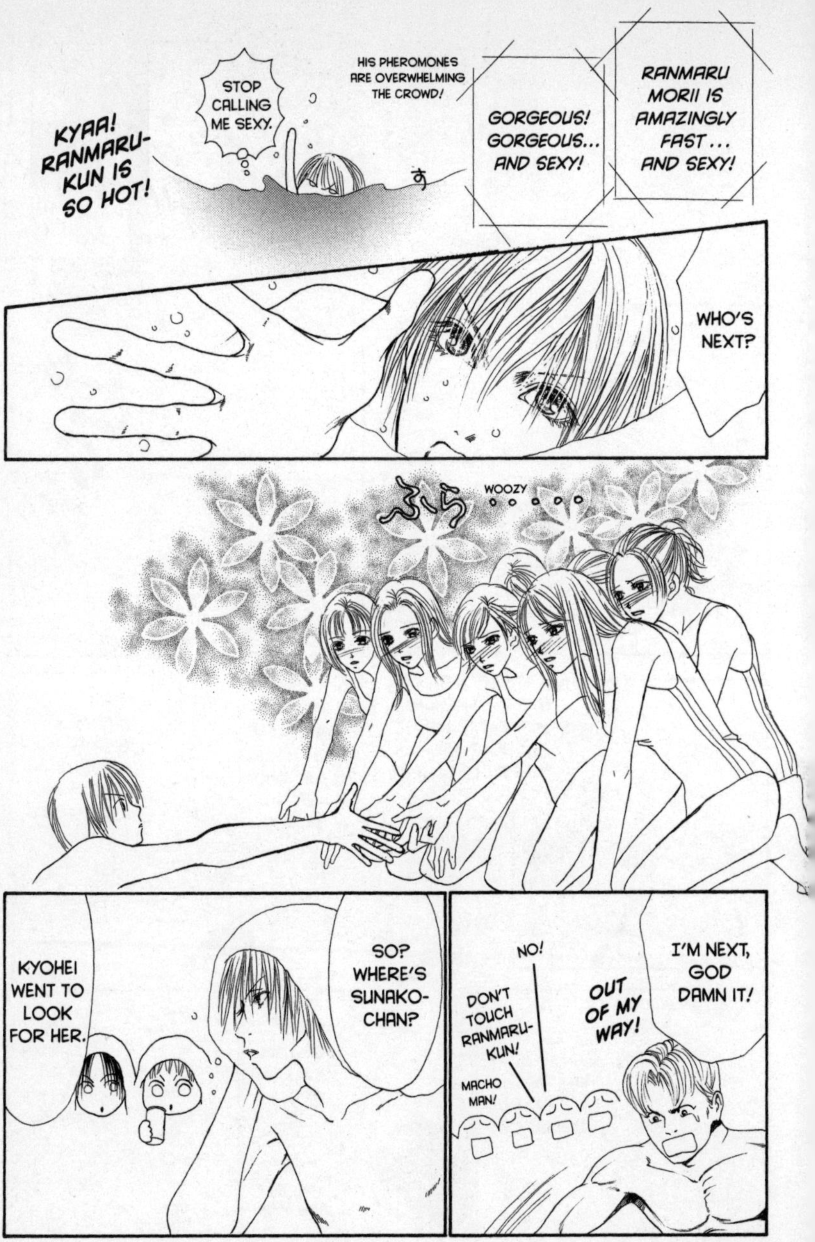
RANMARU MORII IS AMAZINGLY FAST... AND SEXY!
GORGEOUS! GORGEOUS... AND SEXY!
HIS PHEROMONES ARE OVERWHELMING THE CROWD!
す
STOP CALLING ME SEXY.
KYAA! RANMARU-KUN IS SO HOT!
WHO'S NEXT?
ふら
WOOZY
I'M NEXT, GOD DAMN IT!
OUT OF MY WAY!
NO!
DON'T TOUCH RANMARU-KUN!
MACHO MAN!
SO? WHERE'S SUNAKO-CHAN?
KYOHEI WENT TO LOOK FOR HER.

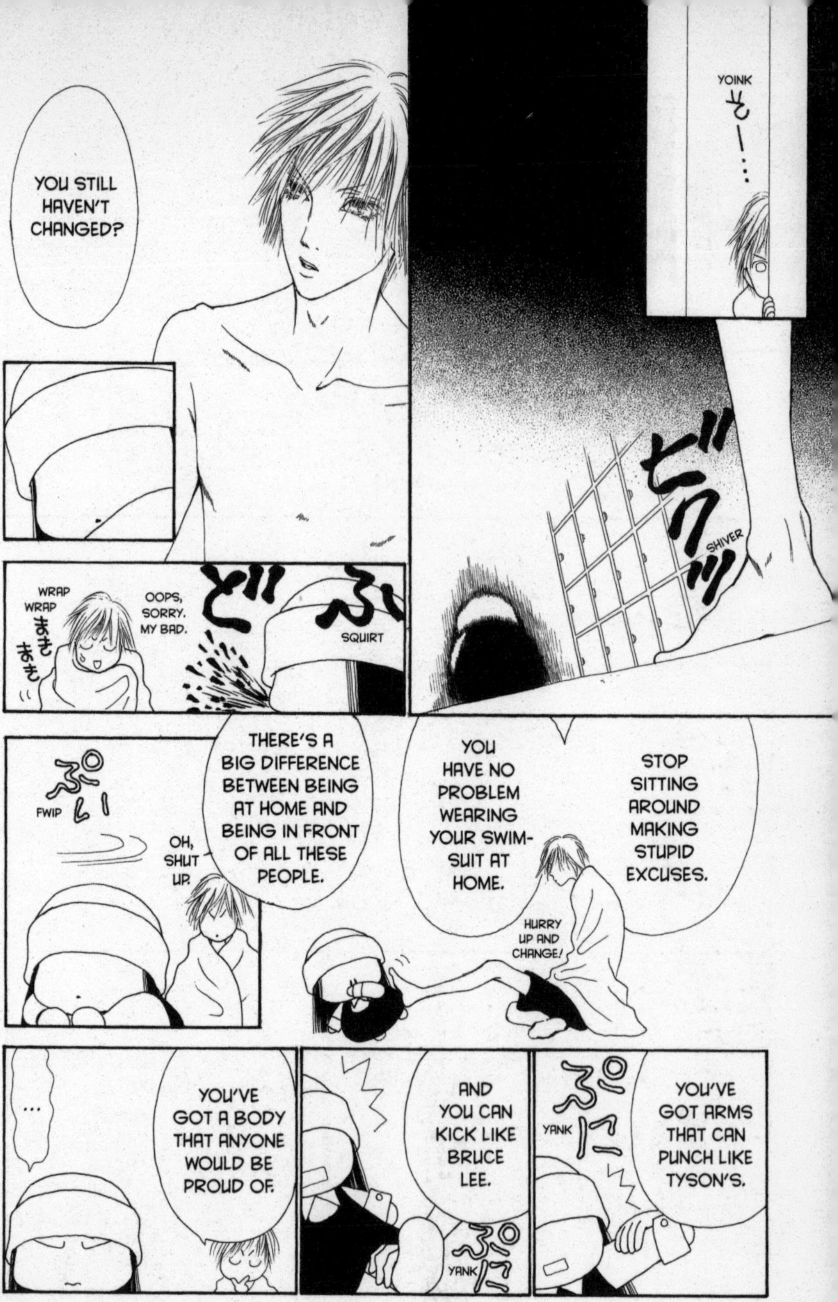
YOINK
SHIVER
YOU STILL HAVEN'T CHANGED?
SQUIRT
OOPS, SORRY. MY BAD.
WRAP WRAP
STOP SITTING AROUND MAKING STUPID EXCUSES.
YOU HAVE NO PROBLEM WEARING YOUR SWIMSUIT AT HOME.
HURRY UP AND CHANGE!
THERE'S A BIG DIFFERENCE BETWEEN BEING AT HOME AND BEING IN FRONT OF ALL THESE PEOPLE.
OH, SHUT UP.
FWIP
YOU'VE GOT ARMS THAT CAN PUNCH LIKE TYSON'S.
YANK
AND YOU CAN KICK LIKE BRUCE LEE.
YANK
YOU'VE GOT A BODY THAT ANYONE WOULD BE PROUD OF.
...

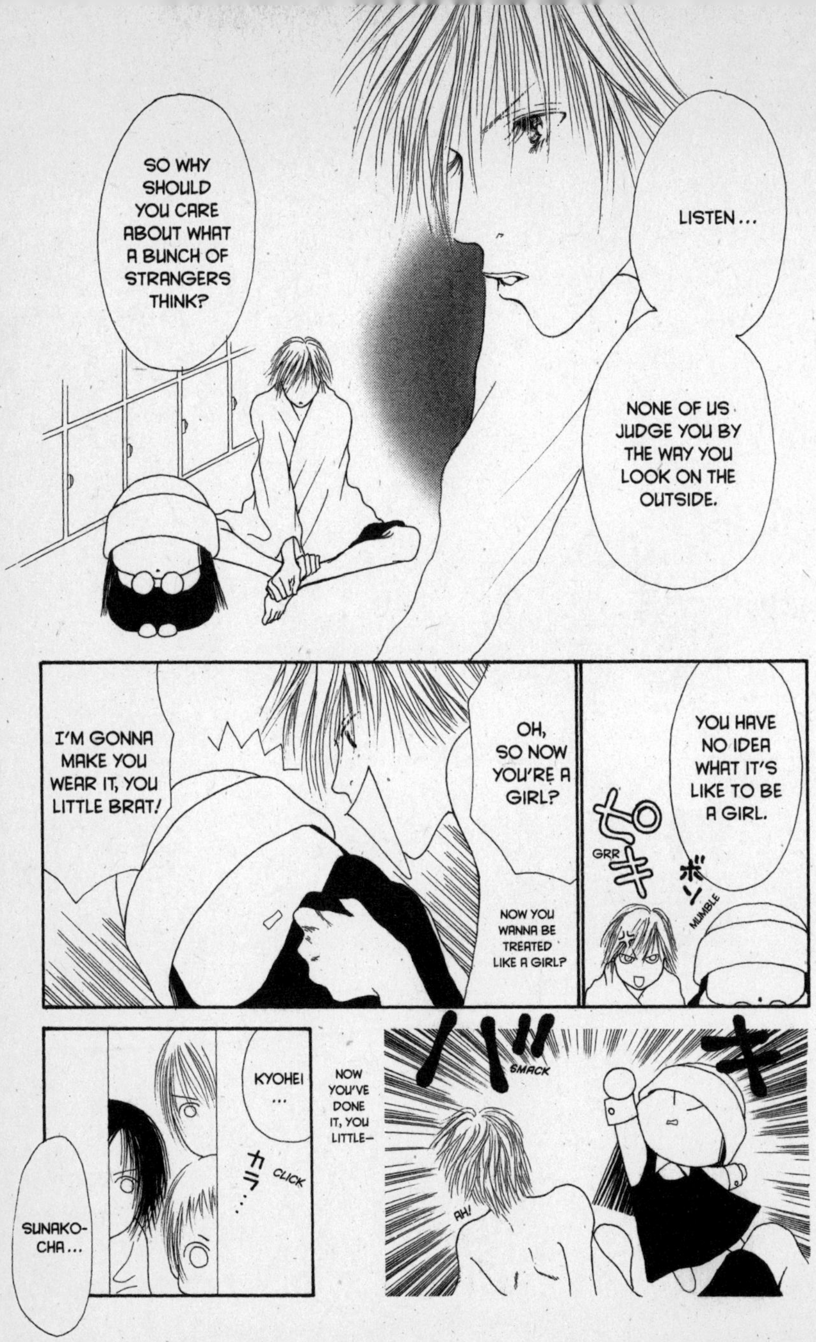
LISTEN...
NONE OF US JUDGE YOU BY THE WAY YOU LOOK ON THE OUTSIDE.
SO WHY SHOULD YOU CARE ABOUT WHAT A BUNCH OF STRANGERS THINK?
YOU HAVE NO IDEA WHAT IT'S LIKE TO BE A GIRL.
MUMBLE
GRR
OH, SO NOW YOU'RE A GIRL?
NOW YOU WANNA BE TREATED LIKE A GIRL?
I'M GONNA MAKE YOU WEAR IT, YOU LITTLE BRAT!
SMACK
AH!
NOW YOU'VE DONE IT, YOU LITTLE—
KYOHEI ...
CLICK
SUNAKO-CHA ...

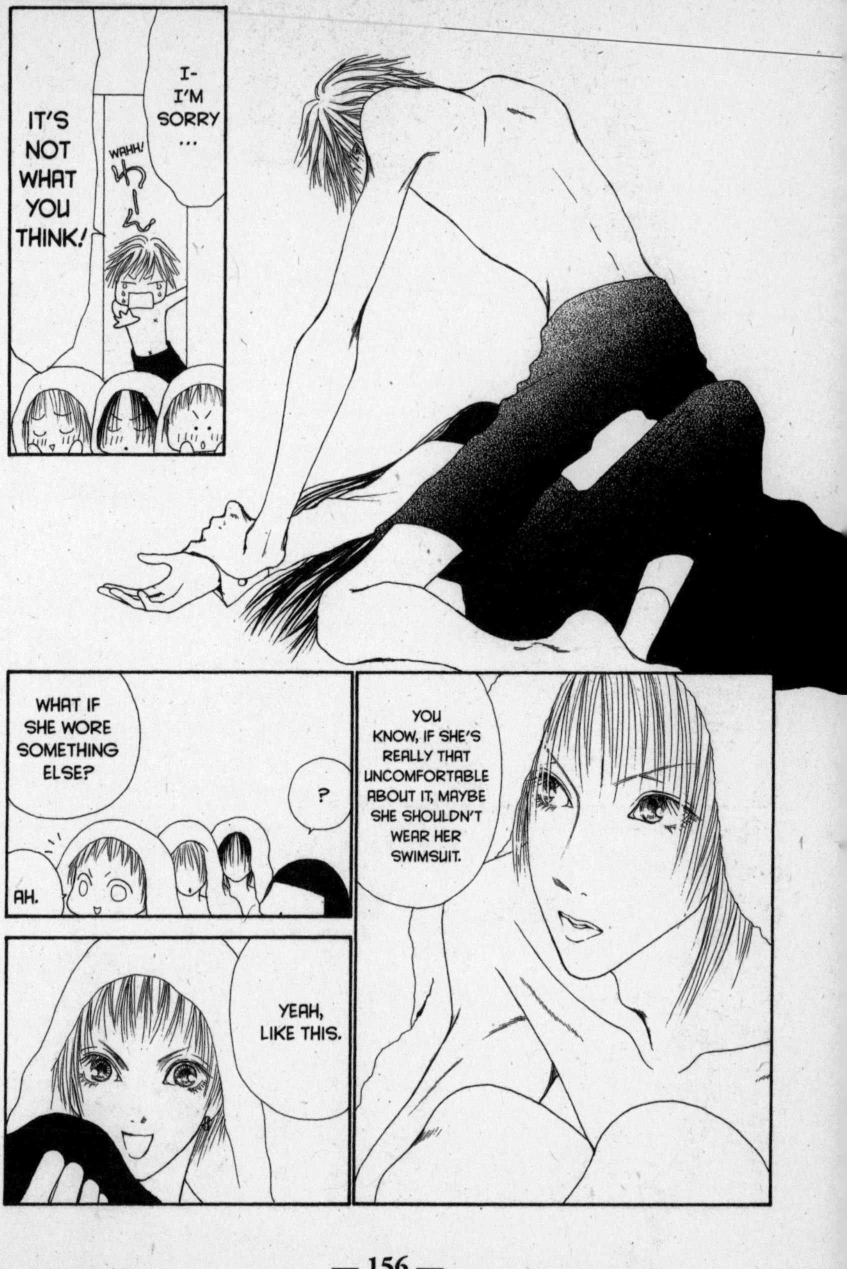
I- I'M SORRY ...
WAHH!
わーん
IT'S NOT WHAT YOU THINK!
YOU KNOW, IF SHE'S REALLY THAT UNCOMFORTABLE ABOUT IT, MAYBE SHE SHOULDN'T WEAR HER SWIMSUIT.
WHAT IF SHE WORE SOMETHING ELSE?
?
AH.
YEAH, LIKE THIS.

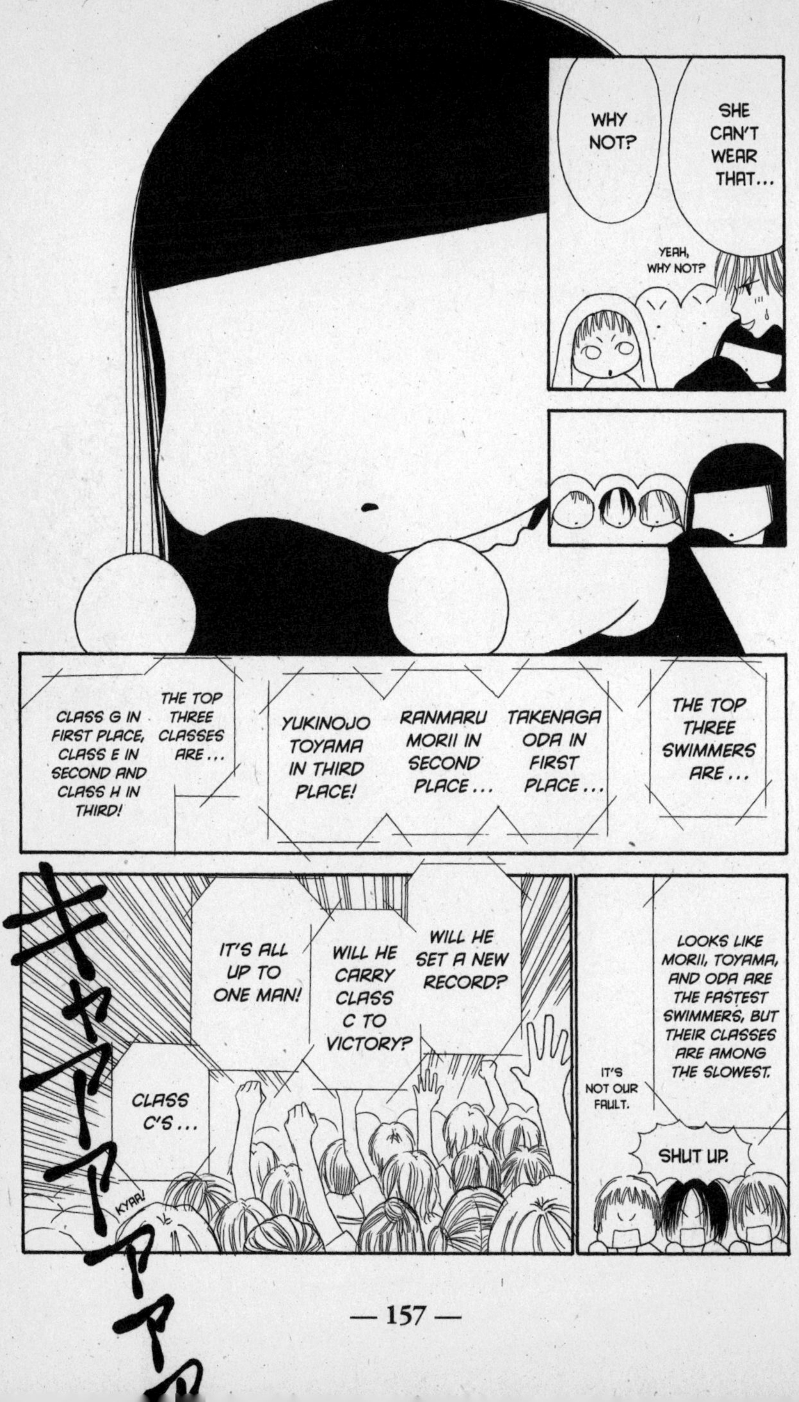
SHE CAN'T WEAR THAT...
WHY NOT?
YEAH, WHY NOT?
THE TOP THREE SWIMMERS ARE...
TAKENAGA ODA IN FIRST PLACE...
RANMARU MORII IN SECOND PLACE...
YUKINOJO TOYAMA IN THIRD PLACE!
THE TOP THREE CLASSES ARE...
CLASS G IN FIRST PLACE, CLASS E IN SECOND AND CLASS H IN THIRD!
LOOKS LIKE MORII, TOYAMA, AND ODA ARE THE FASTEST SWIMMERS, BUT THEIR CLASSES ARE AMONG THE SLOWEST.
IT'S NOT OUR FAULT.
SHUT UP.
WILL HE SET A NEW RECORD?
WILL HE CARRY CLASS C TO VICTORY?
IT'S ALL UP TO ONE MAN!
CLASS C'S...
KYAA!
キャアァア

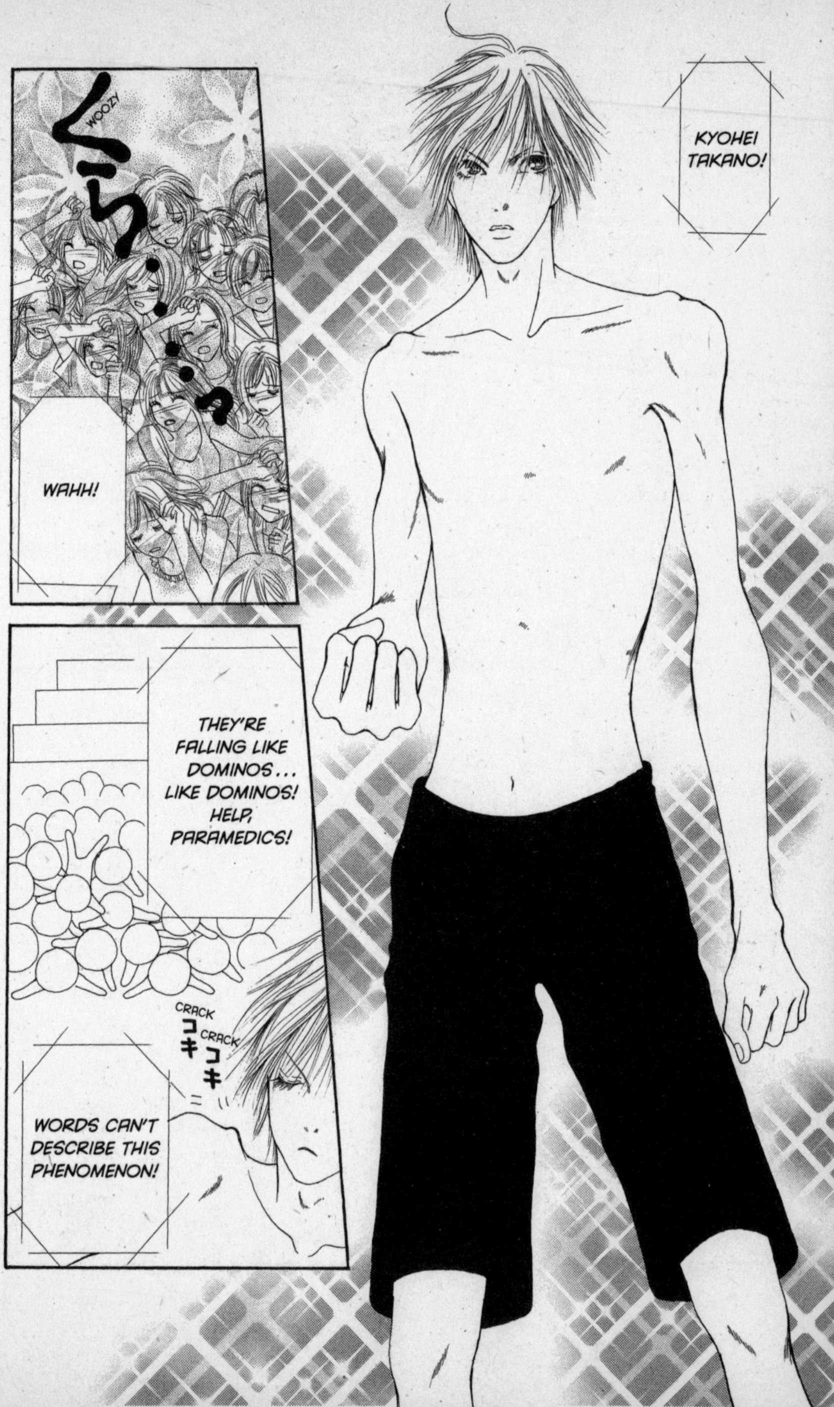
KYOHEI TAKANO!
WOOZY
くら…
WAHH!
THEY'RE FALLING LIKE DOMINOS... LIKE DOMINOS! HELP, PARAMEDICS!
CRACK
コキ
CRACK
コキ
WORDS CAN'T DESCRIBE THIS PHENOMENON!

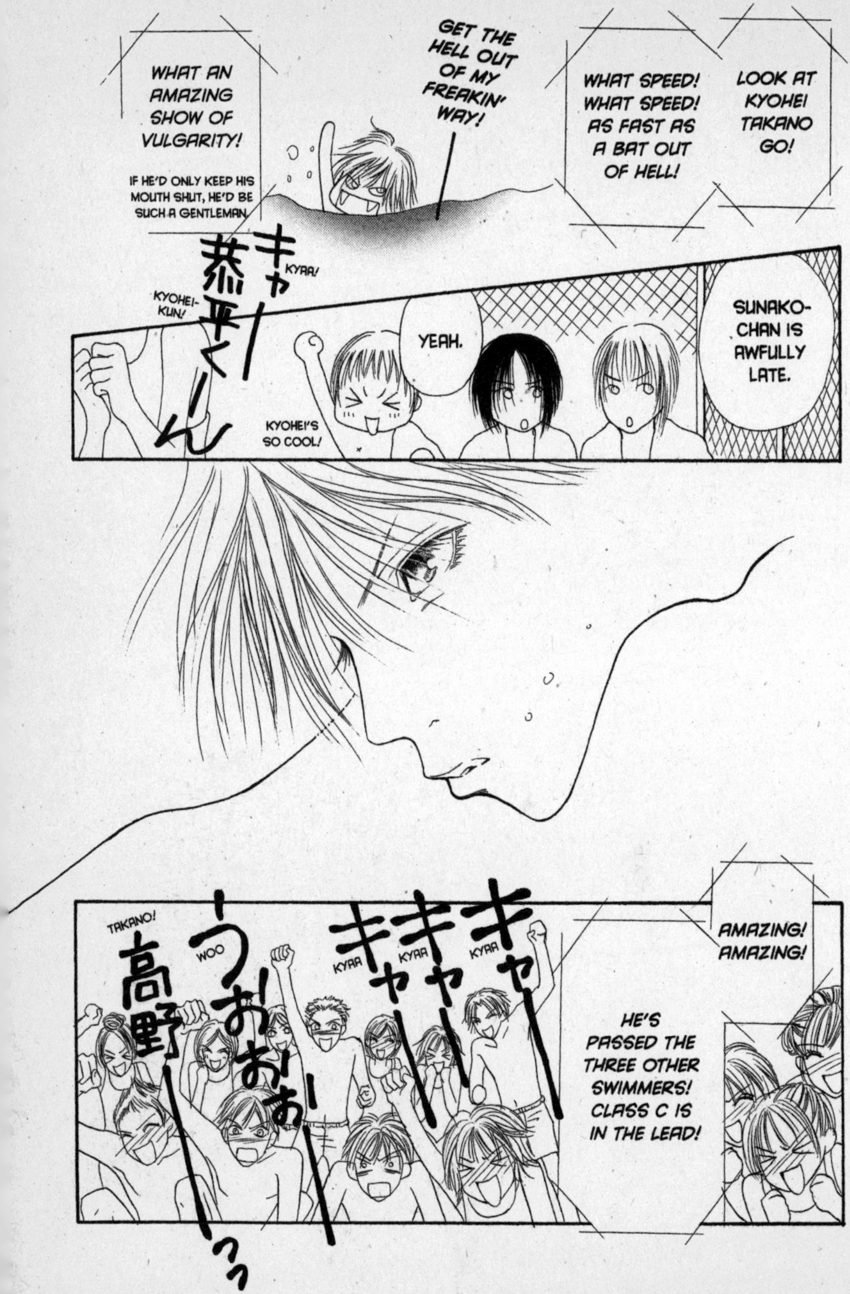
LOOK AT KYOHEI TAKANO GO!
WHAT SPEED! WHAT SPEED! AS FAST AS A BAT OUT OF HELL!
GET THE HELL OUT OF MY FREAKIN' WAY!
WHAT AN AMAZING SHOW OF VULGARITY!
IF HE'D ONLY KEEP HIS MOUTH SHUT, HE'D BE SUCH A GENTLEMAN.
SUNAKO-CHAN IS AWFULLY LATE.
YEAH.
KYOHEI'S SO COOL!
キャー
KYAA!
恭平くーん
KYOHEI-KUN!
AMAZING! AMAZING!
HE'S PASSED THE THREE OTHER SWIMMERS! CLASS C IS IN THE LEAD!
キャー
KYAA
キャー
KYAA
キャー
KYAA
うおおおー
WOO
高野ーっっっ
TAKANO!

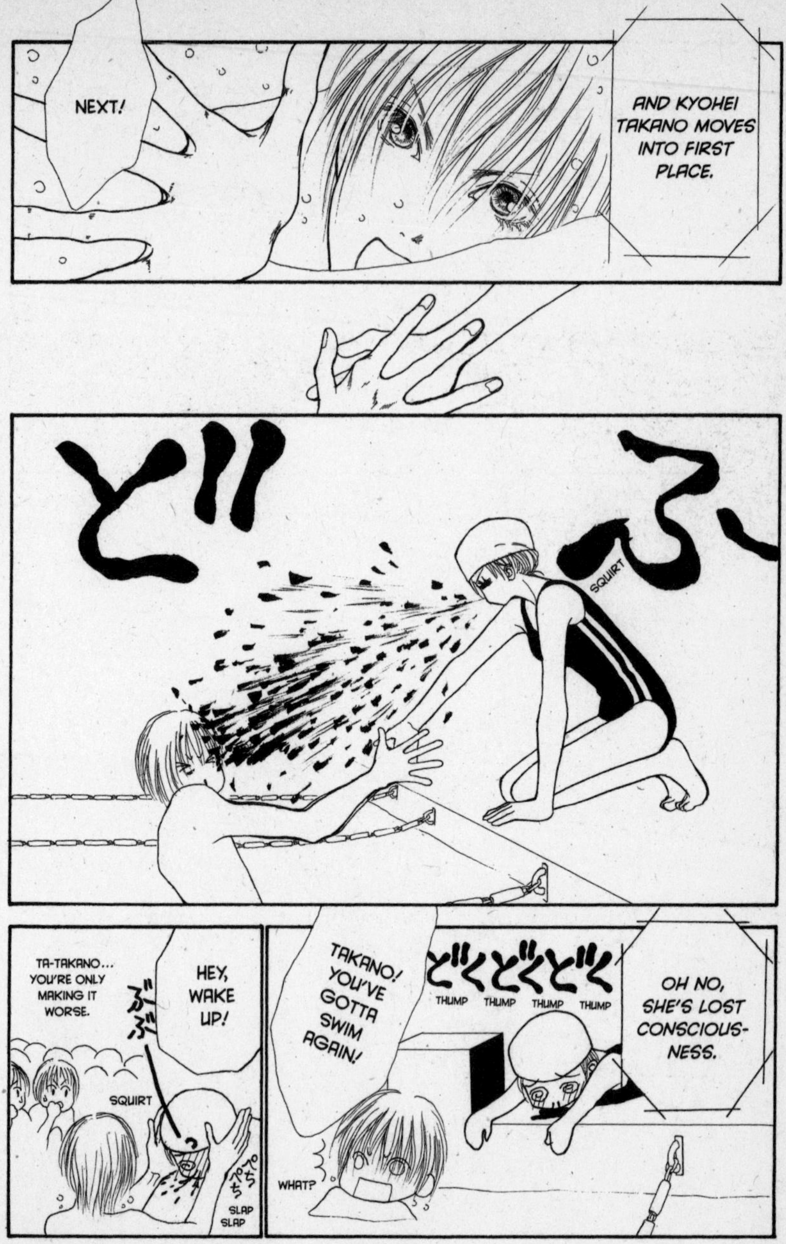
AND KYOHEI TAKANO MOVES INTO FIRST PLACE.
NEXT!
SQUIRT
OH NO, SHE'S LOST CONSCIOUS-NESS.
どくどくどく
THUMP THUMP THUMP THUMP
TAKANO! YOU'VE GOTTA SWIM AGAIN!
WHAT?
HEY, WAKE UP!
SQUIRT
SLAP SLAP
TA-TAKANO... YOU'RE ONLY MAKING IT WORSE.

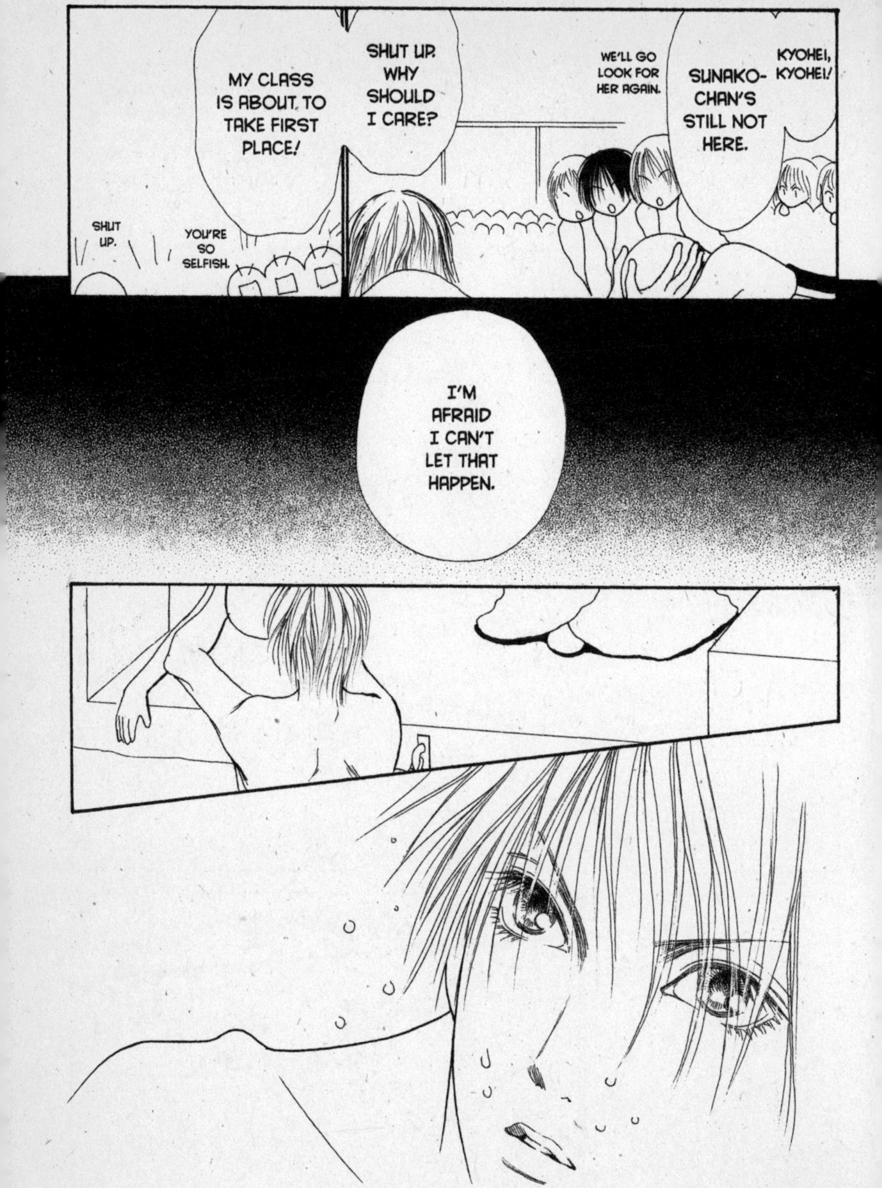
KYOHEI, KYOHEI!
SUNAKO-CHAN'S STILL NOT HERE.
WE'LL GO LOOK FOR HER AGAIN.
SHUT UP. WHY SHOULD I CARE?
MY CLASS IS ABOUT TO TAKE FIRST PLACE!
YOU'RE SO SELFISH.
SHUT UP.
I'M AFRAID I CAN'T LET THAT HAPPEN.

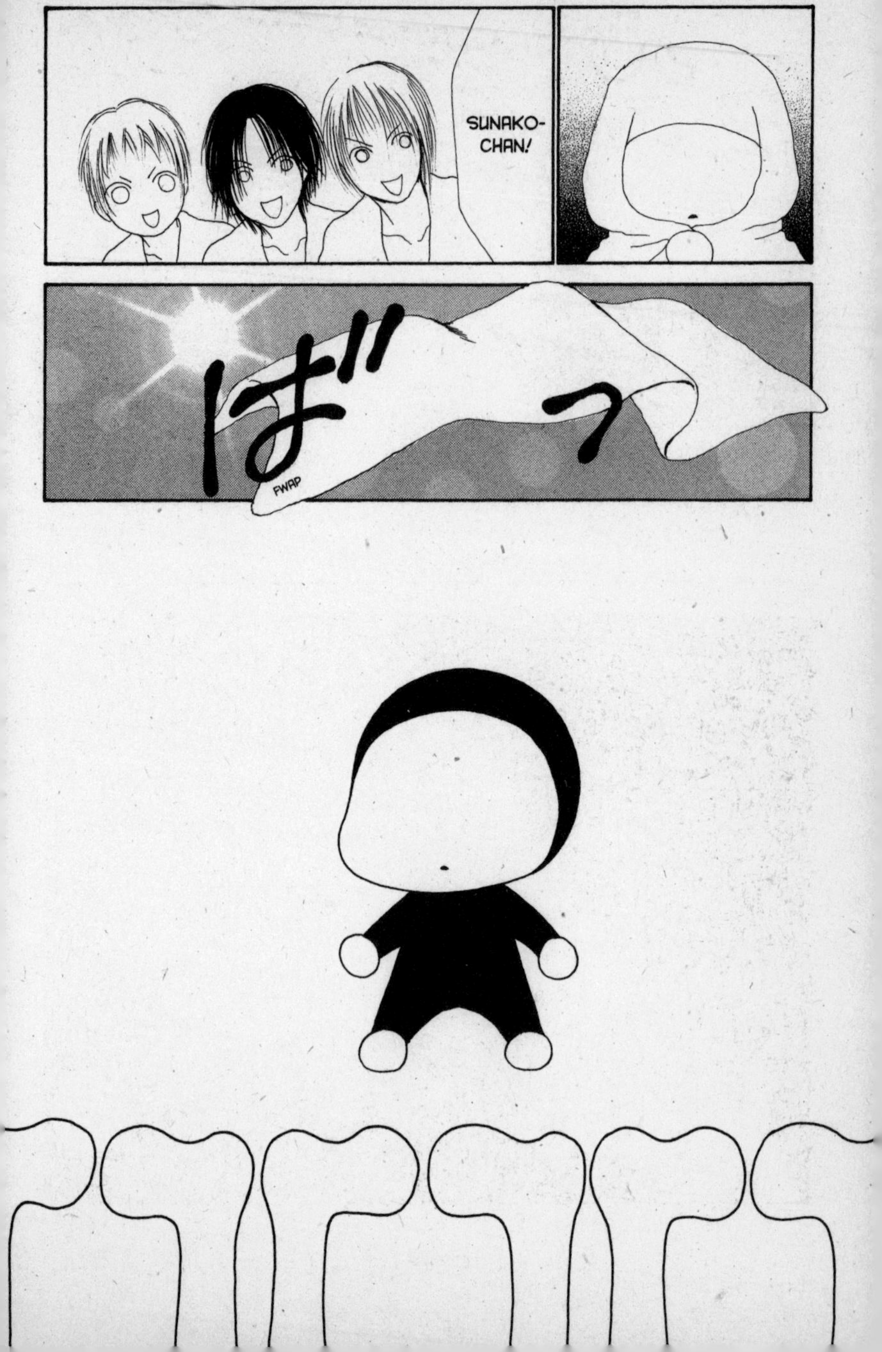
SUNAKO-CHAN!
ばっ
FWAP

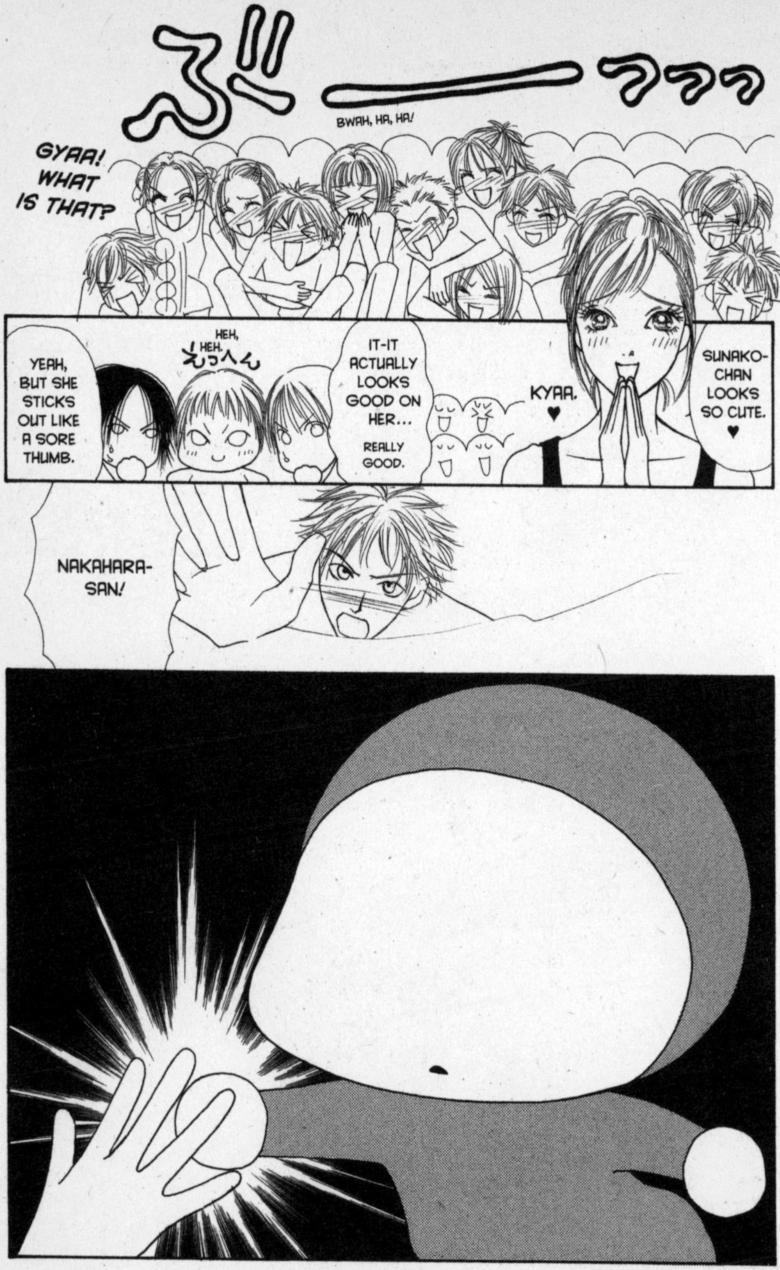
ぶ――っっっ
BWAH, HA, HA!
GYAA! WHAT IS THAT?
SUNAKO-CHAN LOOKS SO CUTE. ♥
KYAA. ♥
IT-IT ACTUALLY LOOKS GOOD ON HER...
REALLY GOOD.
HEH, HEH.
えっへん
YEAH, BUT SHE STICKS OUT LIKE A SORE THUMB.
NAKAHARA-SAN!

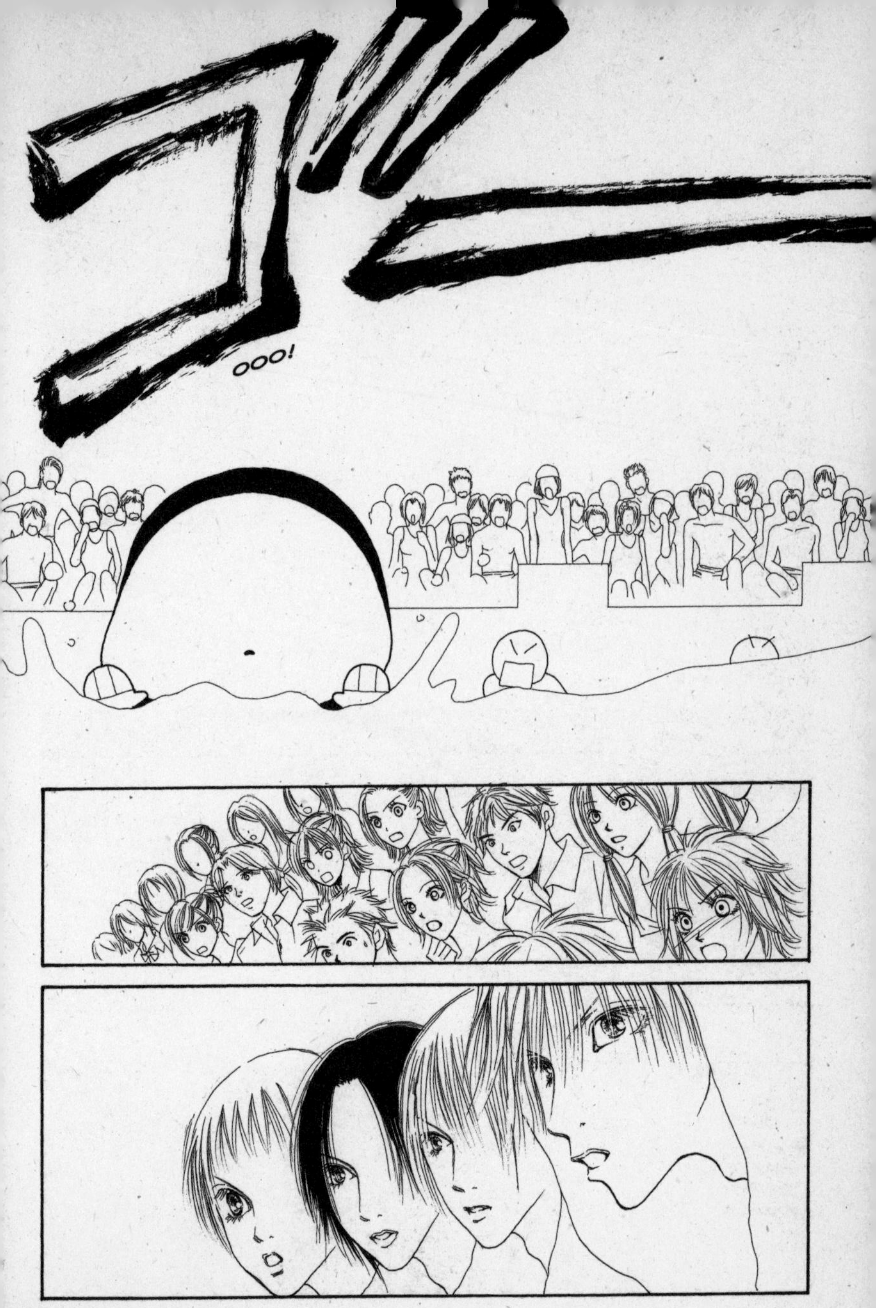
ゴー
OOO!

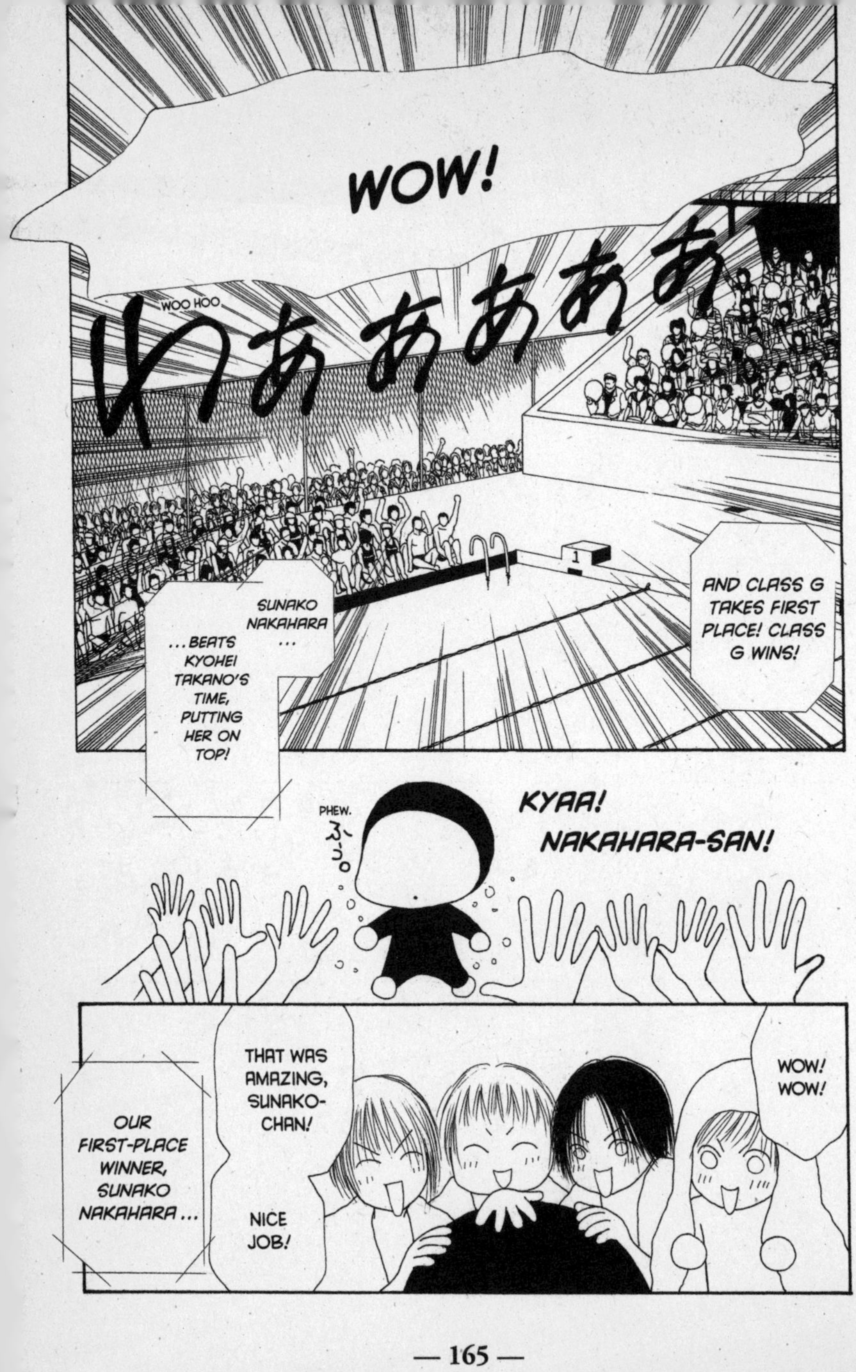
WOW!
WOO HOO
わああああ
AND CLASS G TAKES FIRST PLACE! CLASS G WINS!
SUNAKO NAKAHARA ...
... BEATS KYOHEI TAKANO'S TIME, PUTTING HER ON TOP!
KYAA! NAKAHARA-SAN!
PHEW.
ふぅ
WOW! WOW!
THAT WAS AMAZING, SUNAKO-CHAN!
NICE JOB!
OUR FIRST-PLACE WINNER, SUNAKO NAKAHARA ...

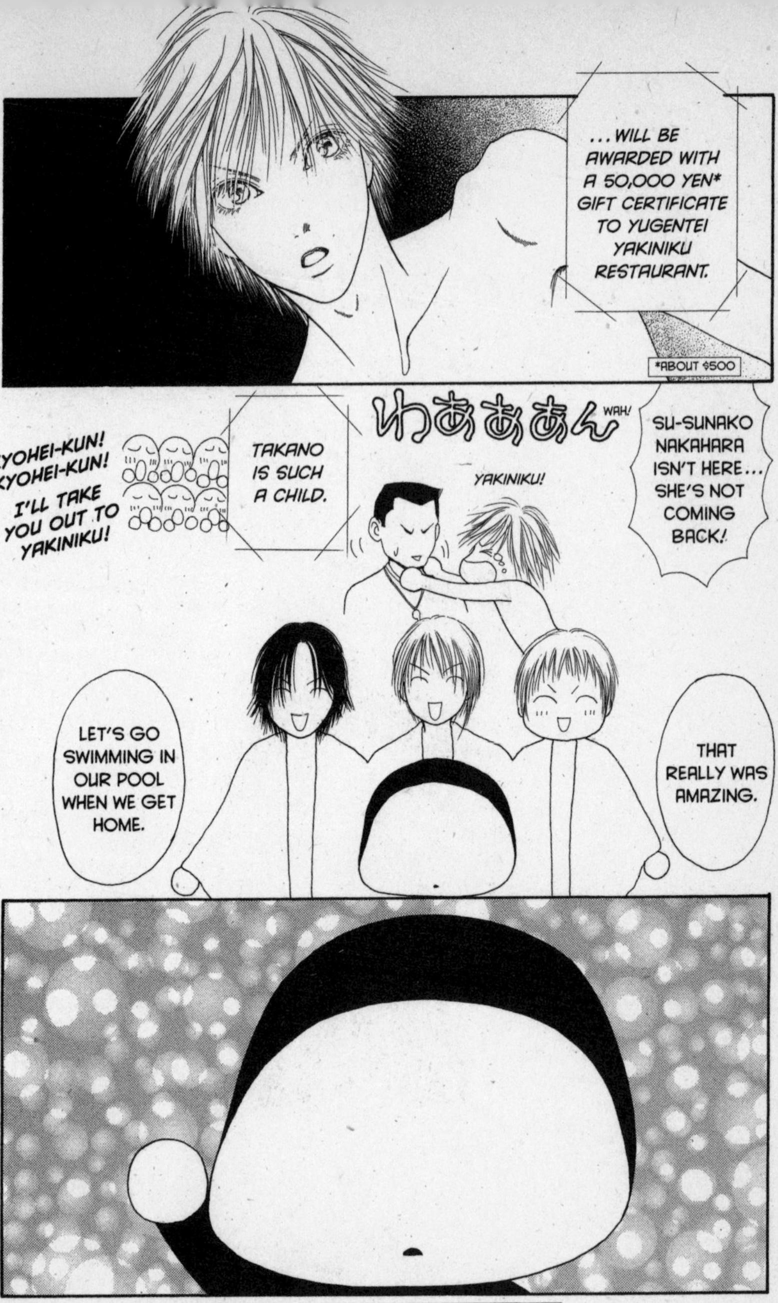
...WILL BE AWARDED WITH A 50,000 YEN* GIFT CERTIFICATE TO YUGENTEI YAKINIKU RESTAURANT.
*ABOUT $500
SU-SUNAKO NAKAHARA ISN'T HERE... SHE'S NOT COMING BACK!
わあああん WAH!
YAKINIKU!
TAKANO IS SUCH A CHILD.
KYOHEI-KUN! KYOHEI-KUN! I'LL TAKE YOU OUT TO YAKINIKU!
THAT REALLY WAS AMAZING.
LET'S GO SWIMMING IN OUR POOL WHEN WE GET HOME.

END OF WALLFLOWER BOOK 6

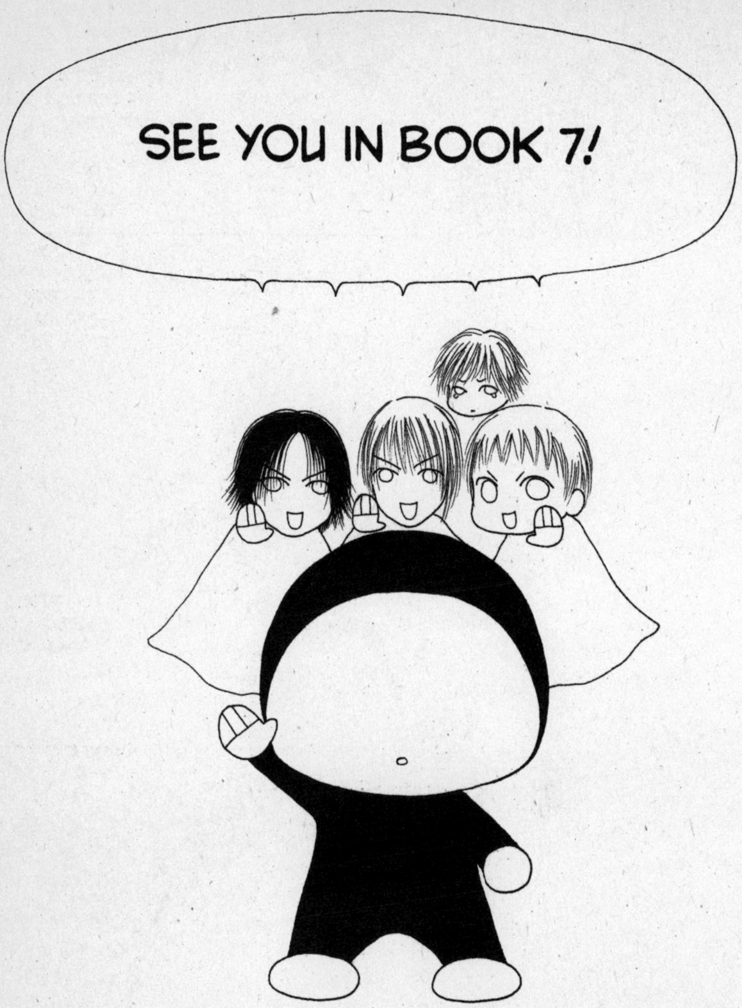
SEE YOU IN BOOK 7!

THANK YOU FOR READING KODANSHA COMICS.

OH, IT LOOKS
JUST LIKE ME.
♥

IF IT WEREN'T FOR ALL YOUR SUPPORT, I WOULDN'T BE
WRITING MANGA TODAY. THANK YOU SO MUCH.

OH NO ... IT KIND OF SCARES ME WHEN I LOOK BACK AT
THE BONUS PAGES AT THE END OF BOOK 5 NOW.

ACTUALLY, BACK THEN I WAS EMOTIONALLY IMBALANCED.

WELL, I WAS ALREADY DEALING WITH THAT AROUND THE TIME I WAS
WORKING ON BOOK 3 OR 4, BUT ANYWAY...I WAS STILL FEELING BLUE
WHEN I WROTE THE FIRST STORY OF BOOK 6 ...

I REALLY DON'T WANT TO REMEMBER WHAT I WAS GOING THROUGH.

I REALLY WAS IN AN *EXTREMELY DARK* PLACE ...

SIGH. I HAVE RECOVERED SINCE THEN, AND I'M FINE NOW. ♥

I STARTED TO FEEL BETTER AROUND THE TIME THAT I WAS WRITING THE
SECOND STORY IN BOOK 6.   (OCCASIONALLY I'D HAVE A RELAPSE, BUT I
                            MANAGED TO HANDLE THEM ON MY OWN.)

I'D LIKE TO THANK EVERYBODY WHO TOOK CARE OF ME. ←— VERY PERSONAL.

*THERE ARE EXTRA BONUS PAGES THIS TIME, SO
I'M GOING TO TAKE FULL ADVANTAGE OF THEM!*

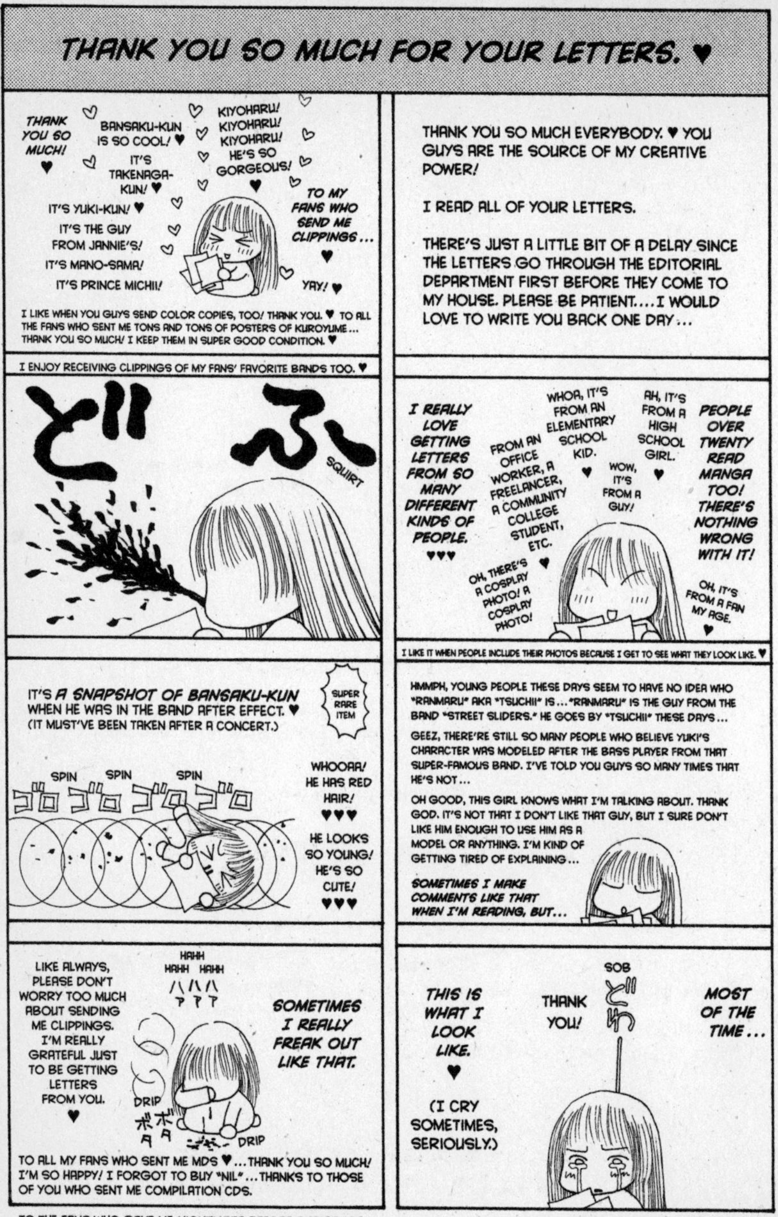
THANK YOU SO MUCH FOR YOUR LETTERS. ♥
THANK YOU SO MUCH EVERYBODY. ♥ YOU GUYS ARE THE SOURCE OF MY CREATIVE POWER!
I READ ALL OF YOUR LETTERS.
THERE'S JUST A LITTLE BIT OF A DELAY SINCE THE LETTERS GO THROUGH THE EDITORIAL DEPARTMENT FIRST BEFORE THEY COME TO MY HOUSE. PLEASE BE PATIENT.... I WOULD LOVE TO WRITE YOU BACK ONE DAY...
TO MY FANS WHO SEND ME CLIPPINGS... ♥
KIYOHARU! KIYOHARU! KIYOHARU! HE'S SO GORGEOUS! ♥
BANSAKU-KUN IS SO COOL! ♥
THANK YOU SO MUCH! ♥
IT'S TAKENAGA-KUN! ♥
IT'S YUKI-KUN! ♥
IT'S THE GUY FROM JANNIE'S!
IT'S MANO-SAMA!
IT'S PRINCE MICHII!
YAY! ♥
I LIKE WHEN YOU GUYS SEND COLOR COPIES, TOO! THANK YOU. ♥ TO ALL THE FANS WHO SENT ME TONS AND TONS OF POSTERS OF KUROYUME... THANK YOU SO MUCH! I KEEP THEM IN SUPER GOOD CONDITION. ♥
I ENJOY RECEIVING CLIPPINGS OF MY FANS' FAVORITE BANDS TOO. ♥
PEOPLE OVER TWENTY READ MANGA TOO! THERE'S NOTHING WRONG WITH IT!
AH, IT'S FROM A HIGH SCHOOL GIRL. ♥
WHOA, IT'S FROM AN ELEMENTARY SCHOOL KID. ♥
WOW, IT'S FROM A GUY!
I REALLY LOVE GETTING LETTERS FROM SO MANY DIFFERENT KINDS OF PEOPLE. ♥♥♥
FROM AN OFFICE WORKER, A FREELANCER, A COMMUNITY COLLEGE STUDENT, ETC. ♥
OH, IT'S FROM A FAN MY AGE. ♥
OH, THERE'S A COSPLAY PHOTO! A COSPLAY PHOTO!
I LIKE IT WHEN PEOPLE INCLUDE THEIR PHOTOS BECAUSE I GET TO SEE WHAT THEY LOOK LIKE. ♥
どぶ
SQUIRT
HMMPH, YOUNG PEOPLE THESE DAYS SEEM TO HAVE NO IDEA WHO "RANMARU" AKA "TSUCHII" IS... "RANMARU" IS THE GUY FROM THE BAND "STREET SLIDERS." HE GOES BY "TSUCHII" THESE DAYS...
GEEZ, THERE'RE STILL SO MANY PEOPLE WHO BELIEVE YUKI'S CHARACTER WAS MODELED AFTER THE BASS PLAYER FROM THAT SUPER-FAMOUS BAND. I'VE TOLD YOU GUYS SO MANY TIMES THAT HE'S NOT...
OH GOOD, THIS GIRL KNOWS WHAT I'M TALKING ABOUT. THANK GOD. IT'S NOT THAT I DON'T LIKE THAT GUY, BUT I SURE DON'T LIKE HIM ENOUGH TO USE HIM AS A MODEL OR ANYTHING. I'M KIND OF GETTING TIRED OF EXPLAINING...
SOMETIMES I MAKE COMMENTS LIKE THAT WHEN I'M READING, BUT...
SUPER RARE ITEM
IT'S A SNAPSHOT OF BANSAKU-KUN WHEN HE WAS IN THE BAND AFTER EFFECT. ♥ (IT MUST'VE BEEN TAKEN AFTER A CONCERT.)
WHOOAA! HE HAS RED HAIR! ♥♥♥
HE LOOKS SO YOUNG! HE'S SO CUTE! ♥♥♥
SPIN SPIN SPIN
ゴロゴロゴロゴロ
MOST OF THE TIME...
SOB
どわ
THANK YOU!
THIS IS WHAT I LOOK LIKE. ♥
(I CRY SOMETIMES, SERIOUSLY.)
SOMETIMES I REALLY FREAK OUT LIKE THAT.
HAHH HAHH HAHH
ハハハ
ァァァ
LIKE ALWAYS, PLEASE DON'T WORRY TOO MUCH ABOUT SENDING ME CLIPPINGS. I'M REALLY GRATEFUL JUST TO BE GETTING LETTERS FROM YOU. ♥
DRIP
ボタボタ
DRIP
TO ALL MY FANS WHO SENT ME MDS ♥... THANK YOU SO MUCH! I'M SO HAPPY! I FORGOT TO BUY "NIL"... THANKS TO THOSE OF YOU WHO SENT ME COMPILATION CDS.

TO THE FANS WHO GAVE ME *NIGHTMARE BEFORE CHRISTMAS* MERCHANDISE ♥... THANK YOU! I PUT ALL THAT STUFF IN MY ROOM! ♥♥♥ I LOVE JACK. ♥

*BANSAKU-KUN: BASSIST FROM THE BAND BAROQUE.
TAKENAGA-KUN: SINGER FROM THE BAND WRISK
YUKI-KUN: DRUMMER FROM THE BAND WRISK
MANO-SAMA: FORMER GUITARIST FROM THE BAND MALICE MIZER
PRINCE MICHII: PRINCE MITSUHIRO OIKAWA

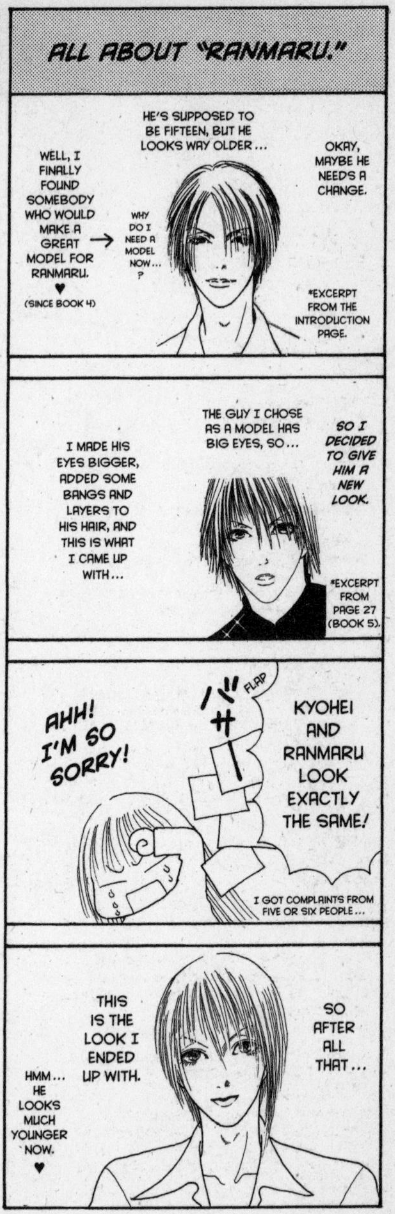
ALL ABOUT "RANMARU."
OKAY, MAYBE HE NEED'S A CHANGE.
HE'S SUPPOSED TO BE FIFTEEN, BUT HE LOOKS WAY OLDER...
WELL, I FINALLY FOUND SOMEBODY WHO WOULD MAKE A GREAT MODEL FOR RANMARU. ♥
(SINCE BOOK 4)
WHY DO I NEED A MODEL NOW...?
*EXCERPT FROM THE INTRODUCTION PAGE.
SO I DECIDED TO GIVE HIM A NEW LOOK.
THE GUY I CHOSE AS A MODEL HAS BIG EYES, SO...
I MADE HIS EYES BIGGER, ADDED SOME BANGS AND LAYERS TO HIS HAIR, AND THIS IS WHAT I CAME UP WITH...
*EXCERPT FROM PAGE 27 (BOOK 5).
KYOHEI AND RANMARU LOOK EXACTLY THE SAME!
バサー
FLAP
AHH! I'M SO SORRY!
I GOT COMPLAINTS FROM FIVE OR SIX PEOPLE...
SO AFTER ALL THAT...
THIS IS THE LOOK I ENDED UP WITH.
HMM... HE LOOKS MUCH YOUNGER NOW. ♥

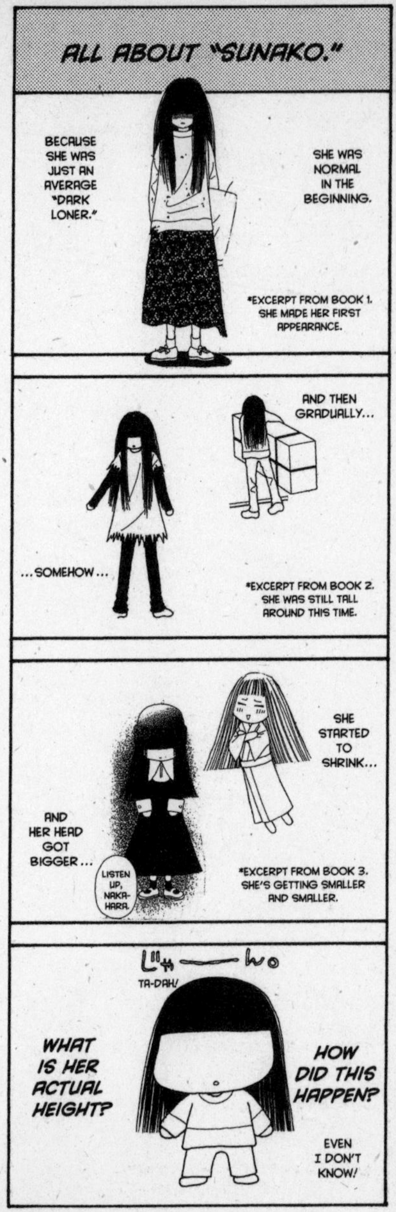
ALL ABOUT "SUNAKO."
SHE WAS NORMAL IN THE BEGINNING.
BECAUSE SHE WAS JUST AN AVERAGE "DARK LONER."
*EXCERPT FROM BOOK 1. SHE MADE HER FIRST APPEARANCE.
AND THEN GRADUALLY...
...SOMEHOW...
*EXCERPT FROM BOOK 2. SHE WAS STILL TALL AROUND THIS TIME.
SHE STARTED TO SHRINK...
AND HER HEAD GOT BIGGER...
*EXCERPT FROM BOOK 3. SHE'S GETTING SMALLER AND SMALLER.
LISTEN UP, NAKA-HARA.
TA-DAH!
HOW DID THIS HAPPEN?
WHAT IS HER ACTUAL HEIGHT?
EVEN I DON'T KNOW!

ANSWERS TO ALL YOUR QUESTIONS.

1

WHY ARE THE GUYS STILL FRESHMEN IN HIGH SCHOOL? DID THEY FAIL?

NO, THEY DIDN'T.

THEY JUST HAVEN'T AGED AT ALL.

THEY MADE IT THROUGH SUMMER AND CELEBRATED NEW YEAR'S, BUT THEY'RE STILL ONLY 15.

2

IS YUKI'S CHARACTER BASED ON THE BASSIST FROM THAT SUPER-FAMOUS BAND?

LIKE I SAID... NO.

I'VE ALREADY DISCUSSED THIS SO MANY TIMES...

OKAY FINE, I'LL JUST TELL YOU WHO HE'S REALLY BASED ON.

THERE'RE ACTUALLY THREE DIFFERENT MODELS FOR HIM. ♡KIYOHARU♡ AROUND THE TIME HE RELEASED "CRUEL" AND "FEMINISM," YUKI-KUN FROM THE BAND WRISK, AND REI FROM THE BAND BAROKKU.

3

WHO IS YOUR FAVORITE CHARACTER?

THE LITTLE VERSIONS OF SUNAKO AND YUKI...

...BECAUSE THEY'RE EASY TO DRAW.

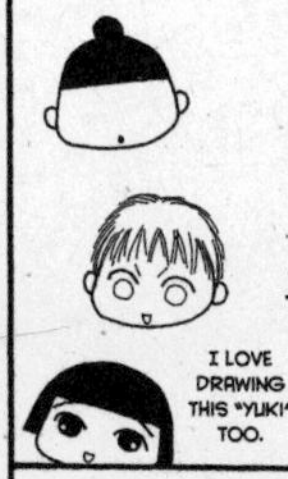
I LOVE DRAWING THIS "YUKI" TOO.

BUT WHEN I'M DRESSING THEM UP IN COSTUMES, ♥ I LIKE...

1. KYOHEI

2. RANMARU

BECAUSE I'M SUCH A BIG FAN OF THE GUY I BASED THEIR CHARACTERS ON.

I LOVE DRESSING THEM UP IN GORGEOUS COSTUMES. ♥

I ACTUALLY CAME UP WITH A LOT OF THE CLOTHES TAKENAGA AND YUKI ARE WEARING.

*THEIR PERSONALITIES ARE SOLELY MY CREATION, AND HAVE NOTHING TO DO WITH THOSE OF THEIR MODELS.

4

ARE KYOHEI AND SUNAKO EVER GOING TO HOOK UP?

I HAVE NO IDEA.

5

PROFILE...

TAKENAGA:
BORN NOVEMBER 6, BLOOD TYPE B

NOI:
BORN SEPTEMBER 29, BLOOD TYPE A

RANMARU:
BORN OCTOBER 29, BLOOD TYPE A

I HAVE FINALLY DECIDED.
THE REST ARE STILL UNDECIDED.

DON'T ASK ME WHY THEY HAVEN'T AGED EVEN THOUGH THEY'VE ALREADY HAD THEIR BIRTHDAYS.

6

IS SUNAKO WEARING CLOTHES FROM THE BRAND NA+H? (WHEN SHE'S NOT IN SWEATS...)

IS KYOHEI WEARING CLOTHES FROM THE BRAND ALICE AUAA? OR IS IT H.NAOTO?

IS THE LANDLADY WEARING JEAN PAUL GAULTIER? OR IS THAT SEXY DYNAMITE LONDON?

THERE AREN'T ANY SPECIFIC DESIGNER BRANDS I USE WHEN I DRAW THEIR WARDROBES, BUT I DO USE MY FAVORITE DESIGNERS AS REFERENCES. SOMETIMES I LOOK AT OLD FASHION MAGAZINES FROM TEN YEARS AGO. I ALSO DESIGN THEM ON MY OWN.

I LOVE ♥ NA+H, H.NAOTO, ALICE AUAA, BLACK PEACE NOW. MY PERSONAL FAVORITE IS JEAN PAUL GAULTIER! ♥♥♥

I OFTEN GO SHOPPING AT ATELIER PIEROT INSIDE THE LAFORLE DEPARTMENT STORE IN HARAJUKU. MY FRIEND WORKS AT H.NAOTO, SO I BUY STUFF THERE TOO. IF YOU'RE EVER THERE, SAY HELLO TO MY FRIEND (A GUY). ♥

WHO IS TOMOKO HAYAKAWA?

I AM A GROUPIE WHO LOVES GORGEOUS BOYS AND GIRLS!

BUT, I GUESS YOU KNOW THAT ALREADY...

I'D LIKE TO SHARE SOME STORIES FROM MY LIFE...

THEY'LL PROBABLY HELP YOU FIND OUT A LITTLE BIT MORE ABOUT ME.

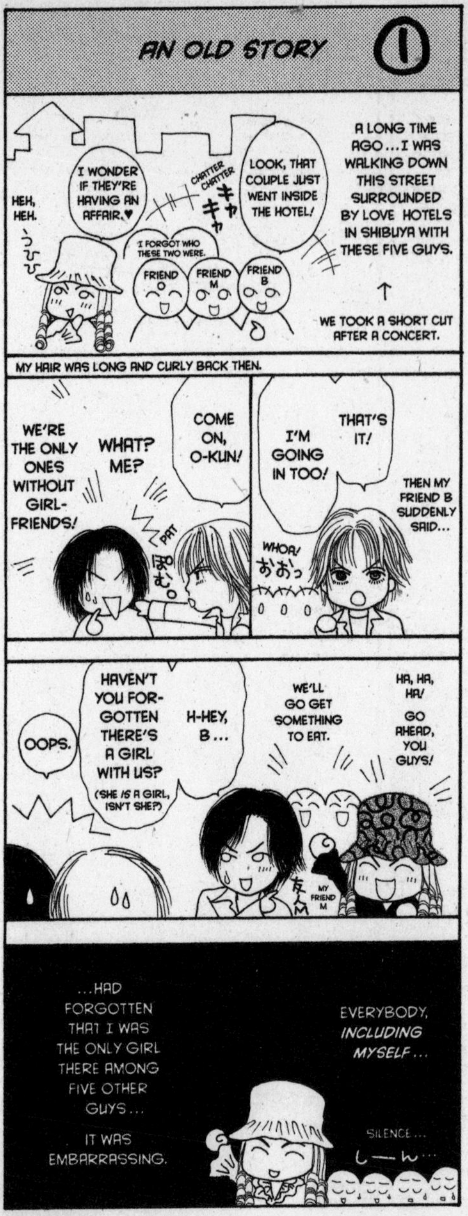
AN OLD STORY ①
A LONG TIME AGO... I WAS WALKING DOWN THIS STREET SURROUNDED BY LOVE HOTELS IN SHIBUYA WITH THESE FIVE GUYS.
WE TOOK A SHORT CUT AFTER A CONCERT.
LOOK, THAT COUPLE JUST WENT INSIDE THE HOTEL!
CHATTER CHATTER
キャキャ
FRIEND B
FRIEND M
I WONDER IF THEY'RE HAVING AN AFFAIR.♥
I FORGOT WHO THESE TWO WERE.
FRIEND
HEH, HEH.
うぷぷ
MY HAIR WAS LONG AND CURLY BACK THEN.
THEN MY FRIEND B SUDDENLY SAID...
THAT'S IT!
I'M GOING IN TOO!
WHOA!
おおっ
COME ON, O-KUN!
WHAT? ME?
WE'RE THE ONLY ONES WITHOUT GIRL-FRIENDS!
PAT
ぽむ。
HA, HA, HA! GO AHEAD, YOU GUYS!
WE'LL GO GET SOMETHING TO EAT.
H-HEY, B...
HAVEN'T YOU FOR-GOTTEN THERE'S A GIRL WITH US?
(SHE IS A GIRL, ISN'T SHE?)
OOPS.
MY FRIEND M
友人M
EVERYBODY, INCLUDING MYSELF...
...HAD FORGOTTEN THAT I WAS THE ONLY GIRL THERE AMONG FIVE OTHER GUYS...
IT WAS EMBARRASSING.
SILENCE...
しーん…

AN OLD STORY ②

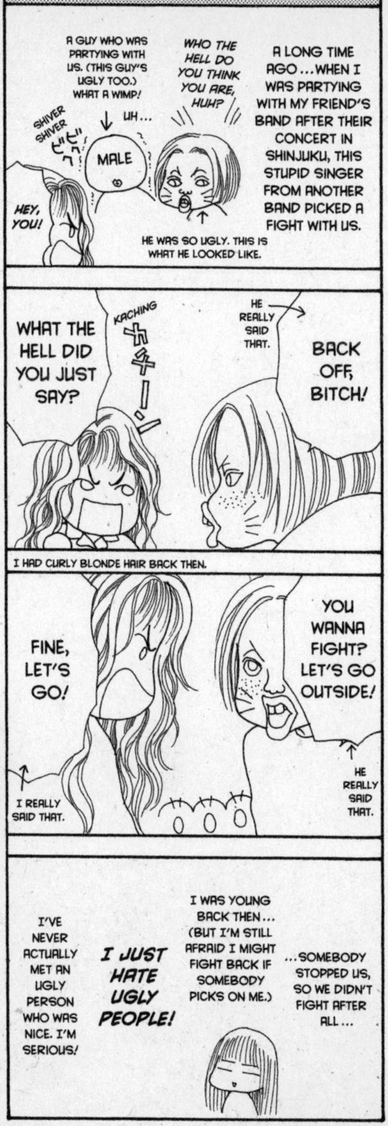
A LONG TIME AGO ... WHEN I WAS PARTYING WITH MY FRIEND'S BAND AFTER THEIR CONCERT IN SHINJUKU, THIS STUPID SINGER FROM ANOTHER BAND PICKED A FIGHT WITH US.
WHO THE HELL DO YOU THINK YOU ARE, HUH?
A GUY WHO WAS PARTYING WITH US. (THIS GUY'S UGLY TOO.) WHAT A WIMP!
UH...
MALE
SHIVER SHIVER
HEY, YOU!
HE WAS SO UGLY. THIS IS WHAT HE LOOKED LIKE.
BACK OFF, BITCH!
HE REALLY SAID THAT.
KACHING
WHAT THE HELL DID YOU JUST SAY?
I HAD CURLY BLONDE HAIR BACK THEN.
YOU WANNA FIGHT? LET'S GO OUTSIDE!
HE REALLY SAID THAT.
FINE, LET'S GO!
I REALLY SAID THAT.
...SOMEBODY STOPPED US, SO WE DIDN'T FIGHT AFTER ALL...
I WAS YOUNG BACK THEN... (BUT I'M STILL AFRAID I MIGHT FIGHT BACK IF SOMEBODY PICKS ON ME.)
I JUST HATE UGLY PEOPLE!
I'VE NEVER ACTUALLY MET AN UGLY PERSON WHO WAS NICE. I'M SERIOUS!

SOME THINGS NEVER CHANGE...

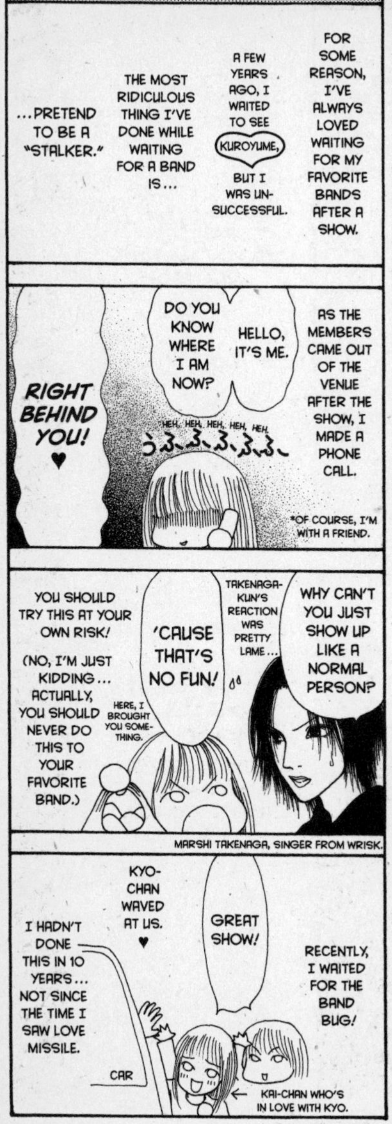
FOR SOME REASON, I'VE ALWAYS LOVED WAITING FOR MY FAVORITE BANDS AFTER A SHOW.
A FEW YEARS AGO, I WAITED TO SEE KUROYUME, BUT I WAS UNSUCCESSFUL.
THE MOST RIDICULOUS THING I'VE DONE WHILE WAITING FOR A BAND IS...
...PRETEND TO BE A "STALKER."
AS THE MEMBERS CAME OUT OF THE VENUE AFTER THE SHOW, I MADE A PHONE CALL.
HELLO, IT'S ME.
DO YOU KNOW WHERE I AM NOW?
HEH, HEH, HEH, HEH, HEH.
RIGHT BEHIND YOU! ♥
*OF COURSE, I'M WITH A FRIEND.
WHY CAN'T YOU JUST SHOW UP LIKE A NORMAL PERSON?
TAKENAGA-KUN'S REACTION WAS PRETTY LAME...
'CAUSE THAT'S NO FUN!
HERE, I BROUGHT YOU SOMETHING.
YOU SHOULD TRY THIS AT YOUR OWN RISK!
(NO, I'M JUST KIDDING... ACTUALLY, YOU SHOULD NEVER DO THIS TO YOUR FAVORITE BAND.)
MARSHI TAKENAGA, SINGER FROM WRISK.
RECENTLY, I WAITED FOR THE BAND BUG!
GREAT SHOW!
KYO-CHAN WAVED AT US. ♥
I HADN'T DONE THIS IN 10 YEARS... NOT SINCE THE TIME I SAW LOVE MISSILE.
CAR
KAI-CHAN WHO'S IN LOVE WITH KYO.

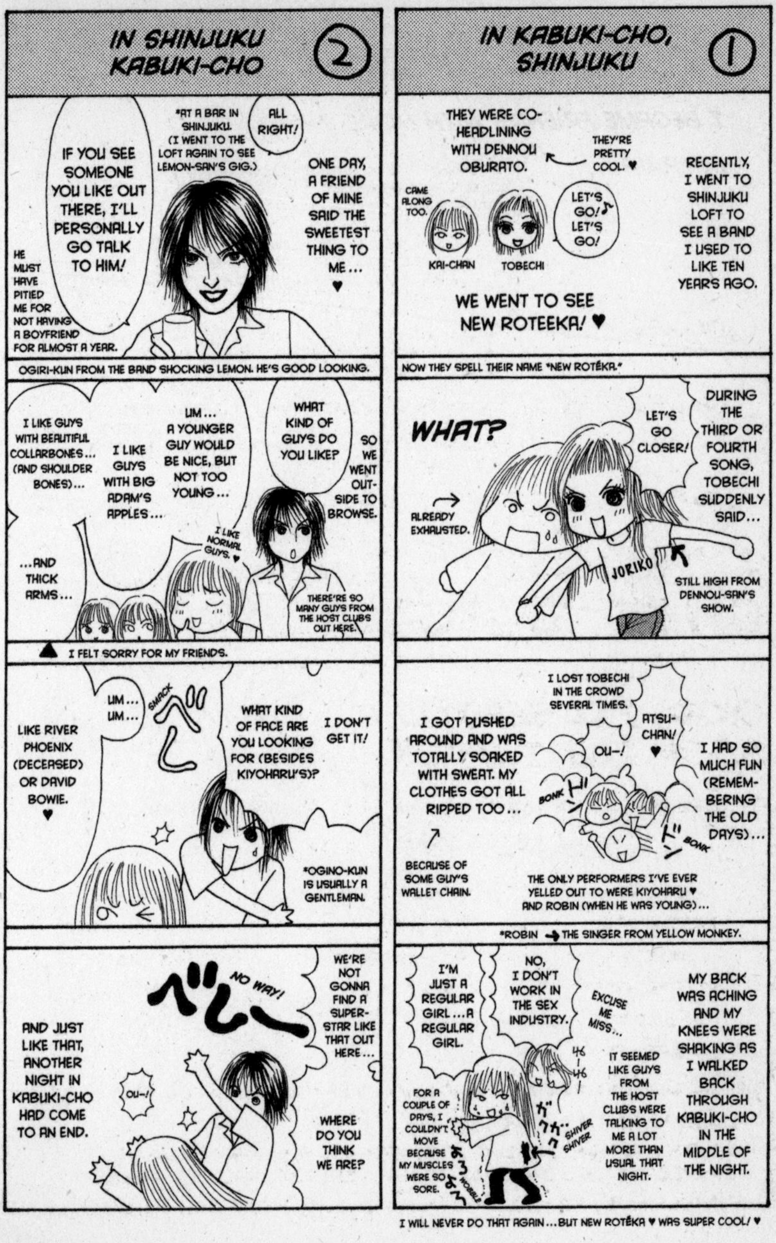
IN KABUKI-CHO, SHINJUKU ①
RECENTLY, I WENT TO SHINJUKU LOFT TO SEE A BAND I USED TO LIKE TEN YEARS AGO.
THEY'RE PRETTY COOL. ♥
THEY WERE CO-HEADLINING WITH DENNOU OBURATO.
LET'S GO! ♪ LET'S GO!
TOBECHI
CAME ALONG TOO.
KAI-CHAN
WE WENT TO SEE NEW ROTEEKA! ♥
NOW THEY SPELL THEIR NAME "NEW ROTÉKA."
DURING THE THIRD OR FOURTH SONG, TOBECHI SUDDENLY SAID...
LET'S GO CLOSER!
WHAT?
JORIKO
STILL HIGH FROM DENNOU-SAN'S SHOW.
ALREADY EXHAUSTED.
I HAD SO MUCH FUN (REMEMBERING THE OLD DAYS)...
I LOST TOBECHI IN THE CROWD SEVERAL TIMES.
ATSU-CHAN! ♥
OU-!
I GOT PUSHED AROUND AND WAS TOTALLY SOAKED WITH SWEAT. MY CLOTHES GOT ALL RIPPED TOO...
BONK
BONK
BECAUSE OF SOME GUY'S WALLET CHAIN.
THE ONLY PERFORMERS I'VE EVER YELLED OUT TO WERE KIYOHARU ♥ AND ROBIN (WHEN HE WAS YOUNG)...
*ROBIN → THE SINGER FROM YELLOW MONKEY.
MY BACK WAS ACHING AND MY KNEES WERE SHAKING AS I WALKED BACK THROUGH KABUKI-CHO IN THE MIDDLE OF THE NIGHT.
EXCUSE ME MISS...
IT SEEMED LIKE GUYS FROM THE HOST CLUBS WERE TALKING TO ME A LOT MORE THAN USUAL THAT NIGHT.
NO, I DON'T WORK IN THE SEX INDUSTRY.
I'M JUST A REGULAR GIRL... A REGULAR GIRL.
SHIVER SHIVER
WOBBLE
FOR A COUPLE OF DAYS, I COULDN'T MOVE BECAUSE MY MUSCLES WERE SO SORE.
I WILL NEVER DO THAT AGAIN... BUT NEW ROTÉKA ♥ WAS SUPER COOL! ♥
IN SHINJUKU KABUKI-CHO ②
ONE DAY, A FRIEND OF MINE SAID THE SWEETEST THING TO ME... ♥
ALL RIGHT!
*AT A BAR IN SHINJUKU. (I WENT TO THE LOFT AGAIN TO SEE LEMON-SAN'S GIG.)
IF YOU SEE SOMEONE YOU LIKE OUT THERE, I'LL PERSONALLY GO TALK TO HIM!
HE MUST HAVE PITIED ME FOR NOT HAVING A BOYFRIEND FOR ALMOST A YEAR.
OGIRI-KUN FROM THE BAND SHOCKING LEMON. HE'S GOOD LOOKING.
SO WE WENT OUT-SIDE TO BROWSE.
WHAT KIND OF GUYS DO YOU LIKE?
UM... A YOUNGER GUY WOULD BE NICE, BUT NOT TOO YOUNG...
I LIKE GUYS WITH BIG ADAM'S APPLES...
I LIKE GUYS WITH BEAUTIFUL COLLARBONES... (AND SHOULDER BONES)...
I LIKE NORMAL GUYS. ♥
...AND THICK ARMS...
THERE'RE SO MANY GUYS FROM THE HOST CLUBS OUT HERE.
▲ I FELT SORRY FOR MY FRIENDS.
I DON'T GET IT!
WHAT KIND OF FACE ARE YOU LOOKING FOR (BESIDES KIYOHARU'S)?
UM... UM...
SMACK
LIKE RIVER PHOENIX (DECEASED) OR DAVID BOWIE. ♥
*OGINO-KUN IS USUALLY A GENTLEMAN.
WE'RE NOT GONNA FIND A SUPER-STAR LIKE THAT OUT HERE...
NO WAY!
WHERE DO YOU THINK WE ARE?
OU-!
AND JUST LIKE THAT, ANOTHER NIGHT IN KABUKI-CHO HAD COME TO AN END.

I'VE BEEN HANGING OUT IN SHINJUKU A LOT LATELY. (WELL, I JUST EAT THERE AND STUFF.) I'VE BEEN DYING TO GET A PET... AND I'VE ALSO BEEN DYING TO MOVE. DAMN, I WISH I COULD MOVE TO A NEW PLACE AND GET A POMERANIAN OR A POODLE!

I BECAME FRIENDS WITH MORE BANDS!

DIMARIA... THE DRUMMER IS MY FRIEND'S BUDDY. HE'S A CUTIE. THEY LOOK LIKE YOUR TYPICAL GLAM BAND. (THEY OFTEN WEAR H.NAOTO CLOTHES ON STAGE.) THEIR SOUND IS "*POSITIVE PUNK (POSI-PUN)", AND FUN TO LISTEN TO.

*BEFORE THE TERM "GLAM BANDS" WAS INVENTED, THIS IS WHAT WE USED TO CALL THIS TYPE OF MUSIC. THERE USED TO BE LOTS AND LOTS OF REALLY COOL "POSI-PUN" BANDS. THIS IS MUSIC FROM THE GOOD OLD DAYS.

DOORMAT... THE DRUMMER IS A FRIEND OF MINE. HE'S SO CUTE ♥ AND NICE TOO! THEY PLAY HARDCORE MUSIC. THEY'RE REALLY COOL. YOU CAN FIND THEM IN MAGAZINES, SO CHECK THEM OUT!

CHOCOLAT S... IS A NEWLY FORMED BAND WITH THE SINGER AND GUITARIST FROM THE BAND ASH. THE TALLER ONE, "G-KUN"... HAS BEAUTIFUL LEGS. MY FRIEND INTRODUCED ME TO THEM OUT OF THE BLUE. THEIR SOUND IS BASICALLY POP ROCK.

THEY'RE ALL OUT THERE PERFORMING, SO PLEASE CHECK THEM OUT!

THANK YOU SO MUCH FOR STICKING AROUND! ♥

I WONDER IF ANYONE ACTUALLY READ THE WHOLE THING...

OKAY, I'LL SEE YOU ALL AGAIN IN BOOK 7! BYE BYE. ♥

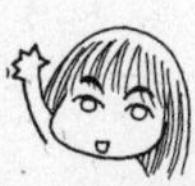

SPECIAL THANKS

MINE-SAMA,
SHIOZAWA-SAMA,
INO-SAMA,
EVERYBODY AT THE EDITORIAL DEPARTMENT.

MY YOUNGER BROTHER HII (HITOSHI),
MY MOM TAKEKO,
YUKO OGAWA.

HANA-CHAN,
AYUAYU WATANABE,
ATSUKO NAMBA-CHAN,
MACHIKO SAKURAI,
IYU KOZAKURA.

CREDITS FOR THE BONUS PAGES...

TOBECHI, KAI-CHAN, OGINO-KUN, TAKENAGA-KUN, SHU-CHAN, MAKO, BUN, EVERYBODY FROM THE HACHIOJI TEAM, AND ALL OF YOU WHO SENT ME LETTERS.

About the Creator

Tomoko Hayakawa was born on March 4.

   Since her debut as a manga creator, Tomoko Hayakawa has worked on many shojo titles with the theme of romantic love—only to realize that she could write about other subjects as well. She decided to pack her newest story with the things she likes most, which led to her current, enormously popular series, *The Wallflower*.

   Her favorite things are: Tim Burton's *The Nightmare Before Christmas*, Jean-Paul Gaultier, and samurai dramas on TV. Her hobbies are collecting items with skull designs and watching *bishonen* (beautiful boys). Her dream is to build a mansion like the one that the Addams family lives in. Her favorite pastime is to lie around at home with her cat, Ten (whose full name is Tennosuke).

   Her zodiac sign is Pisces, and her blood group is AB.

Translation Notes

Japanese is a tricky language for most Westerners, and translation is often more art than science. For your edification and reading pleasure, here are notes on some of the places where we could have gone in a different direction in our translation of the work, or where a Japanese cultural reference is used.

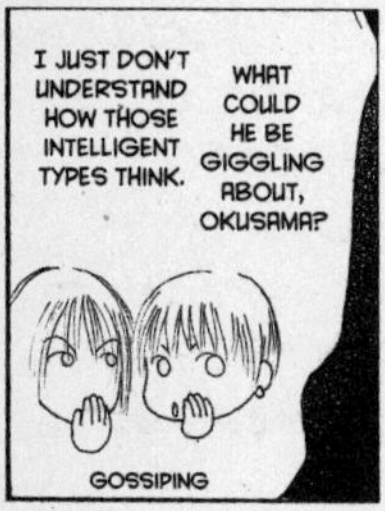
WHAT COULD HE BE GIGGLING ABOUT, OKUSAMA?
I JUST DON'T UNDERSTAND HOW THOSE INTELLIGENT TYPES THINK.
GOSSIPING

Gossip Girls (page 13)

Okusama is an honorific term meaning wife, often used when referring to a married woman. Here Yuki and Ranmaru are pretending to be gossipy housewives.

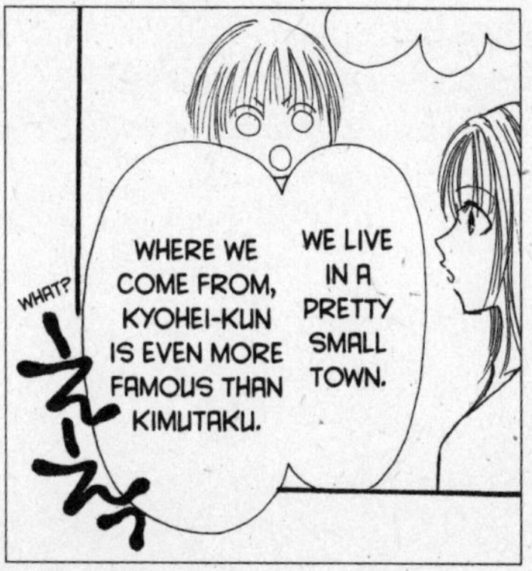
WE LIVE IN A PRETTY SMALL TOWN.
WHERE WE COME FROM, KYOHEI-KUN IS EVEN MORE FAMOUS THAN KIMUTAKU.
WHAT?

Kimutaku (page 17)

Kimutaku (Takuya Kimura) is one of the most popular male celebrities in Japan. He's a member of the boy band SMAP.

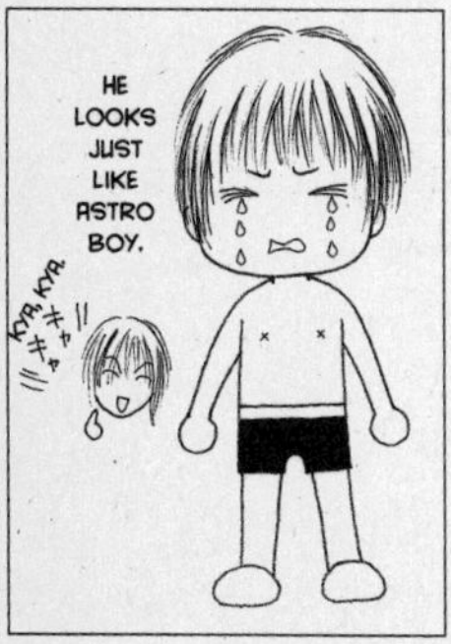
HE LOOKS JUST LIKE ASTRO BOY.
KYA KYA

Astro Boy (page 31)

Astro Boy is a famous manga/anime by Osamu Tezuka. It was published in the United States as *Astro Boy*, but the Japanese title is *Testuwan Atomu*.

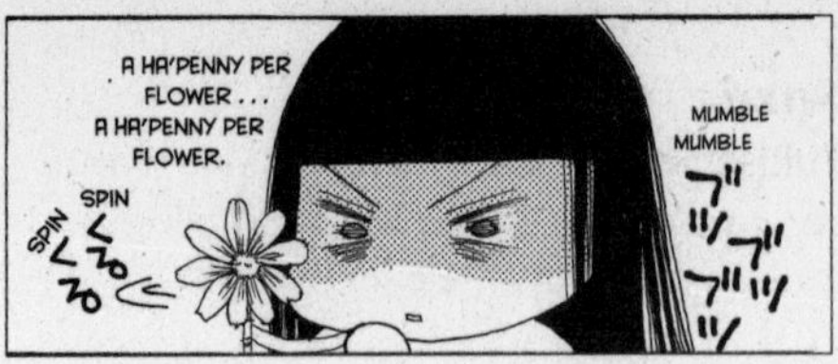
MUMBLE MUMBLE
A HA'PENNY PER FLOWER . . . A HA'PENNY PER FLOWER.
SPIN SPIN

Ha'penny a flower (page 52)

Sunako is actually saying "5 sen" per flower. "Sen" is a very old form of Japanese currency. One sen represents 1/100 of 1 yen. Today, the lowest denomination of currency is the 1 yen coin.

Hokkaido is alrighto (page 53)

Yuki and Kyohei are actually saying, *Hokkaido is dekkaido. Dekai zo* means "It's big." Here they have altered that phrase to create *dekkaido* so that it rhymes with hokkaido. It's a pun. We used "*hokkaido* is alrighto" to try and create a similar-sounding pun.

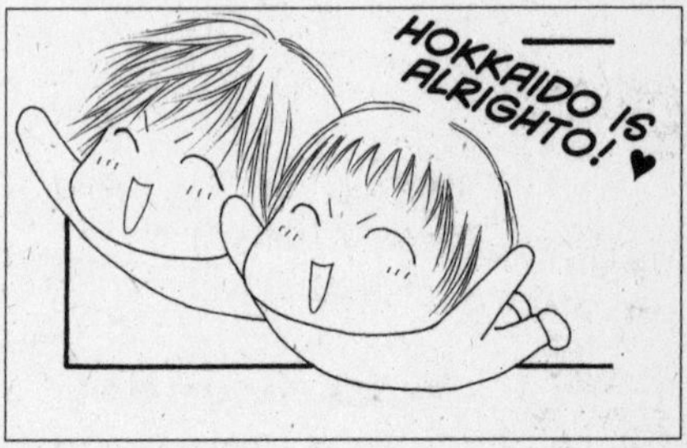
HOKKAIDO IS ALRIGHTO! ♥

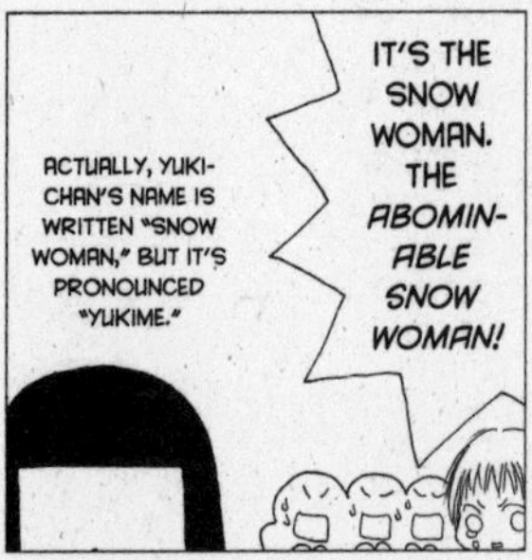
IT'S THE SNOW WOMAN. THE ABOMIN-ABLE SNOW WOMAN!
ACTUALLY, YUKI-CHAN'S NAME IS WRITTEN "SNOW WOMAN," BUT IT'S PRONOUNCED "YUKIME."

Abominable Snow Woman (page 57)

Sunako's friend Yuki's name is written with two characters, *yuki* and *onna*, and literally means "snow woman." Yukinojou screams out, "It's the snow woman!", but Sunako corrects him, saying that her name is actually pronounced "Yukime". The second character, *onna*, meaning woman, can also be read as "me."

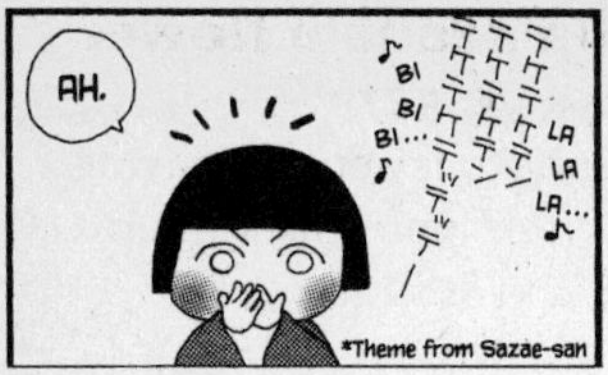
AH.
BI
BI
BI...
LA
LA
LA...
*Theme from Sazae-san

Sazae-san (page 68)

Yuki-chan's cell phone rings the theme song to the long-running anime series *Sazae-san*.

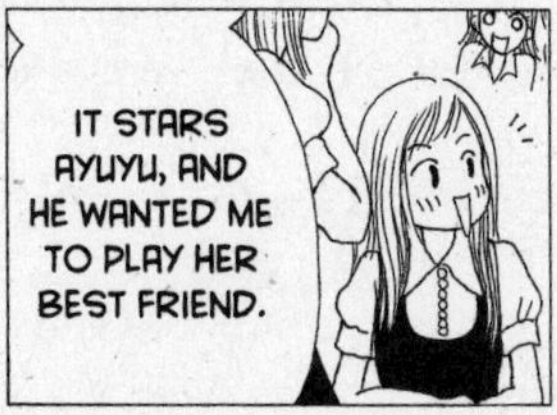
IT STARS AYUYU, AND HE WANTED ME TO PLAY HER BEST FRIEND.

Ayuyu (page 92)

Ayuyu is a play on the Japanese pop idol Ayaya.

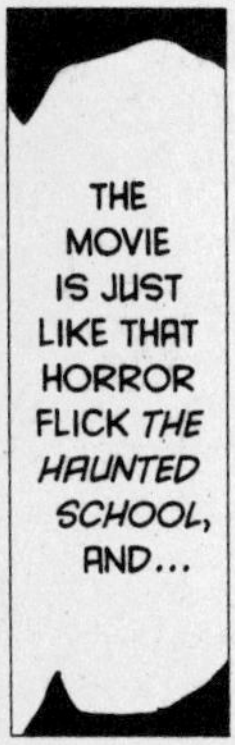
THE MOVIE IS JUST LIKE THAT HORROR FLICK *THE HAUNTED SCHOOL*, AND...

Scary School Stories (page 94)

Noi is referring to the film *Gakko No Kaidan, Scary School Stories*.

Otaku (page 98)

Otaku is a Japanese word for "obsessed fan." The term is generally associated with manga and anime fans, but it can be used to describe virtually any obsession. For example, an American "Trekkie" could be called an *otaku*, and a cheese lover could be called a "cheese *otaku*." In this case, the guys are pretending to be pop idol *otakus*. *Otakus* also tend to dress in very nerdy attire, hence the guys' new outfits. To learn more about the world of the Japanese *otaku*, pick up a copy of the manga *Genshiken* (published by Del Rey).

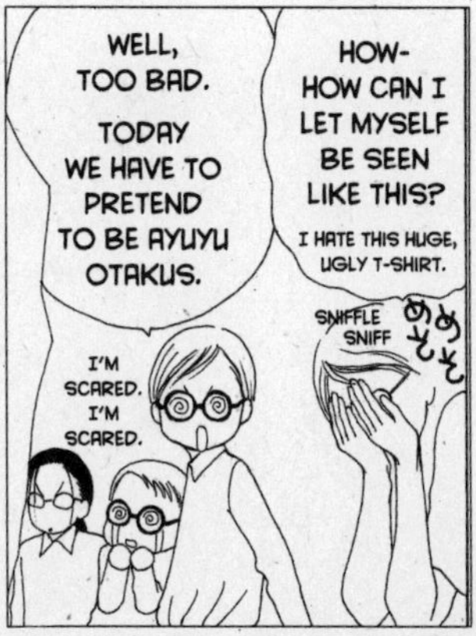
HOW-HOW CAN I LET MYSELF BE SEEN LIKE THIS?
I HATE THIS HUGE, UGLY T-SHIRT.
WELL, TOO BAD.
TODAY WE HAVE TO PRETEND TO BE AYUYU OTAKUS.
SNIFFLE SNIFF
I'M SCARED. I'M SCARED.

Yakiniku (page 110)

Yakiniku is Korean-style barbequed beef. It's very popular in Japan.

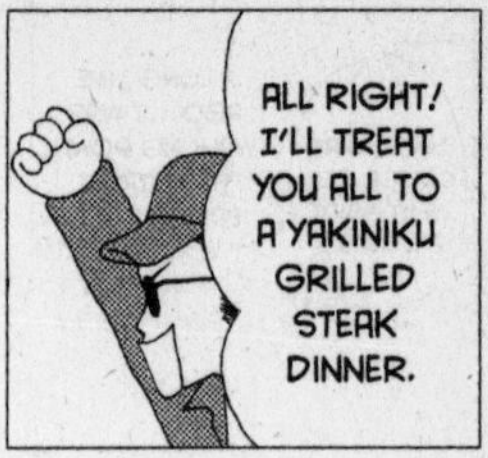
ALL RIGHT! I'LL TREAT YOU ALL TO A YAKINIKU GRILLED STEAK DINNER.

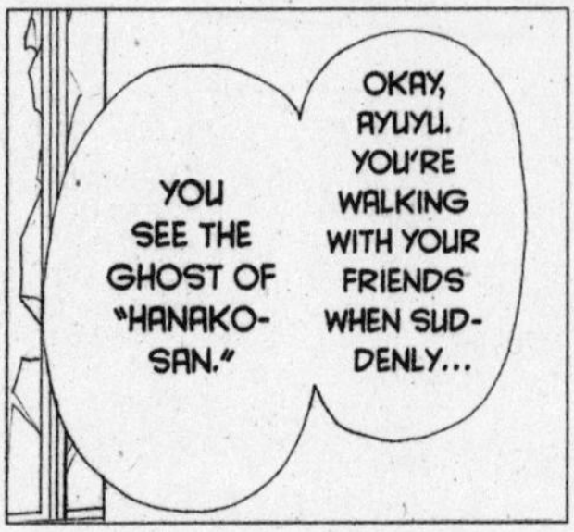
OKAY, AYUYU. YOU'RE WALKING WITH YOUR FRIENDS WHEN SUD-DENLY...
YOU SEE THE GHOST OF "HANAKO-SAN."

Ghost stories (page 111)

This is a reference to "Toire no Hanako-san" or "Hanako-san—Ghost of the Bathroom," a popular urban legend about a ghost named Hanako, who haunts school bathrooms.

More Ghost Stories (page 116)

Sadako is the character from the horror movie *Ringu*, which was remade in America as *The Ring*.

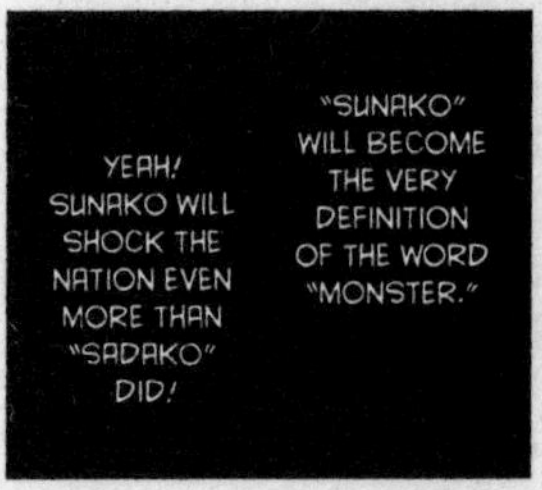
"SUNAKO" WILL BECOME THE VERY DEFINITION OF THE WORD "MONSTER."
YEAH! SUNAKO WILL SHOCK THE NATION EVEN MORE THAN "SADAKO" DID!

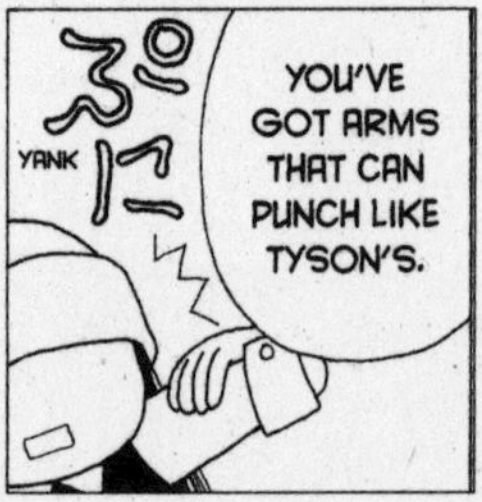
YOU'VE GOT ARMS THAT CAN PUNCH LIKE TYSON'S.
YANK

Arms Like Tyson's (page 154)

Kyohei is actually saying that Sunako's arms are like Jyo's. Jyo is the main character in the boxing anime series *Ashita No Jyo*.

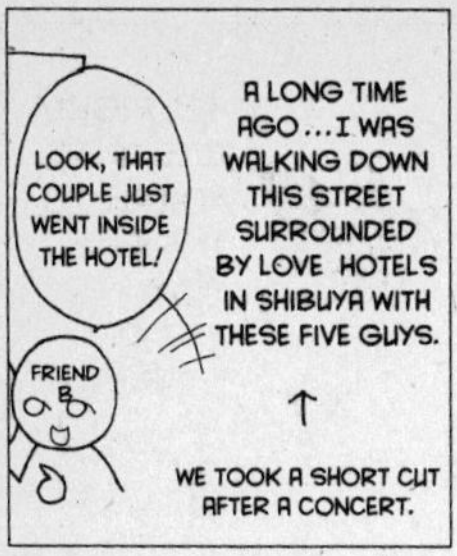
A LONG TIME AGO...I WAS WALKING DOWN THIS STREET SURROUNDED BY LOVE HOTELS IN SHIBUYA WITH THESE FIVE GUYS.
LOOK, THAT COUPLE JUST WENT INSIDE THE HOTEL!
FRIEND B
WE TOOK A SHORT CUT AFTER A CONCERT.

Love Hotels (page 172)

Love hotels are specifically designed for couples seeking privacy. They can be rented by the night or by the hour during the daytime. They often have gaudy, Las Vegas-style decor and themed rooms.

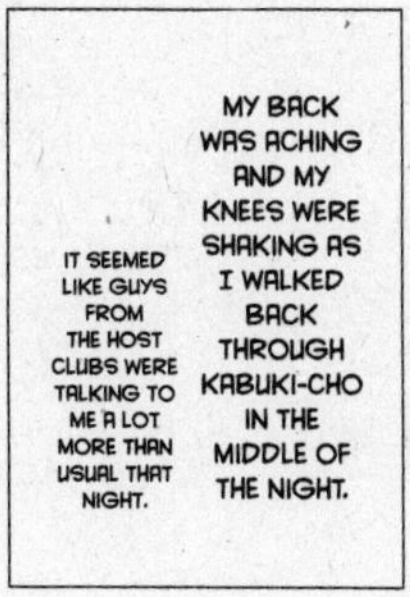
MY BACK WAS ACHING AND MY KNEES WERE SHAKING AS I WALKED BACK THROUGH KABUKI-CHO IN THE MIDDLE OF THE NIGHT.
IT SEEMED LIKE GUYS FROM THE HOST CLUBS WERE TALKING TO ME A LOT MORE THAN USUAL THAT NIGHT.

Kabuki-cho (page 174)

Kabuki-cho is the red-light district of Tokyo and is located in the Shinjuku area.

Preview of Volume 7

We're pleased to present you a preview from Volume 7. This volume is available in English now.

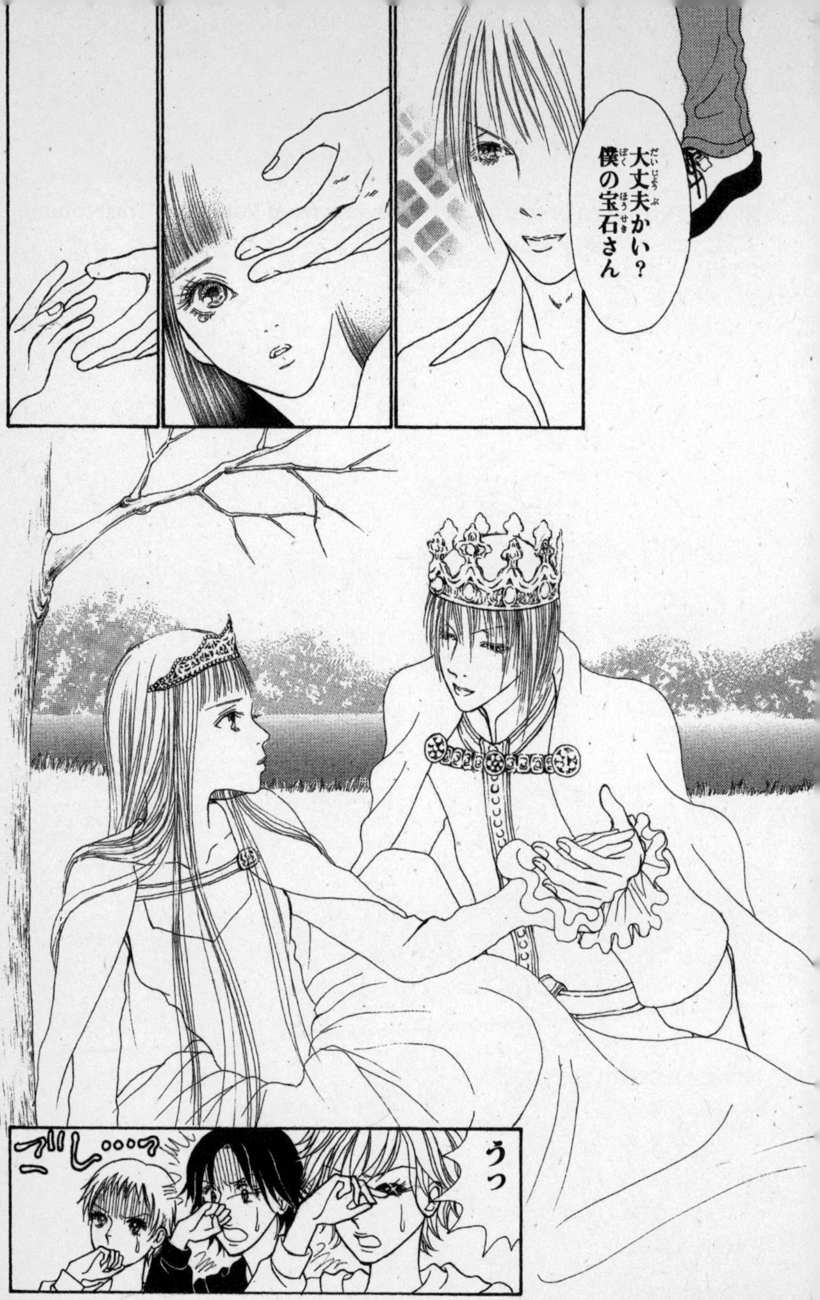
大丈夫かい？僕の宝石さん
うっ
ごし…っ

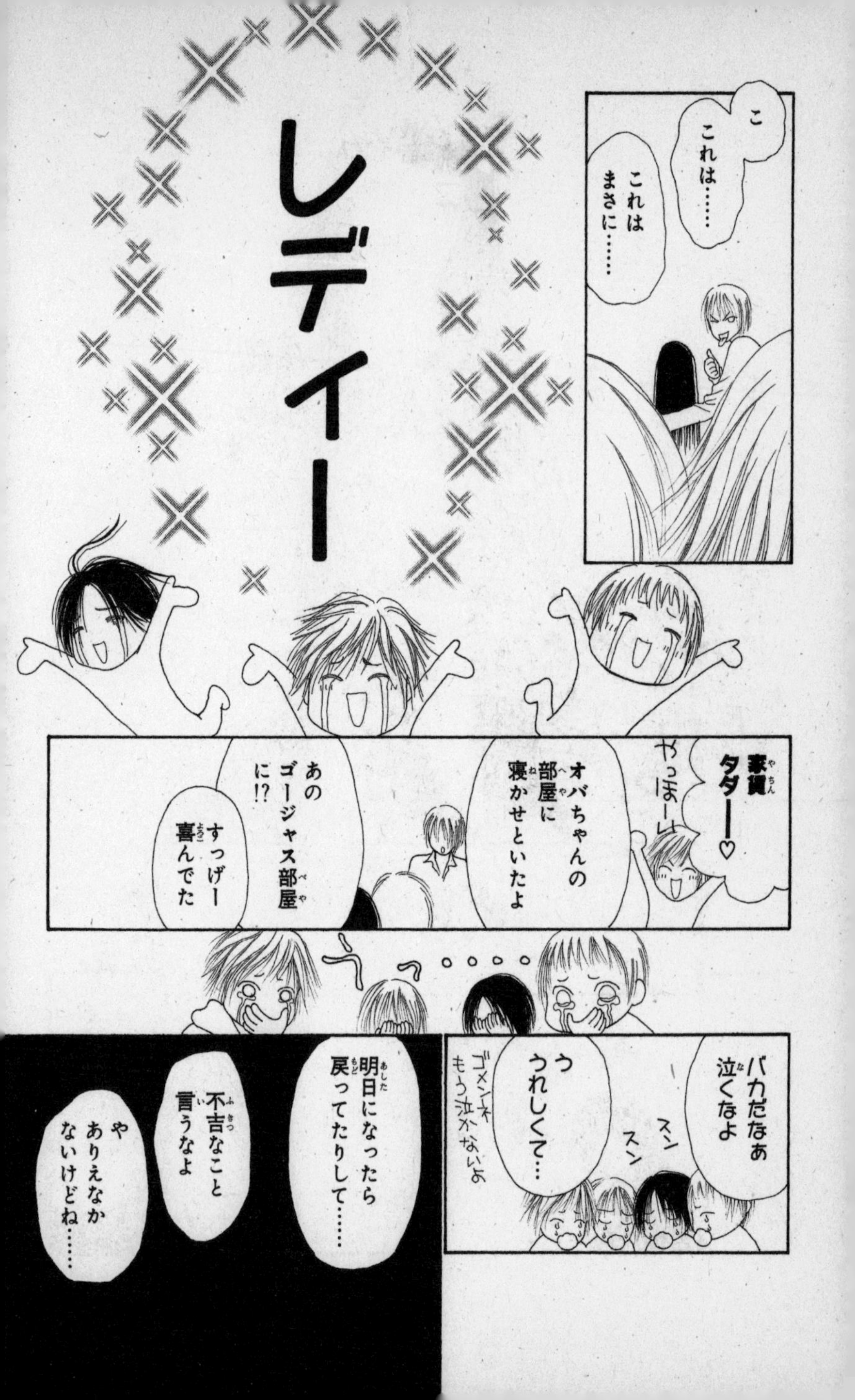

こ
これは……
これはまさに……
レディー
家賃タダーー♡
やっほーい
オバちゃんの部屋に寝かせといたよ
あのゴージャス部屋に!?
すっげー喜んでた
・・・・
バカだなぁ泣くなよ
スン
スン
うれしくて…
ゴメンネもう泣かないよ
明日になったら戻ってたりして……
不吉なこと言うなよ
やありえなかないけどね……

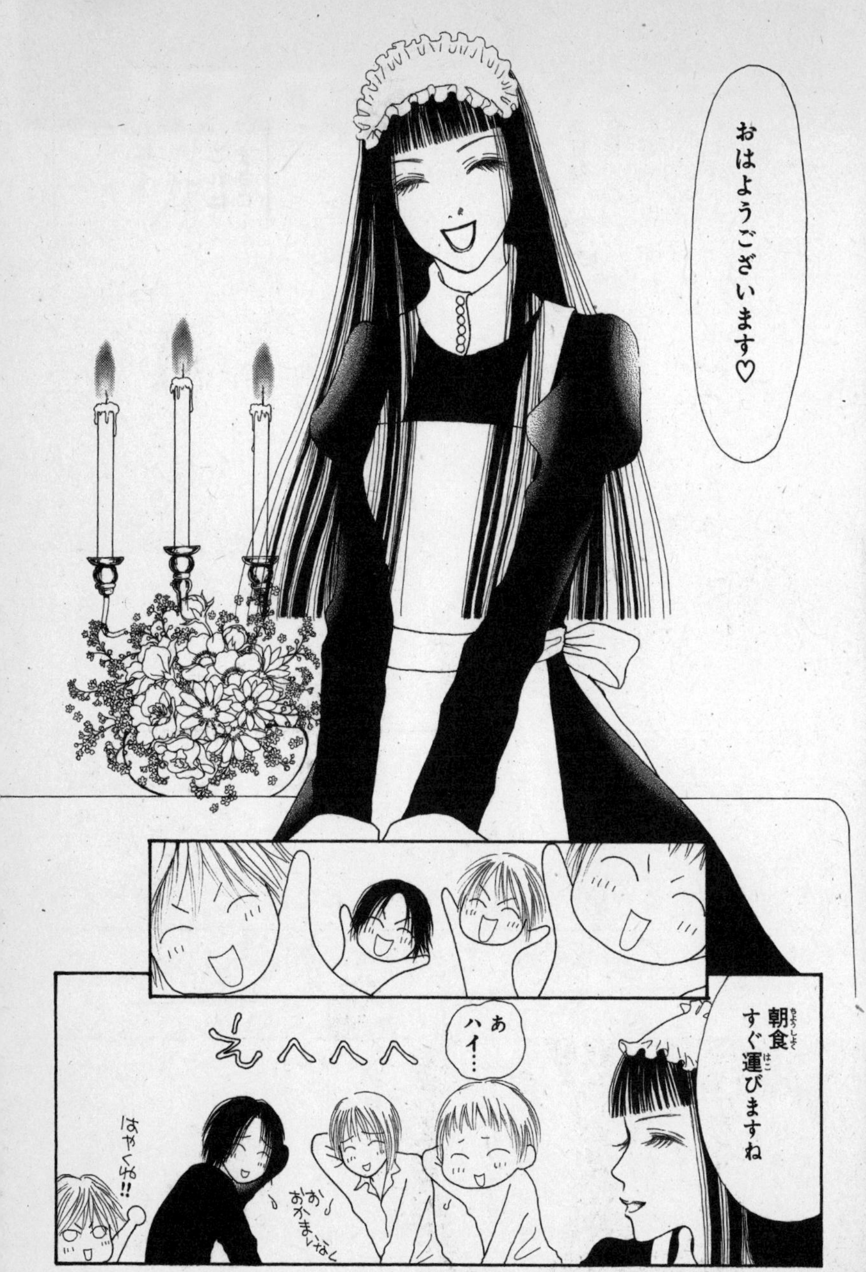
おはようございます♡
朝食すぐ運びますね
あ ハイ…
えへへへ
お♪
おかまいなく
はやくゥ!!

止まれ

[STOP!]

You're going the wrong way!

Manga is a completely different type of reading experience.

To start at the *beginning*, go to the *end*!

That's right! Authentic manga is read the traditional Japanese way—from right to left. Exactly the *opposite* of how American books are read. It's easy to follow: Just go to the other end of the book, and read each page—and each panel—from right side to left side, starting at the top right. Now you're experiencing manga as it was meant to be!